CHILTON BOOK COMPANY

REPAIR & TUNE-UP GUIDE

TOYOTA COROLLA/CARINA TERCEL/STARLET 1970-87

All U.S. and Canadian models of Corolla • Carina • Tercel • Starlet

Y0-AGK-422

President GARY R. INGERSOLL
Senior Vice President, Book Publishing and Research RONALD A. HOXTER
Publisher KERRY A. FREEMAN, S.A.E.
Editor-in-Chief DEAN F. MORGANTINI, S.A.E.
Senior Editor RICHARD J. RIVELE, S.A.E.

CHILTON BOOK COMPANY
Radnor, Pennsylvania
19089

SAFETY NOTICE

Proper service and repair procedures are vital to the safe, reliable operation of all motor vehicles, as well as the personal safety of those performing repairs. This book outlines procedures for servicing and repairing vehicles using safe, effective methods. The procedures contain many NOTES, CAUTIONS and WARNINGS which should be followed along with standard safety procedures to eliminate the possibility of personal injury or improper service which could damage the vehicle or compromise its safety.

It is important to note that repair procedures and techniques, tools and parts for servicing motor vehicles, as well as the skill and experience of the individual performing the work vary widely. It is not possible to anticipate all of the conceivable ways or conditions under which vehicles may be serviced, or to provide cautions as to all of the possible hazards that may result. Standard and accepted safety precautions and equipment should be used when handling toxic or flammable fluids, and safety goggles or other protection should be used during cutting, grinding, chiseling, prying, or any other process that can cause material removal or projectiles.

Some procedures require the use of tools specially designed for a specific purpose. Before substituting another tool or procedure, you must be completely satisfied that neither your personal safety, nor the performance of the vehicle will be endangered.

Although information in this guide is based on industry sources and is as complete as possible at the time of publication, the possibility exists that the manufacturer made later changes which could not be included here. While striving for total accuracy, Chilton Book Company cannot assume responsibility for any errors, changes, or omissions that may occur in the compilation of this data.

PART NUMBERS

Part numbers listed in this reference are not recommendations by Chilton for any product by brand name. They are references that can be used with interchange manuals and aftermarket supplier catalogs to locate each brand supplier's discrete part number.

SPECIAL TOOLS

Special tools are recommended by the vehicle manufacturer to perform their specific job. Use has been kept to a minimum, but where absolutely necessary, they are referred to in the text by the part number of the tool manufacturer. These tools can be purchased, under the appropriate part number, from Kent-Moore Corporation, 29784 Little Mack, Roseville, Michigan, 48066. For Canada, contact Kent-Moore of Canada, Ltd., 2395 Cawthra Mississauga, Ontario, Canada L5A 3P2 or an equivalent tool can be purchased locally from a tool supplier or parts outlet. Before substituting any tool for the one recommended, read the SAFETY NOTICE at the top of this page.

ACKNOWLEDGMENTS

The Chilton Book Company expresses appreciation to Toyota Motor Sales, U.S.A., Inc., 2055 W. 190th Street, Torrance, California 90504, Biscotle Toyota, 1062 W. Main Street, Norristown, Pennsylvania 19401 and Mainline Toyota, Devon, Pennsylvania 19333 for their generous assistance.

Chilton's Repair & Tune-Up Guide: Toyota Corolla/Carina/Tercel/Starlet 1970–87
ISBN 0-8019-7767-3 pbk.
Library of Congress Catalog Card No. 86-47788

CONTENTS

Quick Reference
Specifications For Your Vehicle

Fill in this chart with the most commonly used specifications for your vehicle. Specifications can be found in Chapters 1 through 3 or on the tune-up decal under the hood of the vehicle.

Tune-Up

Firing Order_____

Spark Plugs:

    Type_____

    Gap (in.)_____

Torque (ft. lbs.)_____

Idle Speed (rpm)_____

Ignition Timing (°)_____

    Vacuum or Electronic Advance (Connected/Disconnected)_____

Valve Clearance (in.)

    Intake_____   **Exhaust**_____

Capacities

Engine Oil Type (API Rating)_____

    With Filter Change (qts)_____

    Without Filter Change (qts)_____

Cooling System (qts)_____

Manual Transmission (pts)_____

    Type_____

Automatic Transmission (pts)_____

    Type_____

Front Differential (pts)_____

    Type_____

Rear Differential (pts)_____

    Type_____

Transfer Case (pts)_____

    Type_____

FREQUENTLY REPLACED PARTS
Use these spaces to record the part numbers of frequently replaced parts.

PCV VALVE	**OIL FILTER**	**AIR FILTER**	**FUEL FILTER**
Type_____	**Type**_____	**Type**_____	**Type**_____
Part No._____	**Part No.**_____	**Part No.**_____	**Part No.**_____

General Information and Maintenance

HOW TO USE THIS BOOK

Chilton's Repair and Tune-Up Guide for the Toyota Corolla, Carina, Tercel and Starlet is intended to teach you more about the inner workings of your automobile and save you money on its upkeep. Chapters 1 and 2 will probably be the most frequently used in the book. The first chapter contains all the information that may be required at a moment's notice. Aside from giving the location of various serial numbers and the proper towing instructions, it also contains all the information on basic day-to-day maintenance that you will need to ensure good performance and long component life. Chapter 2 contains the necessary tune-up procedures to assist you not only in keeping the engine running properly and at peak performance levels, but also in restoring some of the more delicate components to operating condition in the event of a failure. Chapters 3 through 9 cover repairs (rather than maintenance) for various portions of your car, with each chapter covering either one separate system or two related systems.

When using the Table of Contents, refer to the bold listings for the subject of the chapter and the smaller listings (or the index) for information on a particular component.

In general, there are three things a proficient mechanic has which must be allowed for when a non-professional does work on his/her car. These are:

1. A sound knowledge of the construction of the parts he is working with; their order of assembly, etc.

2. A knowledge of potentially hazardous situations; particularly how to prevent them.

3. Manual dexterity.

This book provides step-by-step instructions and illustrations whenever possible. Use them carefully and wisely-don't just jump headlong into disassembly. When there is doubt about being able to readily reassemble something, make a careful drawing of the component before taking it apart. Assembly always looks simple when everything is still assembled.

CAUTIONS WARNINGS, AND NOTES will be provided where appropriate to help prevent you from injuring yourself or damaging your car. Consequently, you should always read through the entire procedure before beginning the work so as to familiarize yourself with any special problems which may occur during the given procedure. Since no number of warnings could cover every possible situation, you should work slowly and try to envision what is going to happen in each operation ahead of time.

When it comes to tightening things, there is generally a slimarity between too loose to properly seal or resist vibration and so tight as to risk damage or warping. When dealing with major engine parts, or with any aluminum component, it pays to buy a torque wrench and go by the recommended figures.

When reference is made in this book to the right side or the left side of the car, it should be understood that the positions are always to be viewed from the front seat. This means that the left side of the car is the passenger's side. This will hold true throughout the book, regardless of how you might be looking at the car at the time.

We have attempted to eliminate the use of special tools whenever possible, substituting more readily available hand tools. However, in some cases, the special tools are necessary. These tools can usually be purchased from your local Toyota dealer or from an automotive parts store.

Always be conscious of the need for safety in your work. Never get under a car unless it is firmly supported by jackstands or ramps. Never smoke near, or allow flame to get near the battery or the fuel system. Keep your clothing, hands and hair clear of the fan and pulleys when working near the engine if it is running.

Most importantly, try to be patient; even in the midst of an argument with a stubborn bolt, reaching for the largest hammer in the garage is usually a cause for later regret and more extensive repair. As you gain confidence and experience, working on your car will become a source of pride and satisfaction.

TOOLS AND EQUIPMENT

It would be impossible to catalog each and every tool that you may need to perform all the operations included in this book. It would also not be wise for the amateur to rush out and buy an expensive set of tools on the theory that he may need one of them at some time. The best approach is to proceed slowly, gathering together a good quality set of those tools that are used most frequently. Don't be misled by the low cost of bargain tools. It is far better to spend a little more for quality, name brand tools. Forged wrenches, 10 or 12 point sockets and fine-toothed ratchets are by far preferable to their less expensive counterparts. As any good mechanic can tell you, there are few worse experiences than trying to work on a car or truck with bad tools. Your monetary savings will be far outweighed by frustration and mangled knuckles.

Begin accumulating those tools that are used most frequently; those associated with routine maintenance and tune-up. In addition to the normal assortment of screwdrivers and pliers, you should have the following tools for routing maintenance jobs:

1. Metric wrenches, sockets and combination open end/box end wrenches.
2. Jackstands for support.
3. Oil filter wrench.
4. Oil filler spout or funnel.
5. Grease gun for chassis lubrication.
6. Hydrometer for checking the battery.
7. A low flat pan for draining oil.
8. Lots of rags for wiping up the inevitable mess.

In addition to these items there are several others which are not absolutely necessary, but handy to have around. These include a transmission funnel and filler tube, a drop light on a long cord, and adjustable wrench and a pair of slip joint pliers.

A more advanced set of tools, suitable for tune-up work, can be drawn up easily. While the tools are slightly more sophisticated, they need not be outrageously expensive. The key to these purchases is to make them with an eye towards adaptability and wide range. A basic list of tune-up tools could include:

1. Tachometer/dwell meter;
2. Spark plug gauges and gapping tool;
3. Feeler gauges for valve and point adjustment;
4. Timing light.

A tachometer/dwell meter will ensure accurate tune-up work on cars without electronic ignition. The choice of a timing light should be made carefully. A light which works on the DC current supplied by the car battery is the best choice; it should have a xenon tube for brightness. Since most later models have an electronic ignition system, the timing light should have an inductive pickup which clamps around the No. 1 spark plug cable (the timing light illustrated has one of these pickups).

In addition to these basic tools, there are several other tools and gauges which, though not particularly necessary for basic tune-up work, you may find to be quite useful. These include:

1. A compression gauge. The screw-in type is slower to use but eliminates the possibility of a faulty reading due to escaping pressure;
2. A manifold vacuum gauge;
3. A test light;
4. A combination volt/ohmmeter;
5. An induction meter, used to determine whether or not there is current flowing through a wire. An extremely helpful tool for electrical troubleshooting.

Finally, you will find a torque wrench necessary for all but the most basic of work. The beam-type models are perfectly adequate. The newer click-type (breakaway) torque wrenches are more accurate, but are also much more expensive and must be periodically recalibrated.

SERVICING YOUR CAR SAFELY

It is virtually impossible to anticipate all of the hazards involved with automotive maintenance and service, but care and common sense will prevent most accidents.

The rules of safety for mechanics range from "don't smoke around gasoline", to "use the proper tool for the job". The trick to avoiding injuries is to develop safe work habits and take every possible precaution.

Dos

• Do keep a fire extinguisher and first aid kit within easy reach.
• Do wear safety glasses or goggles when cutting, drilling, grinding or prying, even if you have 20-20 vision. If you wear glasses for the sake of vision, they should be made of hardened glass that can serve also as safety glasses, or wear safety goggles over your regular glasses.

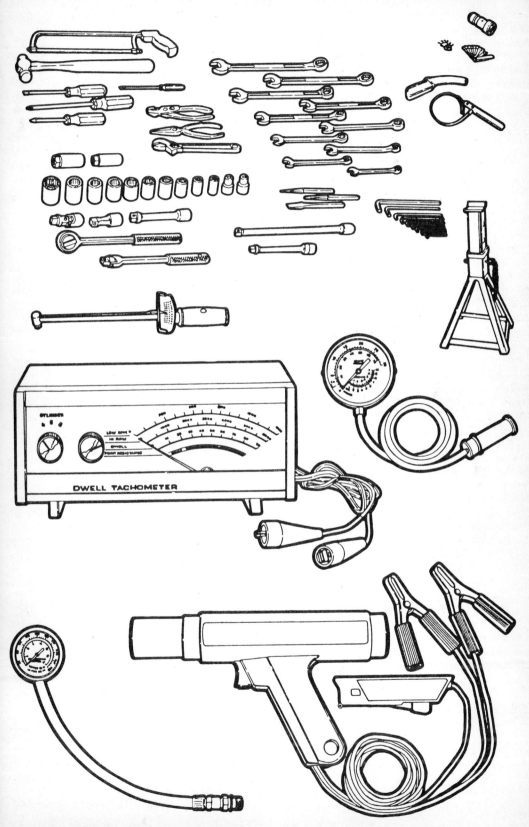

You need only a basic assortment of hand tools for most maintenance and repair jobs

• Do shield your eyes whenever you work around the battery. Batteries contain sulfuric acid. In case of contact with the eyes or skin, flush the area with water or a mixture of water and baking soda and get medical attention immediately.

• Do use safety stands for any undercar service. Jacks are for raising vehicles; safety stands are for making sure the vehicle stays raised until you want it to come down. Whenever the car is raised, block the wheels remaining on the ground and set the parking brake.

• Do use adequate ventilation when working with any chemicals or hazardous materials. Like carbon monoxide, the asbestos dust resulting from brake lining wear can be poisonous in sufficient quantities.

• Do disconnect the negative battery cable when working on the electrical system. The secondary ignition system can contain up to 40,000 volts.

• Do follow manufacturer's directions whenever working with potentially hazardous materials. Both brake fluid and antifreeze are poisonous if taken internally.

• Do properly maintain your tools Loose hammerheads, mushroomed punches and chisels, frayed or poorly grounded electrical cords, excessively worn screwdrivers, spread wrenches (open end), cracked sockets, slipping ratchets, or faulty droplight sockets can cause accidents.

• Do use the proper size and type of tool for the job being done.

• Do when possible, pull on a wrench handle rather than push on it, and adjust your stance to prevent a fall.

• Do be sure that adjustable wrenches are tightly closed on the nut or bolt and pulled so that the face is on the side of the fixed jaw.

• Do select a wrench or socket that fits the nut or bolt. The wrench or socket should be straight, not cocked.

• Do set the parking brake and block the

Always support the car securely with jackstands; never use cinder blocks, tire changing jacks or the like

drive wheels if the work requires the engine running.

Don'ts

• Don't run an engine in a garage or anywhere else without proper ventilation — EVER! Carbon monoxide is poisonous; it takes a long time to leave the human body and you can build up a deadly supply of it in your system by simply breathing in a little every day. You may not realize you are slowly poisoning yourself. Always use power vents, windows, fans or open the garage doors.

• Don't work around moving parts while wearing a necktie or other loose clothing. Short sleeves are much safer than long, loose sleeves; hard-toed shoes with neoprene soles protect your toes and give a better grip on slippery surfaces. Jewelry such as watches, fancy belt buckles, beads or body adornment of any kind is not safe working around a car. Long hair should be hidden under a hat or cap.

• Don't use pockets for toolboxes. A fall or bump can drive a screwdriver deep into your body. Even a wiping cloth hanging from the back pocket can wrap around a spinning shaft or fan.

• Don't smoke when working around gasoline, cleaning solvent or other flammable material.

• Don't smoke when working around the battery. When the battery is being charged, it gives off explosive hydrogen gas.

• Don't use gasoline to wash your hands; there are excellent soaps available. Gasoline may contain lead, and lead can enter the body through a cut, accumulating in the body until you are very ill. Gasoline also removes all the natural oils from the skin so that bone dry hands will suck up oil and grease.

• Don't service the air conditioning system unless you are equipped with the necessary tools and training. The refrigerant, R-12, is extremely cold when compressed, and when released into the air will instantly freeze any surface it contacts, including your eyes. Although the refrigerant is normally non-toxic; R-12 becomes a deadly poisonous gas in the presence of an open flame. One good whiff of the vapors from burning refrigerant can be fatal.

• Don't use screwdrivers for anything other than driving screws! A screwdriver used as a prying tool or chisel can snap when least expected, causing bodily harm. Besides, you ruin a good tool when it is used for purposes other than those intended.

• Don't use a bumper jack (that little scissors or pantograph jack that comes with the car) for anything other than changing a flat tire! If you are serious about repairing and maintaining your own car, then one of the best investments you can make is in a hydraulic floor jack of at least 1½ ton capacity.

SERIAL NUMBER IDENTIFICATION

Vehicle

All models have the vehicle identification number (VIN) stamped on a plate which is attached to the left side of the instrument panel. This plate is visible through the windshield.

The VIN is also stamped on a plate in the engine compartment which is usually located on the firewall.

The serial number on all 1970-80 models con-

Chassis Identification

Model	Year	Chassis Designation
Carina	'72–'73	TA
Corolla 1200	'70–'79	KE
Corolla 1600	'71–'79	TE
Corolla 1800	'80–'82	TE
Corolla (Gas Eng.)	'83–'87	AE
Corolla (Diesel Eng.)	'84–'85	CE
Tercel	'80–'87	AL
Starlet	'81–'84	KP

sists of a series identification number (see the following chart), followed by a 6-digit production number.

The serial number on all 1981 and later models has been changed to the new 17 digit format. The first three digits are the World Manufacturer Identification number. The next five digits are the Vehicle Description Section (same as the series identification number above). The remaining nine numbers are the production numbers.

Engine

The engine serial number consists of an engine series identification number, followed by a 6-digit production number.

VIN plate on the left-side of the instrument panel

VIN plate on the firewall

The VIN plate on later model Toyotas can be found in three different locations

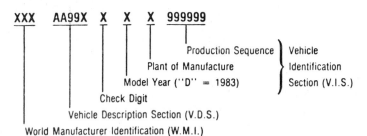

FORMAT: X = Alphabetic or Numeric Characters

A = Alphabetic Characters only

9 = Numeric Characters only

The new 17 digit VIN is used on all 1981 and later models

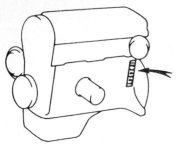

Engine serial number location—all except K-series engines

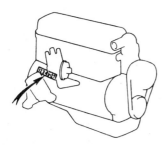

Engine serial number location—K-series engines

The location of this serial number varies from one engine to another. Serial numbers may be found in the following locations:

3K-C, 4K-C, 4K-E

The serial number on the 3K-C, 4K-C and 4K-E engine is stamped on the right side of the engine, below the spark plugs.

1A-C, 1C-L, 2T-C, 3T-C, 3A, 3A-C, 4A-C and 4A-GE

The serial number is stamped on the left side of the engine, behind the dipstick.

ROUTINE MAINTENANCE

Air Cleaner

All of the dust present in the air is kept out of the engine by means of the air cleaner filter element. Proper maintenance is vital, as a clogged element not only restricts the air flow and thus the power, but can also cause premature engine wear.

The filter element should be cleaned every 7,500 miles, or more often if the car is driven under dry, dusty conditions. Remove the filter element and using low pressure compressed air, blow the dirt out.

NOTE: *The filter element used on Toyota vehicles is of the dry, disposable type. It should never be washed, soaked or oiled.*

The filter element should be replaced every 18,000 miles, (1970-72); every 24,000 miles, (1973-74); every 25,000 miles, (1975-77); and every 30,000 miles, (1978 and later); or more often under dry, dusty conditions. Be sure to use the correct one; all Toyota elements are of the same type but they come in a variety of sizes. To replace:

1. Unfasten the wing nut(s) and/or clips that retain the element cover. Remove the cover.

Engine Identification

Model	Year	Engine Displacement cu. in. (cc)	Engine Series Identification	No. of Cylinders	Engine Type
Carina	'72–'73	97 (1588)	2T-C	4	OHV
Corolla 1200	'70–'79	71 (1166)	3K-C	4	OHV
Corolla 1600	'71–'79	97 (1588)	2T-C	4	OHV
Corolla 1800	'80–'82	108 (1770)	3T-C	4	OHV
Corolla (Gas)	'83–'87	97 (1587)	4A-C, 4A-LC	4	SOHC
Corolla (Gas)	'85–'87	97 (1587)	4A-GE	4	DOHC
Tercel	'80–'87	88.6 (1452)	1A-C, 3A, 3A-C	4	SOHC
Tercel	'87	88.9 (1456)	3E	4	SOHC
Starlet	'81–'82	78.7 (1290)	4K-C	4	OHV
Starlet	'83–'84	79 (1290)	4K-E	4	OHV

DOHC—Double-overhead camshaft
OHV—Pushrod-actuated Overhead valves
SOHC—Single-overhead camshaft

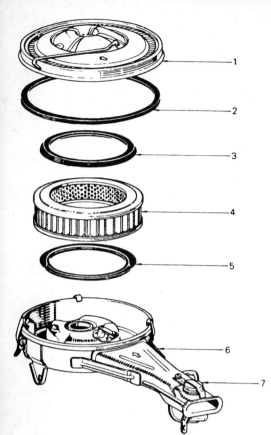

1. Air cleaner case cover
2. Gasket
3. Gasket
4. Cleaner element
5. Gasket
6. Case
7. Diaphragm

Typical air cleaner assembly

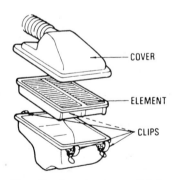

COVER

ELEMENT

CLIPS

Corollas with a diesel engine use a slightly different air filter than other models. Cleaning procedures are still the same

Sometimes the air filter can be cleaned with low pressure compressed air

2. Lift out the air filter element and clean or replace it.

3. Installation the air cleaner element in the reverse order of removal.

Fuel Filter

There are two basic types of fuel filters used: The cartridge type (disposable element) and the totally throwaway type.

The fuel filter should be replaced every 25,000-30,000 miles or sooner if it seems dirty or clogged. Removal and installation procedures differ slightly for certain years.

CAUTION: *Do not smoke or have open flame near the car when working on the fuel system.*

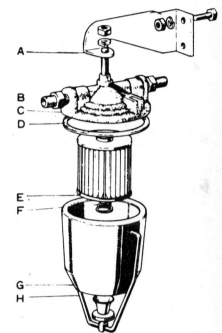

A. Fuel filter bracket
B. Fuel line fitting
C. Body
D. Bowl gasket
E. Filter element
F. Element retaining spring
G. Filter bowl
H. Bowl retaining bail

Cartridge type fuel filter components

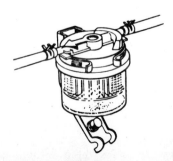

Throwaway type fuel filter

REMOVAL AND INSTALLATION

Cartridge Type

The cartridge type filter is located in the fuel line. To replace the element, proceed as follows:

1. Loosen and remove the nut on the filter bowl.

2. Withdraw the bowl, element spring, element, and gasket.

3. Wash the parts in solvent and examine them for damage.

4. Install a new filter element and bowl gasket.

5. Install the components in the reverse order of their removal. Do not fully tighten the bail nut.

6. Seat the bowl by turning it slightly. Tighten the bail nut fully and check for leaks.

The above service should be performed if the clear glass bowl fills up with gasoline or at normal routine maintenance intervals.

NOTE: *Be sure to specify engine and model when buying the element replacement kit. The kits come in several different sizes.*

Throwaway Type

1971-74

The throwaway type of fuel filter is located in the fuel line. It must be completely removed in order to replace it. The procedure to do this is as follows:

1. Unfasten the fuel intake hose. Use a wrench to loosen the attachment nut and another wrench on the opposite side to keep the filter body from turning (except 1973 and later 3K-C and 2T-C).

2. On 2T-C engines, slip the flexible fuel line off the neck on the other side of the filter. On 1973 and later 3K-C and 2T-C engines, remove the fuel lines from both sides of the filter by loosening the clamp and slipping the rubber hose off.

3. Unfasten the attaching screws from the filter bracket, if so equipped.

4. Install a completely new fuel filter assembly in the reverse order of removal.

1975 AND LATER (EXCEPT 1C-L and 4K-E)

1. Remove the hose clamps from the inlet and outlet hoses.

2. Work the hoses off of the filter necks.

3. Snap the filter out of its bracket and replace it with a new one.

NOTE: *The arrow on the fuel filter must always point toward the carburetor.*

4. Installation of the remaining components is in the reverse order of removal.

5. Run the engine for a few minutes and check the filter for any leaks.

1C-L

1. Disconnect the fuel level warning switch connector at the lower end of the filter.

2. Drain the fuel from the filter (see Chapter 4), loosen the two mounting bolts and remove the filter.

3. Remove the water level warning switch from the filter housing and then unscrew the filter from the housing. An oil filter strap wrench may come in handy when removing the filter.

4. Install the water level warning switch using a new O-ring.

5. Coat the filter gasket lightly with diesel fuel and then screw it in hand tight. DO NOT use a wrench to tighten the fuel filter.

6. Mount the filter assembly, tighten the bolts and connect the warning switch.

7. Using the priming pump on top of the filter, fill the filter with fuel and check for leaks.

4K-E

1. Unbolt the retaining screws and remove the protective shield for the fuel filter (if so equipped).

2. Place a pan under the delivery pipe (large connection) to catch the dripping fuel and SLOWLY loosen the union bolt to bleed off the fuel pressure.

3. Remove the union bolt and drain the remaining fuel.

4. Disconnect and plug the inlet line.

5. Unbolt and remove the fuel filter.

NOTE: *When tightening the fuel line bolts to the fuel filter, you must use a torque wrench. The tightening torque is very important, as under or over tightening may cause fuel leakage. Insure that there is no fuel line interference and that there is sufficient clearance between it and any other parts.*

6. Coat the flare nut, union nut and bolt threads with engine oil.

7. Hand tighten the inlet line to the fuel filter.

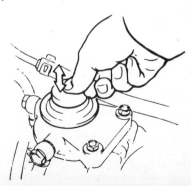

When replacing the diesel fuel filter, always use the priming pump to fill the filter with fuel before starting the engine

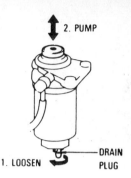

When removing the fuel lines it is always a good idea to place a pan underneath to catch the dripping fuel

When draining water from the diesel fuel filter, turn the drain plug counterclockwise

Draining the Diesel Fuel Filter

CAUTION: *When the fuel filter warning light or buzzer comes on, the water in the fuel filter must be drained immediately.*

1. Raise the hood and position a small pan or jar underneath the drain plug to catch the water about to be released.

2. Reach under the fuel filter and turn the drain plug counterclockwise about 2-2½ turns. NOTE: *Loosening the drain plug more than the suggested amount will cause water to ooze from around the threads of the plug.*

3. Depress the priming pump on top of the filter housing until fuel is the only substance being forced out.

4. Retighten the drain plug by hand only, do not use a wrench.

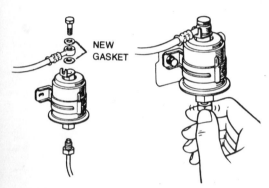

Hand tighten the fuel inlet line

PCV Valve

Gasoline Engines Only

The PCV valve regulates crankcase ventilation during various engine operating conditions. At high vacuum (idle speed and partial load range) it will open slightly and at low vacuum (full throttle) it will open fully. This causes vapor to be removed from the crankcase by the engine vacuum and then sucked into the combustion chamber where it is dissipated.

REMOVAL AND INSTALLATION

1. Check the ventilation hoses for leaks or clogging. Clean or replace as necessary.

2. Locate the PCV valve in the cylinder head cover or in the manifold-to-crankcase line. Remove it.

3. Blow into the crankcase end of the valve. There should be a free passage of air through the valve.

4. Blow into the intake manifold end of the valve. There should be little or no passage of air through the valve.

5. If the PCV valve failed either of the preceding two checks, it will require replacement.

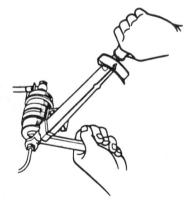

A torque wrench is essential when tightening the fuel lines to the 4K-E fuel filter

8. Install the fuel filter and then tighten the inlet bolt to 23-33 ft.lb.

9. Reconnect the delivery pipe using new gaskets and then tighten the union bolt to 18-25 ft.lb.

10. Run the engine for a few minutes and check for any fuel leaks.

11. Install the protective shield (if so equipped).

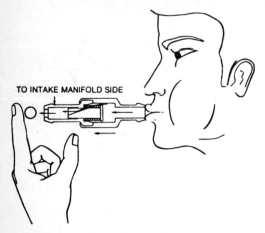

TO INTAKE MANIFOLD SIDE

Air should pass through the PCV valve when blowing into the crankcase side

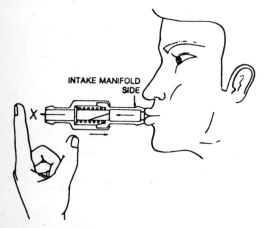

INTAKE MANIFOLD SIDE

Air should not pass through the PCV valve when blowing through the intake manifold side

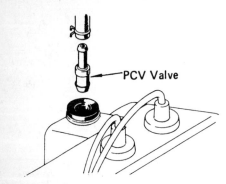

PCV Valve

Removing the PCV valve—typical

6. Installation is in the reverse order of removal.

NOTE: *On models with fuel injection there is no PCV valve. Vapor passage in the ventilation lines is controlled by two orifices.*

To check the PCV system on these models, inspect the hoses for cracks, leaks or other damage. Blow through the orifices to make

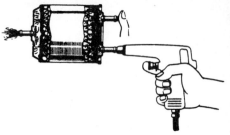

Using compressed air to clean the charcoal canister

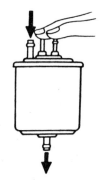

When cleaning the canister on later models, blow air into the outer vent pipe while plugging the other two

sure they are not blocked. Replace all components as necessary.

Evaporative Canister and System
SERVICING
Gasoline Engines Only

Check the evaporation control system every 15,000 miles. Check the fuel and vapor lines and the vacuum hoses for proper connections and correct routing, as well as condition. Replace clogged, damaged or deteriorated parts as necessary.

If the charcoal canister is clogged, it may be cleaned using low pressure compressed air. The entire canister should be replaced every 5 years/50,000 miles (60,000 miles for 1978 and later cars).

The canister is removed by unfastening the various hoses form the canister, and removing the mounting bolts from the mounting bracket or loosening the mounting clamp and removing the canister. Installation is in the reverse order of removal. Refer to Chapter Four for more information on the Emissions System.

Battery
SPECIFIC GRAVITY (EXCEPT MAINTENANCE FREE BATTERIES)

At least once a year, check the specific gravity of the battery. It should be between 1.20 and 1.26 at room temperature.

The specific gravity can be checked with the use of an hydrometer, an inexpensive instrument available from many sources, including auto parts stores. The hydrometer has squeeze bulb at one end and a nozzle at the other. Battery electrolyte is sucked into the hydrometer until the float is lifted from its seat. The specific gravity is then read by noting the position of the float. Generally, if after charging, the specific gravity between any two cells varies more than 50 points (0.050), the battery is bad and should be replaced.

It is not possible to check the specific gravity in this manner on sealed (maintenance free) batteries. Instead, the indicator built into the top of the case must be relied on to display any signs of battery deterioration. If the indicator is dark, the battery can be assumed to be OK. If the indicator is light, the specific gravity is low, and the battery should be charged or replaced.

CABLES AND CLAMPS

Once a year, the battery terminals and the cable clamps should be cleaned. Loosen the clamps and remove the cables, negative cable first. On batteries with posts on top, the use of a puller specially made for the purpose is recommended. These are inexpensive, and available in auto parts stores. Side terminal battery cables are secured with a bolt.

Clean the cable clamps and the battery terminal with a wire brush, until all corrosion, grease, etc., is removed and the metal is shiny. It is especially important to clean the inside of the clamp thoroughly, since a small deposit of foreign material or oxidation there will prevent a sound electrical connection and inhibit either starting or charging. Special tools are available for cleaning these parts, one type for conventional batteries and another type for side terminal batteries.

Before installing the cables, loosen the bat-

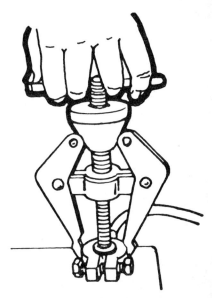

Special pullers are available to remove cable clamps

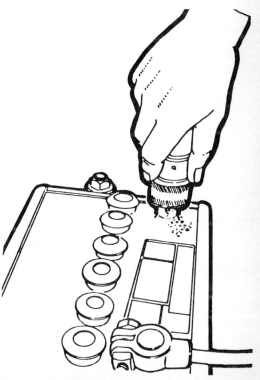

The specific gravity of the battery can be checked with a simple float-type hydrometer

Clean the battery posts with a wire brush, or the special tool shown

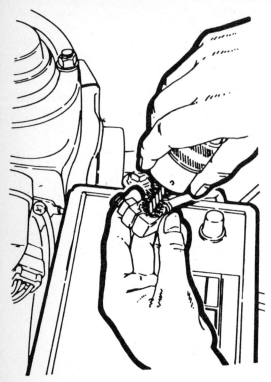

Clean the inside of the clamps with a wire brush, or the special tool

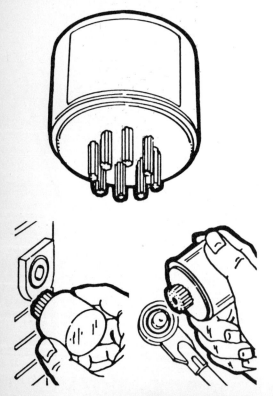

Special tools are also available for cleaning the posts and clamps on side terminal batteries

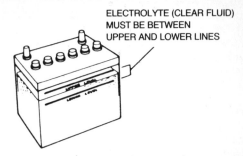

ELECTROLYTE (CLEAR FLUID) MUST BE BETWEEN UPPER AND LOWER LINES

Some batteries have level indicator lines on their sides

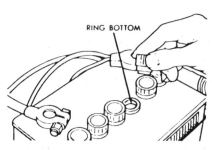

RING BOTTOM

Fill each battery cell to the bottom of the split ring with distilled water

tery holddown clamp or strap, remove the battery and check the battery tray. Clear it of any debris, and check it for soundness. Rust should be wire brushed away, and the metal given a coat of anti-rust paint. Replace the battery and tighten the holddown clamp or strap securely, but be careful not to overtighten, which will crack the battery case.

After the clamps and terminals are clean, reinstall the cables, negative cable last; do not hammer on the clamps to install. Tighten the clamps securely, but do not distort them. Give the clamps and terminals a thin external coat of grease after installation, to retard corrosion.

Check the cables at the same time that the terminals are cleaned. If the cable insulation is cracked or broken, or if the ends are frayed, the cable should be replaced with a new cable of the same length and gauge.

NOTE: *Keep flame or sparks away from the battery; it gives off explosive hydrogen gas. Battery electrolyte contains sulfuric acid. If you should splash any on your skin or in your eyes, flush the affected area with plenty of clear water; if it lands in your eyes, get medical help immediately.*

FLUID LEVEL

Check the battery electrolyte level at least once a month, or more often in hot weather or during periods of extended car operation. The level can be checked through the case on translucent batteries; the cell caps must be removed on other models. The caps must be removed on other models. The electrolyte level in each cell should be kept filled to the split ring inside, or the line marked on the outside of the case.

If the level is low, add only distilled water, or colorless, odorless drinking water, through the opening until the level is correct. Each cell is completely separate from the others, so each must be checked and filled individually.

If water is added in freezing weather, the car should be driven several miles to allow the water to mix with the electrolyte. Otherwise, the battery could freeze.

REPLACEMENT

When it becomes necessary to replace the battery, select a battery with a rating equal to or greater than the battery originally installed. Deterioration and just plain aging of the battery cables, starter motor, and associated wires makes the battery's job harder in successive years. The slow increase in electrical resistance over time makes it prudent to install a new battery with a greater capacity than the old. Details on battery removal and installation are covered in Chapter 3.

Belts

Check the condition of the drive belts and check and adjust the belt tension every 15,000 miles.

1. Inspect the belts for signs of glazing or cracking. A glazed belt will be perfectly smooth from slippage, while a good belt will have a slight texture of fabric visible. Cracks will usually start at the inner edge of the belt and run outward. Replace the belt at the first sign of cracking or if the glazing is severe.

2. Belt tension does not refer to play or droop. By placing your thumb midway between the two pulleys, it should be possible to depress the belt ¼-½". If any of the belts can be depressed more than this, or cannot be depressed this much, adjust the tension. Inadequate tension will result in slippage and wear, while excessive tension will damage bearings and cause belts to fray and crack.

3. All drive belts should be replaced every 60,000 miles regardless of their condition.

ADJUSTMENT

Alternator

To adjust the tension of the alternator drive belt on all models, loosen the pivot and mounting bolts on the alternator. Using a wooden hammer handle, a broomstick or your hand, move the alternator one way or the other until the proper tension is achieved.

CAUTION: *Do not use a screwdriver or any*

other metal device such as a pry bar, as a lever.

Tighten the mounting bolts securely. If a new belt has been installed, recheck the tension after about 200 miles of driving.

1. Loosen the pivot bolt

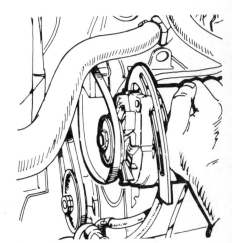

2. Push the component inwards

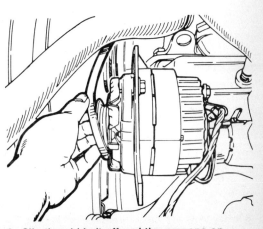

3. Slip the old belt off and the new one on

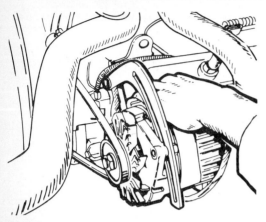

4. Pull outwards to tension the belt

Air Conditioning Compressor

A/C compressor belt tension can be adjusted by turning the tension adjusting bolt which is located on the compressor tensioner bracket. Turn the bolt clockwise to tighten the belt and counterclockwise to loosen it.

Air Pump

To adjust the tension of the air pump drive belt, loosen the adjusting lever bolt and the piv-

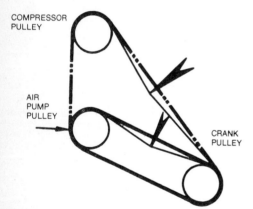

Air pump drive belt tension checking locations with and without A/C

ot bolt. Move the pump in or out until the desired tension is felt.

NOTE: *The tension should be checked between the air pump and the crankshaft pulley on cars without air conditioning. On cars with A/C the tension should be checked between the A/C compressor and the crankshaft pulley.*

Power Steering Pump

Tension on the power steering belt is adjusted by means of an idler pulley. Loosen the lock bolt and turn the adjusting bolt on the idler pulley until the desired tension is felt and then tighten the lock bolt.

Hoses

Upper and lower radiator hoses and all heater hoses should be checked for deterioration, leaks and loose hose clamps every 15,000 miles. To remove the hoses:
1. Drain the radiator.
2. Loosen the hose clamps at each end of the hose to be removed.
3. Working the hose back and forth, slide it off its connection and install the new hose if needed.
4. Position the hose clamps at least ¼" from the end of the hose and tighten them.
NOTE: *Make sure that the hose clamps are beyond the bead and placed in the center of the clamping surface before tightening them.*

Air Conditioning

Regular maintenance for the air conditioning system includes periodic checks of the drive belt tension. In addition, the system should be operated for at least five minutes every month (yes, in the winter too!). This ensures an adequate supply of lubricant to the bearings and also helps to prevent the seals and hoses from drying out. To do this comfortably in the winter, turn the air conditioning **On**, the temperature

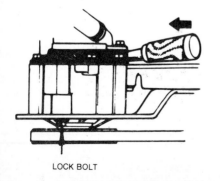

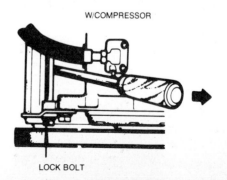

W/COMPRESSOR

LOCK BOLT

LOCK BOLT

Moving the air pump to tension the drive belt (with and without A/C)

HOW TO SPOT WORN V-BELTS

V-Belts are vital to efficient engine operation—they drive the fan, water pump and other accessories. They require little maintenance (occasional tightening) but they will not last forever. Slipping or failure of the V-belt will lead to overheating. If your V-belt looks like any of these, it should be replaced.

This belt has deep cracks, which cause it to flex. Too much flexing leads to heat build-up and premature failure. These cracks can be caused by using the belt on a pulley that is too small. Notched belts are available for small diameter pulleys.

Cracking or weathering

Oil and grease on a belt can cause the belt's rubber compounds to soften and separate from the reinforcing cords that hold the belt together. The belt will first slip, then finally fail altogether.

Softening (grease and oil)

Glazing is caused by a belt that is slipping. A slipping belt can cause a run-down battery, erratic power steering, overheating or poor accessory performance. The more the belt slips, the more glazing will be built up on the surface of the belt. The more the belt is glazed, the more it will slip. If the glazing is light, tighten the belt.

Glazing

The cover of this belt is worn off and is peeling away. The reinforcing cords will begin to wear and the belt will shortly break. When the belt cover wears in spots or has a rough jagged appearance, check the pulley grooves for roughness.

Worn cover

This belt is on the verge of breaking and leaving you stranded. The layers of the belt are separating and the reinforcing cords are exposed. It's just a matter of time before it breaks completely.

Separation

HOW TO SPOT BAD HOSES

Both the upper and lower radiator hoses are called upon to perform difficult jobs in an inhospitable environment. They are subject to nearly 18 psi at under hood temperatures often over 280°F., and must circulate nearly 7500 gallons of coolant an hour—3 good reasons to have good hoses.

A good test for any hose is to feel it for soft or spongy spots. Frequently these will appear as swollen areas of the hose. The most likely cause is oil soaking. This hose could burst at any time, when hot or under pressure.

Swollen hose

Cracked hoses can usually be seen but feel the hoses to be sure they have not hardened; a prime cause of cracking. This hose has cracked down to the reinforcing cords and could split at any of the cracks.

Cracked hose

Weakened clamps frequently are the cause of hose and cooling system failure. The connection between the pipe and hose has deteriorated enough to allow coolant to escape when the engine is hot.

Frayed hose end (due to weak clamp)

Debris, rust and scale in the cooling system can cause the inside of a hose to weaken. This can usually be felt on the outside of the hose as soft or thinner areas.

Debris in cooling system

control lever to **Warm** or **Hi** and turn on the blower to the highest setting. This will engage the compressor, circulating lubricating oils within the system, but preventing the discharge of cold air. The system should also be checked for proper refrigerant charge using the procedure given below.

SYSTEM CHECKS

CAUTION: *Do not attempt to charge or discharge the refrigerant system unless you are thoroughly familiar with its operation and the hazards involved. The compressed refrigerant used in the air conditioning system expands and evaporates (boils) into the atmosphere at a temperature of -29.8°C (-21.7°F) or less. This will freeze any surface that it comes in contact with, including your eyes. In addition, the refrigerant decomposes into a poisonous gas in the presence of flame.*

Factory installed Toyota air conditioners have a sight glass for checking the refrigerant charge. The sight glass is on top of the receiver/drier which is located in the front of the engine compartment, on the right or left side of the radiator depending upon the year of your car.

NOTE: *If your car is equipped with an aftermarket air conditioner, the following system check may not apply. Contact the manufacturer of the unit for instructions on system checks.*

This test works best if the outside air temperature is warm (above 70°F).

1. Place the automatic transmission in Park or the manual transmission in Neutral. Set the parking brake.

2. With the help of a friend, run the engine at a fast idle (about 1500 rpm).

3. Set the controls for maximum cold with the blower on high.

4. Look at the sight glass on top of the receiver/drier. If a steady stream of bubbles is present in the sight glass, the system is low on charge. Very likely there is leak in the system.

5. If no bubbles are present, the system is either fully charged or empty. Feel the high and low pressure lines at the compressor, if no appreciable temperature difference is felt, the system is empty, or nearly so.

6. If one hose is warm (high pressure) and the other is cold (low pressure), the system may be OK. However, you are probably making these tests because there is something wrong with the air conditioning, so proceed to the next step.

7. Either disconnect the compressor clutch wire or have an assistant in the car turn the fan control On and Off to operate the compressor clutch. Watch the sight glass.

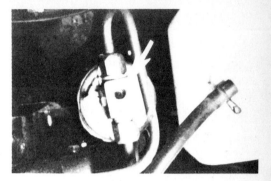

The receiver/drier has a sight glass (arrow)

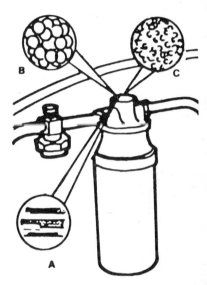

Oil streaks (A), constant bubbles (B) or foam (C) indicate there is not enough refrigerant in the system. Occasional bubbles during initial operation is normal. A clear sight glass indicates a proper charge of refrigerant or no refrigerant at all, which can be determined by the presence of cold air at the outlets in the car. If the glass is clouded with a milky white substance, have the receiver/drier checked professionally

8. If bubbles appear when the clutch is disengaged and disappear when it is engaged, the system is properly charged.

9. If the refrigerant takes more than 45 seconds to bubble when the clutch is disengaged, the system is most likely overcharged. This will usually result in poor cooling at low speeds.

NOTE: *If it is determined that the system has a leak, or needs charging, it should be serviced as soon as possible. Leaks may allow moisture to enter the system, causing an expensive rust problem. More comprehensive testing, diagnosis and service procedures may be found in CHILTON'S GUIDE TO AIR CONDITIONING SERVICE AND REPAIR, book part number 7580, available at your local retailer.*

Windshield Wipers

For maximum effectiveness and longest element life, the windshield and wiper blades should be kept clean. Dirt, tree sap, road tar and so on will cause streaking, smearing and blade deterioration if left on the glass. It is advisable to wash the windshield carefully with a commercial glass cleaner at least once a month. Wipe off the rubber blades with the wet rag afterwards. Do not attempt to move the wipers back and forth by hand; damage to the motor and drive mechanism will result.

If the blades are found to be cracked, broken or torn, they should be replaced immediately. Replacement intervals will vary with usage, although ozone deterioration usually limits blade life to about one year. If the wiper pattern is smeared or streaked, or if the blade chatters across the glass, the blades should be replaced. It is easiest and most sensible to replace them in pairs.

There are basically three different types of wiper blade refills, which differ in their method of replacement. One type has two release buttons, approximately ⅓ of the way up from the ends of the blade frame. Pushing the buttons down releases a lock and allows the rubber blade to be removed from the frame. The new blade slides back into the frame and locks into place.

The second type of refill has two metal tabs which are unlocked by squeezing them together. The rubber blade can then be withdrawn from the frame jaws. A new one is installed by inserting it into the front frame jaws and sliding it rearward to engage the remaining frame jaws. There are usually four jaws; when install-

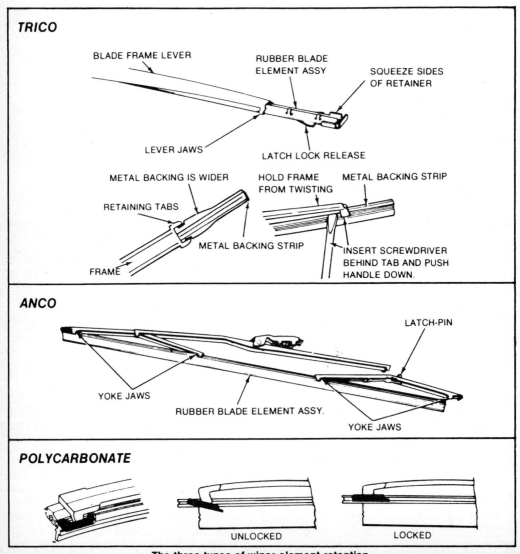

The three types of wiper element retention

ing, be certain that the refill is engaged in all of them. At the end of its travel, the tabs will lock into place on the front jaws of the wiper blade frame.

The third type is a refill made from polycarbonate. The refill has a simple locking device at one end which flexes downward out of the groove into which the jaws of the holder fit, allowing easy release. By sliding the new refill through all the jaws and pushing through the slight resistance when it reaches the end of its travel, the refill will lock into position.

Regardless of the type of refill used, make sure that all of the frame jaws are engaged as the refill is pushed into place and locked. The metal blade holder and frame will scratch the glass if allowed to touch it.

Tires

Tires should be checked weekly for proper air pressure. A chart, located either in the glove compartment or on the driver's or passenger's door, gives the recommended inflation pressures. Maximum fuel economy and tire life will result if the pressure is maintained at the highest figure on the chart. Pressures should be checked before driving since pressure can increase as much as six pounds per square inch (psi) due to heat buildup. It is a good idea to have your own accurate pressure gauge, because not all gauges on service station air pumps can be trusted. When checking pressures, do not neglect the spare tire. Note that some spare tires require pressures considerably higher than those used in the other tires.

While you are about the task of checking air pressure, inspect the tire treads for cuts, bruises and other damage. Check the air valves to be sure that they are tight. Replace any missing valve caps.

Check the tires for uneven wear that might indicate the need for front end alignment or tire rotation. Tires should be replaced when a tread wear indicator appears as a solid band across the tread.

When buying new tires, give some though to the following points, especially if you are considering a switch to larger tires or different profile series:

1. All four tires must be of the same construction type. This rule cannot be violated. Radial, bias, and bias-belted tires must not be mixed.

2. The wheels should be the correct width for the tire. Tire dealers have charts of tire and rim compatibility. A mismatch will cause sloppy handling and rapid tire wear. The tread width should match the rim width (inside bead to inside bead) within an inch. For radial tires, the rim width should be 80% or less of the tire (not tread) width.

3. The height (mounted diameter) of the new tires can change speedometer accuracy, engine speed at a given road speed, fuel mileage, acceleration, and ground clearance. Tire manufacturers furnish full measurement specifications.

4. The spare tire should be usable, at least for short distance and low speed operation, with the new tires.

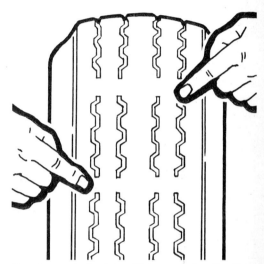

Tread wear indicators will appear when the tire is worn out

Tread depth can also be checked with an inexpensive gauge

A penny works as well as anything for checking tread depth; when the top of Lincoln's head is visible, it's time for new tires

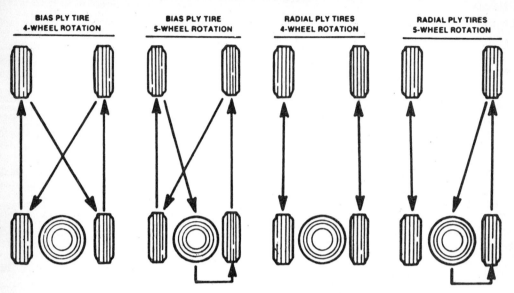

Tire rotation diagrams; note that radials should not be cross-switched

5. There shouldn't be any body interference when loaded, on bumps, or in turns.

TIRE ROTATION

Tire rotation is recommended every 6,000 miles or so, to obtain maximum tire wear. The pattern you use depends on whether or not your car has a usable spare. Radial tires should not be cross-switched (from one side of the car to the other); they last longer if their direction of rotation is not changed. Snow tires sometimes have directional arrows molded into the side of the carcass; the arrow shows the direction of rotation. They will wear very rapidly if the rotation is reversed. Studded tires will lose their studs if their rotational direction is reversed.

NOTE: *Mark the wheel position or direction of rotation on radial tires or studded snow tires before removing them.*

STORAGE

Store the tires at the proper inflation pressure if they are mounted on wheels. Keep them is a cool dry place, laid on their sides. If the tires are stored in the garage or basement, do not let them stand on a concrete floor; set them on strips of wood.

FLUIDS AND LUBRICANTS

Oil and Fuel Recommendations

OIL

The SAE (Society of Automotive Engineers) grade number indicates the viscosity of the engine oil and thus its ability to lubricate at a given temperature. The lower the SAE grade number, the lighter the oil; the lower the viscosity, the easier it is to crank the engine in cold weather.

Oil viscosities should be chosen from those oils recommended for the lowest anticipated temperatures during the oil change interval.

Multi-viscosity oils (10W-30, 20W-50, etc.) offer the important advantage of being adaptable to temperature extremes. They allow easy starting at low temperatures, yet they give good protection at high speeds and engine temperatures. This is a decided advantage in changeable climates or in long distance touring.

The API (American Petroleum Institute) designation indicates the classification of engine oil used under certain given operating conditions. Only oils designated for use "Service SF" should be used. Oils of the SF type perform a variety of functions inside the engine in addition to their basic functions inside the engine in addition to their basic function as a lubricant. Through a balanced system of metallic detergents and polymeric dispersions, the oil prevents the formation of high and low temperature deposits and also keeps sludge and particles of dirt in suspension. Acids, particularly sulfuric acid, as well as other by-products of combustion, are neutralized. Both the SAE grade number and the API designation can be found on top of the oil can.

Diesel engines also require SF engine oil. In addition, the oil must qualify for a CC rating. The API has a number of different diesel engine ratings, including CB, CC, and CD. Any of these other oils are fine as long as the designation CC

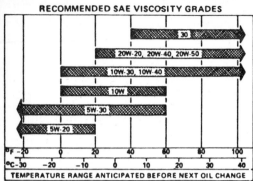

RECOMMENDED SAE VISCOSITY GRADES

NOTICE: Do not use SAE 5W-20 oils for continuous high-speed driving.

Oil viscosity chart

appears on the can along with them. Do not use oil labeled only SF or only CC. Both designations must always appear together.

For recommended oil viscosities, refer to the chart. Note that 10W-30 and 10W-40 grade oils are not recommended for sustained high speed driving when the temperature rises above the indicated limit.

CAUTION: *Non-detergent or straight mineral oils should not be used in your car.*

SYNTHETIC OIL

There are many excellent synthetic and fuel-efficient oils currently available that can provide better gas mileage, longer service life, and in some cases better engine protection. These benefits do not come without a few hitches, however, the main one being the price of synthetic oils, which is three or four times the price per quart of conventional oil.

Synthetic oil is not for every car and ever type of driving, so you should consider your engine's condition and your type of driving. Also, check your car's warranty conditions regarding the use of synthetic oils.

Both brand new engines and older, high mileage engines are the wrong candidates for synthetic oil. The synthetic oils are so slippery that they can prevent the proper break-in of new engines; most manufacturer's recommend that you wait until the engine is properly broken in (5,000 miles) until using synthetic oil. Older engines with wear have a different problem with synthetics: they use consume during operation) more oil as they age. Slippery synthetic oils get past these worn parts easily. If your engine is using conventional oil, it will use synthetics much faster. If your car is leaking oil past old seals you'll have a much greater leak problem with synthetics.

Consider your type of driving. If most of your accumulated mileage is high speed, highway

type driving, the more expensive synthetic oils may be of benefit. Extended highway driving gives the engine chance to warm up, accumulating less acids in the oil and putting less stress on the engine over the long run. Under these conditions, the oil change interval can be extended (as long as your oil filter can last the extended life of the oil) up to the advertised mileage claims of the synthetics. Cars with synthetic oils may show increased fuel economy in highway driving, due to less internal friction. However, many automotive experts agree that 50,000 miles is too long to keep any oil in your engine.

Cars used under harder circumstances, such as stop-and-go, city type driving, short trips, or extended idling, should be serviced more frequently. For the engines in these cars, the much greater cost of synthetic or fuel-efficient oils may not be worth the investment. Internal wear increases much quicker on these cars, causing greater oil consumption and leakage.

NOTE: *The mixing of conventional and synthetic oils is not recommended. If you are using synthetic oil, it might be wise to carry two or three quarts with you no matter where you drive, as not all service stations carry this type of lubricant.*

FUEL

All 1970-76 Corolla and Carina models are designed to operate on regular grade fuel (90 octane or higher). 1975-76 Corollas built for use in California, and all models made in 1977 and later are designed to run on unleaded fuel. The use of leaded fuel in a car requiring unleaded fuel will plug the catalytic converter, rendering it inoperative and will increase exhaust backpressure to the point where engine output will be severely reduced. In all cases, the minimum octane rating of the fuel used must be at least 91 RON (87 CLC). All unleaded fuels sold in the U.S. are required to meet this minimum octane rating.

The use of a fuel too low in octane (a measurement of anti-knock quality) will result in spark knock. Since many factors affect operating efficiency, such as altitude, terrain, air temperature and humidity, knocking may result even though the recommended fuel is being used. If persistent knocking occurs, it may be necessary to switch to a higher grade of fuel. Continuous or heavy knocking may result in engine damage.

NOTE: *Your engine's fuel requirement can change with time, mainly due to carbon buildup, which changes the compression ratio. If your engine pings, knocks or runs on, switch to a higher grade of fuel. Sometimes just changing brands will cure the problem.*

If it becomes necessary to retard the timing from specifications, don't change it more than a few degrees. Retarded timing will reduce power output and fuel mileage and will increase the engine temperature.

Corolla Diesels require the use of diesel fuel. At no time should gasoline be substituted. Two grades of diesel fuel are manufactured, #1 and #2, although #2 grade is generally more available. Better fuel economy results from the use of #2 grade fuel. In some northern parts of the U.S. and in most parts of Canada, #1 grade fuel is available in the winter or a winterized blend of #2 grade is supplied in winter months. When the temperature falls below 20°F (-7°C), #1 grade or winterized #2 grade fuel are the only fuels that can be used. Cold temperatures cause unwinterized #2 to thicken (it actually gels), blocking the fuel lines and preventing the engine from running.

DIESEL CAUTIONS:
- Do not use home heating oil in your car.
- Do not use ether or starting assist fluids in your car.

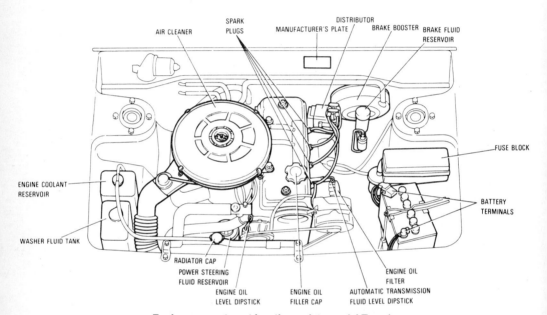

Engine compartment locations—late model Tercels

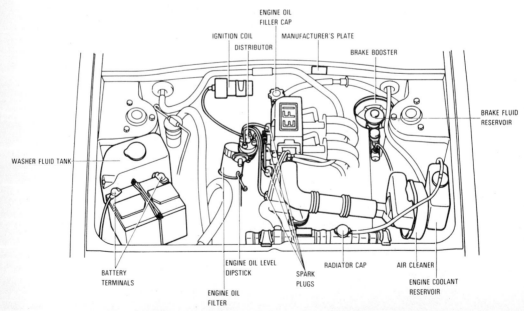

Engine compartment locations—late model Starlets

● Do not use any fuel additives recommended for use in gasoline engines.

It is normal that the engine noise level is louder during the warm-up period in winter. It is also normal that whitish-blue smoke may be emitted from the exhaust after starting and during warm-up. The amount of smoke depends upon the outside temperature.

OPERATION IN FOREIGN COUNTRIES

If you plan to drive your car outside the United States or Canada, there is a possibility that fuels will be too low in anti-knock quality and could produce engine damage. It is wise to consult with local authorities upon arrival in a foreign country to determine the best fuels available.

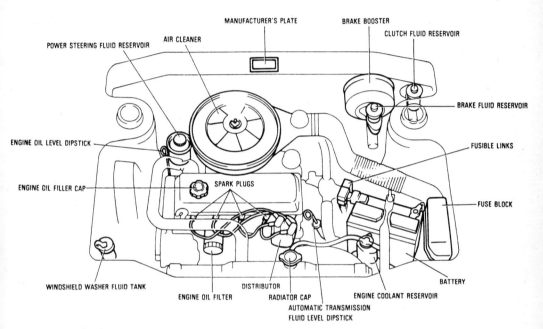

Engine compartment locations—late model Corolla FWD with gasoline engine

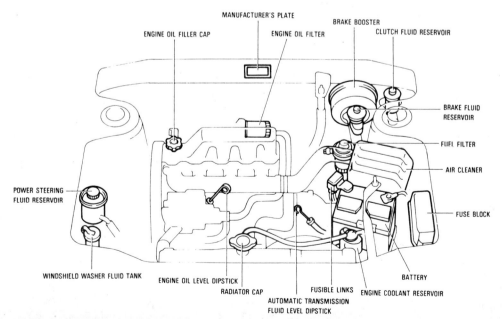

Engine compartment locations—late model Corolla FWD with diesel engine

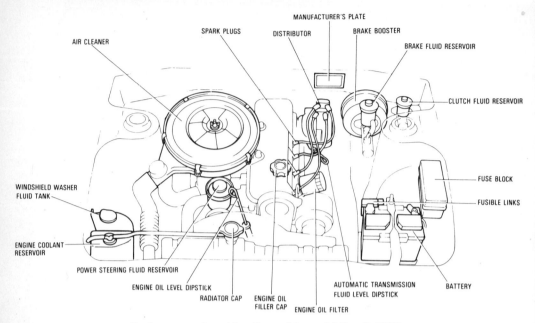

MANUFACTURER'S PLATE

SPARK PLUGS

DISTRIBUTOR

BRAKE BOOSTER

AIR CLEANER

BRAKE FLUID RESERVOIR

CLUTCH FLUID RESERVOIR

FUSE BLOCK

FUSIBLE LINKS

WINDSHIELD WASHER FLUID TANK

ENGINE COOLANT RESERVOIR

POWER STEERING FLUID RESERVOIR

ENGINE OIL LEVEL DIPSTICK

RADIATOR CAP

ENGINE OIL FILLER CAP

ENGINE OIL FILTER

AUTOMATIC TRANSMISSION FLUID LEVEL DIPSTICK

BATTERY

Engine compartment locations—late model Corolla RWD

Engine

OIL LEVEL CHECK

CAUTION: *Prolonged and repeated skin contact with used engine oil, with no effort to remove the oil, may be harmful. Always follow these simple precautions when handling used motor oil.*

• Avoid prolonged skin contact with used motor oil.

• Remove oil from skin by washing thoroughly with soap and water or waterless hand cleaner. Do not use gasoline, thinners or other solvents.

• Avoid prolonged skin contact with oil-soaked clothing.

Every time you stop for fuel, check the engine oil as follows:

1. Park the car on level ground.

2. When checking the oil level it is best for the engine to be at operating temperature, although checking the oil immediately after stopping will lead to a false reading. Wait a few minutes after turning off the engine to allow the oil to drain back into the crankcase.

3. Open the hood and locate the dipstick. Pull the dipstick from its tube, wipe it clean and reinsert it.

4. Pull the dipstick out again and, holding is horizontally, read the oil level. The oil should be between the **F** and **L** or high and low marks on

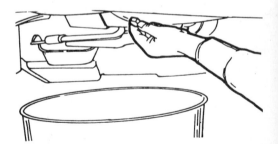

By keeping an inward pressure on the drain plug as you unscrew it, the oil won't escape past the threads

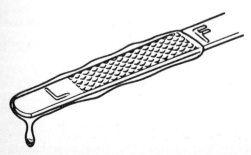

Typical oil dipstick

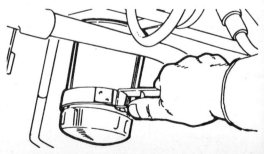

Remove the oil filter with a strap wrench

the dipstick. If the oil is below the **L** or low mark, add oil of the proper viscosity through the capped opening on the top of the cylinder head cover. See the "Oil and Fuel Recommendations" chart in this chapter for the proper viscosity and rating of oil to use.

5. Replace the dipstick and check the oil level again after adding any oil. Be careful not to overfill the crankcase. Approximately one quart of oil will raise the level from the **L** or low mark to the **F** or high mark. Excess oil will generally be consumed at an accelerated rate.

OIL AND FILTER CHANGE

CAUTION: *Prolonged and repeated skin contact with used engine oil, with no effort to*

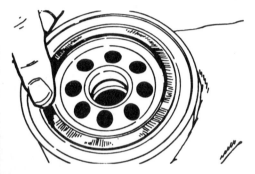

Lubricate the gasket on the new filter with clean engine oil. A dry gasket may not make a good seal and will allow the filter to leak

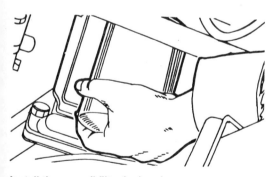

Install the new oil filter by hand

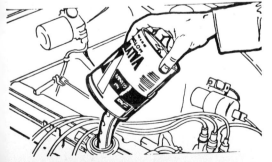

Add oil through the cylinder head cover only

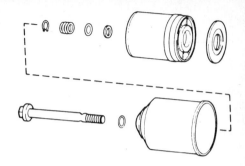

Exploded view of the oil filter used on California diesel engines

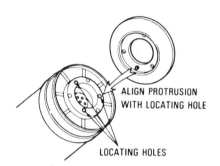

ALIGN PROTRUSION WITH LOCATING HOLE

LOCATING HOLES

On California diesel engines, always make sure that the protrusion on the new gasket aligns with one of the locating holes on the filter

remove the oil, may be harmful. Always follow these simple precautions when handling used motor oil:

- Avoid prolonged skin contact with used motor oil.
- Remove oil from skin by washing thoroughly with soap and water or waterless hand cleaner. Do not use gasoline, thinners or other solvents.
- Avoid prolonged skin contact with oil-soaked clothing.

Except California 1C-L

CAUTION: *The oil should be changed every 6,000 miles on 1970-77 models. All 1978 and later models. All 1978 and later models should have the oil changed every 7,500 miles.*

The oil drain plug is located on the bottom, rear of the oil pan (bottom of the engine, underneath the car).

The mileage figures given are the Toyota recommended intervals assuming normal driving and conditions. If your car is being used under dusty, polluted or off-road conditions, change the oil and filter more frequently than specified. The same goes for cars driven in stop-and-go traffic or only for short distances. Always drain the oil after the engine has been running long enough to bring it to normal operating temperature. Hot oil will flow easier and more contaminants will be removed along with the oil than if it were drained cold. To change the oil and filter:

1. Run the engine until it reaches normal operating temperature.

2. Jack up the front of the car and support on safety stands.

3. Slide a drain pan of at least 6 quart capacity under the oil pan.

4. Loosen the drain plug. Turn the plug out by hand. By keeping an inward pressure on the plug as you unscrew it, oil won't escape past the threads and you can remove it without being burned by hot oil.

5. Allow the oil to drain completely and then install the drain plug. Don't overtighten the plug, or you'll be buying a new pan or a trick replacement plug for stripped threads.

6. Using a strap wrench, remove the oil filter. Keep in mind that it's holding about one quart of dirty, hot oil.

7. Empty the old filter into the drain pan and dispose of the filter.

8. Using a clean rag, wipe off the filter adaptor on the engine block. Be sure that the rag doesn't leave any lint which could clog an oil passage.

9. Coat the rubber gasket on the filter with fresh oil. Spin it onto the engine by hand; when the gasket touches the adaptor surface give it another ½-¾ turn. No more, or you'll squash the gasket and it will leak.

10. Refill the engine with the correct amount of fresh oil. See the Capacities Chart.

11. Check the oil level on the dipstick. It is normal for the level to be a bit above the full mark. Start the engine and allow it to idle for a few minutes.

CAUTION: *Do not run the engine above idle speed until it has built up oil pressure, indicated when the oil light goes out.*

12. Shut off the engine, allow the oil to drain for a minute, and check the oil level. Check around the filter and drain plug for any leaks, and correct as necessary.

California 1C-L

1. Follow Steps 1-5 of the previous procedure. Don't forget any NOTES and CAUTIONS.

2. Loosen the retaining bolt and pull it out. Remove the oil filter case.

3. Lift off the rubber gasket and then take out the filter element.

CAUTION: *Be careful not to lose the rubber washer, washer spring, snap ring and O-ring from inside the oil filter case when removing the filter element.*

4. Using a new rubber gasket, position it on

the oil filter element so that the gasket tab aligns with the hole in the element.

5. Install the snapring washer and new rubber washer into the filter case and then install the new filter element and gasket.

6. Coat the rubber gasket with clean engine oil and install the entire oil filter assembly onto the engine block.

7. Follow Steps 10-12 of the previous procedure.

Transmission/Transaxle
FLUID LEVEL CHECK
Manual

The oil in the manual transmission should be checked at least every 15,000 miles and replaced every 25,000-30,000 miles.

1. With the car parked on a level surface, remove the filler plug from the side of the transmission housing.

2. If the lubricant begins to trickle out of the hole, there is enough. Otherwise, carefully insert your finger (watch out for sharp threads) and check to see if the oil is up to the edge of the hole.

3. If not, add oil through the hole until the level is at the edge of the hole. Most gear lubricants come in a plastic squeeze bottle with a

Recommended Lubricants

Lubricant	Classification
Engine Oil	API SE/SF/CC
Manual Transmission	API GL–4/GL–5 SAE 75W–90 or 80W–90
Manual Transaxle	API GL–4/GL–5 SAE 80W–90
Automatic Transmission	ATF Type Dexron® II ① (A55, A41, A130L & A131L only) ATF Type F (all others)
Differential	API GL–5 SAE 80W–90 ②
Ball Joints	NLGI #1 NLGI #2
Steering Gear	NLGI #2
Power Steering Fluid	ATF Type Dexron® II
Brake Fluid	DOT 3
Wheel Bearing	NLGI #2
Clutch Fluid	DOT 3
Antifreeze	Ethylene Glycol

① Diesel: ATF Dexron® II
② 1984 Corolla FWD: Dexron® II

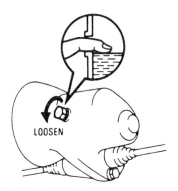

Checking the oil level with your finger

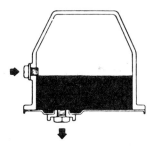

Manual transmission oil level should be up to the bottom of the filler (upper) plug hole

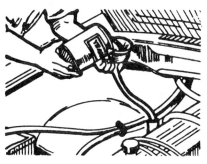

Add automatic transmission fluid through the dipstick tube

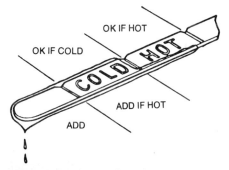

Automatic transmission dipstick—all except the 2 speed Toyoglide

nozzle, making additions simple. You can also use a common everyday kitchen baster. Refer to the Recommended Lubricants chart for the proper oil.

4. Replace the filler plug.

Automatic

Check the automatic transmission fluid level at least every 15,000 miles (more if possible). The dipstick is in the rear of the engine compartment.

2-SPEED TOYOGLIDE

Start the car cold and allow the engine to idle for a few minutes. Set the handbrake and apply the service brakes. Move the gear selector through all of the ranges.

With the engine still running, the parking brake on, and the selector in Neutral (N), remove and clean the transmission dipstick. Insert the dipstick fully, remove it and take a reading. The fluid level should fall between the **L** and **F** marks. If the level is below **L**, add type F fluid to the filler tube until the fluid level is up to the **F** mark.

CAUTION: *Do not overfill the transmission.*

If the fluid contains particles or bubbles, or is burnt, the transmission is defective and should be overhauled.

CAUTION: *Never use type A, DEXRON® or DEXRON®II fluid or gear oil in the transmission. Do not use engine oil supplements either.*

ALL OTHERS

The fluid level should be checked only when the transmission is hot (normal operating temperature). The transmission is considered hot after about 20 miles of highway driving.

1. Park the car on a level surface with the engine idling. Shift the transmission into Neutral and set the parking brake.

2. Remove the dipstick, wipe it clean and reinsert it firmly. Be sure that it has been pushed all the way in. Remove the dipstick and check the fluid level while holding it horizontally. With the engine running, the fluid level should be between the second and third notches on the dipstick.

3. If the fluid level is below the second notch, add the required type of transmission fluid until the proper level is reached. This is easily done with the aid of a funnel. Check the level often as you are filling the transmission. Be extremely careful not to overfill it. Overfilling will cause slippage, seal damage and overheating. Approximately one pint of transmission fluid will raise the level from one notch to the other.

CAUTION: *Use Type F automatic transmission fluid in transmissions EXCEPT, A55,*

A41, A130L and A131L models. The A55, A41, A130L and A131L (and all 1985-87 Corolla and Tercel models) use only DEXRON II (Never use Type F in these units). Check your vehicle owner's manual to be sure.

The fluid on the dipstick should always be a bright red color. If it is discolored (brown or black), or smells burnt, serious transmission troubles, probably due to overheating, should be suspected. The transmission should be inspected by a qualified service technician to locate the cause of the burnt fluid.

DRAIN AND REFILL

Manual

The manual transmission oil should be changed at least every 25,000-30,000 miles. To change, proceed as follows:

1. The oil must be hot before it is drained. If the car is driven until the engine is at normal operating temperature, the oil should be hot enough.

2. Remove the filler plug to provide a vent.

3. The drain plug is on the bottom of the transmission. Place large container underneath the transmission and remove the plug.

4. Allow the oil to drain completely. Clean off the plug and replace it. Tighten it until it is just snug.

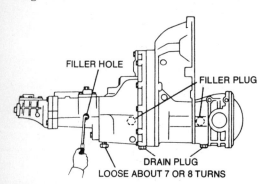

Drain plug and filler plug locations on the 4 x 4 transaxle

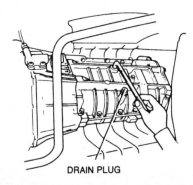

Typical manual transmission drain plug and filler plug locations

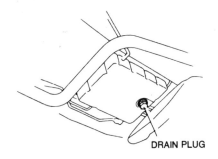

Most Toyota automatic transmissions have a drain plug

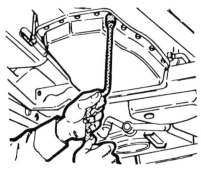

Removing the pan on the automatic transmission

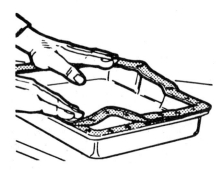

Always replace the gasket when installing the pan

5. Fill the transmission with SAE 80 or SAE 80W/90 gear oil (the transaxle on Corollas with a diesel engine uses Dexron®II automatic transmission fluid). This usually comes in a plastic squeeze bulb or a kitchen baster to squirt the oil in. Refer to the Capacities Chart for the proper amount of oil to put in.

6. The oil level should come up to the top of the filler hole.

7. Replace the filler plug, drive the car for a few minutes, stop, and check for any leaks.

Automatic

The automatic transmission fluid should be changed at least every 25,000-30,000 miles. If the car is normally used in severe service, such as stop-and-go driving, trailer towing or the like, the interval should be halved. The fluid should be hot before it is drained; a 20 minute drive will accomplish this.

Toyota automatic transmissions have a drain plug in them so that if you are in a hurry, you can simply remove the plug, drain the fluid, replace the plug and then refill the transmission. Although this method is fine, a slightly longer procedure may be more effective. If you have the extra time, read on.

1. Remove the plug and drain the fluid. When the fluid stops coming out of the drain hole, loosen the pan retaining screws until the pan can be pulled down at one corner. Lower a corner of the pan and allow any remaining fluid to drain out.

2. After the pan has drained completely, remove the pan retaining screws and then remove the pan and gasket.

3. Clean the pan thoroughly and allow it to air dry. If you wipe it out with a rag you run the risk of leaving bits of lint in the pan which will clog the tiny hydraulic passages in the transmission.

4. Install the pan using a new gasket.

5. Install the drain plug.

6. It is a good idea to measure the amount of fluid drained from the transmission to determine the correct amount of fresh fluid to add. This is because some parts of the transmission may not drain completely and using the dry refill amount specified in the Capacities Chart could lead to overfilling. Fluid is added only through the dipstick tube. Use the proper automatic transmission fluid as specified in the Recommended Lubricants Chart.

7. Replace the dipstick after filling. Start the engine and allow it to idle. DO NOT race the engine.

8. After the engine has idled for a few minutes, shift the transmission slowly through the gears and then return it to Park. With the engine still idling, check the fluid level on the dipstick. If necessary, add more fluid to raise the level to where it is supposed to be.

Differential

FLUID LEVEL CHECK

The oil in the differential should be checked at least every 15,000 miles and replaced every 25,000-30,000 miles.

1. With the car parked on a level surface, remove the filler plug from the back of the differential (all rear drive models and the rear differential on the 4X4 Tercel) or the side (all front drive models).

NOTE: *The plug on the bottom is the drain plug.*

CAUTION: *Do not confuse the differential*

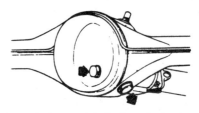

Filler (upper) plug and drain (lower) plug locations on the rear differential—rear wheel drive and 4 x 4 only

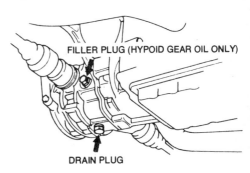

FILLER PLUG (HYPOID GEAR OIL ONLY)

DRAIN PLUG

Filler and drain plug locations on the front differential—front wheel drive only

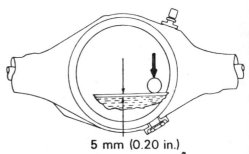

5 mm (0.20 in.)

The fluid level in the differential should be up to the edge of the filler hole (large arrow)

filler plugs on front drive models with the filler plugs for the transaxle (see illustration).

2. If the oil begins to trickle out of the hole, there is enough. Otherwise, carefully insert your finger (watch for sharp threads) into the hole and check to see if the oil is up to the bottom edge of the filler hole.

3. If not, add oil through the hole until the level is at the edge of the hole. Most gear oils come in a plastic squeeze bottle with a nozzle, making additions simple. You can also use a common everyday kitchen baster. Use standard GL-5 hypoid type gear oil, SAE 90W or SAE 80W, if you live in a particularly cold area.

NOTE: *The differential on 1984 Corolla FWD models uses Dexron®II automatic transmission fluid.*

4. Replace the filler plug and run the engine for a while. Turn off the engine and check for leaks.

DRAIN AND REFILL

The gear oil in the differential should be changed at least every 25,000-30,000 miles.

To drain and fill the differential, proceed as follows:

1. Park the vehicle on a level surface. Set the parking brake.

2. Remove the filler (upper) plug. Place a container which is large enough to catch all of the differential oil, under the drain plug.

3. Remove the drain (lower) plug and gasket, if so equipped. Allow all of the oil to drain into the container.

4. Install the drain plug. Tighten it so that it will not leak, but do not overtighten.

5. Refill with the proper grade and viscosity of axle lubricant (See Recommended Lubricants). Be sure that the level reaches the bottom of the filler plug.

6. Install the filler plug and check for leakage.

Cooling System

LEVEL CHECK

It's a good idea to check the coolant every time that you stop for fuel. If the engine is hot, (on models without an expansion tank) let it cool for a few minutes before checking the level. (Models equipped with an expansion tank can be checked by looking at the fluid level in the tank reservoir.

If a hot engine must be checked, (models without an expansion tank) use several folds of rag over the radiator cap, and slowly turn the cap counterclockwise until it reaches the first detent. Allow all of the steam to escape. When the hissing stops, remove the cap the rest of the way.

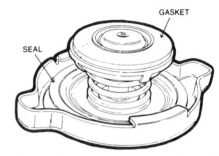

Check the radiator cap seal and gasket condition

Some radiator caps have pressure release levers

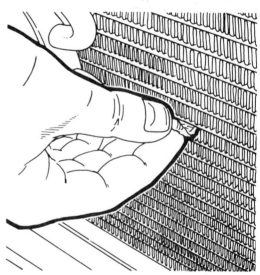

Clean the radiator fins of any debris which impedes air flow

If the engine is hot, cover the radiator cap with a rag

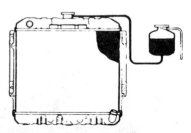

Check the coolant level in the expansion tank on models with a closed cooling system

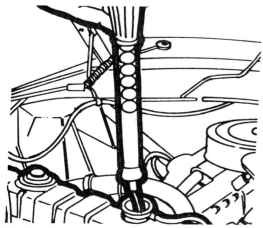

The freezing protection rating can be checked with an antifreeze tester

On models without a coolant expansion tank, the coolant level should be ¾ of an inch below the filler neck (engine cold)

If the coolant level is low, (more than ¾" below the top of the radiator filler neck, or below the low mark on the side of the expansion tank) add equal parts of water and engine coolant/antifreeze. On models without an expansion tank, fill to within ¾" of the top of the filler tube. On models with an expansion tank, fill to the full level mark on the side of the tank.

Check the freezing protection rating at least once a year, preferable just before the winter sets in. This can be done with an antifreeze tester (most service stations will have one on hand will probably check it for you, if not, they are available at an auto parts store). Maintain a protection rating of at least -20°F (-29°C) to prevent engine damage as a result of freezing and to assure the proper engine operating temperature.

SYSTEM SERVICING

1. Remove the radiator cap and the expansion cap (if so equipped).

2. With the caps removed, run the engine until the upper radiator hose is hot. This means that the thermostat is open and the coolant is flowing through the system.

3. Turn off the engine, place a large container underneath the radiator and open the drain valve at the bottom of the radiator.

NOTE: *Drainage may be speeded by removing the drain plugs on the sides of the cylinder block.*

4. Close the drain valve and add water until the system is filled.

5. Repeat Steps 3 and 4 several times until the drained liquid is nearly colorless.

6. Tighten the drain valve and then fill the radiator with a 50/50 mixture of ethylene glycol and water.

7. With the radiator cap still removed, run the engine until the upper radiator hose is hot. Add coolant if necessary, replace the caps and check for any leaks.

Brake and Clutch Master Cylinders
FLUID LEVEL CHECK

The brake and clutch master cylinders are located under the hood, in the left rear section of the engine compartment. They are made of translucent plastic so that the levels may be

Some models have two brake fluid reservoirs, while others have only one

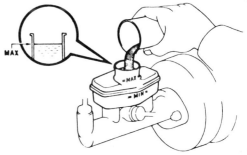

Always fill the master cylinder slowly so as not to create air bubbles in the system

checked without removing the tops. The fluid level in both reservoirs should be checked at least every 15,000 miles. The fluid level should be maintained at the upper most mark on the side of the reservoir. Any sudden decrease in the level indicates a possible leaks in the system and should be checked out immediately.

NOTE: *Some early models may have two separate reservoirs for the brake master cylinder, but most will only have one. All Corollas with a manual transmission will also utilize a clutch master cylinder which is located close to the brake master cylinder, while all Tercels and Starlets have no clutch master cylinder at all since they use a cable-operated clutch.*

When making additions of brake fluid, use only fresh, uncontaminated brake fluid meeting or exceeding DOT 3 standards. Be careful not to spill any brake fluid on painted surfaces, as it eats the paint. Do not allow the brake fluid container or the master cylinder reservoir to remain open any longer than necessary; brake fluid absorbs moisture from the air, reducing its effectiveness and causing corrosion in the lines.

Power Steering Pump
FLUID LEVEL CHECK

The fluid level in the power steering reservoir should be checked at least every 15,000 miles.

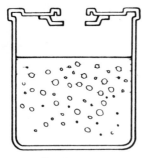

Foaming or emulsification indicates air in the system

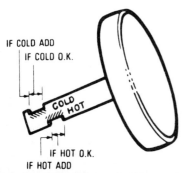

IF COLD ADD
IF COLD O.K.
COLD
HOT
IF HOT O.K.
IF HOT ADD

Power steering pump dipstick on newer models

The vehicle should be parked on level ground, with the engine warm and running at normal idle. Remove the filler cap and check the level on the dipstick; it should be in between the edges of the cross-hatched area on older models or within the **HOT** area on the dipstick on newer models. If the level is low, add Dexron®II type ATF until the proper level is achieved.

Steering Gear
FLUID LEVEL CHECK

The steering gear oil level should be checked at least every 15,000 miles. The filler plug (on models equipped) is on top of the gear housing. The oil level should be kept even with the bottom of the filler hole or slightly lower. Use standard GL-4 hypoid type gear oil SAE 90.

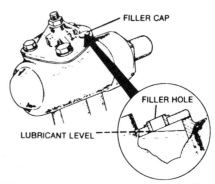

FILLER CAP

FILLER HOLE

LUBRICANT LEVEL

Fill the steering gear to the bottom of the filler hole

Chassis Greasing

Chassis lubrication for these models is limited to greasing the front ball joints every 25,000-30,000 miles.

1. Remove the screw plug from the ball joint. Install a grease nipple.

2. Using a hand-operated grease gun, lubricate the ball joint with NLGI #1 or NLGI #2 molybdenum-disulphide lithium-based grease.

3. Remove the nipped and reinstall the screw plug.

4. Repeat for the other ball joint(s).

Body Lubrication

There is no set period recommended by Toyota for body lubrication. However, it is a good idea to lubricate the following body points at least once a year, especially in the fall before cold weather.

Lubricate with engine oil:
- Door lock latches.
- Door lock rollers.
- Door, hood and hinge pivots.

Lubricate with Lubriplate:

- Trunk lid latch and hinge.
- Glove box door latch.
- Front seat slides.

Lubricate with silicone spray:

- All rubber weather stripping.
- Hood stops.

When finished lubricating a body part, be sure that all the excess lubricant has been wiped off, especially in the areas of the car which may come in contact with clothing.

Wheel Bearings

Refer to the appropriate Chapter for wheel bearing assembly and packing procedures. The front wheel bearings should be repacked every 24,000 miles on 1970-74 vehicles, 25,000 miles on 1975-77 vehicles, and 30,000 miles on 1978 and later vehicles, or every 24 months, whichever occurs first.

PUSHING AND TOWING

Pushing

All Toyotas equipped with a manual transmission can be push started, although more than one car has received a dented fender or bumper from this operation. To push start the car, turn the ignition switch to the ON position, push in the clutch pedal, put the gear shift lever in second or third gear and partially depress the gas pedal. As the car begins to pick up momentum while being pushed, release the clutch pedal and give it gas.

CAUTION: *Never attempt to push start the car while it is in reverse.*

Toyotas that are equipped with an automatic transmission can not be push started no matter how far or how fast they are pushed.

Towing

Cars with a manual transmission can be towed with either end up in the air or with all four wheels on the ground. You need only remember that the transmission must be in Neutral, the parking brake must be off and the ignition switch must be in the **ACC** position.

Cars with an automatic transmission have a few more restrictions when it comes to towing them. The transmission must always be in Neutral, the parking brake must be off and the ignition switch must be in the **ACC** position. On rear wheel drive models, towing with the rear wheels in the air is fine, but remember that the steering column lock is not designed to hold the front wheels in the straight ahead position while the car is being towed.

Front Wheel Drive models, with automatic transmissions, should never be towed with the front wheels on the ground. A dolly or roll back truck should be used.

With the exception of 1974-77 models, Toyotas (RWD) should be towed with the front wheels in the air, but for not more than 50 miles at speeds no greater than 30 mph. Anything more than this will require disconnecting the driveshaft. The same restriction applies when the car is being flat-towed.

1974-77 Toyotas should not be towed with the rear wheels on the ground regardless of the circumstances. If the front end must be raised, either put dollies under the rear wheels or disconnect the driveshaft. The only way that the car can be flat-towed is if the driveshaft has been disconnected.

NOTE: *Most Toyotas are equipped with tow hooks at the front and back of the car. If the car is to be flat-towed, use the hooks. Don't use an unsuspecting suspension member or the bumper.*

JACKING

There are certain safety precautions which should be observed when jacking the vehicle. They are as follows:

1. Always jack the car on a level surface.
2. Set the parking brake, and block the rear wheels, if the front wheels are to be raised. This will keep the car from rolling backward off the jack.
3. If the rear wheels are to be raised, block off the front wheels to keep the car from rolling forward.
4. Block the wheel diagonally opposite the one which is being raised.

NOTE: *The tool kit which is supplied with most Toyota passenger cars includes a wheel block.*

5. If the vehicle is being raised in order to work underneath it, support it with jackstands. Do not place the jackstands against the sheet metal panels beneath the car or they will become distorted.

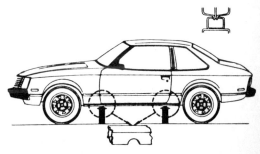

Jacking points for the scissors jack

JUMP STARTING A DEAD BATTERY

The chemical reaction in a battery produces explosive hydrogen gas. This is the safe way to jump start a dead battery, reducing the chances of an accidental spark that could cause an explosion.

Jump Starting Precautions

1. Be sure both batteries are of the same voltage.
2. Be sure both batteries are of the same polarity (have the same grounded terminal).
3. Be sure the vehicles are not touching.
4. Be sure the vent cap holes are not obstructed.
5. Do not smoke or allow sparks around the battery.
6. In cold weather, check for frozen electrolyte in the battery.
7. Do not allow electrolyte on your skin or clothing.
8. Be sure the electrolyte is not frozen.

Jump Starting Procedure

1. Determine voltages of the two batteries; they must be the same.
2. Bring the starting vehicle close (they must not touch) so that the batteries can be reached easily.
3. Turn off all accessories and both engines. Put both cars in Neutral or Park and set the handbrake.
4. Cover the cell caps with a rag—do not cover terminals.
5. If the terminals on the run-down battery are heavily corroded, clean them.
6. Identify the positive and negative posts on both batteries and connect the cables in the order shown.
7. Start the engine of the starting vehicle and run it at fast idle. Try to start the car with the dead battery. Crank it for no more than 10 seconds at a time and let it cool off for 20 seconds in between tries.
8. If it doesn't start in 3 tries, there is something else wrong.
9. Disconnect the cables in the reverse order.
10. Replace the cell covers and dispose of the rags.

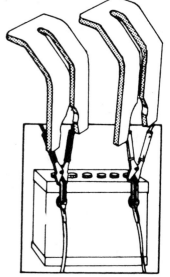

Side terminal batteries occasionally pose a problem when connecting jumper cables. There frequently isn't enough room to clamp the cables without touching sheet metal. Side terminal adaptors are available to alleviate this problem and should be removed after use.

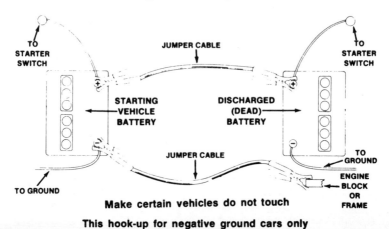

TO STARTER SWITCH   JUMPER CABLE   TO STARTER SWITCH

STARTING VEHICLE BATTERY   DISCHARGED (DEAD) BATTERY

JUMPER CABLE

TO GROUND   TO GROUND   ENGINE BLOCK OR FRAME

Make certain vehicles do not touch

This hook-up for negative ground cars only

CAUTION: *Do not work beneath a vehicle supported only by a tire changing jack.*

6. Do not use a bumper jack to raise the vehicle; the bumpers are not designed for this purpose.

HOW TO BUY A USED CAR

Many people believe that a two or three year old used car is a better buy than a new car. This may be true; the new car suffers the heaviest depreciation in the first two years, but is not old enough to present a lot of costly repair problems. Whatever the age of the used car you might want to buy, this section and a little patience will help you select one that should be safe and dependable.

TIPS

1. First decide what model you want, and how much you want to spend.

2. Check the used car lots and your local newspaper ads. Privately owned cars are usually less expensive, however, you will not get a warranty that, in most cases, comes with a used car purchased from a lot.

3. Never shop at night. The glare of the lights make it easy to miss faults on the body caused by accident or rust repair.

4. Try to get the name and phone number of the previous owner. Contact him/her and ask about the car. If the owner of the lot refuses this information, look for a car somewhere else.

A private seller can tell you about the car and maintenance. Remember, however, there's no law requiring honesty from private citizens selling used cars. There is a law that forbids tampering with or turning back the odometer mileage. This includes both the private citizen and the lot owner. The law also requires that the seller or anyone transferring ownership of the car must provide the buyer with a signed statement indicating the mileage on the odometer at the time of transfer.

5. Write down the year, model and serial number before you buy any used car. Then dial 1-800-424-9393, the toll free number of the National Highway Traffic Safety Administration, and ask if the car has ever been included on any manufacturer's recall list. If so, make sure the needed repairs were made.

6. Use the Used Car Checklist in this section and check all the items on the used car you are considering. Some items are more important than others. you know how much money you can afford for repairs, and depending on the price of the car, may consider doing any needed work yourself. Beware, however, of trouble in areas that will affect operation, safety or emission. Problems in the Used Car Checklist break down as follows:

1-8:Two or more problems in these areas indicate a lack of maintenance. You should beware.

9-13: Indicates a lack of proper care, however, these can usually be corrected with a tune-up or relatively simple parts replacement.

14-17: Problems in the engine or transmission can be very expensive. Walk away from any car with problems in both of these areas.

7. If you are satisfied with the apparent condition of the car, take it to an independent diagnostic center or mechanic for a complete check. If you have a state inspection program, have it inspected immediately before purchase, or specify on the bill of sale that the sale is conditional on passing state inspection.

Capacities

Year	Model	Engine	Crankcase (qts.) W/Filter	Crankcase (qts.) W/O Filter	Transmission (qts.) Manual	Transmission (qts.) Automatic	Drive Axle (pts.)	Fuel Tank (gals.)	Cooling System w/Heater (qts.)
'72–'73	Carina	2T-C	3.9	3.3	1.6	5.0	2.0	13.2	6.9
'70–'79	Corolla	3K-C	3.7	2.9	4S-1.8 5S-2.6	2.6	2.2	12.0	5.1
'71–'79	Corolla	3T-C	4.6	3.7	1.6	2.5	2.4	13.2	8.8
'83–'87	Corolla	4A-C 4A-CL	3.5	3.2	4S-1.8 5S-2.6	2.5	2.2	13.2	①
'85–'87	Corolla	4A-GE	3.9	3.5	1.8	2.5	2.8	13.2	①
'80–'87	Tercel	1A-C 3A, 3A-C	3.5	3.2	2W-3.5 4W-4.1	2.3	2W-2.0 4W-2.2	11.9②	5.4
'87	Tercel	3E	3.4	3.1	5.0	5.2	2.2	11.9	4.9
'81–'84	Starlet	4K-C 4K-E	3.7	3.2	2.6	—	2.2	10.6	5.5

① 1983–84: MT-5.7: AT-6.6
  1985–87-FWD-6.3: RWD MT-5.9, AT-5.8
② 1984–87: 13.2

8. Road test the car — refer to the Road Test Checklist in this section. If your original evaluation and the road test agree — the rest is up to you.

USED CAR CHECKLIST

NOTE: *The numbers on the illustrations refer to the numbers on this checklist.*

1. Mileage: Average mileage is about 12,000 miles per year. More than average mileage may indicate hard usage. 1975 and later catalytic converter equipped models may need converter service at 50,000 miles.

2. Paint: Check around the tailpipe, molding and windows for overspray indicating that the car has been repainted.

3. Rust: Check fenders, doors, rocker panels, window moldings, wheelwells, floorboards, under floormats, and in the trunk for signs of rust. Any rust at all will be a problem. There is no way to check the spread of rust, except to replace the part or panel.

4. Body appearance: Check the moldings, bumpers, grille, vinyl roof, glass, doors, trunk lid and body panels for general overall condition. Check for misalignment, loose holdown clips, ripples, scratches in glass, welding in the trunk, severe misalignment of body panels or ripples may indicate crash work.

5. Leaks: Get down and look under the car. There are no normal leaks, other than water from the air conditioner condenser.

6. Tires: Check the tire air pressure. A common trick is to pump the tire pressure up to make the car roll easier. Check the read wear, open the trunk and check the spare too. Uneven wear is a clue that the front end needs alignment. See the troubleshooting chapter for clues to the causes of tire wear.

7. Shock absorbers: Check the shock absorbers by forcing downward sharply on each corner of the car. Good shocks will not allow the car to bounce more than twice after you let go.

8. Interior: Check the entire interior. You're looking for an interior condition that agrees with the overall condition of the car. Reasonable wear is expected, but be suspicious of new seatcovers on sagging seats, new pedal pads, and worn armrests. These indicate an attempt to cover up hard use. Pull back the carpets and look for evidence of water leaks or flooding. Look for missing hardware, door handles, control knobs, etc. Check lights and signal operations. Make sure all accessories (air conditioner, heater, radio, etc.) work. Check windshield wiper operation.

9. Belts and Hoses: Open the hood and check all belts and hoses for wear, cracks or weak spots.

10. Battery: Low electrolyte level, corroded terminals and/or cracked case indicate a lack of maintenance.

11. Radiator: Look for corrosion or rust in the coolant indicating a lack of maintenance.

12. Air filter: A dirty air filter means a lack of maintenance.

13. Ignition wires: Check the ignition wires for cracks, burned spots, or wear. Worn wires will have to be replaced.

14. Oil level: If the oil level is low, chances are the engine uses oil or leaks. Beware of water in

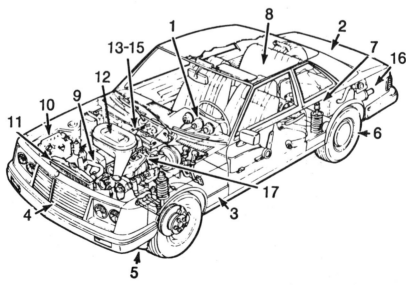

You should check these points when buying a used car. The "Used Car Checklist" gives an explanation of the numbered items

the oil (cracked block), excessively thick oil (used to quiet a noisy engine), or thin, dirty oil with a distinct gasoline smell (internal engine problems).

15. Automatic Transmission: Pull the transmission dipstick out when the engine is running. The level should read Full, and the fluid should be clear or bright red. Dark brown or black fluid that has distinct burnt odor, signals a transmission in need of repair or overhaul.

16. Exhaust: Check the color of the exhaust smoke. Blue smoke indicates, among other problems, worn rings, black smoke can indicate burnt valves or carburetor problems. Check the exhaust system for leaks; it can be expensive to replace.

17. Spark Plugs: Remove one of the spark plugs (the most accessible will do). An engine in good condition will show plugs with a light tan or gray deposit on the firing tip. See the color Tune-Up tips section for spark plug conditions.

ROAD TEST CHECK LIST

1. Engine Performance: The car should be peppy whether cold or warm, with adequate power and good pickup. It should respond smoothly through the gears.

2. Brakes: They should provide quick, firm stops with no noise, pulling or brake fade.

3. Steering: Sure control with no binding harshness, or looseness and no shimmy in the wheel should be expected. Noise or vibration from the steering wheel when turning the car means trouble.

4. Clutch (Manual Transmission): Clutch action should give quick, smooth response with easy shifting. The clutch pedal should have about 1-1½" of free-play before it disengages the clutch. Start the engine, set the parking brake, put the transmission in first gear and slowly release the clutch pedal. the engine should begin to stall when the pedal is ½-¾ of the way up.

5. Automatic Transmission: The transmission should shift rapidly and smoothly, with no noise, hesitation, or slipping.

6. Differential: No noise or thumps should be present. Differentials have no normal leaks.

7. Driveshaft, Universal Joints: Vibration and noise could mean driveshaft problems. Clicking at low speed or coast conditions means worn U-joints.

8. Suspension: Try hitting bumps at different speeds. A car that bounces has weak shock absorbers. Clunks mean worn bushings or ball joints.

9. Frame: Wet the tires and drive in a straight line. Tracks should show two straight lines, not four. Four tire tracks indicate a frame bent by collision damage. If the tires can't be wet for this purpose, have a friend drive along behind you and see if the car appears to be traveling in a straight line.

Troubleshooting Basic Air Conditioning Problems

Problem	Cause	Solution
There's little or no air coming from the vents (and you're sure it's on)	• The A/C fuse is blown • Broken or loose wires or connections • The on/off switch is defective	• Check and/or replace fuse • Check and/or repair connections • Replace switch
The air coming from the vents is not cool enough	• Windows and air vent wings open • The compressor belt is slipping • Heater is on • Condenser is clogged with debris • Refrigerant has escaped through a leak in the system • Receiver/drier is plugged	• Close windows and vent wings • Tighten or replace compressor belt • Shut heater off • Clean the condenser • Check system • Service system
The air has an odor	• Vacuum system is disrupted • Odor producing substances on the evaporator case • Condensation has collected in the bottom of the evaporator housing	• Have the system checked/repaired • Clean the evaporator case • Clean the evaporator housing drains
System is noisy or vibrating	• Compressor belt or mountings loose • Air in the system	• Tighten or replace belt; tighten mounting bolts • Have the system serviced
Sight glass condition Constant bubbles, foam or oil streaks	• Undercharged system	• Charge the system

Troubleshooting Basic Air Conditioning Problems (cont.)

Problem	Cause	Solution
Clear sight glass, but no cold air Clear sight glass, but air is cold Clouded with milky fluid	• No refrigerant at all • System is OK • Receiver drier is leaking dessicant	• Check and charge the system • Have system checked
Large difference in temperature of lines	• System undercharged	• Charge and leak test the system
Compressor noise	• Broken valves • Overcharged • Incorrect oil level • Piston slap • Broken rings • Drive belt pulley bolts are loose	• Replace the valve plate • Discharge, evacuate and install the correct charge • Isolate the compressor and check the oil level. Correct as necessary. • Replace the compressor • Replace the compressor • Tighten with the correct torque specification
Excessive vibration	• Incorrect belt tension • Clutch loose • Overcharged • Pulley is misaligned	• Adjust the belt tension • Tighten the clutch • Discharge, evacuate and install the correct charge • Align the pulley
Condensation dripping in the passenger compartment	• Drain hose plugged or improperly positioned • Insulation removed or improperly installed	• Clean the drain hose and check for proper installation • Replace the insulation on the expansion valve and hoses
Frozen evaporator coil	• Faulty thermostat • Thermostat capillary tube improperly installed • Thermostat not adjusted properly	• Replace the thermostat • Install the capillary tube correctly • Adjust the thermostat
Low side low—high side low	• System refrigerant is low • Expansion valve is restricted	• Evacuate, leak test and charge the system • Replace the expansion valve
Low side high—high side low	• Internal leak in the compressor—worn • Cylinder head gasket is leaking • Expansion valve is defective • Drive belt slipping	• Remove the compressor cylinder head and inspect the compressor. Replace the valve plate assembly if necessary. If the compressor pistons, rings or cylinders are excessively worn or scored replace the compressor • Install a replacement cylinder head gasket • Replace the expansion valve • Adjust the belt tension
Low side high—high side high	• Condenser fins obstructed • Air in the system • Expansion valve is defective • Loose or worn fan belts	• Clean the condenser fins • Evacuate, leak test and charge the system • Replace the expansion valve • Adjust or replace the belts as necessary
Low side low—high side high	• Expansion valve is defective • Restriction in the refrigerant hose • Restriction in the receiver/drier • Restriction in the condenser	• Replace the expansion valve • Check the hose for kinks—replace if necessary • Replace the receiver/drier • Replace the condenser
Low side and high side normal (inadequate cooling)	• Air in the system • Moisture in the system	• Evacuate, leak test and charge the system • Evacuate, leak test and charge the system

Troubleshooting Basic Wheel Problems

Problem	Cause	Solution
The car's front end vibrates at high speed	• The wheels are out of balance • Wheels are out of alignment	• Have wheels balanced • Have wheel alignment checked/adjusted
Car pulls to either side	• Wheels are out of alignment • Unequal tire pressure • Different size tires or wheels	• Have wheel alignment checked/adjusted • Check/adjust tire pressure • Change tires or wheels to same size
The car's wheel(s) wobbles	• Loose wheel lug nuts • Wheels out of balance • Damaged wheel • Wheels are out of alignment • Worn or damaged ball joint • Excessive play in the steering linkage (usually due to worn parts) • Defective shock absorber	• Tighten wheel lug nuts • Have tires balanced ' • Raise car and spin the wheel. If the wheel is bent, it should be replaced • Have wheel alignment checked/adjusted • Check ball joints • Check steering linkage • Check shock absorbers
Tires wear unevenly or prematurely	• Incorrect wheel size • Wheels are out of balance • Wheels are out of alignment	• Check if wheel and tire size are compatible • Have wheels balanced • Have wheel alignment checked/adjusted

Troubleshooting Basic Tire Problems

Problem	Cause	Solution
The car's front end vibrates at high speeds and the steering wheel shakes	• Wheels out of balance • Front end needs aligning	• Have wheels balanced • Have front end alignment checked
The car pulls to one side while cruising	• Unequal tire pressure (car will usually pull to the low side) • Mismatched tires • Front end needs aligning	• Check/adjust tire pressure • Be sure tires are of the same type and size • Have front end alignment checked
Abnormal, excessive or uneven tire wear See "How to Read Tire Wear"	• Infrequent tire rotation • Improper tire pressure • Sudden stops/starts or high speed on curves	• Rotate tires more frequently to equalize wear • Check/adjust pressure • Correct driving habits
Tire squeals	• Improper tire pressure • Front end needs aligning	• Check/adjust tire pressure • Have front end alignment checked

Troubleshooting the Cooling System

Problem	Cause	Solution
High temperature gauge indication—overheating	• Coolant level low • Fan belt loose • Radiator hose(s) collapsed • Radiator airflow blocked • Faulty radiator cap • Ignition timing incorrect • Idle speed low • Air trapped in cooling system	• Replenish coolant • Adjust fan belt tension • Replace hose(s) • Remove restriction (bug screen, fog lamps, etc.) • Replace radiator cap • Adjust ignition timing • Adjust idle speed • Purge air

Troubleshooting the Cooling System (cont.)

Problem	Cause	Solution
High temperature gauge indication—overheating (cont.)	• Heavy traffic driving	• Operate at fast idle in neutral intermittently to cool engine
	• Incorrect cooling system component(s) installed	• Install proper component(s)
	• Faulty thermostat	• Replace thermostat
	• Water pump shaft broken or impeller loose	• Replace water pump
	• Radiator tubes clogged	• Flush radiator
	• Cooling system clogged	• Flush system
	• Casting flash in cooling passages	• Repair or replace as necessary. Flash may be visible by removing cooling system components or removing core plugs.
	• Brakes dragging	• Repair brakes
	• Excessive engine friction	• Repair engine
	• Antifreeze concentration over 68%	• Lower antifreeze concentration percentage
	• Missing air seals	• Replace air seals
	• Faulty gauge or sending unit	• Repair or replace faulty component
	• Loss of coolant flow caused by leakage or foaming	• Repair or replace leaking component, replace coolant
	• Viscous fan drive failed	• Replace unit
Low temperature indication—undercooling	• Thermostat stuck open	• Replace thermostat
	• Faulty gauge or sending unit	• Repair or replace faulty component
Coolant loss—boilover	• Overfilled cooling system	• Reduce coolant level to proper specification
	• Quick shutdown after hard (hot) run	• Allow engine to run at fast idle prior to shutdown
	• Air in system resulting in occasional "burping" of coolant	• Purge system
	• Insufficient antifreeze allowing coolant boiling point to be too low	• Add antifreeze to raise boiling point
	• Antifreeze deteriorated because of age or contamination	• Replace coolant
	• Leaks due to loose hose clamps, loose nuts, bolts, drain plugs, faulty hoses, or defective radiator	• Pressure test system to locate source of leak(s) then repair as necessary
	• Faulty head gasket	• Replace head gasket
	• Cracked head, manifold, or block	• Replace as necessary
	• Faulty radiator cap	• Replace cap
Coolant entry into crankcase or cylinder(s)	• Faulty head gasket	• Replace head gasket
	• Crack in head, manifold or block	• Replace as necessary
Coolant recovery system inoperative	• Coolant level low	• Replenish coolant to FULL mark
	• Leak in system	• Pressure test to isolate leak and repair as necessary
	• Pressure cap not tight or seal missing, or leaking	• Repair as necessary
	• Pressure cap defective	• Replace cap
	• Overflow tube clogged or leaking	• Repair as necessary
	• Recovery bottle vent restricted	• Remove restriction
Noise	• Fan contacting shroud	• Reposition shroud and inspect engine mounts
	• Loose water pump impeller	• Replace pump
	• Glazed fan belt	• Apply silicone or replace belt
	• Loose fan belt	• Adjust fan belt tension
	• Rough surface on drive pulley	• Replace pulley
	• Water pump bearing worn	• Remove belt to isolate. Replace pump.
	• Belt alignment	• Check pulley alignment. Repair as necessary.

Troubleshooting the Cooling System (cont.)

Problem	Cause	Solution
No coolant flow through heater core	• Restricted return inlet in water pump	• Remove restriction
	• Heater hose collapsed or restricted	• Remove restriction or replace hose
	• Restricted heater core	• Remove restriction or replace core
	• Restricted outlet in thermostat housing	• Remove flash or restriction
	• Intake manifold bypass hole in cylinder head restricted	• Remove restriction
	• Faulty heater control valve	• Replace valve
	• Intake manifold coolant passage restricted	• Remove restriction or replace intake manifold

NOTE: *Immediately after shutdown, the engine enters a condition known as heat soak. This is caused by the cooling system being inoperative while engine temperature is still high. If coolant temperature rises above boiling point, expansion and pressure may push some coolant out of the radiator overflow tube. If this does not occur frequently it is considered normal.*

Tire Size Comparison Chart

"Letter" sizes			Inch Sizes	Metric-inch Sizes		
"60 Series"	"70 Series"	"78 Series"	1965–77	"60 Series"	"70 Series"	"80 Series"
			5.50-12, 5.60-12	165/60-12	165/70-12	155-12
		Y78-12	6.00-12			
		W78-13	5.20-13	165/60-13	145/70-13	135-13
		Y78-13	5.60-13	175/60-13	155/70-13	145-13
			6.15-13	185/60-13	165/70-13	155-13, P155/80-13
A60-13	A70-13	A78-13	6.40-13	195/60-13	175/70-13	165-13
B60-13	B70-13	B78-13	6.70-13	205/60-13	185/70-13	175-13
			6.90-13			
C60-13	C70-13	C78-13	7.00-13	215/60-13	195/70-13	185-13
D60-13	D70-13	D78-13	7.25-13			
E60-13	E70-13	E78-13	7.75-13			195-13
			5.20-14	165/60-14	145/70-14	135-14
			5.60-14	175/60-14	155/70-14	145-14
			5.90-14			
A60-14	A70-14	A78-14	6.15-14	185/60-14	165/70-14	155-14
	B70-14	B78-14	6.45-14	195/60-14	175/70-14	165-14
	C70-14	C78-14	6.95-14	205/60-14	185/70-14	175-14
D60-14	D70-14	D78-14				
E60-14	E70-14	E78-14	7.35-14	215/60-14	195/70-14	185-14
F60-14	F70-14	F78-14, F83-14	7.75-14	225/60-14	200/70-14	195-14
G60-14	G70-14	G77-14, G78-14	8.25-14	235/60-14	205/70-14	205-14
H60-14	H70-14	H78-14	8.55-14	245/60-14	215/70-14	215-14
J60-14	J70-14	J78-14	8.85-14	255/60-14	225/70-14	225-14
L60-14	L70-14		9.15-14	265/60-14	235/70-14	
	A70-15	A78-15	5.60-15	185/60-15	165/70-15	155-15
B60-15	B70-15	B78-15	6.35-15	195/60-15	175/70-15	165-15
C60-15	C70-15	C78-15	6.85-15	205/60-15	185/70-15	175-15
	D70-15	D78-15				
E60-15	E70-15	E78-15	7.35-15	215/60-15	195/70-15	185-15
F60-15	F70-15	F78-15	7.75-15	225/60-15	205/70-15	195-15
G60-15	G70-15	G78-15	8.15-15/8.25-15	235/60-15	215/70-15	205-15
H60-15	H70-15	H78-15	8.45-15/8.55-15	245/60-15	225/70-15	215-15
J60-15	J70-15	J78-15	8.85-15/8.90-15	255/60-15	235/70-15	225-15
	K70-15		9.00-15	265/60-15	245/70-15	230-15
L60-15	L70-15	L78-15, L84-15	9.15-15			235-15
	M70-15	M78-15				255-15
		N78-15				

Note: Every size tire is not listed and many size comparisons are approximate, based on load ratings. Wider tires than those supplied new with the vehicle, should always be checked for clearance.

Tune-Up and Performance Maintenance

TUNE-UP PROCEDURES

In order to extract the full measure of performance and economy from your engine it is essential that it be properly tuned at regular intervals. A regular tune-up will keep your Toyota's engine running smoothly and will prevent the annoying minor breakdowns and poor performance associated with an untuned engine.

NOTE: *All Toyotas use a conventional breaker points ignition through 1974. In 1975 Toyota switched to a transistorized ignition system. This system was much like the previous system with one basic difference; instead of the breaker points switching the primary current to the coil on and off, they triggered a transistor which did it for them. In 1977, certain Toyotas sold in California came equipped with a fully transistorized electronic ignition system. In 1978, this system became standard on all models (except the Canadian Tercel with the 3A engine which continues to use breaker points through 1982).*

A complete tune-up should be performed every 15,000 miles or twelve months, whichever comes first. This interval should be halved if the car is operated under severe conditions, such as trailer towing, prolonged idling, continual stop and start driving, or if starting or running problems are noticed. It is assumed that the routine maintenance (described in Chapter 1) has been kept up, as this will have a decided effect on the results of a tune-up. All of the applicable steps of a tune-up should be followed in order, as the result is a cumulative one.

If the specifications on the tune-up sticker in the engine compartment of your Toyota disagree with the Tune-Up Specifications chart in this chapter, the figures on the sticker must be used. The sticker often reflects changes made during the production run.

Spark Plugs

Spark plugs ignite the air and fuel mixture in the cylinder as the piston reaches the top of the compression stroke. The controlled explosion that results forces the piston down, turning the crankshaft and the rest of the drive train.

The average life of a normal, spark plug is 15,000 miles, although manufacturers are now claiming spark plug lives of up to 30,000 miles or more. This is, however, dependent on a number of factors: the mechanical condition of the engine; the type of fuel; the driving conditions; and the driver.

When you remove the spark plugs, check their condition. They are a good indicator of the condition of the engine. It is a good idea to remove the spark plugs every 6,000 miles to keep an eye on the mechanical state of the engine.

A small deposit of light tan or gray material (or rust red with unleaded fuel) on a spark plug that has been used for any period of time is to be considered normal. Any other color or abnormal amounts of deposit, indicates that there is something amiss in the engine.

The gap between the center electrode and the side or ground electrode can be expected to increase not more than 0.001" (0.0254mm) every 1,000 miles under normal conditions.

When a spark plug is functioning normally or, more accurately, when the plug is installed in an engine that is functioning properly, the plugs can be taken out, cleaned, gapped, and reinstalled without doing the engine any harm.

When, and if, a plug fouls and being to misfire, you will have to investigate, correct the cause of the fouling, and either clean or replace the plug.

There are several reasons why a spark plug will foul and you can learn which is at fault by just looking at the plug. A few of the most common reasons for plug fouling, and a description

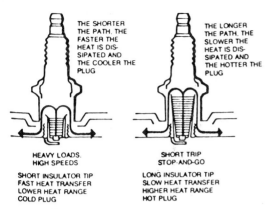

THE SHORTER THE PATH, THE FASTER THE HEAT IS DISSIPATED AND THE COOLER THE PLUG

THE LONGER THE PATH, THE SLOWER THE HEAT IS DISSIPATED AND THE HOTTER THE PLUG

HEAVY LOADS.
HIGH SPEEDS

SHORT INSULATOR TIP
FAST HEAT TRANSFER
LOWER HEAT RANGE
COLD PLUG

SHORT TRIP
STOP-AND-GO

LONG INSULATOR TIP
SLOW HEAT TRANSFER
HIGHER HEAT RANGE
HOT PLUG

Spark plug heat range

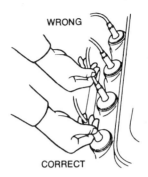

WRONG

CORRECT

When removing the spark plug wire, always grasp it by the rubber boot

of the fouled plug's appearance, are listed in the Color Insert, which also offers solutions to the problems.

Spark plugs suitable for use in your Toyota's engine are offered in a number of different heat ranges. The amount of heat which the plug absorbs is determined by the length of the lower insulator. The longer the insulator, the hotter the plug will operate; the shorter the insulator, the cooler it will operate. A spark plug that absorbs (or retains) little heat and remains too cool will accumulate deposits of lead, oil, and carbon, because it is not hot enough to burn them off. This leads to fouling and consequent misfiring. A spark plug that absorbs too much heat will have no deposits, but the electrodes will burn away quickly and, in some cases, pre-ignition may result. Pre-ignition occurs when the spark plug tips get so hot that they ignite the fuel/air mixture before the actual spark fires. This premature ignition will usually cause a pinging sound under conditions of low speed and heavy load. In severe cases, the heat may become high enough to start the fuel/air mixture burning throughout the combustion chamber rather than just to the front of the plug. In this case, the resultant explosion will be strong enough to damage pistons, rings, and valves.

In most cases the factory recommended heat range is correct; it is chosen to perform well under a wide range of operating conditions. How-

ever, if most of your driving is long distance, high speed travel, you may want to install a spark plug one step colder than standard. If most of your driving is of the short trip variety, when the engine may not always reach operating temperature, a hotter plug may help burn off the deposits normally accumulated under those conditions.

REMOVAL

1. Number the wires so that you won't cross them when you replace them.
2. Remove the wire from the end of the spark plug by grasping the wire by the rubber boot. If the boot sticks to the plug, remove it by twisting and pulling at the same time. Do not pull the wire itself or you will damage the core.
3. Use a $^{13}/_{16}''$ spark plug socket to loosen all of the plugs about two turns.
NOTE: *The cylinder head is cast from aluminum. Remove the spark plugs when the engine is cold, if possible, to prevent damage to the threads.*
If removal of the plugs is difficult, apply a few drops of penetrating oil or silicone spray to the area around the base of the plug, and allow it a few minutes to work.
4. If compressed air is available, apply it to the area around the spark plug holes. Otherwise, use a rag or a brush to clean the area. Be careful not to allow any foreign material to drop into the spark plug holes.
5. Remove the plugs by unscrewing them the rest of the way from the engine.

Diesel Engine Tune-Up Specifications

| Model | Year | Engine Type | Warm Valve Clearance (in.) | | Intake Valve Opens (deg) | Injection Pump Setting (deg) | Injection Nozzle Pressure (psi) | | Idle Speed (rpm) | Compression Pressure (psi) |
			In	Ex			New	Used		
Corolla	1984	1C–L	0.008–0.012	0.010–0.014	NA	25–30B	2062–2205	2062–2205	700	356–427

Gasoline Engine Tune-Up Specifications—1970–87

When analyzing compression test results, look for uniformity among cylinders, rather than specific pressures.

Model	Year	Engine Type	Spark Plugs Type (ND)	Spark Plugs Gap (in.)	Distributor Point Dwell (deg)	Distributor Point Gap (in.)	Ignition Timing (deg) ▲● MT	Ignition Timing (deg) ▲● AT	Compression Pressure (psi)**	Fuel Pump Pressure (psi)	Idle Speed (rpm)▲ MT	Idle Speed (rpm)▲ AT	Valve Clearance (in.)‡ In	Valve Clearance (in.)‡ Ex
Carina	'72–'73	2T–C	W20EP	.031	52	.018	5	5	170	2.8–4.3	750	650	.007	.013
Corolla 1200	'70–'77	3K–C	W20EP	.031	52	.018	5	—	156	2.8–4.3	750	—	.008	.012
	'78–'79	3K–C	W16EX–U	.031	①	.008–.016②	8	8	156	3.0–4.5	750	750	.008	.012
Corolla 1600	'71–'74	2T–C	W20EP	.031	52	.018	5	5	171	2.8–4.3	750	650	.007	.013
	'75–'77	2T–C	W16EP	.030	52③	.018	10④	10④	171	2.8–4.3⑤	850	850	.008	.013
	'78–'79	2T–C	⑥	.030	①	.008–.016②	10	10	171	3.0–4.5	850	850	.008	.013
Corolla	'80	3T–C	⑦	.043⑧	①	.008–.016②	10	10	163	NA	700⑨	750⑨	.008	.013
	'81–'82	3T–C	⑩	.043⑧	①	.008–.016②	7⑪	7⑪	163	NA	⑫	⑫	.008	.013
	'83	4A–C	⑩	.043⑧	①	.008–.016②	5	5	178	2.5–3.5	⑬	⑬	.008	.012
	'84	4A–C	⑩	.043⑧	①	.008–.016②	5	5	178	2.5 3.5	㉕	㉕	.008	.012
Tercel	'80–'82	1A–C	W20ETR–S	.039	①	.008–.016②	5	—	177	NA	650	800	.008	.012
		3A	W16EXR–U	.031	52	.018	5	5	177	NA	650	800	.008	.012
		3A–C	⑭	.043	①	.008–.016②	5	5	177	NA	⑮	800	.008	.012
	'83–'84	3A	⑯	.031	①	.008–.016②	5	5	178	NA	⑰	⑰	.008	.012

Starlet	3A–C	⑱	.043 ⑲	①	.008–.016 ②	5	5	178	NA	⑳	⑳	.008	.012
'81–'82	4K–C	㉑	㉒	①	.008–.016 ②	8	—	156	2.8–4.2	650 ㉓	—	.008	.012
'83–'84	4K–E	㉔	.043 ㉖	①	.008–.016 ②	5	—	185	36–38	700	—	HYD.	HYD.

NOTE: *The underhood specifications sticker often reflects tune-up specification changes made while the car is in production. Sticker figures must always be used if they disagree with those in the chart.*

▲ With the manual transmission in Neutral or the automatic transmission in Drive (D)
● All figures are Before Top Dead Center (BTDC)
** The difference between cylinders should never exceed 14 psi
‡ Valves clearances are with the engine at normal operating temperature
NA Not available at time of publication

① Electronic ignition; dwell is set automatically
② Figure given is for distributor air gap
③ Dual point models: main—57; sub—52
④ Dual point models: main—12B; sub—19B–25B
⑤ California models w/electric fuel pump: 2.4–3.8
⑥ USA: W14EX–U
    W16EX–U
  Canada: W16EPR
    W16EXR–U
⑦ USA: W16EX–U11
    W14EX–U11
  Canada: W16EPR
    W16EXR–U
    W14EXR–U
⑧ Canada: .031
⑨ W/PS: 850
⑩ California: W16EXR–U11
  Federal: W16EXR–U11
    W14EXR–U11
  Canada: W16EPR (83 only)
    W16EXR–U
    W14EXR–U
⑪ Canada: 10B
⑫ USA: w/PS—850
    MT w/o PS—650
    AT w/o PS—750
  Canada: w/PS—850
    MT w/o PS—700
    AT w/o PS—750

⑬ W/PS: MT—650
    AT—800
  w/o PS: MT—800
    AT—900
⑭ California: W16EXR–U11
  Federal & Canada: W16EXR–U11
    W14EXR–U11
⑮ 4 spd: 550
  5 spd: 650
⑯ W16EXR–U
    W14EXR–U
⑰ W/PS: MT—800
    AT—900
  w/o PS: MT—650
    AT—800
⑱ California: W16EXR–U11
  Federal & Canada: W16EXR–U11
    W14EXR–U11
  Canada 4WD wagon: W16EXR–U11
    W14EXR–U
⑲ Canada 4WD wagon: .031
⑳ W/PS: 5 & 6 spd—800
    AT—900
  w/o PS: 4 spd—550

    5 & 6 spd—650
    AT—700
㉑ California: W14EXR–U
    W16EXR–U
  Federal & Canada: W14EXR–U11
    W16EXR–U11
㉒ California: .031
  Federal & Canada: .043
㉓ California: 700
㉔ 4 spd: P16R (platinum)
  5 spd: J16BR–U11 (extended tip)
㉕ FWD: MT—650
    AT—800
  RWD: MT w/o PS—700
    MT w/PS—800
    AT w/o PS—800
    AT w/PS—900
㉖ 1984: extended electrode—0.039–0.043
    platinum tipped—0.039–0.043 (new)
      0.055 (used)
  NEVER adjust gap on used platinum tipped plug.

Gasoline Engine Tune-Up Specifications—1985–87

Year	Model	Engine Displacement cu. in. (cc)	Spark Plugs Type	Gap (in.)	Ignition Timing (deg.) MT	AT	Com-pression Pressure (psi)	Fuel Pump (psi)	Idle Speed (rpm) MT	AT	Valve Clearance In.	Ex.
1985	Tercel	88.6 (1452)	BPR5EY	0.031	5B	5B	178	2.6–3.5	①	①	0.008	0.012
		88.6 (1452)	BPR5EY-11(14)	0.043	5B	5B	178	2.6–3.5	①	①	0.008	0.012
	Corolla	97.0 (1587)	BPR5EY-11(15)	0.043	5B	5B	178	2.5–3.5	①	①	0.008	0.012
		97.0 (1597)	BCPR5EP-11	0.043	10B	—	179	33–39	800	—	0.008	0.012
1986	Tercel	88.6 (1452)	BPR5EY	0.031	5B	5B	178	2.6–3.5	①	①	0.008	0.012
		88.6 (1452)	BPR5EY-11	0.043	5B	5B	178	2.6–3.5	①	①	0.008	0.012
	Corolla	97.0 (1587)	BPR5EY-11	0.043	5B	5B	178	2.5–3.5	①	①	0.008	0.012
		97.0 (1597)	BCPR5EP-11	0.043	10B	10B	179	33–38	800	800	0.008	0.012
1987	Tercel	88.6 (1452)	BPR5EY-11(14)	0.043	5B	5B	178	2.6–3.5	①		0.008	0.012
		88.9 (1456)	BPR5EY-11	0.043	3B	3B	184	2.6–3.5	①		0.008	0.008
	Corolla	97.0 (1587)	BPR5EY-11	0.043	5B	5B	163	2.5–3.5	①		0.008	0.012
		97.0 (1597)	BCPR5EP-11	0.043	10B	10B	179	33–38	①		0.008	0.010

① See underhood emissions sticker

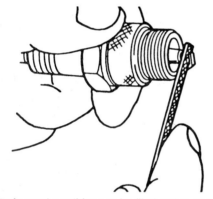

Plugs in good condition can be filed and re-used

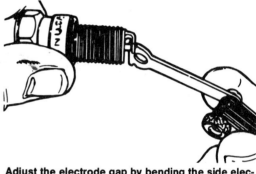

Adjust the electrode gap by bending the side electrode

INSPECTION

Check the plugs for deposits and wear. if they are not going to be replaced, clean the plugs thoroughly. Remember that any kind of deposit will decrease the efficiency of the plug. Plugs can be cleaned on a spark plug cleaning machine, which can sometimes be found in service stations, or you can do an acceptable job of cleaning with a stiff brush. If the plugs are cleaned, the electrodes must be filed flat. Use an ignition point file, not an emery board or the like, which will leave deposits. The electrodes must be filed perfectly flat with sharp edges; rounded edges reduce the spark plug voltage by as much as 50%.

Check spark plug gap before installation. The ground electrode (the L-shaped one connected to the body of the plug) must be parallel to the center electrode and the specified size wire gauge (see Tune-Up Specifications) should pass through the gap with a slight drag.

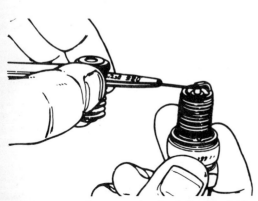

Always use a wire gauge to check the electrode gap

CAUTION: *Never adjust the gap on a used platinum tipped spark plug.*

Always check the gap on new plugs, too; they are not always set correctly at the factor. Do not use a flat feeler gauge when measuring the gap, because the reading will be inaccurate. Wire gapping tools usually have a bending tool attached. use that to adjust the side electrode until the proper distance is obtained. Absolutely never bend the center electrode. Also, be careful not to bend the side electrode too far or too often; it may weaken and break off within the engine, causing damage and a lot of work.

INSTALLATION

1. Lubricate the threads of the spark plugs with a drop of oil. Install the plugs and tighten them hand tight. Take care not to cross-thread them.

2. Tighten the spark plugs with the socket. Do not apply the same amount of force you would use for a bolt; just snug them in. If a torque wrench is available, tighten to 11-15 ft.lb.

3. Install the wires on their respective plugs. Make sure the wires are firmly connected. You will be able to feel them click into place.

Spark Plug Wires

CHECKING AND REPLACING

At every tune-up, visually inspect the spark plug cables for burns, cuts, or breaks in the insulation. Check the boots and the nipples on the distributor cap and coil. Replace any damaged wiring.

Every 36,000 miles or so, the resistance of the wires should be checked with an ohmmeter. Wires with excessive resistance will cause misfiring, and may make the engine difficult to start in damp weather. Generally the useful life of the cables is 36,000-50,000 miles.

To check resistance, remove the distributor cap, leaving the wires attached. Connect one lead of an ohmmeter to an electrode within the

cap; connect the other lead to the corresponding spark plug terminal (remove it from the plug for this test). Replace any wire which shows a resistance over 25,000Ω. Test the high tension lead from the coil by connecting the ohmmeter between the center contact in the distributor cap and either of the primary terminals of the coil. If resistance is more than 25,000Ω, remove the cable from the coil and check the resistance of the cable alone. Anything over 15,000Ω is cause for replacement. It should be remembered that resistance is also a function of length; the longer the cable, the greater the resistance. Thus, if the cables on your car are longer than the factory originals, resistance will be higher, quite possibly outside these limits.

When installing new cables, replace them one at a time to avoid mixups. Start by replacing the longest one first. Install the boot firmly over the spark plug. Route the wire over the same path as the original. Insert the nipple firmly into the tower on the cap or the coil.

Firing Order

NOTE: *To avoid confusion, spark plug wires should be replaced one at a time. Distributor*

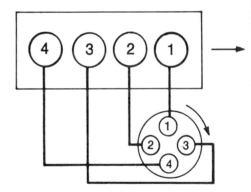

2T-C, 3T-C, 3K-C, 4K-C and 4K-E

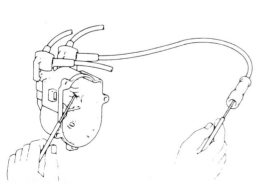

Checking the spark plug cable resistance

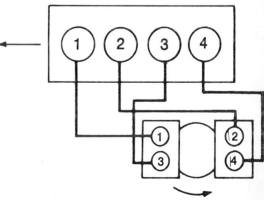

1A-C, 3A, 3A-C and 4A-C (1983 shown, others similar)

terminal position may differ slightly from that which is illustrated.

Breaker Points and Condenser

The points function as a circuit breaker for the primary circuit of the ignition system. The ignition coil must boost the 12 volts of electrical pressure supplied by the battery to as much as 25,000 volts in order to fire the plugs. To do this, the coil depends on the points and the condenser to make a clean break in the primary circuit.

The coil has both primary and secondary circuits. When the ignition is turned on, the battery supplies voltage through the coil and onto the points. The points are connected to ground, completing the primary circuit. As the current passes through the coil, a magnetic field is created in the iron center core of the coil. When the cam in the distributor turns, the points open, breaking the primary circuit. The magnetic field in the primary circuit of the coil then collapses and cuts through the secondary circuit windings around the iron core. Because of the physical principle called electromagnetic induction, the battery voltage is increased to a level sufficient to fire the spark plugs.

When the points open, the electrical charge in the primary circuit tries to jump the gap created between the two open contacts of the points. If this electrical charge were not transferred elsewhere, the metal contacts of the points would start to change rapidly.

The function of the condenser is to absorb excessive voltage from the points when they open and thus prevent the points from becoming pitted or burned.

If you have ever wondered why it is necessary to tune your engine occasionally, consider the fact that the ignition system must complete the above cycle each time spark plug fires. On a 4-cylinder, 4-cycle engine, two of the four plugs must fire once for ever engine revolution. If the idle speed of your engine is 800 revolutions per minute (800 rpm), the breaker points open and close 1,600 times (2 x 800 = 1,600). And that is just at idle. What about at 60 mph?

There are two ways to check breaker point gap; with a feeler gauge or with a dwell meter. Either way you set the points, you are adjusting the amount of time (in degrees of distributor rotation) that the points will remain open. If you adjust the points with a feeler gauge, you are setting the maximum amount the points will open when the rubbing block on the points is on a high point of the distributor cam. When you adjust the points with a dwell meter, you are measuring the number of degrees (of distributor cam rotation) that the points will

remain closed before they start to open as a high point of the distributor cam approaches the rubbing block of the points.

If you still do not understand how the points function, take a friend, go outside, and remove the distributor cap from your engine. Have your friend operate the starter (make sure that the transmission is not in gear) as you look at the exposed parts of the distributor.

There are two rules that should always be followed when adjusting or replacing points. The points and condenser are a matched set; never replace one without replacing the other. If you change the point gap or dwell of the engine, you also change the ignition timing. Therefore, if you adjust the points, you must also adjust the timing.

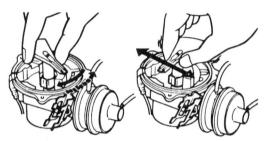

The rotor should return to its original position when rotated slightly and then let go

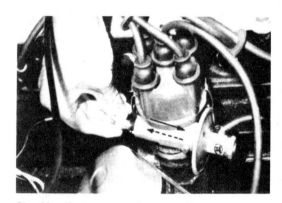

Checking the vacuum advance unit

INSPECTION AND CLEANING

The breaker points should be inspected and cleaned at 6,000 mile intervals. To do so, perform the following steps:

1. Disconnect the high tension lead from the coil.

2. Unsnap the two distributor cap retaining clips and lift the cap straight up. Leave the leads connected to the cap and position it out of the way.

3. Remove the rotor and dust cover by pulling them straight up.

4. Place a screwdriver against the breaker

points and pry them open. Examine their condition. If they are excessively worn, burned, or pitted, they should be replaced.

5. Polish the points with a point file. Do not use emery cloth or sandpaper; these may leave particles on the points causing them to arc.

6. Clean the distributor cap and rotor with alcohol. Inspect the cap terminals for looseness and corrosion. Check the rotor tip for excessive burning. Inspect both cap and rotor for cracks. Replace either if they show any of the above signs of wear or damage.

7. Check the operation of the centrifugal advance mechanism by turning the rotor clockwise. Release the rotor; it should return to its original position. If it doesn't, check for binding parts.

8. Check the vacuum advance unit, by removing the plastic cap and pressing on the octane selector. It should return to its original position. Check for binding if it doesn't.

9. If the points do not require replacement, proceed with the adjustment section below. Otherwise perform the point and condenser replacement procedures.

POINT REPLACEMENT

1971-77

The points should be replaced ever 12,000 miles (24,000 miles with transistorized ignition), or if they are badly pitted, worn, or burned. To replace them, proceed as follows:

1. If you have not already done so, perform Steps 1-3 of the preceding Inspection and Cleaning procedure.

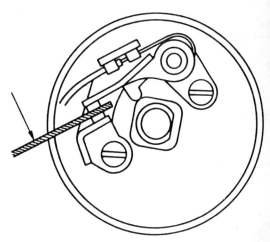

The arrow indicates the feeler gauge used to check the point gap (1971–74)

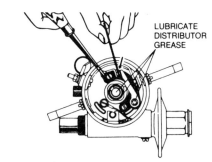

LUBRICATE DISTRIBUTOR GREASE

Adjustment of the points and distribution lubrication—1971–74

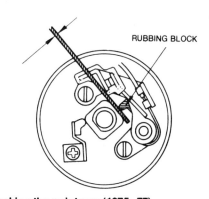

RUBBING BLOCK

Checking the point gap (1975–77)

2. Unfasten the point lead connector.

3. Remove the point retaining clip and unfasten the point holddown screw(s). It is a good idea to use a magnetic or locking screwdriver to remove the small screws inside the distributor, since they are almost impossible to find once they have been dropped.

4. Lift out the points set.

5. Install the new point set in the reverse order of removal. Adjust the points as detailed below, after completing installation.

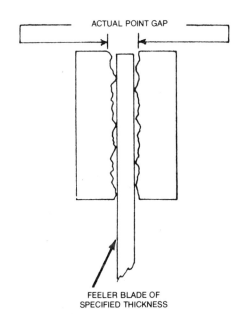

ACTUAL POINT GAP

FEELER BLADE OF SPECIFIED THICKNESS

The feeler gauge method of checking point gap is less accurate than the dwell meter method

CONDENSER REPLACEMENT

1971-74

Replace the condenser whenever the points are replaced, or if it is suspected of being defective. On Toyota passenger cars the condenser is located on the outside of the distributor. To replace it, proceed as follows:

1. Carefully remove the nut and washer from the condenser lead terminal.
2. Use a magnetic or locking screwdriver to remove the condenser mounting screw.
3. Remove the condenser.
4. Installation of a new condenser is performed in the reverse order of removal.

ADJUSTMENT

Perform the gap adjustment procedure whenever new points are installed, or as part of routine maintenance. If you are adjusting an old set of points, you must check the dwell as well, since the feeler gauge is really only accurate with a new point set. The points on all 1975-77 models and the 1980-82 Canadian Tercel (3A engine) are adjusted in a slightly different manner than you may be familiar with so make sure that you follow the correct adjustment procedure below.

1971-74

1. Rotate the engine by hand (or by using a remote starter switch), so that the edge of the point set rubbing block is on the high point of the distributor cam lobe.
2. Insert a 0.018″ (0.46mm) feeler gauge between the points; a slight drag should be felt.
3. If no drag is felt or if the feeler gauge cannot be inserted at all, loosen, but do not remove, the point holddown screw.
4. Insert a screwdriver into the adjustment slot. Rotate the screwdriver until the proper point gap is attained. The point gap is increased by rotating the screwdriver counterclockwise and decreased by rotating it clockwise.
5. Tighten the point holddown screw.
NOTE: *Lubricate the cam lobes, breaker arm, rubbing block, arm pivot, and distributor shaft with special high temperature distributor grease.*

1975-77 and 1980-82 Tercel w/3A Engine

The point set on this ignition system is covered by a piece of protective plastic shielding. Because of this, the gap must be checked between the point rubbing block and the distributor cam lobe instead of between the two point tips. Do not try to remove the plastic shielding as it will damage the point set.

1. Using your hands or a remote starter switch, rotate the engine so that the rubbing block is resting on the low point (flat side) of the cam lobe.
2. Insert a 0.018″ (0.46mm) flat feeler gauge between the rubbing block and the cam lobe; a slight drag should be felt.
3. If no drag can be felt or if the feeler gauge cannot be inserted at all, loosen, but do not remove, the point holddown screw.
4. Insert a screwdriver into the point adjustment slot. Rotate the screwdriver until the proper gap is achieved. The gap is increased by rotating the screwdriver counterclockwise and decreased by rotating it clockwise.
5. Tighten the point holddown screw. Lubricate the cam lobes, breaker arm, rubbing block, arm pivot and distributor shaft with special high temperature distributor grease.

Transistorized Ignition

In 1975, Toyota introduced its transistorized ignition system. This system works very much like the conventional system previously described. Regular breaker points are used, but instead of switching primary current to the coil off-and-on, they are used to trigger a switching transistor. The transistor, in turn, switches the coil primary current on and off.

Since only a very small amount of current is needed to operate the transistor, the points will not become burned or pitted as they would if they had full primary current passing through them. This also allows the primary current to be higher than usual because the use of a higher current would normally cause the points to fail much more rapidly.

As already stated the condenser is used to absorb any extra high voltage passing through the points. Since, in the transistorized system, there is no high current, no condenser is needed or used.

As a result of the lower stress placed on them, the points only have to be replaced every 24,000 miles instead of the usual 12,000 miles.

The Toyota transistorized ignition system may be quickly identified by the lack of a condenser on the outside of the distributor and by the addition of a control box, which is connected between the distributor and the primary side of the coil.

SERVICE PRECAUTIONS

Basically, the transistorized ignition is serviced just like its conventional counterpart. The points must be checked, adjusted, and replaced in the same manner. Point gap and dwell must be checked and set. The points should also be kept clean and should be replaced at 24,000 mile intervals. Of course, since there is no condenser, it does not have to be replaced when the points are.

However, there are several precautions to observe when servicing the transistorized ignition system:

1. Use only pure alcohol to clean the points. Shop solvent or an oily rag will leave a film on the points which will not allow the low current to pass.

2. Hook up a tachometer, dwell meter, or a combination dwell/tachometer to the negative (–) side of the coil: NOT to the distributor or the positive (+) side. Damage to the switching transistor will result if the meter is connected in the usual manner.

3. See the previous section for the remaining service procedures which are identical to those for the conventional ignition system.

Dwell Angle

The dwell angle is the number of degrees of distributor cam rotation through which the points remain closed (conducting electricity). Increasing the point gap decreases dwell, while decreasing the gap increases dwell.

The dwell angle may be checked with the distributor cap and rotor installed and the engine running, or with the cap and rotor removed and the engine cranking at starter speed. The meter gives a constant reading with the engine running. With the engine cranking, the meter will

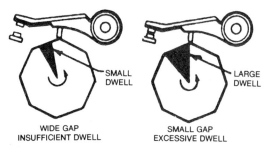

Dwell as a function of point gap

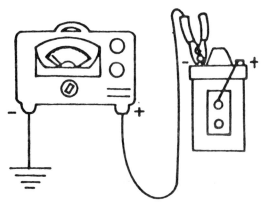

Dwell meter connections with transistorized ignition

fluctuate between 0 dwell and the maximum figure for that setting. Never attempt to adjust the points when the ignition is on, or you may receive a shock.

NOTE: *On cars with electronic ignition (1978 and later), the dwell is pre-set at the factor and is not adjustable.*

ADJUSTMENT WITH A DWELL METER

1. Connect a dwell meter to the ignition system, according to the manufacturer's instructions.

  a. When checking the dwell on a conventional ignition system, connect one meter lead (usually black) to a metallic part of the car to ground the meter; the other lead (usually red) is connected to the coil primary post (the one with the small lead which runs to the distributor body);

  b. When checking dwell on a model with transistorized ignition, ground one meter lead (usually black) to a metallic part of the car; hook up the other lead (usually red) to the negative (–) coil terminal. Under no circumstances should the meter be connected to the distributor or the positive (+) side of the coil. (See the preceding Service Precautions).

2. If the dwell meter has a set line, adjust the needle until it rests on the line.

3. Start the engine. It should be warmed up and running at the specified idle speed.

NOTE: *It is not necessary to check the dwell on the transistorized system for certain 1977 California models. It is set at the factory and requires no adjustment.*

CAUTION: *Be sure to keep fingers, tools, clothes, hair, and wires clear of the engine fan. The transmission should be in Neutral (or Park), parking brake set, and running in a well ventilated area.*

4. Check the reading on the dwell meter. If your meter doesn't have a 4-cylinder scale, multiply the 8-cylinder reading by two.

5. If the meter reading is within the range specified in the Tune-Up Specifications chart, shut the engine off and disconnect the dwell meter.

6. If the dwell is not within specifications, shut the engine off and adjust the point gap as previously outlined. Increasing the point gap decreases the dwell angle and vice versa.

7. Adjust the points until dwell is within specifications, then disconnect the dwell meter. Adjust the timing as detailed in the following section.

Electronic Ignition

Electronic ignition systems offer many advantages over the conventional breaker point ignition system. By eliminating the points maintenance requirements are greatly reduced. An electronic ignition system is capable of producing much higher voltage, which in turn aids in starting, reduces spark plug fouling and provides better emission control.

In 1977, certain Corollas made for California came equipped with electronic ignition. In 1978, Toyota decided to make electronic ignition standard equipment on all models (except the 1980-82 Canadian Tercel w/3A engine) and the same basic system is still used today.

The system Toyota uses consists of a distributor with a signal generator, an ignition coil and an electronic igniter. The signal generator is used to activate the electronic components of the igniter. It is located in the distributor and consists of three main components; the signal rotor, the pick-up coil and the permanent magnet. The signal rotor (not to be confused with the normal rotor) revolves with the distributor shaft, while the pickup coil and the permanent magnet are stationary. As the signal rotor spins, the teeth on it pass a projection leading from the pickup coil. When this happens, voltage is allowed to flow through the system, firing the spark plugs. There is no physical contact and no electrical arcing, hence no need to replace burnt or worn parts.

Service consists of inspection of the distributor cap, rotor and the ignition wires; replacing them as necessary. In addition, the air gap between the signal rotor and the projection on the pickup coil should be checked periodically.

AIR GAP ADJUSTMENT

1. Remove the distributor cap as detailed earlier. Inspect the cap for cracks, carbon tracks or a worn center contact. Replace it if necessary, transferring the wires one at a time from the old cap to the new one.

2. Pull the ignition rotor (not the signal rotor) straight up and remove it. Replace it if the contacts are worn, burned or pitted. Do not file the contacts.

3. Turn the engine over (you may use a socket wrench on the front pulley bolt to do this) until the projection on the pickup coil is directly opposite the signal rotor tooth.

4. Get a non-ferrous (paper, brass, or plastic) feeler gauge of 0.012″ (0.30mm), and insert it into the pick-up air gap. DO NOT USE AN ORDINARY METAL FEELER GAUGE! The gauge should just touch either side of the gap. The permissible range is 0.008-0.016″ (0.20-0.40mm).

NOTE: *The air gap on 1983-84 3A-C and 4A-C engines is NOT adjustable. If the gap is not within specifications, the pick-up coil (igniter) must be replaced.*

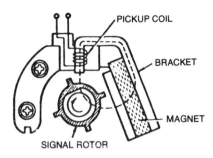

Components of the electronic ignition signal generator

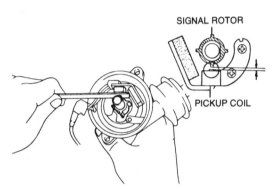

Checking the air gap—all engines except 1983 and later 3A-C and 4A-C

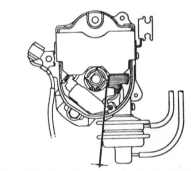

Checking the air gap on the electronic ignition system—3A-C and 4A-C

5. If the gap is either too wide or too narrow, loosen the two phillips screws mounting the pickup coil onto the distributor base plate. Then, wedge a screwdriver between the notch in the pickup coil assembly and the two dimples on the base plate, and turn the screwdriver back and forth until the pickup gap is correct.

6. Tighten the screws and recheck gap, readjusting if necessary.

Ignition Timing

Ignition timing is the measurement in degrees of crankshaft rotation of the instant the spark plugs in the cylinders fire, in relation to the location of the piston, while the piston is on its compression stroke.

Ignition timing is adjusted by loosening the distributor locking device and turning the distributor in the engine.

Ideally, the air/fuel mixture in the cylinder will be ignited (by the spark plug) and just beginning its rapid expansion as the piston passes top dead center (TDC) of the compression stroke. If this happens, the piston will be beginning the power stroke just as the compressed (by the movement of the piston) and ignited (by the spark plug) air/fuel mixture starts to expand. The expansion of the air/fuel mixture will

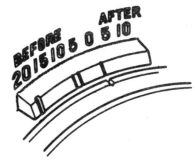

Timing marks—1A-C, 3A, 1980–82 3A-C

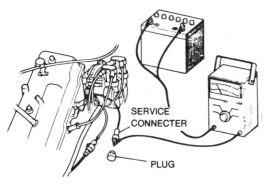

1983 and later A-series engines require a special tachometer hook-up

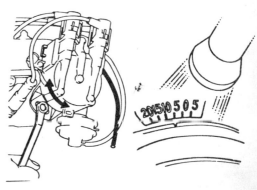

Timing marks—4A-C and 1983 and later 3A-C engines (note the disconnected vacuum hose)

Timing marks—3K-C and 2T-C

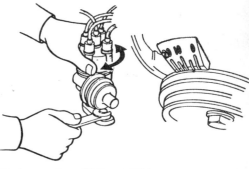

Timing marks—4K-C and 4K-E

Timing marks—3T-C

Timing marks—4A-GE

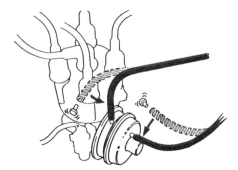

Vacuum hose disconnected—4K-C and 4K-E

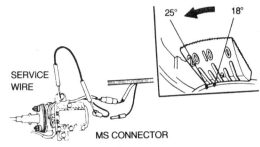

The second time the MS connector is short-circuited, ignition timing should advance from 18° BTDC to 25° BTDC

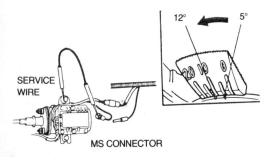

The first time the MS connector is short-circuited, ignition timing should advance from 5° BTDC to 12° BTDC

then force the piston down on the power stroke and turn the crankshaft.

It takes a fraction of a second for the spark from the plug to completely ignite the mixture in the cylinder. Because of this, the spark plug must fire before the piston reaches TDC, if the mixture is to be completely ignited as the piston passes TDC. This measurement is given in degrees (of crankshaft rotation) before the piston reaches top dead center (BTDC). If the ignition timing setting for your engine is 7° BTDC, this means that the spark plug must fire at a time

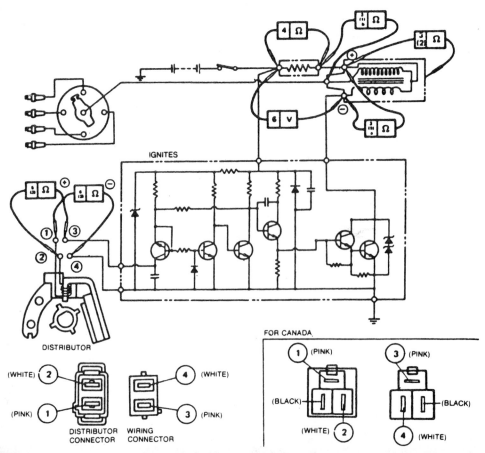

Electronic ignition system schematic

when the piston for that cylinder is 7° before top dead center of its compression stroke. However, this only holds true while your engine is at idle speed.

As you accelerate from idle, the speed of your engine (rpm) increases. The increase in rpm means that the pistons are now traveling up and down much faster. Because of this, the spark plugs will have to fire even even sooner if the mixture is to be completely ignited as the piston passes TDC. To accomplish this, the distributor incorporates means to advance the timing of the spark as engine speed increases.

The distributor in your Toyota has two means of advancing the ignition timing. One is called centrifugal advance and is actuated by weights in the distributor. The other is called vacuum advance and is controlled by that larger circular housing on the side of the distributor (models equipped).

In addition, some distributors have a vacuum/retard mechanism which is contained in the same housing on the side of the distributor as the vacuum advance. The function of this mechanism is to retard the timing of the ignition spark under certain engine conditions. This causes more complete burning of the air/fuel mixture in the cylinder and consequently lower exhaust emissions.

Because these mechanisms change ignition timing, it is necessary to disconnect and plug the one or two vacuum lines from the distributor when setting the basic ignition timing. (Consult the emissions sticker under the hood of your vehicle. Follow those instructions if they differ from the ones listed here).

If ignition timing is set too far advanced (BTDC), the ignition and expansion of the air/fuel mixture in the cylinder will try to force the piston down the cylinder while it is still traveling upward. This causes engine ping, a sound which resembles marbles being dropped into an empty tin can. If the ignition timing is too far retarded (after, or ATDC), the piston will have already started down on the power stroke when the air/fuel mixture ignites and expands. This will cause the piston to be forced down only a portion of its travel. This will result in poor engine performance and lack of power.

Ignition timing adjustment is checked with a timing light. This instrument is usually connected to the number one (No. 1) spark plug of the engine (see the equipment manfacturer's instructions). The timing light flashes every time an electrical current is sent from the distributor, through the No. 1 spark plug wire, to the spark plug. The crankshaft pulley and the front cover of the engine are marked with a timing pointer and a timing scale. When the timing

pointer is aligned with the **0** mark on the timing scale, the piston in the No. 1 cylinder is at TDC of its compression stroke. With the engine running, and the timing light aimed at the timing pointer and timing scale, the stroboscopic flashes from the timing light will allow you to check the ignition timing setting of the engine. The timing light flashes every time the spark plug in the No. 1 cylinder of the engine fires. Since the flash from the timing light makes the crankshaft pulley seem stationary for a moment, you will be able to read the exact position of the piston in the No. 1 cylinder on the timing scale.

There are three basic types of timing light available. the first is a simple neon bulb with two wire connections (one for the spark plug and one for the plug wire, connecting the light in series). This type of light is quite dim, and must be held closely to the marks to be seen, but it is inexpensive. The second type of light operates from the car battery. Two alligator clips connect to the batter terminals, while a third wire connects to the spark plug with an adaptor. This type of light is more expensive, but the zenon bulb provides a nice bright flash which can even be seen in sunlight. the third type replaces the battery source with 110 volt house current. Some timing lights have other functions built into them, such as dwell meters, tachometers, or remote starting switches. These are convenient, in that they reduce the tangle of wires under the hood, but may duplicate the functions of tools you already have.

If your Toyota has electronic ignition, you should use a timing light with an inductive pickup. This pickup simple clamps onto the No. 1 plug wire, eliminating the adaptor. It is not susceptible to crossfiring or false triggering, which may occur with a conventional light, due to the greater voltages produced by electronic ignition.

CHECKING AND ADJUSTMENT

Single Point and Electronic Distributors

1. Warm-up the engine. Connect a tachometer and check the engine idle speed to be sure that it is within the specification given in the Tune-Up Specifications chart at the beginning of the chapter.

NOTE: *Before hooking up a tachometer to a 1975-77 car with a transistorized ignition system, see the preceding service precautions in the Breaker Points and Condenser section.*

1983 and later A-series engines require a special type of tachometer which hooks up to the service connector wire coming out of the distributor. As many tachometers are not compatible with this hook-up, we recommend that you consult with the manufacturer before purchasing a certain type.

On models with electronic ignition, hook the dwell meter or tachometer to the negative (–) side of the coil, not to the distributor primary lead; damage to the ignition control unit will result.

2. If the timing marks are difficult to see, use a dab of paint or chalk to make them more visible.

3. Connect a timing light according to the manufacturer's instructions.

4. Disconnect the vacuum line(s) from the distributor vacuum unit. Plug it (them) with a pencil or golf tee(s).

5. Be sure that the timing light wires are clear of the fan and start the engine.

CAUTION: *Keep fingers, clothes, tools, hair, and leads clear of the spinning engine fan. Be sure that you are running the engine in a well ventilated area.*

6. Allow the engine to run at the specified idle speed with the gearshift in Neutral with manual transmission and Drive (D) with automatic transmission.

CAUTION: *Be sure that the parking brake is set and that the front wheels are blocked to prevent the car from rolling forward, especially when Drive is selected with an automatic.*

7. Point the timing light at the marks indicated in the chart and illustrations. With the engine at idle, timing should be at the specification given on the Tune-Up Specifications chart at the beginning of the chapter.

8. If the timing is not at the specification, loosen the pinch bolt at the base of the distributor just enough so that the distributor can be turned. Turn the distributor to advance or retard the timing as required. Once the proper marks are seen to align with the timing light, timing is correct.

9. Stop the engine and tighten the pinch bolt. Start the engine and recheck the timing. Stop the engine; disconnect the tachometer and timing light. Connect the vacuum line(s) to the distributor vacuum unit.

NOTE: *After tightening the distributor pinch bolt on the 4K-E engine (5 speed only), but before disconnecting the timing light and tachometer, it is a good idea to check the Mechatro Spark (MS) System.*

Disconnect the MS connector at the igniter and then connect a jumper wire between the side of the igniter and the MS connector. Ignition timing should advance to 12° BTDC. Reconnect the MS connector and the vacuum hose at the distributor diaphragm, the timing should now advance to about 18° BTDC. Disconnect the MS connector once again (isn't this fun?)

and make sure that the timing advances to above 25° BTDC. Reconnect the MS connector.

DUAL POINT DISTRIBUTOR

A dual point distributor is offered as an option on some Corolla models, sold outside of California, in 1975. To adjust the dual point system, proceed as follows:

1. Adjust the timing for the main set of points as previously outlined in the Single Point section.

2. Use a jumper wire to ground the terminal on the thermoswitch connector after removing the connector from the thermoswitch. The thermoswitch is threaded into the intake manifold and is connected to the dual point system relay. Be careful not to confuse it with any of the emission control system switches which are connected to the computer.

3. Check the timing with a light as described above, the timing should be 22° before top dead center (BTDC).

4. If the timing is off, connect a dwell meter to the negative side of the coil, and adjust the sub-points so that the dwell angle is 52°. The sub-points are adjusted in the same manner as the main points.

5. Remove the test equipment and reconnect the thermoswitch.

Electronic Ignition System Troubleshooting

NOTE: *This book contains simple testing procedures for your electronic ignition system. More comprehensive testing on this system and other electronic control systems can be found in CHILTON'S GUIDE TO ELECTRONIC ENGINE CONTROLS, book part number 7535, available at your local retailer.*

Troubleshooting this system is easy, but you must have an accurate ohmmeter and voltmeter. The numbers in the diagram correspond to the numbers of the following troubleshooting steps. Be sure to perform each step in order.

1. Check for a spark at the spark plugs by hooking up a timing light in the usual manner. If the light flashes, it can be assumed that voltage is reaching the plugs, which should then be inspected, along with the fuel system. If no flash is generated, go on to the following ignition checks.

2. Check all wiring and plastic connectors for tight and proper connections.

3. (1) With an ohmmeter, check between the positive (+) and negative (–) primary terminals of the ignition coil. The resistance (cold) should be 1.3-1.7Ω. Between the primary terminal and the high tension terminal, the resistance (cold) should be 12-16kΩ. (2) The insulation resis-

tance between the (+) primary terminal and the ignition coil case should be infinite.

4. The resistor wire (brown and yellow) resistance should be 1.2Ω (cold). To measure, disconnect the plastic connector at the igniter and connect one wire of the ohmmeter to the yellow wire and one to the brown.

5. Remove the distributor cap and ignition rotor. (1) Check the air gap between the timing rotor spoke and the pick-up coil. When aligned, the air gap should be 0.008-0.016″ (0.20-0.40mm). You will probably have to bump the engine around with the starter to line up the timing rotor. (2) Unplug the distributor connector at the distributor. Connect one wire of the ohmmeter to the white wire, and one wire to the pink wire. The resistance of the signal generator should be 130-190Ω.

6a. Checking the igniter last, connect the (–) voltmeter wire to the (–) ignition coil primary terminal, and the (+) voltmeter wire to the yellow resistor wire at the connector unplugged in Step 4. With the ignition switch turned on **On** (not Start) the voltage should measure 12 volts.

6b. Check the voltage between the (–) ignition coil primary terminal and the yellow resistor wire again, but this time use the ohmmeter as resistance. Using the igniter end of the distributor connector unplugged in Step 5, connect the positive (+) ohmmeter wire to the pink distributor wire, and the negative (–) ohmmeter wire to the white wire.

CAUTION: *Do not intermix the (+) and (–) terminals of the ohmmeter.*

Select either the 1Ω or 10Ω range of the ohmmeter. With the voltmeter connected as in Step 6 (1), and the ignition switch turned to **On** (not Start), the voltage should measure nearly zero.

Octane Selector

The octane selector is used as a fine adjustment to match the vehicle's ignition timing to the grade of gasoline being used. It is located near the distributor vacuum unit (models equipped), beneath a plastic dust cover. Normally the octane selector should not require adjustment, however, adjustment is as follows:

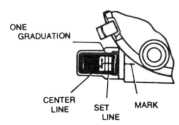

Octane selector

Octane Selector Test Speeds

Engine Type	Test Speed (mph)
3K-C	19–21
2T-C	16–22

1. Align the setting line with the threaded end of the housing and then align the center line with the setting mark on the housing.

2. Drive the car to the speed specified in the Octane Selector Test Speeds chart in High gear on a level road.

3. Depress the accelerator pedal all the way to the floor. A slight pinging sound should be heard. As the car accelerates, the sound should gradually go away.

4. If the pinging sound is low or if it fails to disappear as the vehicle speed increases, retard the timing by turning the knob toward **R** (Retard).

5. If there is no pinging sound at all, advance the timing by turning the knob toward **A** (Advance).

NOTE: *On 1973-79 models, do not turn the octane selector more than ½ turn toward **R**.* Do not turn it toward **A** at all.

6. When the adjustment is completed, replace the plastic dust cover.

NOTE: *One graduation of the octane selector is equal to about 10° of crankshaft angle.*

Valve Lash

Since all Toyota models (with the exception of the 4K-E, which uses hydraulic valve lash adjusters) are equipped with mechanical valve lifters, they should be adjusted at the factory recommended intervals (1970-77, every 12,000 miles; 1978-84, every 15,000 miles; 1985-87, every 30,000 miles).

Valve lash is one factor which determines how far the intake and exhaust valves will open into the cylinder.

If the valve clearance is too large, part of the lift of the camshaft will be used up in removing the excessive clearance, thus the valves will not be opened far enough. This condition has two effects, the valve train components will emit a tapping noise as they take up the excessive clearance, and the engine will perform poorly, since the less the intake valve opens, the smaller the amount of air/fuel mixture admitted to the cylinders will be. The less the exhaust valves open, the greater the back-pressure in the cylinder which prevents the proper air/fuel mixture from entering the cylinder.

If the valve clearance is too small, the intake and exhaust valves will not fully seat on the cylinder head when they close. When a valve seats on the cylinder head it does two things, it seals the combustion chamber so none of the gases in the cylinder can escape and it cools itself by transferring some of the heat it absorbed from the combustion process through the cylinder

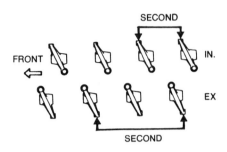

Adjust these valves second on the 2T-C and 3T-C engines

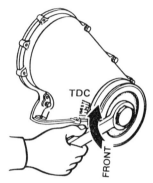

Turn the crankshaft to set the engine at TDC

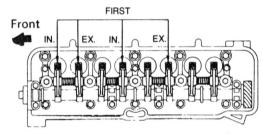

Adjust these valves first on the A-series engines

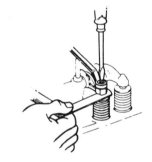

Checking the valve lash on A-series engines

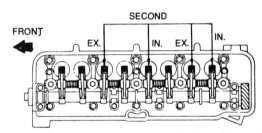

Adjust these valves second on the A-series engines

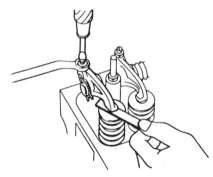

Checking the valve lash on all other engines

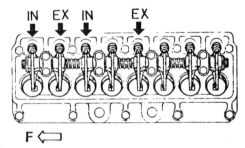

Adjust these valves first on the 3K-C and 4K-C engines

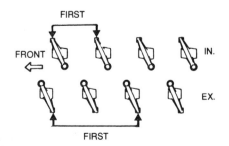

Adjust these valves first on the 2T-C and 3T-C engines

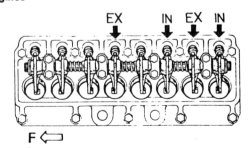

Adjust these valves second on the 3K-C and 4K-C engines

head and into the engine cooling system. Therefore, if the valve clearance is too small, the engine will run poorly (due to gases escaping from the combustion chamber), and the valves will overheat and warp (since they cannot transfer heat unless they are touching the seat in the cylinder head).

NOTE: *While all valve adjustments must be as accurate as possible, it is better to have the valve adjustment slightly loose than slightly tight, as burnt valves may result form overly tight adjustments.*

ADJUSTMENT

All Engines Except 4K-E, 4A-GE and 1C-L

NOTE: *Although Toyota recommends that the valve lash on certain models be set while the engine is running, we feel that for the average backyard mechanic it is more convenient to adjust the valves statically (engine off). Thus, running valve lash adjustment procedures have been omitted from this manual.*

1. Start the engine and run it until it reaches normal operating temperature.

2. Stop the engine. Remove the air cleaner assembly. Remove any other hoses, cables, etc. which are attached to, or in the way of, the, cylinder head cover. Remove the cylinder head cover.

CAUTION: *Be careful when removing components as the engine will be hot.*

3. Turn the crankshaft until the pointer or notch on the pulley aligns with the **O** or **T** mark on the timing scale. This will insure that the engine is at TDC.

NOTE: *Check that the rocker arms on the No. 1 cylinder are loose and those on the No. 4 cylinder are tight. If not, turn the crankshaft one complete revolution (360°).*

4. Retighten the cylinder head bolts on all 3K-C engines to the proper torque specifications (see Torque Specifications in Chapter 3). Also on the 3K-C, retighten the valve rocker support bolts to 13-17 ft.lb.

CAUTION: *Tighten all of the bolts in Step 4 in the proper sequence and stages (see Chapter 3).*

5. Using a flat feeler gauge, check the clearance between the bottom of the rocker arm and the top of the valve stem. This measurement should correspond to the one given in the Tune-Up Specifications chart in this chapter. Check only the valves listed under **First** in the accompanying valve arrangement illustrations for your particular engine.

6. If the clearance is not within specifications, the valves will require adjustment. Loosen the locknut on the other end (A-series engines have the locknut on the same end) of the rocker arm and, still holding the nut with an open end wrench, turn the adjustment screw to achieve the correct clearance.

7. Once the correct valve clearance is achieved, keep the adjustment screw from turning with your screwdriver and tighten the locknut. Recheck the valve clearances.

8. Turn the engine one complete revolution (360°) and adjust the remaining valves. Follow Steps 5-7 and use the valve arrangement illustration marked 'Second'.

9. Use a new gasket and then install the cylinder head cover. Install anyother components which were removed in Step 2.

4A-GE and 1C-L Diesel Engine

1. Follow Steps 1-2 of the previous procedure. Don't forget the CAUTION after Step 2.

2. Use a wrench and turn the crankshaft until the notch in the pulley aligns with the timing pointer in the front cover. This will insure that the engine is at TDC.

NOTE: *Check that the valve lifters on the No. 1 cylinder are loose and that those on the No. 4 cylinder are tight. If not, turn the crankshaft one complete revolution (360°) and then realign the marks.*

3. Using a flat feeler gauge, measure the clearance between the camshaft lobe and the valve lifter. This measurement should corre-

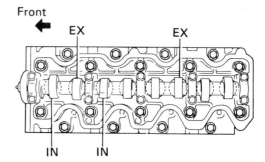

Adjust these valves first on the 1C-L engine

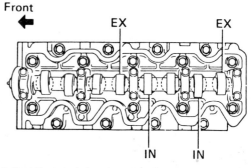

Adjust these valves second on the 1C-L engine

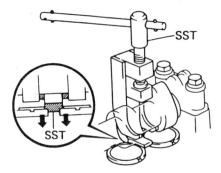

Installing the special tool to depress the valve lifters

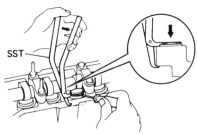

Depressing the valve lifter to remove the shim—4A-GE

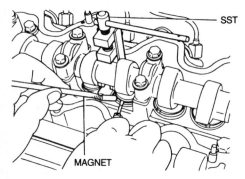

Use a magnet and a screwdriver to remove the old valve shims

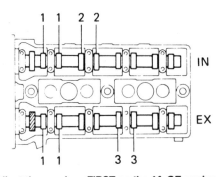

Adjust these valves FIRST on the 4A-GE engine

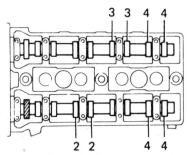

Adjust these valves SECOND on the 4A-GE engine

spond to the one given in the Tune-Up chart. Check only the valves listed under **First** in the accompanying valve arrangement illustrations for your particular engine.

NOTE: *If the measurement is within specifications, go on to the next step. If not, record the measurement taken for each individual valve.*

4. Turn the crankshaft one complete revolution and realign the timing marks as previously described.

5. Measure the clearance of the valves shown in the valve arrangement illustration marked **Second**.

NOTE: *If the measurement for this set of valves (and also the previous one) is within specifications, you need go no further, the procedure is finished. If not, record the measurements and proceed to Step 6.*

6. Turn the crankshaft to position the intake camshaft lobe of the cylinder to be adjusted, upward.

7. Using a small screwdriver, turn the valve lifter so that the notch is easily accessible.

8. Install SST #09248-64010 (Diesel) or SST 09248-70012 (4A-GE) between the two camshaft lobes and then turn the handle so that the tool presses down both (intake and exhaust) valve lifters evenly. On the 4A-GE engine, the tool will work on only one lifter at a time.

9. Using a small screwdriver and a magnet, remove the valve shims.

10. Measure the thickness of the old shim with a micrometer. Locate that particular measurement in the Installed Shim Thickness column of the accompanying chart, then locate the already recorded measurement for that valve in the Measured Clearance column of the chart. Index the two columns to arrive at the proper replacement shim thickness.

NOTE: *On Diesel engines, replacement shims are available in 25 sizes, in increments of 0.050mm (0.0020"), from 2.200mm (0.00866") to 3.400mm (0.1399"). On the 4A-GE engine, shims are available from 2.500mm (0.984") to 3.300mm (0.1299").*

Intake

Installed shim thickness (mm) — across the top; Measured clearance (mm) — down the side.

Measured clearance (mm)	2.500	2.525	2.550	2.575	2.600	2.625	2.650	2.675	2.700	2.725	2.750	2.775	2.800	2.825	2.850	2.875	2.900	2.925	2.950	2.975	3.000	3.025	3.050	3.075	3.100	3.125	3.150	3.175	3.200	3.225	3.250	3.275	3.300
0.000–0.025								02	02	04	04	06	06	08	08	10	10	12	12	14	14	16	16	18	18	20	20	22	22	24	24	26	26
0.026–0.050							02	02	04	04	06	06	08	08	10	10	12	12	14	14	16	16	18	18	20	20	22	22	24	24	26	26	28
0.051–0.075						02	02	04	04	06	06	08	08	10	10	12	12	14	14	16	16	18	18	20	20	22	22	24	24	26	26	28	28
0.076–0.100					02	02	04	04	06	06	08	08	10	10	12	12	14	14	16	16	18	18	20	20	22	22	24	24	26	26	28	28	30
0.101–0.125				02	02	04	04	06	06	08	08	10	10	12	12	14	14	16	16	18	18	20	20	22	22	24	24	26	26	28	28	30	30
0.126–0.149			02	02	04	04	06	06	08	08	10	10	12	12	14	14	16	16	18	18	20	20	22	22	24	24	26	26	28	28	30	30	32
0.150–0.250																																	
0.251–0.275	04	06	06	08	08	10	10	12	12	14	14	16	16	18	18	20	20	22	22	24	24	26	26	28	28	30	30	32	32	34	34	34	
0.276–0.300	06	06	08	08	10	10	12	12	14	14	16	16	18	18	20	20	22	22	24	24	26	26	28	28	30	30	32	32	34	34	34		
0.301–0.325	06	08	08	10	10	12	12	14	14	16	16	18	18	20	20	22	22	24	24	26	26	28	28	30	30	32	32	34	34	34			
0.326–0.350	08	08	10	10	12	12	14	14	16	16	18	18	20	20	22	22	24	24	26	26	28	28	30	30	32	32	34	34	34				
0.351–0.375	08	10	10	12	12	14	14	16	16	18	18	20	20	22	22	24	24	26	26	28	28	30	30	32	32	34	34	34					
0.376–0.400	10	10	12	12	14	14	16	16	18	18	20	20	22	22	24	24	26	26	28	28	30	30	32	32	34	34	34						
0.401–0.425	10	12	12	14	14	16	16	18	18	20	20	22	22	24	24	26	26	28	28	30	30	32	32	34	34	34							
0.426–0.450	12	12	14	14	16	16	18	18	20	20	22	22	24	24	26	26	28	28	30	30	32	32	34	34	34								
0.451–0.475	12	14	14	16	16	18	18	20	20	22	22	24	24	26	26	28	28	30	30	32	32	34	34	34									
0.476–0.500	14	14	16	16	18	18	20	20	22	22	24	24	26	26	28	28	30	30	32	32	34	34	34										
0.501–0.525	14	16	16	18	18	20	20	22	22	24	24	26	26	28	28	30	30	32	32	34	34	34											
0.526–0.550	16	16	18	18	20	20	22	22	24	24	26	26	28	28	30	30	32	32	34	34	34												
0.551–0.575	16	18	18	20	20	22	22	24	24	26	26	28	28	30	30	32	32	34	34	34													
0.576–0.600	18	18	20	20	22	22	24	24	26	26	28	28	30	30	32	32	34	34	34														
0.601–0.625	18	20	20	22	22	24	24	26	26	28	28	30	30	32	32	34	34	34															
0.626–0.650	20	20	22	22	24	24	26	26	28	28	30	30	32	32	34	34	34																
0.651–0.675	20	22	22	24	24	26	26	28	28	30	30	32	32	34	34	34																	
0.676–0.700	22	22	24	24	26	26	28	28	30	30	32	32	34	34	34																		
0.701–0.725	22	24	24	26	26	28	28	30	30	32	32	34	34	34																			
0.726–0.750	24	24	26	26	28	28	30	30	32	32	34	34	34																				
0.751–0.775	24	26	26	28	28	30	30	32	32	34	34	34																					
0.776–0.800	26	26	28	28	30	30	32	32	34	34	34																						
0.801–0.825	26	28	28	30	30	32	32	34	34	34																							
0.826–0.850	28	28	30	30	32	32	34	34	34																								
0.851–0.875	28	30	30	32	32	34	34	34																									
0.876–0.900	30	30	32	32	34	34	34																										
0.901–0.925	30	32	32	34	34	34																											
0.926–0.950	32	32	34	34	34																												
0.951–0.975	32	34	34	34																													
0.976–1.000	34	34	34																														
1.001–1.025	34	34																															
1.026–1.050	34																																

Intake valve clearance (cold):
0.15 – 0.25 mm (0.006 – 0.010 in.)

Example: 2.800 mm Installed is
Measured clearance is 0.450 mm
Replace 2.800 mm shim with
shim No. 24 (3.050 mm).

Shim Selection Chart—4A-GE

Shim thickness mm (in.)

Shim No.	Thickness	Shim No.	Thickness
02	2.500 (0.0984)	20	2.950 (0.1161)
04	2.550 (0.1004)	22	3.000 (0.1181)
06	2.600 (0.1024)	24	3.050 (0.1201)
08	2.650 (0.1043)	26	3.100 (0.1220)
10	2.700 (0.1063)	28	3.150 (0.1240)
12	2.750 (0.1083)	30	3.200 (0.1260)
14	2.800 (0.1102)	32	3.250 (0.1280)
16	2.850 (0.1122)	34	3.300 (0.1299)
18	2.900 (0.1142)		

SHIM SELECTION USING CHART

Exhaust

Installed shim thickness (mm)

Measured clearance (mm)	2.500	2.525	2.550	2.575	2.600	2.625	2.650	2.675	2.700	2.725	2.750	2.775	2.800	2.825	2.850	2.875	2.900	2.925	2.950	2.975	3.000	3.025	3.050	3.075	3.100	3.125	3.150	3.175	3.200	3.225	3.250	3.275	3.300
0.000–0.025										02	02	04	04	06	06	08	08	10	10	12	12	14	14	16	16	18	18	20	20	22	22	24	24
0.026–0.050									02	02	04	04	06	06	08	08	10	10	12	12	14	14	16	16	18	18	20	20	22	22	24	24	26
0.051–0.075								02	02	04	04	06	06	08	08	10	10	12	12	14	14	16	16	18	18	20	20	22	22	24	24	26	26
0.076–0.100							02	02	04	04	06	06	08	08	10	10	12	12	14	14	16	16	18	18	20	20	22	22	24	24	26	26	28
0.101–0.125						02	02	04	04	06	06	08	08	10	10	12	12	14	14	16	16	18	18	20	20	22	22	24	24	26	26	28	28
0.126–0.150					02	02	04	04	06	06	08	08	10	10	12	12	14	14	16	16	18	18	20	20	22	22	24	24	26	26	28	28	30
0.151–0.175				02	02	04	04	06	06	08	08	10	10	12	12	14	14	16	16	18	18	20	20	22	22	24	24	26	26	28	28	30	30
0.176–0.199			02	02	04	04	06	06	08	08	10	10	12	12	14	14	16	16	18	18	20	20	22	22	24	24	26	26	28	28	30	30	32
0.200–0.300																																	
0.301–0.325	04	06	06	08	08	10	10	12	12	14	14	16	16	18	18	20	20	22	22	24	24	26	26	28	28	30	30	32	32	34	34		
0.326–0.350	06	06	08	08	10	10	12	12	14	14	16	16	18	18	20	20	22	22	24	24	26	26	28	28	30	30	32	32	34	34			
0.351–0.375	06	08	08	10	10	12	12	14	14	16	16	18	18	20	20	22	22	24	24	26	26	28	28	30	30	32	32	34	34				
0.376–0.400	08	08	10	10	12	12	14	14	16	16	18	18	20	20	22	22	24	24	26	26	28	28	30	30	32	32	34	34					
0.401–0.425	08	10	10	12	12	14	14	16	16	18	18	20	20	22	22	24	24	26	26	28	28	30	30	32	32	34	34						
0.426–0.450	10	10	12	12	14	14	16	16	18	18	20	20	22	22	24	24	26	26	28	28	30	30	32	32	34	34							
0.451–0.475	10	12	12	14	14	16	16	18	18	20	20	22	22	24	24	26	26	28	28	30	30	32	32	34	34								
0.476–0.500	12	12	14	14	16	16	18	18	20	20	22	22	24	24	26	26	28	28	30	30	32	32	34	34									
0.501–0.525	12	14	14	16	16	18	18	20	20	22	22	24	24	26	26	28	28	30	30	32	32	34	34										
0.526–0.550	14	14	16	16	18	18	20	20	22	22	24	24	26	26	28	28	30	30	32	32	34	34											
0.551–0.575	14	16	16	18	18	20	20	22	22	24	24	26	26	28	28	30	30	32	32	34	34												
0.576–0.600	16	16	18	18	20	20	22	22	24	24	26	26	28	28	30	30	32	32	34	34													
0.601–0.625	16	18	18	20	20	22	22	24	24	26	26	28	28	30	30	32	32	34	34														
0.626–0.650	18	18	20	20	22	22	24	24	26	26	28	28	30	30	32	32	34	34															
0.651–0.675	18	20	20	22	22	24	24	26	26	28	28	30	30	32	32	34	34																
0.676–0.700	20	20	22	22	24	24	26	26	28	28	30	30	32	32	34	34																	
0.701–0.725	20	22	22	24	24	26	26	28	28	30	30	32	32	34	34																		
0.726–0.750	22	22	24	24	26	26	28	28	30	30	32	32	34	34																			
0.751–0.775	22	24	24	26	26	28	28	30	30	32	32	34	34																				
0.776–0.800	24	24	26	26	28	28	30	30	32	32	34	34																					
0.801–0.825	24	26	26	28	28	30	30	32	32	34	34																						
0.826–0.850	26	26	28	28	30	30	32	32	34	34																							
0.851–0.875	26	28	28	30	30	32	32	34	34																								
0.876–0.900	28	28	30	30	32	32	34	34																									
0.901–0.925	28	30	30	32	32	34	34																										
0.926–0.950	30	30	32	32	34	34																											
0.951–0.975	30	32	32	34	34																												
0.976–1.000	32	32	34	34																													
1.001–1.025	32	34	34																														
1.026–1.060	34	34																															
1.051–1.075	34																																

Shim thickness — mm (in.)

Shim No.	Thickness	Shim No.	Thickness
02	2.500 (0.0984)	20	2.950 (0.1161)
04	2.550 (0.1004)	22	3.000 (0.1181)
06	2.600 (0.1024)	24	3.050 (0.1201)
08	2.650 (0.1043)	26	3.100 (0.1220)
10	2.700 (0.1063)	28	3.150 (0.1240)
12	2.750 (0.1083)	30	3.200 (0.1260)
14	2.800 (0.1102)	32	3.250 (0.1280)
16	2.850 (0.1122)	34	3.300 (0.1299)
18	2.900 (0.1142)		

Exhaust valve clearance (cold):
0.20 – 0.30 mm (0.008 – 0.012 in.)

Example: 2.800 mm Installed is
Measured clearance is 0.450 mm
Replace 2.800 mm shim with

SHIM SELECTION CHART

Intake

Installed Shim Thickness (mm)

(Large shim selection matrix cross-referencing Measured Clearance (mm) rows against Installed Shim Thickness (mm) columns from 2.200 through 3.400. Each cell gives the replacement shim number.)

Shim Thickness

Shim No.	Thickness mm (in.)	Shim No.	Thickness mm (in.)
01	2.20 (0.0866)	27	2.85 (0.1122)
03	2.25 (0.0886)	29	2.90 (0.1142)
05	2.30 (0.0906)	31	2.95 (0.1161)
07	2.35 (0.0925)	33	3.00 (0.1181)
09	2.40 (0.0945)	35	3.05 (0.1201)
11	2.45 (0.0965)	37	3.10 (0.1220)
13	2.50 (0.0984)	39	3.15 (0.1240)
15	2.55 (0.1004)	41	3.20 (0.1260)
17	2.60 (0.1024)	43	3.25 (0.1280)
19	2.65 (0.1043)	45	3.30 (0.1299)
21	2.70 (0.1063)	47	3.35 (0.1319)
23	2.75 (0.1083)	49	3.40 (0.1339)
25	2.80 (0.1102)		

Intake Valve Clearance (cold):   0.20 – 0.30 mm (0.008 – 0.012 in.)

Example: 2.700 mm (0.1063 in.) shim installed
Measured clearance is 0.350 mm (0.0138 in.).
Replace 2.700 mm (0.1063 in.) sh m with shim No. 25.

SHIM SELECTION CHART

Exhaust

Measured Clearance (mm)	Installed Shim Thickness (mm)																																																
	2.200	2.225	2.250	2.275	2.300	2.325	2.350	2.375	2.400	2.425	2.450	2.475	2.500	2.525	2.550	2.575	2.600	2.625	2.650	2.675	2.700	2.725	2.750	2.775	2.800	2.825	2.850	2.875	2.900	2.925	2.950	2.975	3.000	3.025	3.050	3.075	3.100	3.125	3.150	3.175	3.200	3.225	3.250	3.275	3.300	3.325	3.350	3.375	3.400
0.000-0.025											01	01	01	03	03	05	05	07	07	09	09	11	11	13	13	15	15	17	17	19	19	21	21	23	23	25	25	27	27	29	29	31	31	33	33	35	35	37	37
0.026-0.050										01	01	01	03	03	05	05	07	07	09	09	11	11	13	13	15	15	17	17	19	19	21	21	23	23	25	25	27	27	29	29	31	31	33	33	35	35	37	37	39
0.051-0.075									01	01	01	03	03	05	05	07	07	09	09	11	11	13	13	15	15	17	17	19	19	21	21	23	23	25	25	27	27	29	29	31	31	33	33	35	35	37	37	39	39
0.076-0.100								01	01	01	03	03	05	05	07	07	09	09	11	11	13	13	15	15	17	17	19	19	21	21	23	23	25	25	27	27	29	29	31	31	33	33	35	35	37	37	39	39	41
0.101-0.125							01	01	01	03	03	05	05	07	07	09	09	11	11	13	13	15	15	17	17	19	19	21	21	23	23	25	25	27	27	29	29	31	31	33	33	35	35	37	37	39	39	41	41
0.126-0.150						01	01	01	03	03	05	05	07	07	09	09	11	11	13	13	15	15	17	17	19	19	21	21	23	23	25	25	27	27	29	29	31	31	33	33	35	35	37	37	39	39	41	41	43
0.151-0.175					01	01	01	03	03	05	05	07	07	09	09	11	11	13	13	15	15	17	17	19	19	21	21	23	23	25	25	27	27	29	29	31	31	33	33	35	35	37	37	39	39	41	41	43	43
0.176-0.200				01	01	01	03	03	05	05	07	07	09	09	11	11	13	13	15	15	17	17	19	19	21	21	23	23	25	25	27	27	29	29	31	31	33	33	35	35	37	37	39	39	41	41	43	43	45
0.201-0.225			01	01	01	03	03	05	05	07	07	09	09	11	11	13	13	15	15	17	17	19	19	21	21	23	23	25	25	27	27	29	29	31	31	33	33	35	35	37	37	39	39	41	41	43	43	45	45
0.226-0.249		01	01	01	03	03	05	05	07	07	09	09	11	11	13	13	15	15	17	17	19	19	21	21	23	23	25	25	27	27	29	29	31	31	33	33	35	35	37	37	39	39	41	41	43	43	45	45	47
0.250-0.350																																																	
0.351-0.375	03	05	05	07	07	09	09	11	11	13	13	15	15	17	17	19	19	21	21	23	23	25	25	27	27	29	29	31	31	33	33	35	35	37	37	39	39	41	41	43	43	45	45	47	47	49	49	49	
0.376-0.400	05	05	07	07	09	09	11	11	13	13	15	15	17	17	19	19	21	21	23	23	25	25	27	27	29	29	31	31	33	33	35	35	37	37	39	39	41	41	43	43	45	45	47	47	49	49	49		
0.401-0.425	05	07	07	09	09	11	11	13	13	15	15	17	17	19	19	21	21	23	23	25	25	27	27	29	29	31	31	33	33	35	35	37	37	39	39	41	41	43	43	45	45	47	47	49	49	49			
0.426-0.450	07	07	09	09	11	11	13	13	15	15	17	17	19	19	21	21	23	23	25	25	27	27	29	29	31	31	33	33	35	35	37	37	39	39	41	41	43	43	45	45	47	47	49	49	49				
0.451-0.475	07	09	09	11	11	13	13	15	15	17	17	19	19	21	21	23	23	25	25	27	27	29	29	31	31	33	33	35	35	37	37	39	39	41	41	43	43	45	45	47	47	49	49	49					
0.476-0.500	09	09	11	11	13	13	15	15	17	17	19	19	21	21	23	23	25	25	27	27	29	29	31	31	33	33	35	35	37	37	39	39	41	41	43	43	45	45	47	47	49	49	49						
0.501-0.525	09	11	11	13	13	15	15	17	17	19	19	21	21	23	23	25	25	27	27	29	29	31	31	33	33	35	35	37	37	39	39	41	41	43	43	45	45	47	47	49	49	49							
0.526-0.550	11	11	13	13	15	15	17	17	19	19	21	21	23	23	25	25	27	27	29	29	31	31	33	33	35	35	37	37	39	39	41	41	43	43	45	45	47	47	49	49	49								
0.551-0.575	11	13	13	15	15	17	17	19	19	21	21	23	23	25	25	27	27	29	29	31	31	33	33	35	35	37	37	39	39	41	41	43	43	45	45	47	47	49	49	49									
0.576-0.600	13	13	15	15	17	17	19	19	21	21	23	23	25	25	27	27	29	29	31	31	33	33	35	35	37	37	39	39	41	41	43	43	45	45	47	47	49	49	49										
0.601-0.625	13	15	15	17	17	19	19	21	21	23	23	25	25	27	27	29	29	31	31	33	33	35	35	37	37	39	39	41	41	43	43	45	45	47	47	49	49	49											
0.626-0.650	15	15	17	17	19	19	21	21	23	23	25	25	27	27	29	29	31	31	33	33	35	35	37	37	39	39	41	41	43	43	45	45	47	47	49	49	49												
0.651-0.675	15	17	17	19	19	21	21	23	23	25	25	27	27	29	29	31	31	33	33	35	35	37	37	39	39	41	41	43	43	45	45	47	47	49	49	49													
0.676-0.701	17	17	19	19	21	21	23	23	25	25	27	27	29	29	31	31	33	33	35	35	37	37	39	39	41	41	43	43	45	45	47	47	49	49	49														
0.701-0.725	17	19	19	21	21	23	23	25	25	27	27	29	29	31	31	33	33	35	35	37	37	39	39	41	41	43	43	45	45	47	47	49	49	49															
0.726-0.750	19	19	21	21	23	23	25	25	27	27	29	29	31	31	33	33	35	35	37	37	39	39	41	41	43	43	45	45	47	47	49	49	49																
0.751-0.775	19	21	21	23	23	25	25	27	27	29	29	31	31	33	33	35	35	37	37	39	39	41	41	43	43	45	45	47	47	49	49	49																	
0.776-0.800	21	21	23	23	25	25	27	27	29	29	31	31	33	33	35	35	37	37	39	39	41	41	43	43	45	45	47	47	49	49	49																		
0.801-0.825	21	23	23	25	25	27	27	29	29	31	31	33	33	35	35	37	37	39	39	41	41	43	43	45	45	47	47	49	49	49																			
0.826-0.850	23	23	25	25	27	27	29	29	31	31	33	33	35	35	37	37	39	39	41	41	43	43	45	45	47	47	49	49	49																				
0.851-0.875	23	25	25	27	27	29	29	31	31	33	33	35	35	37	37	39	39	41	41	43	43	45	45	47	47	49	49	49																					
0.876-0.900	25	25	27	27	29	29	31	31	33	33	35	35	37	37	39	39	41	41	43	43	45	45	47	47	49	49	49																						
0.901-0.925	25	27	27	29	29	31	31	33	33	35	35	37	37	39	39	41	41	43	43	45	45	47	47	49	49	49																							
0.926-0.950	27	27	29	29	31	31	33	33	35	35	37	37	39	39	41	41	43	43	45	45	47	47	49	49	49																								
0.951-0.975	27	29	29	31	31	33	33	35	35	37	37	39	39	41	41	43	43	45	45	47	47	49	49	49																									
0.976-1.000	29	29	31	31	33	33	35	35	37	37	39	39	41	41	43	43	45	45	47	47	49	49	49																										
1.001-1.025	29	31	31	33	33	35	35	37	37	39	39	41	41	43	43	45	45	47	47	49	49	49																											
1.026-1.050	31	31	33	33	35	35	37	37	39	39	41	41	43	43	45	45	47	47	49	49	49																												
1.051-1.075	31	33	33	35	35	37	37	39	39	41	41	43	43	45	45	47	47	49	49	49																													
1.076-1.100	33	33	35	35	37	37	39	39	41	41	43	43	45	45	47	47	49	49	49																														
1.101-1.125	33	35	35	37	37	39	39	41	41	43	43	45	45	47	47	49	49	49																															
1.126-1.150	35	35	37	37	39	39	41	41	43	43	45	45	47	47	49	49	49																																
1.151-1.175	35	37	37	39	39	41	41	43	43	45	45	47	47	49	49	49																																	
1.176-1.200	37	37	39	39	41	41	43	43	45	45	47	47	49	49	49																																		
1.201-1.225	37	39	39	41	41	43	43	45	45	47	47	49	49	49																																			
1.226-1.250	39	39	41	41	43	43	45	45	47	47	49	49	49																																				
1.251-1.275	39	41	41	43	43	45	45	47	47	49	49	49																																					
1.276-1.300	41	41	43	43	45	45	47	47	49	49	49																																						
1.301-1.325	41	43	43	45	45	47	47	49	49	49																																							
1.326-1.350	43	43	45	45	47	47	49	49	49																																								
1.351-1.375	43	45	45	47	47	49	49	49																																									
1.376-1.400	45	45	47	47	49	49	49																																										
1.401-1.425	45	47	47	49	49	49																																											
1.426-1.450	47	47	49	49	49																																												
1.451-1.475	47	49	49	49																																													
1.476-1.500	49	49	49																																														
1.501-1.525	49	49																																																
1.526-1.550	49																																																	

Exhaust Valve Clearance (cold): 0.25 – 0.35 mm (0.0010 – 0.014 in.)

Example: 2.700 mm (0.1063 in.) shim installed Measured clearance is 0.450 mm (0.0177 in.). Replace 2.700 mm (0.1063 in.) shim with shim No. 27.

Shim Thickness

Shim No.	Thickness mm (in.)	Shim No.	Thickness mm (in.)
01	2.20 (0.0866)	27	2.85 (0.1122)
03	2.25 (0.0886)	29	2.90 (0.1142)
05	2.30 (0.0906)	31	2.95 (0.1161)
07	2.35 (0.0925)	33	3.00 (0.1181)
09	2.40 (0.0945)	35	3.05 (0.1201)
11	2.45 (0.0965)	37	3.10 (0.1220)
13	2.50 (0.0984)	39	3.15 (0.1240)
15	2.55 (0.1004)	41	3.20 (0.1260)
17	2.60 (0.1024)	43	3.25 (0.1280)
19	2.65 (0.1043)	45	3.30 (0.1299)
21	2.70 (0.1063)	47	3.35 (0.1319)
23	2.75 (0.1083)	49	3.40 (0.1339)
25	2.80 (0.1102)		

11. Install the new shim, remove the special tool and then recheck the valve clearance.

12. Installation of the remaining components is in the reverse order of removal. Check and adjust (if necessary), both the ignition timing and the idle speed.

4K-E Engine

These engines are equipped with hydraulic lash adjusters in the valve train. These adjusters maintain a zero clearance between the rocker arm and valve stem; no adjustment is possible or necessary.

Carburetor/Fuel Injection

This section contains only adjustments as they normally apply to engine tune-up. Descriptions of the carburetor and fuel injection systems and other adjustment procedures can be found in Chapter 4.

When the engine in your Toyota is running, air/fuel mixture from the carburetor is being drawn into the engine by a partial vacuum which is created by the downward movement of the pistons on the intake stroke of the 4-stroke cycle of the engine. The amount of air/fuel mixture that enters the engine is controlled by throttle plates in the bottom of the carburetor. When the engine is not running, the throttle plates are closed, completely blocking off the bottom of the carburetor from the inside of the engine. The throttle plates are connected, through the throttle linkage, to the gas pedal in the passenger compartment of the car. After you start the engine and put the transmission in gear, you depress the gas pedal to start the car moving. What you actually are doing when you depress the gas pedal is opening the throttle plate in the carburetor to admit more of the air/fuel mixture to the engine. The further you open the throttle plates in the carburetor, the higher the engine speed becomes.

As previously stated, when the engine is not running, the throttle plates in the carburetor are closed. When the engine is idling, it is necessary to open the throttle plates slightly. To prevent having to keep your foot on the gas pedal when the engine is idling, an idle speed adjusting screw was added to the carburetor. This screw has the same effect as keeping your foot slightly depressed on the gas pedal. The idle speed adjusting screw contacts a lever (the throttle lever) on the outside of the carburetor. When the screw is turned in, it opens the throttle plate on the carburetor, raising the idle speed of the engine. This screw is called the curb idle adjusting screw, and the procedures in this section will tell you how to adjust it.

Since it is difficult for the engine to draw the air/fuel mixture from the carburetor with the small amount of throttle plate opening that is present when the engine is idling, an idle mixture passage is provided in the bottom of the carburetor below the throttle plates. This idle mixture passage contains an adjusting screw which restricts the amount of air/fuel mixture that enters the engine at idle. the procedure given in this section will tell how to set the idle mixture adjusting screw.

IDLE SPEED AND MIXTURE

1970-74

NOTE: *Perform the following adjustments with the air cleaner in place. When adjusting the idle speed and mixture, the gear selector should be placed in Drive (D) on 1970-73 models equipped with an automatic transmission. Be sure to set the parking brake and block the front wheels. On all cars equipped with manual transmissions and all 1974 automatics, adjust the idle speed with the gearshift in Neutral (N).*

1. Run the engine until it reaches normal operating temperature. Stop the engine.

2. Connect a tachometer to the engine as detailed in the manufacturer's instructions.

   a. On models having a conventional ignition system, one lead (usually black) goes to a good chassis ground. The other lead (usually red) goes to the distributor primary side of the coil (the terminal with small wire running to the distributor body);

   b. On models with transistorized ignition, connect one lead (usually black) of the tachometer to a good chassis ground. Connect

Vacuum at Idle
(in. Hg)

Year	Engine	Transmission	Minimum Vacuum Gauge Reading
1970-72	3K-C	All	16.9
	2T-C	All	16.9
1973	3K-C	MT	16.5
	2T-C	MT	16.9
		AT	14.1
1974	3K-C	MT	16.5
	2T-C ①	All	16.9
	2T-C ②	All	15.7

MT—anual transmission
AT—Automatic transmission
① All US cars except California
② California only

the other lead (usually red) to the negative (–) coil terminal; NOT to the distributor or positive (+) side. Connecting the tach to the wrong side will damage the switching transistor.

3. Remove the plug and install a vacuum gauge in the manifold vacuum port by using a suitable metric adaptor.

4. Start the engine and allow it to stabilize at idle.

5. Turn the idle speed screw until the engine runs smoothly at the lowest possible engine speed without stalling.

6. Turn the idle speed screw until the vacuum gauge indicates the highest specified reading (see the Vacuum At Idle chart) at the specified idle speed. (See the Tune-Up Specifications chart at the beginning of the chapter).

7. Tighten the idle speed screw to the point just before the engine rpm and vacuum readings drop off.

8. Remove the tachometer and the vacuum gauge. Install the plug back in the manifold vacuum port. Road test the vehicle.

9. In some states, emission inspection is required. In such cases, you should take your car to a diagnostic center which has an HC/CO meter, and have the idle emission level checked to be sure that it is in accordance with state regulations. Starting 1974, CO levels at idle are given on the engine tune-up decal under the hood.

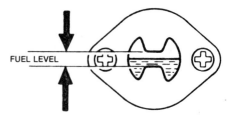

Check the fuel level in the float bowl

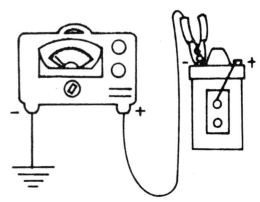

Tachometer connection with transistorized ignition

1975 and Later (Except 1C-L Diesel)

The idle speed and mixture should be adjusted under the following conditions: the air cleaner must be installed, the choke fully opened, the

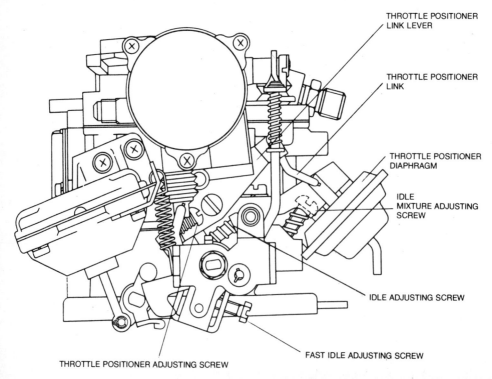

THROTTLE POSITIONER LINK LEVER

THROTTLE POSITIONER LINK

THROTTLE POSITIONER DIAPHRAGM

IDLE MIXTURE ADJUSTING SCREW

IDLE ADJUSTING SCREW

FAST IDLE ADJUSTING SCREW

THROTTLE POSITIONER ADJUSTING SCREW

Carburetor adjustments for 2T-C engines—1971–74

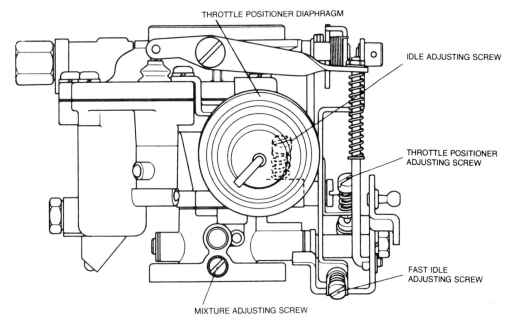

THROTTLE POSITIONER DIAPHRAGM

IDLE ADJUSTING SCREW

THROTTLE POSITIONER
ADJUSTING SCREW

FAST IDLE
ADJUSTING SCREW

MIXTURE ADJUSTING SCREW

Carburetor adjustments for 3K-C engine—1971–77

transmission should be in Neutral (N), all accessories should be turned off, all vacuum lines should be connected, and the ignition timing should be set to specification.

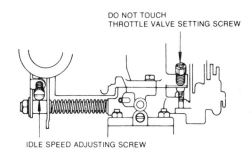

DO NOT TOUCH
THROTTLE VALVE SETTING SCREW

IDLE SPEED ADJUSTING SCREW

Carburetor adjustment for 1978 and later 3K-C engine

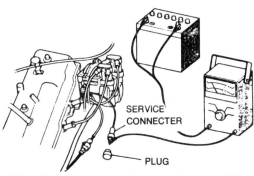

SERVICE
CONNECTER

PLUG

1983 and late A-series engines require a special tachometer hook-up

1. Start the engine and allow it to reach normal operating temperature (180°).

2. Check the float setting; the fuel level should be just about even with the spot on the sight glass. If the fuel level is too high or low, adjust the float level. (See Chapter 4).

NOTE: *1983 and later A-series and the 3E engine(s) require a special type of tachometer which hooks up to the service connector wire coming out of the distributor. As many tachometers are not compatible with this hook-up, we recommend that you consult with the*

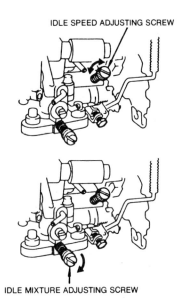

IDLE SPEED ADJUSTING SCREW

IDLE MIXTURE ADJUSTING SCREW

4K-C carburetor adjustment points

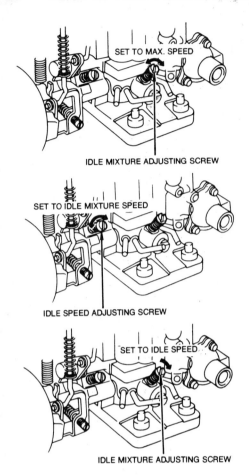

3T-C carburetor adjustment points

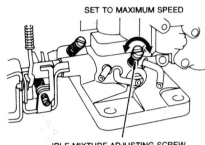

Carburetor adjustment points—1A-C and 3A; 3A-C and 4A-C similar

manufacturer before purchasing a certain type.

3. Connect a tachometer in accordance with the manufacturer's instructions. However, connect the tachometer positive (+) lead to the coil. Negative (–) terminal. Do NOT hook it up to the distributor or positive (+) side; damage to the transistorized ignition will result.

NOTE: *On 1980 and later models, all of*

which have tamper-proof idle mixture screws, merely turn the idle speed adjusting screw until the proper idle speed is obtained (refer to the Tune-Up Specifications chart). Disregard the following steps. Disconnect the ta-

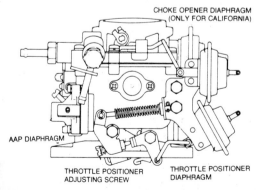

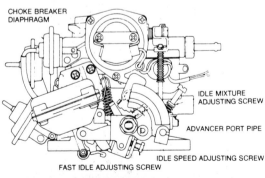

Carburetor adjustments for the 1975–79 2T-C engine

IDLE SPEED ADJUSTING SCREW

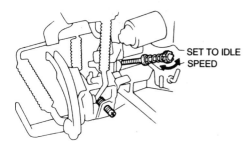

SET TO IDLE SPEED

Idle speed adjustment on 4A—C engines

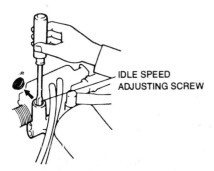

IDLE SPEED ADJUSTING SCREW

Idle speed adjustment for the 4K-E engine

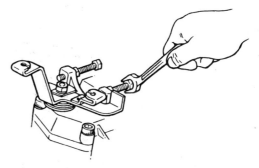

Adjusting the idle speed on the diesel engine

Adjusting the maximum speed on the diesel engine

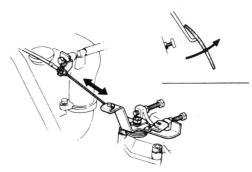

Connect the accelerator cable and then adjust it so there is no slack

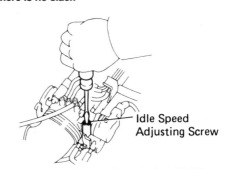

Idle Speed Adjusting Screw

Adjusting the idle speed—typical of 4A-GE engine

chometer after the adjustment is complete. On the 1983 Starlet, race the engine at 2,500 rpm for 2 min. before adjusting the idle speed.

4. Turn the idle speed adjusting screw to obtain the correct curb idle speed.

5. Turn the idle mixture adjusting screw to increase the idle speed as much as is possible.

6. Next turn the idle speed screw to again obtain the correct curb idle speed.

7. If possible, turn the idle mixture screw to increase the idle speed again.

8. Keep repeating Steps 6 and 7 until the idle mixture adjusting screw will no longer increase the idle speed.

9. Disconnect the tachometer.

1C-L Diesel Engine

1. Run the engine until it reaches normal operating temperature.

NOTE: *The air cleaner should be in place, all accessories should be turned off and the transmission should be in Neutral.*

2. Install a tachometer that is compatible with diesel engines.

3. Disconnect the accelerator cable from the injection pump and then check that the idle speed is within specifications. If not, adjust it with the adjustment screw on the injection pump.

4. With the tachometer still connected, check the engine maximum speed by fully depressing

the adjusting lever on the injection pump. Maximum speed should be approximately 5,100 rpm.

5. If maximum speed is not within specifications, turn the adjusting screw until it is.

Troubleshooting Engine Performance

Problem	Cause	Solution
Hard starting (engine cranks normally)	• Binding linkage, choke valve or choke piston	• Repair as necessary
	• Restricted choke vacuum diaphragm	• Clean passages
	• Improper fuel level	• Adjust float level
	• Dirty, worn or faulty needle valve and seat	• Repair as necessary
	• Float sticking	• Repair as necessary
	• Faulty fuel pump	• Replace fuel pump
	• Incorrect choke cover adjustment	• Adjust choke cover
	• Inadequate choke unloader adjustment	• Adjust choke unloader
	• Faulty ignition coil	• Test and replace as necessary
	• Improper spark plug gap	• Adjust gap
	• Incorrect ignition timing	• Adjust timing
	• Incorrect valve timing	• Check valve timing; repair as necessary
Rough idle or stalling	• Incorrect curb or fast idle speed	• Adjust curb or fast idle speed
	• Incorrect ignition timing	• Adjust timing to specification
	• Improper feedback system operation	• Refer to Chapter 4
	• Improper fast idle cam adjustment	• Adjust fast idle cam
	• Faulty EGR valve operation	• Test EGR system and replace as necessary
	• Faulty PCV valve air flow	• Test PCV valve and replace as necessary
	• Choke binding	• Locate and eliminate binding condition
	• Faulty TAC vacuum motor or valve	• Repair as necessary
	• Air leak into manifold vacuum	• Inspect manifold vacuum connections and repair as necessary
	• Improper fuel level	• Adjust fuel level
	• Faulty distributor rotor or cap	• Replace rotor or cap
	• Improperly seated valves	• Test cylinder compression, repair as necessary
	• Incorrect ignition wiring	• Inspect wiring and correct as necessary
	• Faulty ignition coil	• Test coil and replace as necessary
	• Restricted air vent or idle passages	• Clean passages
	• Restricted air cleaner	• Clean or replace air cleaner filler element
	• Faulty choke vacuum diaphragm	• Repair as necessary
Faulty low-speed operation	• Restricted idle transfer slots	• Clean transfer slots
	• Restricted idle air vents and passages	• Clean air vents and passages
	• Restricted air cleaner	• Clean or replace air cleaner filter element
	• Improper fuel level	• Adjust fuel level
	• Faulty spark plugs	• Clean or replace spark plugs
	• Dirty, corroded, or loose ignition secondary circuit wire connections	• Clean or tighten secondary circuit wire connections
	• Improper feedback system operation	• Refer to Chapter 4
	• Faulty ignition coil high voltage wire	• Replace ignition coil high voltage wire
	• Faulty distributor cap	• Replace cap
Faulty acceleration	• Improper accelerator pump stroke	• Adjust accelerator pump stroke
	• Incorrect ignition timing	• Adjust timing
	• Inoperative pump discharge check ball or needle	• Clean or replace as necessary
	• Worn or damaged pump diaphragm or piston	• Replace diaphragm or piston

Troubleshooting Engine Performance (cont.)

Problem	Cause	Solution
Faulty acceleration (cont.)	• Leaking carburetor main body cover gasket	• Replace gasket
	• Engine cold and choke set too lean	• Adjust choke cover
	• Improper metering rod adjustment (BBD Model carburetor)	• Adjust metering rod
	• Faulty spark plug(s)	• Clean or replace spark plug(s)
	• Improperly seated valves	• Test cylinder compression, repair as necessary
	• Faulty ignition coil	• Test coil and replace as necessary
	• Improper feedback system operation	• Refer to Chapter 4
Faulty high speed operation	• Incorrect ignition timing	• Adjust timing
	• Faulty distributor centrifugal advance mechanism	• Check centrifugal advance mechanism and repair as necessary
	• Faulty distributor vacuum advance mechanism	• Check vacuum advance mechanism and repair as necessary
	• Low fuel pump volume	• Replace fuel pump
	• Wrong spark plug air gap or wrong plug	• Adjust air gap or install correct plug
	• Faulty choke operation	• Adjust choke cover
	• Partially restricted exhaust manifold, exhaust pipe, catalytic converter, muffler, or tailpipe	• Eliminate restriction
	• Restricted vacuum passages	• Clean passages
	• Improper size or restricted main jet	• Clean or replace as necessary
	• Restricted air cleaner	• Clean or replace filter element as necessary
	• Faulty distributor rotor or cap	• Replace rotor or cap
	• Faulty ignition coil	• Test coil and replace as necessary
	• Improperly seated valve(s)	• Test cylinder compression, repair as necessary
	• Faulty valve spring(s)	• Inspect and test valve spring tension, replace as necessary
	• Incorrect valve timing	• Check valve timing and repair as necessary
	• Intake manifold restricted	• Remove restriction or replace manifold
	• Worn distributor shaft	• Replace shaft
	• Improper feedback system operation	• Refer to Chapter 4
Misfire at all speeds	• Faulty spark plug(s)	• Clean or replace spark plug(s)
	• Faulty spark plug wire(s)	• Replace as necessary
	• Faulty distributor cap or rotor	• Replace cap or rotor
	• Faulty ignition coil	• Test coil and replace as necessary
	• Primary ignition circuit shorted or open intermittently	• Troubleshoot primary circuit and repair as necessary
	• Improperly seated valve(s)	• Test cylinder compression, repair as necessary
	• Faulty hydraulic tappet(s)	• Clean or replace tappet(s)
	• Improper feedback system operation	• Refer to Chapter 4
	• Faulty valve spring(s)	• Inspect and test valve spring tension, repair as necessary
	• Worn camshaft lobes	• Replace camshaft
	• Air leak into manifold	• Check manifold vacuum and repair as necessary
	• Improper carburetor adjustment	• Adjust carburetor
	• Fuel pump volume or pressure low	• Replace fuel pump
	• Blown cylinder head gasket	• Replace gasket
	• Intake or exhaust manifold passage(s) restricted	• Pass chain through passage(s) and repair as necessary
	• Incorrect trigger wheel installed in distributor	• Install correct trigger wheel

Troubleshooting Engine Performance (cont.)

Problem	Cause	Solution
Power not up to normal	• Incorrect ignition timing	• Adjust timing
	• Faulty distributor rotor	• Replace rotor
	• Trigger wheel loose on shaft	• Reposition or replace trigger wheel
	• Incorrect spark plug gap	• Adjust gap
	• Faulty fuel pump	• Replace fuel pump
	• Incorrect valve timing	• Check valve timing and repair as necessary
	• Faulty ignition coil	• Test coil and replace as necessary
	• Faulty ignition wires	• Test wires and replace as necessary
	• Improperly seated valves	• Test cylinder compression and repair as necessary
	• Blown cylinder head gasket	• Replace gasket
	• Leaking piston rings	• Test compression and repair as necessary
	• Worn distributor shaft	• Replace shaft
	• Improper feedback system operation	• Refer to Chapter 4
Intake backfire	• Improper ignition timing	• Adjust timing
	• Faulty accelerator pump discharge	• Repair as necessary
	• Defective EGR CTO valve	• Replace EGR CTO valve
	• Defective TAC vacuum motor or valve	• Repair as necessary
	• Lean air/fuel mixture	• Check float level or manifold vacuum for air leak. Remove sediment from bowl
Exhaust backfire	• Air leak into manifold vacuum	• Check manifold vacuum and repair as necessary
	• Faulty air injection diverter valve	• Test diverter valve and replace as necessary
	• Exhaust leak	• Locate and eliminate leak
Ping or spark knock	• Incorrect ignition timing	• Adjust timing
	• Distributor centrifugal or vacuum advance malfunction	• Inspect advance mechanism and repair as necessary
	• Excessive combustion chamber deposits	• Remove with combustion chamber cleaner
	• Air leak into manifold vacuum	• Check manifold vacuum and repair as necessary
	• Excessively high compression	• Test compression and repair as necessary
	• Fuel octane rating excessively low	• Try alternate fuel source
	• Sharp edges in combustion chamber	• Grind smooth
	• EGR valve not functioning properly	• Test EGR system and replace as necessary
Surging (at cruising to top speeds)	• Low carburetor fuel level	• Adjust fuel level
	• Low fuel pump pressure or volume	• Replace fuel pump
	• Metering rod(s) not adjusted properly (BBD Model Carburetor)	• Adjust metering rod
	• Improper PCV valve air flow	• Test PCV valve and replace as necessary
	• Air leak into manifold vacuum	• Check manifold vacuum and repair as necessary
	• Incorrect spark advance	• Test and replace as necessary
	• Restricted main jet(s)	• Clean main jet(s)
	• Undersize main jet(s)	• Replace main jet(s)
	• Restricted air vents	• Clean air vents
	• Restricted fuel filter	• Replace fuel filter
	• Restricted air cleaner	• Clean or replace air cleaner filter element
	• EGR valve not functioning properly	• Test EGR system and replace as necessary
	• Improper feedback system operation	• Refer to Chapter 4

TROUBLESHOOTING BASIC POINT-TYPE IGNITION SYSTEM PROBLEMS

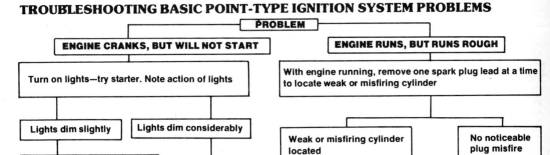

PROBLEM

ENGINE CRANKS, BUT WILL NOT START

Turn on lights—try starter. Note action of lights

Lights dim slightly

Lights dim considerably

Battery or starter and battery connections OK if cranking speed is good

Battery good, but engine will still not run

Battery weak or defective. Check for corroded or loose terminals

Remove spark plug wire and hold ¼" from engine while cranking

No spark

1. Points not closing
2. Points not opening
3. Points dirty, pitted, or burned
4. Broken primary wire or loose connection.
5. Shorted condenser
6. Grounded contact arm
7. Short or ground in primary circuit
8. High tension wire from coil to distributor defective
9. Defective coil or condenser
10. Cracked/burned rotor or cracked distributor cap
11. Wet coil, distributor or spark plug wires
12. Defective spark plugs

Weak spark

1. Dirty, pitted or burned points
2. Poor electrical connections
3. Defective plug wires
4. Defective condenser
5. Defective coil
6. Defective rotor
7. Cracked distributor cap or burned contacts
8. Wet coil, distributor or high tension wires

Good spark

Problem is not in ignition system. Check fuel supply.

ENGINE RUNS, BUT RUNS ROUGH

With engine running, remove one spark plug lead at a time to locate weak or misfiring cylinder

Weak or misfiring cylinder located

No noticeable plug misfire

Check condition of spark plug against chart in this chapter to determine cause of misfire—replace spark plug

Possible cause of misfiring may be:

1. Plugs worn out
2. Plug gap too wide
3. Defective coil or condenser
4. Breaker points worn out
5. Spark advanced too far
6. Incorrect point gap
7. Loose primary circuit connections
8. Cracked distributor cap
9. Vacuum advance defective
10. Defective rotor
11. Defective plug wires

---

6. Connect the accelerator cable and adjust it so that there is no slack.

7. Check to see that the adjusting lever is stopped by the maximum speed adjusting screw when the accelerator pedal is depressed all the way to the floor.

4A-GE Engine

1. Connect a tachometer (follow the tachometer manufacturer's directions) to the engine. Run the engine until the normal operating temperature is reached. Make sure that the air cleaner is installed, all pipes and hoses of the air intake system are installed and all vacuum hoses are connected.

2. Check that all electrical connectors are fastened and tight. Switch off all accessories.

3. Run the engine up to 2,500 rpm for about two minutes. Allow the engine to return to the normal idle speed. Adjust the speed as necessary by turning the curb idle speed screw (rear upper side of unit).

Engine and Engine Rebuilding

3

UNDERSTANDING BASIC ELECTRICITY

Understanding the basic theory of electricity makes electrical troubleshooting much easier. Several gauges are used in electrical troubleshooting to see inside the circuit being tested. Without a basic understanding, it will be difficult to understand testing procedures.

Electricity is the flow of electrons, hypothetical particles thought to constitute the basic stuff of electricity. In a comparison with water flowing in a pipe, the electrons would be the water. As the flow of water can be measured, the flow of electricity can be measured. The unit of measurement is amperes, frequently abbreviated amps. An ammeter will measure the actual amount of current flowing in the circuit.

Just as the water pressure is measured in units such as pounds per square inch, electrical pressure is measured in volts. When a voltmeter's two probes are placed on two live portions of an electrical circuit with different electrical pressures, current will flow through the voltmeter and produce a reading which indicates the difference in electrical pressure between the two parts of the circuit.

While increasing the voltage in a circuit will increase the flow of current, the actual flow depends not only on voltage, but on the resistance of the circuit. The standard unit for measuring circuit resistance is an ohm, measured by an ohmmeter. The ohmmeter is somewhat similar to an ammeter, but incorporates its own source of power so that a standard voltage is always present.

An actual electric circuit consists of four basic parts. These are: the power source, such as a generator or battery; a hot wire, which conducts the electricity under a relatively high voltage to the component supplies by the circuit; the load, such as a lamp, motor, resistor, or relay coil; and the ground wire, which carries the current back to the source under very low voltage. In such a circuit the bulk of the resistance exists between the point where the hot wire is connected to the load, and the point where the load is grounded. In an automobile, the vehicle's frame, which is made of steel, is used as a part of the ground circuit for many of the electrical devices.

Remember that, in electrical testing, the voltmeter is connected in parallel with the circuit being tested (without disconnecting any wires) and measures the difference in voltage between the locations of the two probes; that the ammeter is connected in series with the load (the circuit is separated at one point and the ammeter inserted so it becomes a part of the circuit); and the ohmmeter is self-powered, so that all the power in the circuit should be off and the portion of the circuit to be measured contacted at either end by one of the probes of the meter.

For any electrical system to operate, it must make a complete circuit. This simply means that the power flow from the battery must make a complete circle. When an electrical component is operating, power flows from the battery to the component, passes through the component causing it to perform its function (lighting a light bulb) and then returns to the battery through the ground of the circuit. This ground is usually (but not always) the metal part of the car on which the electrical component is mounted.

Perhaps the easiest way to visualize this is to think of connecting a light bulb with two wires attached to it to your car battery. The battery in your car has two posts (negative and positive). If one of the two wires attached to the light bulb was attached to the negative post of the battery and the other wire was attached to the positive post of the battery, you would have a complete circuit. Current from the battery would flow out one post, through the wire attached to it and then to the light bulb, where it would pass through causing it to light. It would then leave the light bulb, travel through the other wire, and return to the other post of the battery.

The normal automotive circuit differs from this simple example in two ways. First, instead of having a return wire from the bulb to the battery, the light bulb returns the current to the battery through the chassis of the vehicle. Since the negative battery cable is attached to the chassis and the chassis is made of electrically conductive metal, the chassis of the vehicle can serve as a ground wire to complete the circuit. Secondly, most automotive circuits contain switches to turn components on and off.

Some electrical components which require a large amount of current to operate also have a relay in their circuit. Since these circuits carry a large amount of current, the thickness of the wire in the circuit (gauge size) is also greater. If this large wire were connected from the component to the control switch on the instrument panel, and then back to the component, a voltage drop would occur in the circuit. To prevent this potential drop in voltage, an electromagnetic switch (relay) is used. The large wires in the circuit are connected from the car battery to one side of the relay, and from the opposite side of the relay to the component. The relay is normally open, preventing current from passing through the circuit. An additional, smaller, wire is connected from the relay to the control switch for the circuit. When the control switch is turned on, it grounds the smaller wire from the relay and completes the circuit. When the control switch is turned on, it grounds the smaller wire from the relay. If you were to disconnect the light bulb (from the previous example of a light bulb being connected to the battery by two wires) from the wires and touch the two wires together (please take our word for this; don't try it), the result will be a shower of sparks. A similar thing happens (on a smaller scale) when the power supply wire to a component or the electrical component itself becomes grounded before the normal ground connection for the circuit. To prevent damage to the system, the fuse for the circuit blows to interrupt the circuit, protecting the components from damage. Because grounding a wire from a power source makes a complete circuit, less the required component to use the power, the phenomenon is called a short circuit. The most common causes of short circuits are: the rubber insulation on a wire breaking or rubbing through to expose the current carrying core of the wire to a metal part of the car, or a shorted switch.

Some electrical systems on the car are protected by a circuit breaker which is, basically, a self-repairing fuse. When either of the above de-

scribed events takes place in a system which is protected by a circuit breaker, the circuit breaker opens the circuit the same way a fuse does. However, when either the short is removed from the circuit or the surge subsides, the circuit breaker resets itself and does not have to be replaced as a fuse does.

The final protective device in the chassis electrical system is a fuse link. A fuse link is a wire that acts as a fuse. It is connected between the starter relay and the main wiring harness for the car. This connection is under the hood, very near a similar fuse link which protects the engine electrical system. Since the fuse link protects all the chassis electrical components, it is the probable cause of trouble when none of the electrical components function, unless the battery is disconnected or dead.

Electrical problems generally fall into one of three areas:

1. The component that is not functioning is not receiving current.

2. The component itself is not functioning.

3. The component is not properly grounded.

Problems that fall into the first category are by far the most complicated. It is the current supply system to the component which contains all the switches, relays, fuses, etc.

The electrical system can be checked with a test light and a jumper wire. A test light is a device that looks like a pointed screwdriver with a wire attached to it. It has a light bulb in its handle. A jumper wire is a piece of insulated wire with an alligator clip attached to each end.

If a light bulb is not working, you must follow a systematic plan to determine which of the three causes is the villain.

1. Turn on the switch that controls the inoperable bulb.

2. Disconnect the power supply wire from the bulb.

3. Attach the ground wire on the test light to a good metal ground.

4. Touch the probe end of the test light to the end of the power supply wire that was disconnected from the bulb. If the bulb is receiving current, the test light will go on.

NOTE: *If the bulb is one which works only when the ignition key is turned on (turn signal), make sure the key is turned on.*

If the test light does not go on, then the problem is in the circuit between the battery and the bulb. As mentioned before, this includes all the switches, fuses, and relays in the system. Turn to the wiring diagram and find the bulb on the diagram. Follow the wire that runs back to the battery. The problem is an open circuit between the battery and the bulb. As mentioned before, this includes all the switches, fuses, and relays in the system. Turn to the wiring diagram and find the bulb on the diagram. Follow the wire that runs back to the battery. The problem is an open circuit between the battery and the bulb. If the fuse is blown and, when replaced, immediately blows again, there is a short circuit in the system which must be located and repaired. If there is a switch in the system, bypass it with a jumper wire. This is done by connecting one end of the jumper wire to the wire coming out of the switch. Again, consult the wiring diagram. If the test light lights with the jumper wire installed, the switch or whatever was bypasses is defective.

NOTE: *Never substitute the jumper wire for the bulb, as the bulb is the component required to use the power from the power source.*

5. If the bulb in the test light goes on, then the current is getting to the bulb that is not working in the car. This eliminates the first of the three possible causes. Connect the power supply wire and connect a jumper wire from the bulb to a good metal ground. Do this with the switch which controls the bulb turned on, and also the ignition switch turned on if it is required for the light to work. If the bulb works with jumper wire installed, then it has a bad ground. This is usually caused by the metal area on which the bulb mounts to the car being coated with some type of foreign matter.

6. If neither test located the source of the trouble, then the light bulb itself is defective.

The above test procedure can be applied to any of the components of the chassis electrical system by substituting the component that is not working for the light bulb. Remember that for any electrical system to work, all connections must be clean and tight.

Battery and Starting System

The battery is the first link in the chain of mechanisms which work together to provide cranking of the automobile engine. In most modern cars, the battery is a lead-acid electrochemical device consisting of six 2V subsections connected in series to the unit is capable of producing approximately 12 V of electrical pressure. Each subsection, or cell, consists of a series of positive and negative plates held a short distance apart in a solution of sulfuric and water. The two types of plates are of dissimilar metals. This causes a chemical reaction to be set up, and it is this reaction which produces current flow from the battery when its positive and negative terminals are connected to an electrical appliance such as a lamp or motor. The continued transfer of electrons would eventually convert the sulfuric acid in the electrolyte to water, and make the two plates identical in chemical composition. As electrical energy is removed from the battery, its voltage output tends to drop. Thus, measuring battery voltage and battery electrolyte composition are two ways of checking the ability of the unit to supply power. During the starting of the engine, electrical energy is removed from the battery. However, if the charging circuit is in good condition and the operating conditions are normal, the power removed from the battery will be replaced by the generator (or alternator) which will force electrons back through the battery, reversing the normal flow, and restoring the battery to its original chemical state.

The battery and starting motor are linked by very heavy electrical cables designed to minimize resistance to the flow of current. Generally, the major power supply cable that leave the battery goes directly to the starter, while other electrical system needs are supplied by a smaller cable. During the starter operation, power flows from the battery to the starter and is grounded through the car's frame and the battery's negative ground strap.

The starting motor is a specially designed, direct current electric motor capable of producing a very great amount of power for its size. One thing that allows the motor to produce a great deal of power is its tremendous rotating speed. It drives the engine through a tiny piston gear (attached to the starter's armature), which drives the very large flywheel ring gear at a greatly reduced speed. Another factor allowing it to produce so much power is that only intermittent operation is required of it. Thus, little allowance for air circulation is required, and the windings can be built into a very small space.

The starter solenoid is a magnetic device which employs the small current supplied by the starting switch circuit of the ignition switch. This magnetic action moves a plunger which mechanically engages the starter and electrically closes the heavy switch which connects it to the battery. The starting switch circuit consists of the starting switch contained within the ignition switch, a transmission neutral safety switch or clutch pedal switch, and the wiring necessary to connect these with the starter solenoid or relay.

A pinion, which is a small gear, is mounted to a one-way drive clutch. This clutch is splined to the starter armature shaft. When the ignition switch is moved to the start position, the solenoid plunger slides the pinion toward the flywheel ring gear via a collar and spring. If the teeth on the pinion and flywheel match properly, the pinion will engage the flywheel immediately. If the gear teeth butt one another, the spring will be compressed and will force the gears to mesh as soon as the starter turns far enough to allow them to do so. As the solenoid plunger reaches the end of its travel, it closes the contacts that connect the battery and starter and then the engine is cranked.

As soon as the engine starts, the flywheel ring gear begins turning fast enough to drive the pinion at an extremely high rate of speed. At this point, the one-way clutch begins allowing the pinion to spin faster than the starter shaft so that the starter will not operate at excessive speed. When the ignition switch is released from the starter position, the solenoid is de-energized, and a spring contained within the solenoid assembly pulls the gear out of mesh and interrupts the current flow to the starter.

Some starters employ a separate relay, mounted away from the starter, to switch the motor and solenoid current on and off. The relay thus replaces the solenoid electrical switch, but does not eliminate the need for a solenoid mounted on the starter used to mechanically engage the starter drive gears. The relay is used to reduce the amount of current the starting switch must carry.

The Charging System

The automobile charging system provides electrical power for operation of the vehicle's ignition and starting systems and all the electrical accessories. The battery serves as an electrical surge or storage tank, storing (in chemical form) the energy originally produced by the engine driven generator. The system also provides a means of regulating generator output to protect the battery from being overcharged and to avoid excessive voltage to the accessories.

The storage battery is a chemical device incorporating parallel lead plates in a tank containing a sulfuric acid/water solution. Adjacent plates are slightly dissimilar, and the chemical reaction of the two dissimilar plates produces electrical energy when the battery is connected to a load such as the starter motor. The chemical reaction is reversible, so that when the generator is producing a voltage (electrical pressure) greater than that produced by the battery, electricity is forced into the battery, and the battery is returned to its fully charged state.

The vehicle's generator is driven mechanically, through V belts, by the engine crankshaft. It consists of two coils of fine wire, one stationary (the stator), and one movable (the rotor). The rotor may also be known as the armature, and consists of fine wire wrapped around an iron core which is mounted on a shaft. The electricity which flows through the two coils of wire (provided initially by the battery in some cases) creates an intense magnetic field around both rotor and stator, and the interaction between the two fields creates voltage, allowing the generator to power the accessories and charge the battery.

There are two types of generators; the earlier is the direct current (DC) type. The current produced by the DC generator is generated in the armature and carried off the spinning armature by stationary brushes contacting the commutator. The commutator plates, which are separated from one another by a very short gap, are connected to the armature circuits so that current will flow in one direction only in the wires carrying the generator output. The generator stator consists of two stationary coils of wire which draw some of the output current of the generator to form a powerful magnetic field and create the interaction of fields which generates the voltage. The generator field is wired in series with the regulator.

Newer automobiles use alternating current generators because they are more efficient, can be rotated at higher speeds, and have fewer brush problems. In an alternator, the field rotates while all the current produced passes only through the stator windings. The brushes bear against continuous slip rings rather than a commutator. This causes the current produced to periodically reverse the direction of its flow. Diodes (electrical one-way switches) block the flow of current from traveling in the wrong direction. A series of diodes is wired together to permit the alternating flow of the stator to be converted to a pulsating, but unidirectional flow at the alternator output. The alternator's field is wired in series with the voltage regulator.

The regulator consists of several circuits. Each circuit has a core, or magnetic coil of wire, which operates a switch. Each switch is connected to ground through one or more resistors. The coil of wire responds directly to system voltage. When the voltage reaches the required level, the magnetic field created by the winding of wire closes the switch and inserts a resistance into the generator field circuit, thus reducing the output. The contacts of the switch cycle open and close many times each second to precisely control voltage.

While alternators are self-limiting as far as maximum current is concerned, DC generators employ a current regulating circuit which responds directly to the total amount of current flowing through the generator circuit rather than to the output voltage. The current regulator is similar to the voltage regulator except that all system current must flow through the energizing coil on its way to the various accessories.

SAFETY PRECAUTIONS

Observing these precautions will ensure safe handling of the electrical system components, and will avoid damage to the vehicle's electrical system:

1. Be absolutely sure of the polarity of a booster battery before making connections. Connect the cables positive to positive, and negative to negative. Connect positive cables first and then make the last connection to a ground on the body of the booster vehicle so that arching cannot ignite hydrogen gas that may have accumulated near the battery. Even momentary connection of a booster battery with the polarity reserved will damage alternator diodes.

2. Disconnect both vehicle battery cable before attempting to charge a battery.

3. Never ground the alternator or generator output or battery terminal. Be cautious when using metal tools around a battery to avoid creating a short circuit between the terminals.

4. Never ground the field circuit between the alternator and regulator.

5. Never run an alternator or generator without load unless the field circuit is disconnected.

6. Never attempt to polarize an alternator.

7. Keep the regulator cover in place when taking voltage and current limiter readings.

8. Use insulated tools when adjusting the regulator.

9. Whenever DC generator-to-regulator wires have been disconnected, the generator must be polarized. To do this with an externally grounded, light duty generator, momentarily place a jumper wire between the battery terminal and the generator terminal of the regulator. With an internally grounded heavy duty unit, disconnect the wire to the regulator field terminal and touch the regulator battery terminal with it.

ENGINE ELECTRICAL

Ignition Coil

PRIMARY RESISTANCE CHECK

In order to check the coil primary resistance, you must first disconnect all wires from the ignition coil terminals. Using an ohmmeter, check the resistance between the positive and the negative terminals on the coil. The resistance should be:

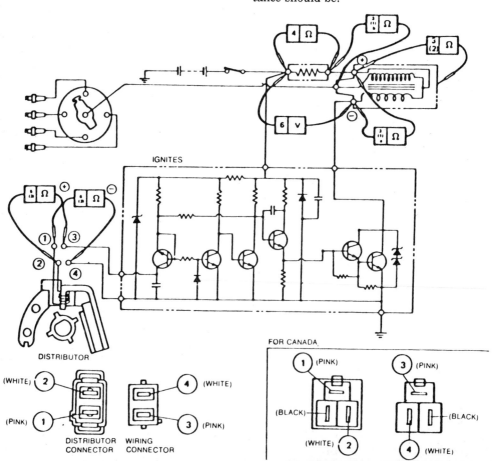

Fully transistorized electronic ignition system troubleshooting—typical

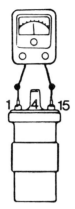

Checking the coil primary resistance—all except 1983 and later A-series

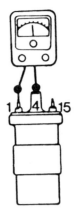

Checking the coil secondary resistance—all except 1983 and later A-series

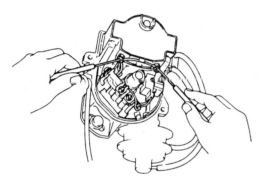

Checking the coil primary resistance—1983 and later A-series engines

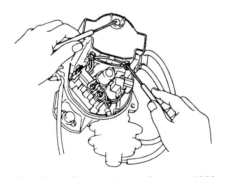

Checking the coil secondary resistance—1983 and later A-series engine

- 2T-C: 1.3-1.6Ω.
- 3T-C and 1A-C to 1980: Federal and Canada: 0.4-0.5Ω; California: 0.8-1.0Ω.
- 1981-82 3T-C: 0.8-1.0Ω.
- 1980-81 3A and 4K-C: 1.3-1.7Ω.
- 1982 3A: 1.3-1.6Ω.
- 1981-82 3A-C: 0.8-1.0Ω.
- 1983 and later 3A-C (exc. Canada 4WD wagon) and USA 4A-C: 0.4-0.5Ω.
- 1983 and later Canada 4WD wagon and Canadian 4A-C: 1.2-1.5Ω.

- 3K-C-w/o igniter: 1.2-1.5Ω; w/igniter: 1.3-1.6Ω.
- 4A-GE: 0.5-0.7Ω.
- 3E: USA 1.3-1.5Ω; Canada 0.4-0.5Ω.

If the resistance is not within those tolerances, the coil will require replacement.

SECONDARY RESISTANCE CHECK

In order to check the coil secondary resistance, you must first disconnect all wires from the ignition coil terminals. Using an ohmmeter, check the resistance between the negative terminal and the coil wire terminal. The resistance should be:

- 2T-C: 10,200-13,800Ω.
- 1980 3T-C and 1A-C: Federal and Canada: 8,500-11,500Ω; California: 11,500-15,500Ω.
- 1981-82 3T-C: 11,500-15,500Ω.
- 1980-81 3A and 4K-C: 11,900-16,100Ω.
- 1982 3A: 10,700-14,500Ω.
- 1981 3A-C: 11,500-15,500Ω.
- 1982 3A-C: 10,700-14,500Ω.
- 1983 and later 3A-C and 4A-C: 7,700-10,400Ω.
- 3K-C-w/o igniter: 8,000-12,000Ω; w/igniter: 10,000-15,000Ω.
- 4K-E - 10,700-14,500Ω.
- 4A-GE: 11,000-16,000Ω.
- 3E: 10,200-13,800Ω.

If the resistance is not within these tolerances, the coil will require replacement.

Distributor

REMOVAL

Except 1983 and Later A-Series Engines

To remove the distributor, proceed in the following order:
1. Unfasten the retaining clips and lift the

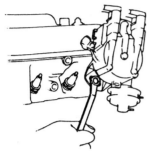

Loosen the pinch bolt and then pull the distributor straight out

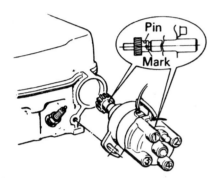

1980–82 A-series distributor alignment

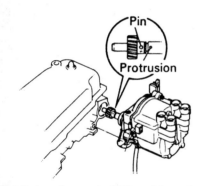

Distributor alignment—1983 and later A-series engine

distributor cap straight up. It will be easier to install the distributor if the wiring is left connected to the cap. If the wires must be removed from the cap, mark their positions to aid in installation.

2. Remove the dust cover and mark the position of the rotor relative to the distributor body; then mark the position of the body relative to the block.

3. Disconnect the coil primary wire and the vacuum line(s). If the distributor vacuum unit has two vacuum lines, mark which is which for installation.

4. Remove the pinch bolt and lift the distributor straight up or out, away from the engine.

The rotor and body are marked so that they can be returned to the position from which they were removed. Do not turn or disturb the engine (unless absolutely necessary, such as for engine rebuilding), after the distributor has been removed.

1983 and Later A-Series Engines

1. Disconnect the negative battery cable.

2. Disconnect the two electrical leads at the distributor.

3. Grasp each spark plug wire by its rubber boot and remove it from the spark plug.

NOTE: *Don't forget to tag each spark plug wire before removal.*

4. Tag and disconnect the vacuum advance hose(s).

5. Remove the distributor holddown bolt and lift out the distributor.

INSTALLATION – TIMING NOT DISTURBED

Except 1983 and Later A-Series Engines

1. Insert the distributor in the block and align the matchmarks made during removal.

2. Engage the distributor driven gear with the distributor drive.

NOTE: *Before installing the distributor on A-series engines, there is one further step. On 1980-82 models: Align the drilled mark on the driven gear (not the driven gear straight pin) with the center of the No. 1 terminal on the distributor cap and then align the stationary flange center with the bolt hole center.*

3. Install the distributor clamp and secure it with the pinch bolt.

4. Install the cap, primary wire, and vacuum line(s).

5. Install the spark plug leads. Consult the marks made during removal to be sure that the proper lead goes to each plug. Install the high tension wire if it was removed.

6. Start the engine. Check the timing and adjust it and the octane selector, as outlined in Chapter 2.

1983 and Later A-Series Engines

1. Set the No. 1 cylinder to TDC of the compression stroke. This can be accomplished by removing the No. 1 spark plug and then turning the engine (crankshaft) by hand while your thumb is over the spark plug hole. As the No. 1 piston comes up on its firing stroke, you should be able to feel the pressure on your thumb. Make sure the timing pointer is at the **0** mark on the scale and then replace the spark plug.

2. Coat the distributor drive gear and the governor shaft tip with clean engine oil.

3. Align the protrusion on the housing with the pin of the spiral driven drill mark side and

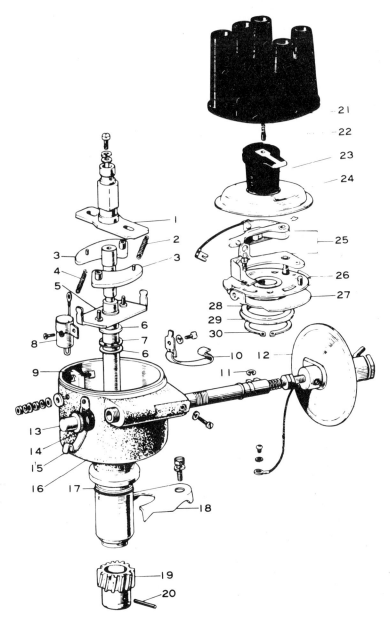

1. Cam
2. Governor spring
3. Governor weight
4. Governor spring
5. Distributor shaft
6. Metal washer
7. Bakelite washer
8. Condenser (not used
   w/transistor ignition)
9. Insulator
10. Cap spring clip
11. Snap-ring
12. Vacuum advance unit
13. Octane selector assembly
14. Rubber washer
15. Cap spring clip

16. Distributor housing
17. O-ring
18. Distributor clamp
19. Spiral gear
20. Pin
21. Distributor cap
22. Spring
23. Rotor
24. Dust cover
25. Breaker point assembly
26. Movable plate
27. Stationary plate
28. Adjusting washer
29. Wave washer
30. Snap-ring

An exploded view of the breaker points distributor

then align the center of the flange with the center of the bolt hole in the cylinder head.

4. Tighten the holddown bolt.

5. Install the spark plug wires and the vacuum hoses.

6. Connect the electrical leads and the negative battery cable.

7. Start the engine and check the ignition timing. Adjust if necessary.

INSTALLATION – TIMING LOST

If the engine has been cranked, dismantled, or the timing otherwise lost, proceed as follows:

1. Determining top dead center (TDC) of the No. 1 cylinder's compression stroke by removing the spark plug from the No. 1 cylinder and placing your finger on a vacuum gauge over the spark plug hole. This is important because the

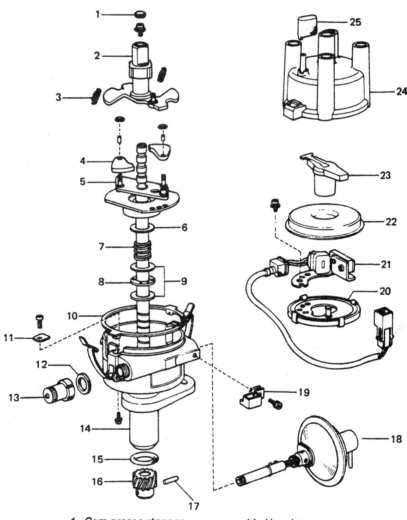

1. Cam grease stopper	14. Housing
2. Signal rotor	15. O ring
3. Governor spring	16. Spiral gear
4. Governor weight	17. Pin
5. Governor shaft	18. Vacuum advancer
6. Plate washer	19. Cord clamp
7. Compression coil spring	20. Breaker plate
8. Thrust bearing	21. Signal generator
9. Washer	22. Dustproof cover
10. Dustproof packing	23. Distributor rotor
11. Steel plate washer	24. Distributor cap
12. Rubber washer	25. Rubber cap
13. Octane selector cap	

An exploded view of a distributor with the fully transistorized ignition system

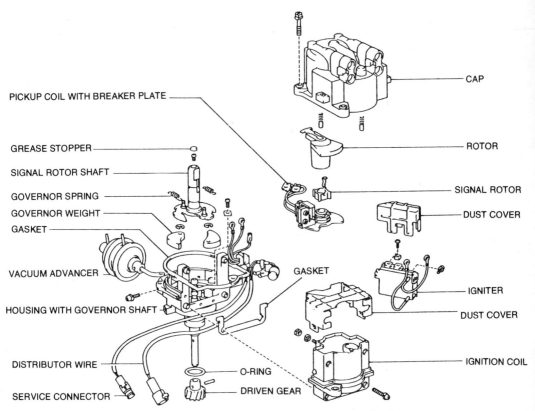

PICKUP COIL WITH BREAKER PLATE

CAP

GREASE STOPPER

ROTOR

SIGNAL ROTOR SHAFT

GOVERNOR SPRING

SIGNAL ROTOR

GOVERNOR WEIGHT

DUST COVER

GASKET

VACUUM ADVANCER

GASKET

HOUSING WITH GOVERNOR SHAFT

IGNITER

DUST COVER

DISTRIBUTOR WIRE

O-RING

IGNITION COIL

SERVICE CONNECTOR

DRIVEN GEAR

Exploded view of a late model A-series electronic distributor

timing marks will also line up with the last cylinder in the firing order in its exhaust stroke.

CAUTION: *On engines which have the spark plugs buried in the exhaust manifold, use a compression gauge or a screwdriver handle, not your finger, if the manifold is still hot.*

Crank the engine until compression pressure starts to build up. Continue cranking the engine until the timing marks indicate TDC or **0**.

2. Next align the timing marks to the specifications given in the Ignition Timing column of the Tune-Up Specifications chart at the beginning of Chapter 2.

3. Temporarily install the rotor in the distributor without the dust cover. Turn the distributor shaft so that the rotor is pointing toward the No. 1 terminal in the distributor cap. The points should just be about to open.

4. Use a small screwdriver to align the slot on the distributor drive (oil pump driveshaft) with the key on the bottom of the distributor shaft.

5. Align the matchmarks on the distributor body and the block which were made during the removal. Install the distributor in the block by rotating it slightly (no more than one gear tooth in either direction) until the driven gear meshes with the drive.

NOTE: *Oil distributor spiral gear and the oil pump driveshaft end before distributor installation.*

6. Rotate the distributor, once it is installed, so that the points are just about to open or the projection on the pickup coil is almost opposite the signal rotor tooth. Temporarily tighten the pinch bolt.

7. Remove the rotor and install the dust cover. Replace the rotor and the distributor cap.

8. Install the primary wire and the vacuum line(s).

9. Install the No. 1 spark plug. Connect the cables to the spark plugs in the proper order by using the marks made during removal. Install the high tension lead if it was removed.

10. Start the engine. Adjust the ignition timing and the rotor selector, as outlined in Chapter 2.

Alternator

All models covered in this manual use a 12 volt alternator. Amperage ratings vary according to the year and model. All 1970-79 models utilize a separate, adjustable regulator, while most 1980 and later models (except the 1983-84 Starlet) come equipped with either a separate,

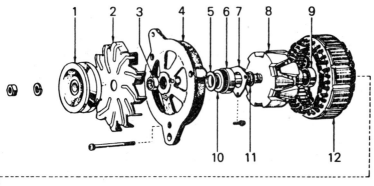

1. Pulley
2. Fan
3. Spacer collar
4. Drive end frame
5. Felt ring
6. Bearing
7. Bearing retainer
8. Rotor
9. Bearing
10. Felt cover
11. Spacer ring
12. Stator assembly
13. (+) Rectifier holder
14. (−) Rectifier holder
15. Insulator
16. Rear end frame
17. Rear end cover
18. Insulator
19. Brush
20. Brush spring
21. Brush holder
22. Insulator
23. Insulator

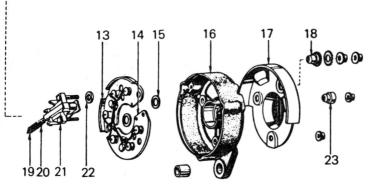

Exploded view of a typical alternator—1970–79

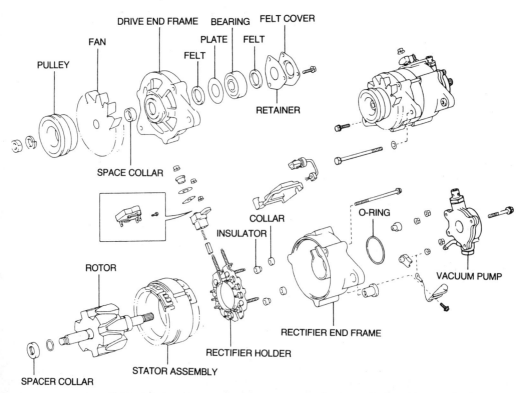

Exploded view of the alternator used on the 1C-L diesel engine

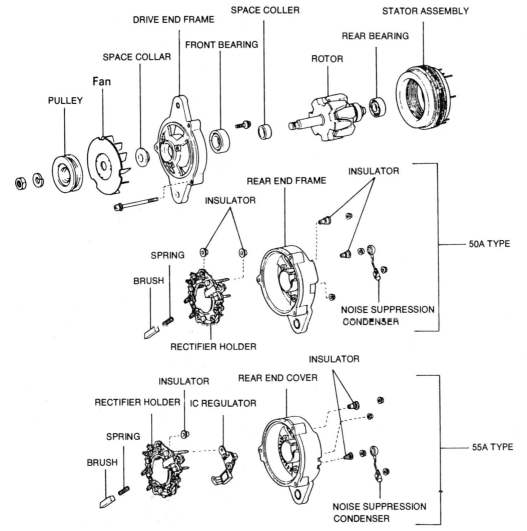

Exploded view of a typical alternator used in 1980 and later—separate regulator (50A type); IC regulator (55A type)

adjustable regulator or a transistorized, non-adjustable IC regulator, integral with the alternator.

ALTERNATOR PRECAUTIONS

To prevent damage to the alternator and regulator, the following precautionary measures must be taken when working with the electrical system.

1. Never reverse battery connections. Always check the batter polarity visually. This is to be done before any connections are made to ensure that all of the connections correspond to the battery ground polarity of the car.

2. Booster batteries must be connected properly. Make sure the positive cable of the booster battery is connected to the positive terminal of the battery which is getting the boost.

3. Disconnect the battery cables before using a fast charger; the charger has a tendency to force current through the diodes in the opposite direction for which they were designed.

4. Never use a fast charger as a booster for starting the car.

5. Never disconnect the voltage regulator while the engine is running, unless as noted for testing purposes.

6. Do not ground the alternator output terminal.

7. Do not operate the alternator on an open circuit with the field energized.

8. Do not attempt to polarize the alternator.

9. Disconnect the battery cables and remove the alternator before using an electric arc welder on the car.

10. Protect the alternator from excessive

Alternator and Regulator Specifications

Engine Type	Alternator Manufacturer	Alternator Output (amps)	Regulator Manufacturer	Field Relay Contact Spring Deflection (in.)	Field Relay Point Gap (in.)	Field Relay Volts to Close	Regulator Air Gap (in.)	Regulator Point Gap (in.)	Volts
2T–C	Nippondenso	40 ①	Nippondenso	.008–.024	.016–.047	4.5–5.8	.012	.010–.018	13.8–14.8
3K–C	Nippondenso	25 ②	Nippondenso	.008–.024	.016–.047	4.5–5.8	.012	.010–.018	13.8–14.8
3T–C, 1A–C, 3A, 3A–C, 4A–C	Nippondenso	50	Nippondenso	.008–.024	.016–.047	4.5–5.8	.012	.010–.018	13.8–14.8
		55	Nippondenso	IC REGULATOR—NOT ADJUSTABLE					13.8–14.4 ③
4K–C	Nippondenso	45	Nippondenso	.008–.024	.016–.047	4.5–5.8	.012	.010–.018	13.8–14.8
		45	Nippondenso	IC REGULATOR—NOT ADJUSTABLE					13.8–14.4
4K–E	Nippondenso	55	Nippondenso	IC REGULATOR—NOT ADJUSTABLE					13.8–14.4
1C–L	Nippondenso	50	Nippondenso	—NOT ADJUSTABLE—					13.8–14.4

① 50 amp optional 1978–79: 50 or 55 amp
② 1977: 40 amp ③ 3T–C: 14.0–14.7

moisture. If the engine is to be steam cleaned, cover or remove the alternator.

REMOVAL AND INSTALLATION

NOTE: *On some models the alternator is mounted very low on the engine. On these models it may be necessary to remove the gravel shield and work from underneath the car in order to gain access to the alternator.*

1. Disconnect the negative battery cable from the battery. Unfasten the starter-to-battery cable at the battery end.
2. Remove the air cleaner, if necessary, to gain access to the alternator.
3. Unfasten the bolts which attach the adjusting link to the alternator. Remove the alternator drive belt.
4. Unfasten the alternator wiring connections.

NOTE: *Diesel engine alternators are equipped with a vacuum pump. Before removal, two oil lines and a vacuum hose must first be disconnected.*

5. Remove the alternator attaching bolt and then withdraw the alternator from its bracket.
6. Installation is performed in the reverse order of removal. After installing the alternator, adjust the belt tension as detailed in Chapter 1.

Regulator

All 1970-79 models are equipped with a separate, adjustable regulator. Most 1980 and later models are equipped with the same as above or a transistorized regulator which is attached to the brush assembly on the side of the alternator housing. If faulty, it must be replaced; there are no adjustments which can be made.

REMOVAL AND INSTALLATION

Separate (not on alternator)

1. Disconnect the negative battery cable.
2. Disconnect the wiring harness connector at the back of the regulator.
3. Remove the regulator mounting bolts.
4. Remove the regulator.
5. Installation is in the reverse order of removal.

IC (mounted on alternator)

1. Remove the alternator as detailed earlier.
2. Remove the two screws on the back of the alternator housing and then remove the regulator end cover.
3. Underneath the end cover there are three terminal screws, remove them.
4. Remove the two regulator mounting screws and remove the regulator.

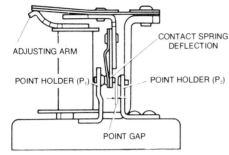

ADJUSTING ARM

CONTACT SPRING
DEFLECTION

POINT HOLDER (P₁)

POINT HOLDER (P₂)

POINT GAP

Field-relay components

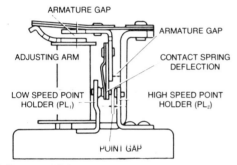

ARMATURE GAP

ARMATURE GAP

ADJUSTING ARM

CONTACT SPRING
DEFLECTION

LOW SPEED POINT
HOLDER (PL₁)

HIGH SPEED POINT
HOLDER (PL₂)

POINT GAP

Voltage regulator components

5. Using a suitable tool, pry out the plastic housing and the rubber seal around the regulator terminals.

6. Installation is in the reverse order of removal.

ADJUSTMENT

NOTE: *Only regulators which are separate from the alternator are adjustable. IC regulators are NOT adjustable.*

Voltage

1. Connect a voltmeter up to the battery terminals. Negative (black) lead to the negative (–) terminal; positive (red) lead to positive (+) terminal.

2. Start the engine and gradually increase its speed to about 1,500 rpm.

3. At this speed, the voltage reading should fall within the range specified in the Alternator and Regulator Specifications chart.

4. If the voltage does not fall within the specifications, remove the cover from the regulator and adjust it by bending the adjusting arm.

5. Repeat Steps 2 and 3 if the voltage cannot be brought to specification, proceed with the mechanical adjustments which follow.

Mechanical

NOTE: *Perform the voltage adjustment outlined above, before beginning the mechanical adjustments.*

FIELD RELAY

1. Remove the cover from the regulator assembly.

2. Use a feeler gauge to check the amount that the contact spring is deflected while the armature is being depressed.

3. If the measurement is not within specifications (see the Alternator and Regulator Specifications chart), adjust the regulator by bending the point holder P2 (see the illustration).

4. Check the point gap with a feeler gauge against the specifications in the chart.

5. Adjust the point gap, as required, by bending the point holder P1 (see the illustration).

6. Clean off the points with emery cloth if they are dirty and wash them with solvent.

VOLTAGE REGULATOR

1. Use a feeler gauge to measure the air (armature) gap. If it is not within the specifications (see the Alternator and Regulator Specifications chart), adjust it by bending the low speed point holder (see the illustration).

2. Check the point gap with a feeler gauge. If it is not within specifications, adjust it by bending the high speed point holder (see the illustration). Clean the points with emery cloth and wash them off with solvent.

3. Check the amount of contact spring deflection while depressing the armature. The specification should be the same as that for the contact spring on the field relay. If the amount of deflection is not within specification, replace, do not adjust, the voltage regulator. Go back and perform the steps outlined under Voltage Adjustment. If the voltage cannot be brought within specifications, replace the voltage regulator. If the voltage still fails to come within specifications, the alternator is probably defective and should be replaced.

Starter

REMOVAL AND INSTALLATION

1. Disconnect the negative battery cable from the battery. Disconnect the cable which runs from the starter to the battery at the battery end.

2. Remove the air cleaner assembly, if necessary, to gain access to the starter.

NOTE: *On some models with automatic transmissions, it may be necessary to unfasten the throttle linkage connecting rod.*

3. On Corolla 1200 models, perform the following: Disconnect the manual choke cable and the accelerator cable from the carburetor. Unfasten the front exhaust pipe flange from the manifold and then remove the complete manifold assembly.

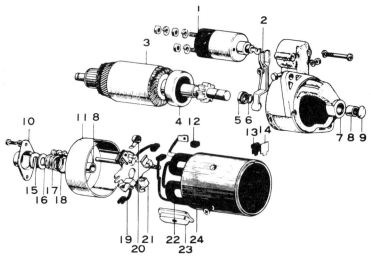

1. Solenoid	9. Bearing cover	17. Brake spring
2. Engagement lever	10. Bearing cover	18. Gasket
3. Armature	11. Commutator end frame	19. Brush
4. Overrunning clutch	12. Rubber bushing	20. Brush spring
5. Clutch stop	13. Rubber grommet	21. Brush holder
6. Snap-ring	14. Plate	22. Field coil
7. Drive housing	15. Lockplate	23. Pole shoes
8. Bushing	16. Washer	24. Field yoke

Components of the direct-drive starter motor

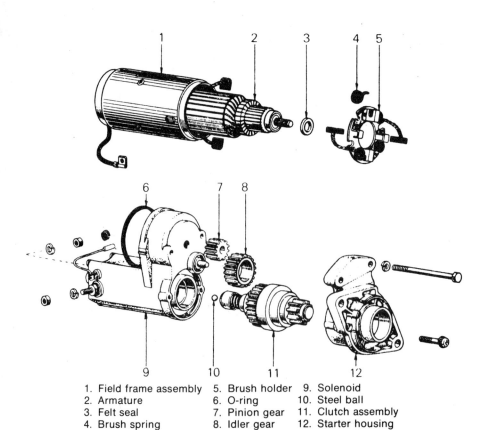

1. Field frame assembly	5. Brush holder	9. Solenoid
2. Armature	6. O-ring	10. Steel ball
3. Felt seal	7. Pinion gear	11. Clutch assembly
4. Brush spring	8. Idler gear	12. Starter housing

Components of the gear reduction starter motor

NOTE: *Radiator removal will facilitate starter removal on diesel engines.*

4. On the Starlet, remove the exhaust pipe and its bracket. Also, remove the intermediate shaft.

5. On Corollas with gasoline engines and automatic transmissions, remove the transmission oil filler tube.

6. Disconnect all of the wiring at the starter.

7. Unfasten the starter securing nuts and withdraw the starter assembly toward the front of the car.

8. Installation is in the reverse order of removal.

STARTER OVERHAUL

Solenoid Replacement — Direct Drive Type

1. Remove the starter.

2. Unscrew the two solenoid switch (magnetic switch) retaining screws.

3. Remove the solenoid. In order to unhook the solenoid from the starter drive lever, lift it up at the same time that you are pulling it out of the starter housing.

4. Installation is in the reverse order of removal. Make sure that the solenoid switch is properly engaged with the drive lever before tightening the mounting screws.

Brush Replacement — Direct Drive Type

1. Remove the starter.

2. Remove the solenoid (magnetic switch).

3. Remove the two end frame cap mounting bolts and remove the end frame cap.

4. Remove the O-ring and the lock plate from the armature shaft groove and then slide the shims off the shaft.

5. Unscrew the two long housing screws (they are found at the front of the starter) and carefully pull off the end plate.

6. Using a screwdriver, separate the brushes and the brush springs and then remove the brushes from the brush holder.

7. Slide the brush holder off of the armature shaft.

8. Crush the old brushes off of the copper braid and file away any remaining solder.

9. Fit the new brushes to the braid and spread the braid slightly.

NOTE: *Use a soldering iron of at least 250 watts.*

10. Using radio solder, solder the brush to the braid. Grip the copper braid with flat pliers to prevent the solder from flowing down its length.

11. File off any extra solder and then repeat the procedure for the remaining three brushes.

12. Installation is in the reverse order of removal.

NOTE: *When installing the brush holder, make sure that the brushes line up properly.*

Brush Replacement — Reduction Gear Type

1. Remove the starter.

2. Disconnect the lead from the solenoid (magnetic switch) terminal.

3. Unscrew the two mounting bolts and remove the field frame assembly from the solenoid housing.

4. Remove the O-ring and the felt seal.

5. Unscrew the mounting screws and remove the starter housing from the solenoid housing.

6. Pull out the clutch assembly and then remove the pinion and idler gears.

7. Remove the steel ball from the clutch shaft hole.

8. Perform Steps 6-12 of the direct drive replacement procedure.

Starter Drive Replacement — Direct Drive Type

1. Perform Steps 1-7 of the Brush Replacement-Direct Drive Type procedure.

2. Pull the field frame away from the drive housing and remove it.

3. Remove the drive lever pivot bolt from the drive housing.

4. Pull the armature from the drive housing.

5. Take a 14mm socket and slide it over the armature shaft until it rests on the stop collar.

6. Tap the stop collar down with a hammer.

7. Pry off the exposed stop ring and then remove the stop collar from the shaft.

8. Remove the starter drive clutch assembly.

9. Installation is in the reverse order of removal.

Battery

Refer to Chapter 1 for details on battery maintenance.

REMOVAL AND INSTALLATION

1. Disconnect the negative cable from the terminal, then disconnect the positive cable. Special pullers are available to remove the clamps.

NOTE: *To avoid sparks, always disconnect the negative cable first and connect it last.*

2. Unscrew and remove the battery holddown clamp.

3. Remove the battery, being careful not to spill any of the acid.

NOTE: *Spilled acid can be neutralized with a baking soda and water solution. If you somehow get acid into your eyes, flush it out with lots of clean water and get to a doctor as quickly as possible.*

4. Clean the battery posts thoroughly before reinstalling or when installing a new one.

5. Clean the cable clamps, using the special tools or a wire brush, both inside and out.

6. Install the battery and the holddown clamp. Connect the positive and then the negative cable. Do not hammer them into place. The terminals should be coated with grease to prevent corrosion.

CAUTION: *Make absolutely sure that the batter is connected properly before you turn on the ignition switch. Reversed polarity can burn out your alternator and regulator in a matter of seconds.*

ENGINE MECHANICAL

Understanding the Engine

The basic piston engine is a metal block containing a series of chambers. The upper engine block is usually an iron or aluminum alloy casting, consisting of outer walls, which form hollow jackets around the cylinder walls. The lower block provides a number of rigid mounting points for the bearings which hold the crankshaft in place, and is known as the crankcase. The hollow jackets of the upper block add to the rigidity of the engine and contain the liquid coolant which carries the heat away from the cylinders and other engine parts. The block of an air cooled engine consists of a crankcase which provides for the rigid mounting of the crankshaft and for studs which hold the cylinders in place. The cylinders are individual, single-wall castings, finned for cooling, and are usually bolted to the crankcase, rather than cast integrally with the block. In a water-cooled engine, only the cylinder head is bolted to the top of the block. The water pump is mounted directly to the block.

The crankshaft is a long, iron or steel shaft mounted rigidly in the bottom of the crankcase, at a number of points (usually 4-7). The crankshaft is free to turn and contains a number of counterweighted crankpins (one for each cylinder) that are offset several inches from the center of the crankshaft and turn in a circle as the crankshaft turns. The crankpins are centered under each cylinder. Pistons with circular rings to seal the small space between the pistons and wall of the cylinders are connected to the crankpins by steel connecting rods. The rods connect the pistons at their upper ends with the crankpins at their lower ends.

When the crankshaft spins, the pistons move up and down in the cylinder, depending on the position of the piston. Two openings in each cylinder head (above the cylinders) allow the intake of the air/fuel mixture and the exhaust of the burned gases. The volume of the combustion chamber must be variable for the engine to compress the fuel charge before combustion, to make use of the expansion of the burning gases and to exhaust the burned gases and take in a fresh fuel mixture. As the pistons are forced downward by the expansion of burning fuel, the connecting rods convert the reciprocating (up and down) motion of the pistons into rotary (turning) motion of the crankshaft. A round flywheel at the rear of the crankshaft provides a large, stable mass to smooth out the rotation.

The cylinder head(s) form(s) tight cover(s) for the tops of the cylinders and contain machined chambers into which the fuel mixture is forced as it is compressed by the pistons reaching the upper limit of their travel. Each com-

Battery and Starter Specifications

Engine Type	Battery			Starter							Minimum Brush Tension (oz)	Minimum Brush Length (in.)
	Ampere Hour Capacity	Volts	Terminal Grounded	Lock Test			No-Load Test					
				Amps	Volts	Torque (ft. lbs.)	Amps	Volts	RPM			
1970–77												
3K-C	48	12	Neg	450	8.5	8	55	11	3,500		21	0.51
2T-C	50	12	Neg	Not Recommended			①	11.5	3,500		52.8	0.55
1977 3K-C	50	12	Neg	600	7.0	13	50	11	5,000		21	0.47
2T-C	60	12	Neg	Not Recommended			90	11.5	4,000		21	0.33
1978–87												
2T-C, 1A-C 3A-C, 4A-C 4A-GE, 3E	50, 60, 110	12	N	Not Recommended			90	11.5	3,500		31.6	.57

① Less than 90 amps

bustion chamber contains one intake valve, one exhaust valve and one spark plug per cylinder. The spark plugs are screwed into holes in the cylinder head so that the tips protrude into the combustion chambers. The valve in each open-ing in the cylinder head is opened and closed by the action of the camshaft. The camshaft is driven by the crankshaft through a chain or belt at ½ crankshaft speed (the camshaft gear is twice the size of the crankshaft gear). The

General Engine Specifications

Model	Year	Engine Type	Engine Displacement Cu. In. (cc)	Carburetor Type	Horsepower (@ rpm)	Torque @ rpm (ft. lbs.)	Bore x Stroke (in.)	Compression Ratio
Carina	'72–'73	2T-C	96.9 (1588)	2-bbl	88 @ 6000	98 @ 3800	3.35 x 2.76	8.5:1
Corolla 1200	'70–'71	3K-C	71 (1166)	2-bbl	73 @ 6000	70 @ 4200	2.95 x 2.60	9.0:1
	'72–'77	3K-C	71 (1166)	2-bbl	65 @ 6000	67 @ 3800	2.95 x 2.60	9.0:1
	'78–'79	3K-C	71 (1166)	2-bbl	58 @ 5800	63 @ 3800	2.95 x 2.60	9.0:1
Corolla 1600	'71	2T-C	96.9 (1588)	2-bbl	102 @ 6000	101 @ 0000	3.35 x 2.76	8.5:1
	'72–'74	2T-C	96.9 (1588)	2-bbl	88 @ 6000	98 @ 3800	3.35 x 2.76	8.5:1
	'75–'77	2T-C	96.9 (1588)	2-bbl	75 @ 5800	83 @ 3800	3.35 x 2.76	9.0:1
	'78–'79	2T-C	96.9 (1588)	2-bbl	75 @ 5400	85 @ 2800	3.35 x 2.76	9.0:1
Corolla 1800	'80–'81	3T-C	108 (1770)	2-bbl	75 @ 5000 ①	95 @ 2600 ②	3.35 x 3.07	9.0:1
	'82	3T-C	108 (1770)	2-bbl	70 @ 4600	93 @ 2400	3.35 x 3.07	9.0:1
Corolla	'83–'85	4A-C	97 (1587)	2-bbl	70 @ 4800	85 @ 2800	3.94 x 3.03	9.0:1
	'84	1C-L	112.2 (1839)	DFI	56 @ 4500	76 @ 3000	3.27 x 3.35	22.5:1
	'85–'87	4A-GE	97 (1587)	EFI	112 @ 6600	97 @ 4800	3.19 x 3.03	9.4:1
	'86–'87	4A-C	97 (1587)	2-bbl	74 @ 5200	86 @ 2800	3.19 x 3.03	9.0:1
Tercel	'80–'84	1A-C, 3A	88.6 (1452)	2-bbl	60 @ 4800	72 @ 2800	3.05 x 3.03	8.7:1
	'81	3A-C	88.6 (1452)	2-bbl	62 @ 4800	75 @ 2800	3.05 x 3.03	9.0:1
	'82–'87	3A-C	88.6 (1452)	2-bbl	62 @ 5200	75 @ ③ 2800	3.05 x 3.03	9.0:1
	'87	3E	88.9 (1456)	2-bbl	78 @ 6000	87 @ 4000	2.87 x 3.54	9.3:1 ②
Starlet	'81–'82	4K-C	79 (1290)	2-bbl	58 @ 5200	67 @ 3600	2.95 x 2.87	9.0:1
	'83–'84	4K-E	79 (1290)	EFI	58 @ 4200	74 @ 3400	2.95 x 2.87	9.5:1

EFI Electronic Fuel Injection
DFI Diesel Fuel Injection
① Calif: 73 @ 5000

② Calif: 90 @ 2600
③ 1983 4SM: 75 @ 2400

valves are operated either through rocker arms and pushrods (overhead cam engine).

Lubricating oil is stored in a pan at the bottom of the engine and is force fed to all parts of the engine by a gear type pump, driven from the crankshaft. The oil lubricates the entire engine and also seals the piston rings, giving good compression.

Engine

REMOVAL AND INSTALLATION

3K-C, 4K-C and 4K-E

1. Drain the entire cooling system. Remove any emissions systems hoses which are in the way, but mark them beforehand so that you'll know where to put them back.

CAUTION: *When draining the coolant, keep in mind that cats and dogs are attracted by the ethylene glycol antifreeze, and are quite likely to drink any that is left in an uncovered container or in puddles on the ground. This will prove fatal in sufficient quantity. Always drain the coolant into a sealable container. Coolant should be reused unless it is contaminated or several years old.*

2. Unfasten the cable which runs from the battery to the starter at the battery terminal; first disconnect the ground (-) cable.

3. Scribe marks on the hood and hinges to aid in hood alignment during assembly. Remove the hood.

4. Unfasten the headlight bezel retaining screws and remove the bezels. Remove the radiator grille attachment screws and remove the grille.

5. Remove the hood lock assembly after detaching the release cable.

6. Unfasten the nuts from the horn retainers and disconnect the wiring. Withdraw the horn assembly.

7. Remove the air cleaner from its bracket after unfastening the hoses from it.

8. Remove the windshield washer tank from its bracket but first drain its contents into a clean container.

9. Remove both the upper and lower radiator hoses from the engine after loosening the hose clamps.

NOTE: *On models with automatic transmissions, disconnect and plug the oil line from the oil cooler.*

10. Detach the radiator mounting bolts and remove the radiator.

11. Remove the accelerator cable from its support on the cylinder head cover. Unfasten the

Valve Specifications

Engine Type	Seat Angle (deg)	Face Angle (deg)	Spring Pressure (lbs.)		Spring Installed Height (in.)		Stem-To-Guide Clearance (in.)		Stem Diameter (in.)	
			Inner	Outer	Inner	Outer	Intake	Exhaust	Intake	Exhaust
3K-C	45	44.5	—	70.1	—	1.512	0.0010–0.0020 ①	0.0021–0.0030 ②	0.3140 ⌃	0.3140
4K-C, 4K-E	45	44.5	—	70.1 ④	—	1.512	0.0012–0.0026	0.0014–0.0028	0.3136–0.3142	0.3134–0.3140
2T-C	45	44.5	—	58.4 ③	—	1.484	0.0012–0.0020	0.0012–0.0024	0.3140	0.3140
1A-C, 3A, 3A-C, 4A-C	45	44.5	—	52.0	—	1.520	0.0010–0.0024	0.0012–0.0026	0.2744–0.2750	0.2742–0.2748
3T-C	45	44.5	—	57.9	—	1.484	0.0010–0.0024	0.0012–0.0026	0.3139	0.3139
IC-L	45	44.5	—	53.0	—	1.587	0.0008–0.0022	0.0014–0.0028	0.3140–0.3146	0.3134–0.3140
3E	45	44.5	—	35.1	—	1.384	0.0010–0.0024	0.0012–0.0026	0.2350–0.2356	0.2348–0.2354
4A-LC	45	44.5	—	52.0	—	1.520	0.0010–0.0024	0.0012–0.0026	0.2744–0.2750	0.2742–0.2748
4A-GEC, 4A-GELC	45	44.5	—	35.9	—	1.366	0.0010–0.0024	0.0012–0.0026	0.2350–0.2356	0.2348–0.2354

① 1978 and later: 0.0012–0.0026
② 1978 and later: 0.0014–0.0028
③ 1978 and later: 57.9
④ 4K-E: 77.2

cable at the carburetor throttle arm (except 4K-E). Unfasten the choke cable from the carburetor (except 4K-E).

12. Detach the water hose retainer from the cylinder head.

13. Disconnect the by-pass and heater hoses at the water pump. Disconnect the other end of the heater hose from the water valve. Remove the heater control cable from the wiring harness multi-connectors.

Crankshaft and Connecting Rod Specifications

All measurements in inches

| Engine Type | Crankshaft | | | | Connecting Rod | | |
	Main Brg. Journal Dia.	Main Brg. Oil Clearance	Shaft End-Play	Thrust on No.	Journal Diameter	Oil Clearance	Side Clearance
3K-C	1.9675–1.9685	0.0005–0.0015	0.0020–0.0090 ①	3	1.6525–1.6535	0.0006–0.0015 ②	0.0040–0.0080 ③
2-TC	2.2827–2.2834	0.0012–0.0024 ②	0.0030–0.0070 ④	3	1.8889–1.8897	0.0008–0.0020	0.0063–0.0102
1A-C, 3A, 3A-C, 4A-C	1.8892–1.8898	0.0005–0.0019 ⑤	0.0008–0.0073	3	1.5742–1.5748	0.0008–0.0020	0.0059–0.0098
3T-C	2.2825–2.2835	0.0009–0.0019	0.0008–0.0087	3	1.8889–1.8897	0.0009–0.0019	0.0063–0.0012
4K-C, 4K-E	1.9676–1.9685	0.0006–0.0016	0.0016–0.0095	3	1.6526–1.6535	0.0006–0.0016	0.0079–0.0150 ⑥
1C-L	2.2435–2.2441	0.0013–0.0026	0.0016–0.0094	3	1.9877–1.9882	0.0014–0.0025	0.0031–0.0118
3E	1.9683–1.9685	0.0006–0.0014	0.0008–0.0087	3	1.8110–1.8113	0.0006–0.0019	0.0059–0.0138
4A-LC	1.8891–1.8898	0.0006–0.0013	0.0008–0.0087	3	1.5742–1.5748	0.0008–0.0020	0.0059–0.0098
4A-GEC, 4A-GELC	1.8891–1.8898	0.0005–0.0015	0.0008–0.0087	3	1.5742–1.5748	0.0008–0.0020	0.0059–0.0098

① 1978 and later: 0.0016–0.0087
② 1978 and later: 0.0009–0.0019
③ 1978 and later: 0.0043–0.0084
④ 1978 and later: 0.0010–0.0090
⑤ 1984 3A-C: 0.0012–0.0026
⑥ 1984 4K-E: 0.0079–0.0120

Camshaft Specifications

All measurements in inches

| Year | Engine | Journal Diameter | | | | | Bearing Clearance | Lobe Lift | | Camshaft End Play |
		1	2	3	4	5		Intake	Exhaust	
'71–'82	2T-C, 3T-C	1.8291–1.8297	1.8292–1.8199	1.8094–1.8100	1.7996–1.8002	1.7897–1.7904	0.0010–0.0026	—	—	0.003–0.006
'70–'84	3K-C, 4K-C, 4K-E	1.7011–1.7018	1.6911–1.6917	1.6813–1.6819	1.6716–1.6722	—	①	—	—	0.003–0.006
'80–'84	1A-C, 3A, 3A-C, 4A-C, 1C-L	1.1015–1.1022	1.1015–1.1022	1.1015–1.1022	1.1015–1.1022	—	0.0015–0.0029	—	—	0.0031–0.0071
	3E	1.0622–1.0628	1.0622–1.0628	1.0622–1.0628	1.0622–1.0628	—	0.0015–0.0029	—	—	0.0031–0.0071
	4A-LC	1.1015–1.1022	1.1015–1.1022	1.1015–1.1022	1.1015–1.1022	—	0.0015–0.0029	—	—	0.0031–0.0071
	4A-GEC, 4A-GELC	1.0610–1.0616	1.0610–1.0616	1.0610–1.0616	1.0610–1.0616	—	0.0014–0.0028	—	—	0.0031–0.0075

① 3K-C, 4K-C: Nos. 1 & 4—0.0010–0.0026
           Nos. 2 & 3—0.0014–0.0028
4K-E: Nos. 1 & 4—0.0010–0.0026
       Nos. 2 & 3—0.0016–0.0030

Piston and Ring Specifications

All measurements in inches

Engine Type	Piston Clearance	Ring Gap			Ring Side Clearance		
		Top Compression	Bottom Compression	Oil Control	Top Compression	Bottom Compression	Oil Control
3K-C	0.0010–0.0020	0.0006–0.0014 ①	0.0006–0.0014 ①	0.0006–0.0014 ②	0.0011–0.0027	0.0007–0.0023 ③	0.0006–0.0023
4K-C	0.0012–0.0020	0.0039–0.0110	0.0039–0.0018	0.0080–0.0350	0.0012–0.0028	0.0008–0.0024	snug
4K-E	0.0012–0.0020	⑨	⑩	⑪	0.0012–0.0028	0.0008–0.0024	snug
2T-C	0.0024–0.0031	0.0008–0.0016 ④	0.0004–0.0012 ⑤	0.0004–0.0012 ⑥	0.0008–0.0024	0.0008–0.0024 ⑦	0.0008–0.0024 ⑧
3T-C	0.0020–0.0028	0.0039–0.0098	0.0059–0.0118	0.0079–0.0276	0.0008–0.0024	0.0006–0.0022	snug
2A-C, 3A, 3A-C	0.0039–0.0047	0.0079–0.0157 ⑫	0.0059–0.0138 ⑬	0.0039–0.0236 ⑭	0.0016–0.0031	0.0012–0.0028	snug
4A-C	0.0039–0.0047	⑮	⑯	⑰	0.0016–0.0031 ⑱	0.0012–0.0028 ⑲	snug
1C-L	0.0016–0.0024	0.0098–0.0193	0.0079–0.0173	0.0079–0.0193	0.0079–0.0081	0.0079–0.0081	snug
3E	0.0028–0.0035	0.0102–0.0142	0.0118–0.0177	0.0059–0.0157	0.0016–0.0031	0.0012–0.0028	snug
4A-LC	0.0035–0.0043	0.0098–0.0138	0.0059–0.0165	0.0078–0.0276	0.0016–0.0031	0.0012–0.0028	snug
4A-GEC, 4A-GELC	0.0039–0.0047	0.0098–0.0138	0.0078–0.0118	0.0078–0.0276	0.0016–0.0031	0.0012–0.0028	snug

FWD Front Wheel Drive
RWD Rear Wheel Drive
① '78 and later: 0.004–0.011
② '78 and later: 0.008–0.035
③ '78 and later: 0.001–0.003
④ '78 and later: 0.006–0.011
⑤ '78 and later: 0.008–0.013
⑥ '78 and later: 0.008–0.028
⑦ '78 and later: 0.0006–0.0022
⑧ '78–'79: 0.008–0.035
⑨ '83: 0.0063–0.0118
　'84: 0.0079–0.0154
⑩ '83: 0.0059–0.0118
　'84: 0.0059–0.0154
⑪ '83: TP—0.008–0.028
　Riken—0.012–0.035
　'84: TP—0.0079–0.0311
　Riken—0.0118–0.0390
⑫ '83: TP—0.0079–0.0157
　Riken—0.0079–0.0138

'84: TP—0.0079–0.0193
　Riken—0.0079–0.0173
⑬ '83: TP—0.0059–0.0138
　Riken—0.0059–0.0118
　'84: TP—0.0059–0.0173
　Riken—0.0059–0.0154
⑭ '83: TP—0.0039–0.0236
　Riken—0.0118–0.0354
　'84: TP—0.0039–0.0272
　Riken—0.0118–0.0390
⑮ '83 and '84 FWD: TP—0.0098–0.0138
　　　　　Riken—0.0079–0.0138
　'84 RWD: 0.0098–0.0185
⑯ '83 and '84: FWD: 0.0059–0.0118
　'84 RWD: 0.0059–0.0165
⑰ '83 and '84 FWD: TP—0.0079–0.0276
　　　　　Riken—0.0118–0.0354
　'84 RWD: 0.0118–0.0390
⑱ '84 FWD: 0.0012–0.0028
⑲ '84 FWD: 0.0008–0.0024

14. Detach the exhaust pipe from the exhaust manifold.

15. Detach the wires from the water temperature and oil pressure sending units.

16. Remove the nut from the front left hand engine mount.

17. Remove the fuel line from the fuel pump.

18. Detach the battery ground cable from the cylinder block.

19. Remove the nut from the front right hand engine mount.

20. Remove the clip and detach the cable from the clutch release lever.

21. Remove the primary and high tension wires from the coil.

22. Detach the back-up light switch wire at its connector on the right side of the extension housing.

Torque Specifications
All Readings in ft. lbs.

Engine Type	Cylinder Head Bolts	Rod Bearing Bolts	Main Bearing Bolts	Crankshaft Pulley Bolt	Flywheel-to-Crankshaft Bolts	Manifold	
						Intake	Exhaust
3K-C	39.0–47.7	28.9–37.6	39.0–47.7	29–43 ④	39–48	14–22 ①	
2T-C	52.0–63.5 ⑤	28.9–36.1	52.0–63.5	28.9–43.3 ②	41.9–47.7 ③	7.2–11.6 ⑥	7.2–11.6 ⑦
1A-C, 3A 3A-C, 4A-C	40–47	26–32 ⑨	40–47	55–61 ⑧	55–61	15–21	15–21
3T-C	62–68	29–36	53–63	47–61	42–47	14–18	22–32
4K-C, 4K-E	40–47	29–37	40–47	55–75	40–47	15–21 ①	
1C-L	60–65	45–50	75–78	70–75	63–68	10–15	32–36
3E	Text	27–31	40–47	105–117	60–70	11–17	33–42
4A-LC	40–47	32–40	40–47	80–94	55–61	15–21	15–21
4A-GE	40–47	32–40	40–47	100–110	50–58	15–21	15–21

① Intake and exhaust manifolds combined
② 1975: 43–51 ft. lbs.; 1976: 116–145 ft. lbs.
③ 1975–76: 58–64 ft. lbs.
④ 1977: 32.5–39.8
⑤ 1977–79: 61.5–68.7
⑥ 1978–79: 14–18
⑦ 1978–79: 22–32
⑧ 1981–83: 80–94
⑨ Connecting rods purchased after 2/15/84: 34–39

The following steps apply to Corolla models with manual transmissions and Starlet:

23. Remove the carpet from the transmission tunnel. Remove the boots from the shift lever.

24. Remove the snapring from the gearshift selector lever base. Withdraw the selector lever assembly.

The following steps apply to Corolla models with automatic transmissions:

25. Disconnect the accelerator linkage torque rod at the carburetor.

26. Disconnect the throttle linkage connecting rod from the bellcrank lever.

27. Drain the oil from the transmission oil pan. (See Chapter 1.)

28. Detach the transmission gear selector shift rod from the control shaft.

The following steps apply to Corollas with both manual and automatic transmissions and Starlet:

29. Raise the rear wheels of the car. Support the car with jackstands.

CAUTION: *Be sure that the car is supported securely; remember, you will be working underneath it!*

30. Disconnect the driveshaft from the transmission.

NOTE: *Drain the oil from the manual transmission first, to prevent it from leaking out. (See Chapter 1.)*

31. Detach the exhaust pipe support bracket from the extension housing.

32. Remove the insulator bolt from the rear engine mount.

33. Place a jack under the transmission and remove the four bolts from the rear (engine support) crossmember.

34. Install lifting hooks on the engine lifting brackets. Attach a suitable hoist.

35. Lift the engine slightly; then move it toward the front of the car. Bring the engine the rest of the way out at an angle.

CAUTION: *Use care not to damage other parts of the automobile.*

36. Engine installation is the reverse order of removal. Adjust all transmission and carburetor linkages, as detailed in the appropriate chapter. Install and adjust the hood. Refill the engine, radiator, and transmission to capacity, as detailed in Chapter 1.

2T-C, 3T-C and 4A-C (RWD)

1. Drain the radiator, cooling system, transmission, and engine oil.

CAUTION: *When draining the coolant, keep in mind that cats and dogs are attracted by the ethylene glycol antifreeze, and are quite likely to drink any that is left in an uncovered container or in puddles on the ground. This will prove fatal in sufficient quantity. Always drain the coolant into a sealable container. Coolant should be reused unless it is contaminated or several years old.*

2. Disconnect the battery-to-starter cable at the positive battery terminal after first disconnecting the negative cable.

3. Scribe marks on the hood and its hinges to aid in alignment during installation.

4. Remove the hood supports from the body. Remove the hood.

NOTE: *Do not remove the supports from the hood.*

5. On Carina models, remove the headlight bezels. Disconnect the hood release cable then remove the grille, lower grille molding, hood lock base and base support.

6. On Corolla models, perform Steps 4-6 as previously detailed in the 3K-C Engine Removal section.

7. Detach both the upper and lower hoses from the radiator. On cars with automatic transmissions, disconnect and plug the lines from the oil cooler. Remove the radiator.

8. Unfasten the clamps and remove the heater and by-pass hoses from the engine. Remove the heater control cable from the water valve.

9. Remove the wiring from the coolant temperature and oil pressure sending units.

10. Remove the air cleaner from its bracket, complete with its attendant hoses.

11. Unfasten the accelerator torque rod from the carburetor. On models equipped with automatic transmissions, remove the transmission linkage as well.

12. Remove the emission control system hoses and wiring, as necessary (mark them to aid in installation).

13. Remove the clutch hydraulic line support bracket.

14. Unfasten the high tension and primary wires from the coil.

15. Mark the spark plug cables and remove them from the distributor.

16. Detach the right hand front engine mount.

17. Remove the fuel line at the pump (filter on 1975-76 models with electric pumps).

18. Detach the downpipe from the exhaust manifold.

19. Detach the left hand front engine mount.

20. Disconnect all of the wiring harness multi-connectors.

21. On cars equipped with manual transmissions, remove the shift lever boot and the shift lever cap boot.

22. Unfasten the four gear selector lever cap retaining screws, remove the gasket and withdraw the gear selector lever assembly from the top of the transmission.

NOTE: *On all Carina models and on Corolla 5-speed models, the floor console must be removed first.*

23. Lift the rear wheels of the car off the ground and support the car with jackstands.

CAUTION: *Be sure that the car is securely supported!*

24. On cars equipped with automatic transmissions, disconnect the gear selector control rod.

25. Detach the exhaust pipe support bracket.

26. Disconnect the driveshaft from the rear of the transmission.

27. Unfasten the speedometer cable from the transmission. Disconnect the wiring from the back-up light switch and the neutral safety switch (automatic only).

28. Detach the clutch release cylinder assembly, complete with hydraulic lines. Do not disconnect the lines.

29. Unbolt the rear support member mounting insulators.

30. Support the transmission and detach the rear support member retaining bolts. Withdraw the support member from under the car.

31. Install lifting hooks on the engine lifting brackets. Attach a suitable hoist to the engine.

32. Remove the jack from under the transmission.

33. Raise the engine and move it toward the front of the car. Use care to avoid damaging the components which remain on the car.

34. Support the engine on a workstand.

35. Install the engine by following the removal steps in reverse order. Adjust all of the linkages as detailed in the appropriate chapter. Install the hood and adjust it. Replenish the fluid levels in the engine, radiator, and transmission as detailed in Chapter 1.

4A-GE Series (RWD)

1. Disconnect the battery cables (negative cable first) and then remove the battery.

2. Remove the hood and the engine undercover splash shield.

3. Remove the No. 2 air cleaner hose. Disconnect the actuator and accelerator cables from their bracket on the cylinder head.

4. From inside the vehicle; remove the center console, lift up the shift boot and remove the shifter.

5. Drain the engine oil and transmission fluid. On automatic transmission equipped vehicles, disconnect the two cooler lines from the radiator.

6. Drain the radiator and engine coolant. Remove the radiator hoses and then remove the radiator and shroud.

CAUTION: *When draining the coolant, keep in mind that cats and dogs are attracted by the ethylene glycol antifreeze, and are quite likely to drink any that is left in an uncovered container or in puddles on the ground. This will prove fatal in sufficient quantity. Always drain the coolant into a sealable container. Coolant should be reused unless it is contaminated or several years old.*

7. Remove the air cleaner assembly.

8. Remove the power steering pump and the pump mounting bracket.

9. Loosen the water pump pulley set nuts, remove the drive belt adjusting bolt and remove the drive belt.

10. Remove the set nuts and remove the fluid coupling with the fan and water pump pulley.

11. Remove the air conditioning compressor and its mounting bracket. DO NOT DISCONNECT THE TWO HOSES. Position the compressor (with the hoses connected) to the side and out of the way. Wire the compressor to the frame so it can not slip, and so there is no tension on the hoses.

12. Remove the spark plug wires from the plugs and cover mounting brackets. Disconnect the coil wire. Remove the distributor.

13. Remove the exhaust pipe bracket from the pipe and clutch housing.

14. Disconnect, and separate, the exhaust pipe from the exhaust manifold.

15. Disconnect the starter wire harness.

16. Remove the fuel hose from the pulsation damper and pressure regulator

17. Remove the cold start injector pipe. Remove the PCV hose from the intake manifold.

18. Tag and disconnect all related vacuum hoses: Brake booster hose; Charcoal canister hose from the intake manifold; VSV hose from the air valve; Two air valve hoses from the vacuum pipe; and the Vacuum sensing hose from the pressure regulator.

19. Remove the wiring harness and the vacuum pipe from the No.3 timing cover.

20. Tag and disconnect all the related wires: Two ingiter connections; Oil pressure sender gauge connector; Noise filter connector; Relay block connector; Ground strap (between the oil filter retainer and the body); Ground strap connector; Solenoid resistor connector; Four injector connectors; Ground strap from the intake manifold; Ground strap (between the cylinder head and body); Water temperature sender gauge connector; VSV connector; and the Throttle position sensor connector. Position the harness to one side without disconnecting it frm the engine.

21. Raise and safely support the front of the vehicle.

22. Remove the engine mounting bolts on either side of the engine.

23. Unbolt the clutch release cylinder without disconnecting the hydraulic line and position it out of the way.

24. Disconnect the driveshaft. Tag and disconnect the speedometer cable and the back-up switch connector. Remove the O-ring.

25. Disconnect the bond cables from the clutch and extension housings. Lower the vehicle.

26. Attach a suitable engine sling and hoist to the lift bracket on the engine. Support the en-

gine rear mounting on a jack. Remove the rear mounting bolts. Carefully raise the engine and transmission and remove from the vehicle.

27. Remove the starter, the two stiffner plates and then remove the transmission from the engine.

28. Install the engine and transmission in the reverse order of removal.

1A-C, 3A, 3A-C, 4A-C and 4A-LC (FWD)

1. Disconnect the negative battery terminal.
2. Remove the hood.
3. Remove the air cleaner and all necessary lines attached to it.
4. Drain the radiator.

CAUTION: *When draining the coolant, keep in mind that cats and dogs are attracted by the ethylene glycol antifreeze, and are quite likely to drink any that is left in an uncovered container or in puddles on the ground. This will prove fatal in sufficient quantity. Always drain the coolant into a sealable container. Coolant should be reused unless it is contaminated or several years old.*

5. Cover both driveshaft boots with a shop towel.

6. Remove the solenoid valve connector, water temperature switch connector, and the electric fan connector.

7. Remove the exhaust support plate bolts, and the exhaust pipe.

8. Remove the top radiator support.

9. Remove the top and bottom radiator hoses and remove the radiator with the fan.

NOTE: *On cars equipped with automatic transmissions remove the coolant lines before removing the radiator.*

10. Remove the windshield washer tank.

11. Remove the heater hoses and the lines to the fuel pump.

12. Remove the accelerator cable, choke cable, and the ground strap.

13. Remove the brake booster vacuum lines.

14. Remove the coil wire and unplug the alternator.

15. Remove the clutch release cable.

16. Remove the wires on the starter.

17. Remove the temperature sending and oil pressure switch connectors.

18. Remove the batter ground strap from the block.

19. Jack up your vehicle and support it with jackstands.

20. Remove the engine mounting bolts and the engine shock absorbers.

21. Support the differential with a jack.

22. Remove the transaxle mounting bolts.

NOTE: *It is probably easier to remove these bolts from underneath the car.*

23. Remove the engine. See the paragraph be-

low if your vehicle is equipped with an automatic transmission.

24. Tie the bell housing to the cowl to keep support on the transaxle.

NOTE: *The grille may be removed, if necessary, to give better leverage when removing the engine.*

25. Installation is the reverse of removal. Adjust all linkages as covered in the appropriate section. Refill all fluids to the proper levels. Tighten the transaxle bolts 37-57 ft.lb.

On cars with automatic transmissions, the following procedures are necessary.

1. Remove the starter.

2. Remove the cooling lines from the transmission.

3. Support the transmission with a jack.

4. Remove the transaxle mounting bolts.

5. Remove the torque converter mounting bolts.

NOTE: *In order to turn the converter, place a wrench on the crankshaft pulley and turn it until you see a bolt appear in the area where the starter was.*

6. While the engine is suspended from your hoist, pull it forward about 2".

7. Insert a pry bar in this opening and gently separate the torque converter from the engine.

8. Installation is the reverse of removal.

9. Confirm that the converter contact surface is 1.02" from the housing. Install a guide bolt in one of the mounting bolt holes. Remove the engine mounting insulator (left side) and the mounting bracket (right side). To secure the transaxle to the engine temporarily install the top two mounting bolts. This will facilitate easier engine installation.

3E Sedans (FWD)

1. Remove the battery and radiator overflow tank. Disconnect the negative battery cable first, when removing the battery.

2. Scribe the hood hinge locations on the reverse side of the hood and remove the hood. Scribing the hinge locations will make installation alignment easier. Remove the under engine splash shields.

3. Drain the engine coolant from the radiator. Remove the radiator and windshield washer tank.

CAUTION: *When draining the coolant, keep in mind that cats and dogs are attracted by the ethylene glycol antifreeze, and are quite likely to drink any that is left in an uncovered container or in puddles on the ground. This will prove fatal in sufficient quantity. Always drain the coolant into a sealable container. Coolant should be reused unless it is contaminated or several years old.*

4. On models equipped with cruise control: Disconnect the acuator control cable, disconnect the wire harness connector and remove the mounting bolts and acuator.

5. Disconnect the accelerator cable and throttle valve cable (automatic transaxle equipped vehicles).

6. Disconnect the fuel lines at the fuel pump and plug the lines.

7. Remove the charcoal canister. Disconnect the vacuum hose from the power brake booster.

8. Disconnect the heater hoses from the water outlet housing and from the heater water valve.

9. Disconnect the speedometer cable from the transaxle housing.

10. Disconnect the transaxle shift control cables from the transaxle connection.

11. On manual transaxle equipped vehicles, remove the clutch release cylinder from the transaxle case. Remove the bell crank selector from the case.

12. Disconnect the following wires: Ground strap from the left hand front apron. Oxygen sensor wire. Oil pressure switch wire. Water temperature switch sender wire. Water temperature switch wire from the CMH. Backup light/neutral safety switch wire. Ignition control wire. Water temperature switch for the electric fan control.

13. Disconnect the wire harness from the intake manifold.

14. Remove the intake manifold stay support.

15. Disconnect the connectors for the: Solenoid and CMH. Alternator wire and connector. Starter connector and wire.

16. Remove the vacuum suction valve.

17. On models equipped: Remove the power steering pump drive belt. Remove the power steering pump with the hoses attached and secure it out of the way.

18. On models equipped: Remove the AC compressor drive belt. Remove the compressor WITHOUT DISCONNECT THE LINES. Position and secure the compressor out of the way.

19. Disconnect the exhaust pipe from the exhaust manifold.

20. Disconnect the drive axle shafts.

21. Attach an engine hoist to engine hangers provided on the engine. Remove the rear mounting through bolt. Remove the four bolts and rear mounting insulator.

22. Remove the front mounting through bolt. Remove the three bolts and mounting bracket from the engine block.

23. Remove the two bolts, through bolt and right hand mounting insulator. Remove the five bolts and left hand mounting bracket.

24. Carefully hoist the engine and transaxle assembly from the vehicle.

25. Service the engine as required and install in the reverse order.

3A-C Wagons (FWD)

1. Disconnect and remove the battery. Remove the battery carrier. Remove the hood.

2. Drain the coolant. Disconnect and plug the transaxle fluid lines, if equipped. Remove the radiator. Remove the washer tank. Disconnect the heater hoses. If the vehicle is equipped with air conditioning, remove the condenser fan assembly.

CAUTION: *When draining the coolant, keep in mind that cats and dogs are attracted by the ethylene glycol antifreeze, and are quite likely to drink any that is left in an uncovered container or in puddles on the ground. This will prove fatal in sufficient quantity. Always drain the coolant into a sealable container. Coolant should be reused unless it is contaminated or several years old.*

3. Remove the power steering pump, with lines connected, and position it to the side.

4. Disconnect the engine ground strap, the oxygen sensor wire, the distributor connector, the ground strap from the dash panel, the oil pressure switch wire, the coolant fan wire, the water temperature gauge wire, the back-up light switch and neutral safety switch wires.

5. Disconnect the accelerator control cable, and the kick down cable (if equipped.

6. Disconnect and plug the fuel lines hoses. Disconnect the vacuum hose from the VSV idle-up. Disconnect the power brake booster vacuum line.

7. Disconnect the air suction filter from the cylinder block. Remove the transaxle upper mount bolts.

8. Raise and support the vehicle safely. Remove the front exhaust pipe. Remove the oil cooler lines (if equipped).

9. If equipped, disconnect the clutch cable. Remove the stiffener plates. Disconnect the engine mounted shock/roll absorber.

10. Remove the engine mount bolts. **On vehicles equipped with an automatic transaxle:**Remove the torque converter lower cover. Remove the torque converter to flywheel mounting bolts.

11. Wrap both of the halfshafts (drive axles) with protective material. Disconnect and remove the starter motor. Lower the vehicle, but leave enough room to remove the transaxle lower mounting bolts.

12. Support the transaxle assembly with a floorjack. Remove the lower transaxle mounting bolts.

13. Attach an engine hoist to the engine lift brackets, lift the engine slightly and separate the transaxle. Carefully lift the engine from the vehicle. Make sure all wires, hoses, and controls are disconnect prior to lifting.

14. Service as required and install the engine in the reverse order of removal. Make sure the front transaxle spline or torque converter mounting is aligned with the flywheel. Lubricate the converter hub/shaft tip with MP grease prior to engine installation. The rear bolt (close to firewall) is torqued to 47 ft.lb. The upper bolt (toward the front of the vehicle) is torqued to 29 ft.lb. The middle front bolt is torqued to 47 ft.lb. and the lower front bolt is torqued to 17 ft.lb.

4A-GE Series (FWD)

1. Remove the battery and hood. Disconnect the negative cable first when removing the battery. Scribe the hood hinge outline on the underhood to help with installation alignment.

2. Remove the under engine splash shields. Drain the engine oil.

3. Drain the engine coolant from the radiator. If the vehicle is equipped with and automatic transaxle, drain the transaxle fluid.

CAUTION: *When draining the coolant, keep in mind that cats and dogs are attracted by the ethylene glycol antifreeze, and are quite likely to drink any that is left in an uncovered container or in puddles on the ground. This will prove fatal in sufficient quantity. Always drain the coolant into a sealable container. Coolant should be reused unless it is contaminated or several years old.*

4. Remove the air cleaner assembly. Remove the coolant reservoir tank.

5. Remove the radiator and electric cooling fan assembly. Disconnect the heater hoses from the eater inlet housing.

6. Disconnect the fuel hose from the inlet of the fuel filter. Disconnect the heater and air hoses from the air valve and disconnect the fuel return line from the pressure regulator.

7. If the vehicle is equipped with a manual transaxle, remove the clutch release cylinder from the transaxle case.

8. Disconnect the charcoal canister vacuum hose. Disconnect the transaxle control cables from the shift levers.

9. Disconnect the speedometer cable from the transaxle case. Disconnect the accelerator link and cruise control cable. Remove the cruise control actuator.

10. Remove the ignition coil. Disconnect the main engine wire by: Remove the right cowl panel. Disconnect the No. 4 junction block connectors. Remove the ECU cover and disconnect the ECU connectors. Pull out the engine main wire to the engine compartment.

11. Disconnect the following: No. 2 junction block connectors. Starter cable from the bat-

tery positive post terminal (if not already disconnected). Washer charge valve connector. Cruise control vacuum pump connector. Cruise control vacuum switch connector. Solenoid resistor connector.

12. Disconnect the brake booster vacuum line.

13. Disconnect the AC compressor and vane pump by: Remove the vane pump pulley nut and loosen the pulley. Loosen the idler pulley adjusting bolt and pulley bolt, remove the drive belt. Remove the four compressor mounting bolts and move the compressor WITH THE LINES ATTACHED to the side and secure out of the way. Loosen the bolts mounting the compressor bracket. Disconnect the oil pressure connector. Loosen the vane pump lock bolt and pivot bolts. Remove the vane pump with its mounting bracket and secure it out of the way.

14. Remove the oxygen sensor.

15. Disconnect the oil cooler lines.

16. Raise and safely support the front of the vehicle.

17. Disconnect the exhaust pipe from the exhaust manifold.

18. Disconnect the front and rear mounting from the crossmember by: Remove the two hole covers and remove the two bolts from each mounting.

19. Remove the front mounting bolt and mount.

20. Remove the center engine mounting crossmember.

21. Disconnect the drive axle shafts from the transaxle.

22. Lower the front of the vehicle.

23. Attach an engine hoist to the engine.

24. Remove the right hand mounting bracket. Remove the left hand mounting bracket from the transaxle bracket.

25. Carefully lift the engine from the vehicle.

26. Service as required. Install in the reverse order of removal.

1C-L Diesel

1. Drain the engine coolant.

CAUTION: *When draining the coolant, keep in mind that cats and dogs are attracted by the ethylene glycol antifreeze, and are quite likely to drink any that is left in an uncovered container or in puddles on the ground. This will prove fatal in sufficient quantity. Always drain the coolant into a sealable container. Coolant should be reused unless it is contaminated or several years old.*

2. Remove the hood.

3. Remove the battery.

4. Disconnect and tag all cables attached to various engine parts.

5. Disconnect and tag all electrical wires attached to various engine parts.

6. Disconnect and tag all vacuum liens connected to various engine parts.

7. Remove the cruise control actuator and bracket.

8. Disconnect the radiator and heater hoses.

9. Disconnect the automatic transmission cooler lines at the radiator.

10. Unbolt the two radiator supports and lift out the radiator.

11. Remove the air cleaner assembly.

12. Disconnect all wiring and linkage at the transmission.

13. Pull out the injection system wiring harness and secure to the right side fender apron.

14. Disconnect the fuel lines at the fuel filter and return pipes.

15. Disconnect the speedometer cable at the transmission.

16. Remove the clutch release cylinder without disconnect the fluid line.

17. Unbolt the air conditioning compressor and secure it out of the way.

18. Raise and support the car on jackstands.

19. Drain the transaxle fluid.

20. While someone holds the brake pedal depressed, unbolt both axle shafts. It's a good idea to wrap the boots with shop towels to prevent grease loss.

21. Unbolt the power steering pump and secure it out of the way.

22. Disconnect the exhaust pipe from the manifold.

23. Disconnect the front and rear engine mounts at the frame member.

24. Lower the vehicle.

25. Attach an engine crane at the lifting eyes.

26. Take up the engine weight with the crane and remove the right and left side engine mounts.

27. Slowly and carefully, remove the engine and transaxle assembly.

28. Installation is the reverse of removal. Torque the engine mount bolts to 29 ft.lb. Torque the axle shaft bolts to 27 ft.lb. Torque the fuel line connectors to 22 ft.lb.

Cylinder Head Cover
REMOVAL AND INSTALLATION

1. Remove the air cleaner and its assorted hoses and lines.

2. Tag and disconnect any wires, hoses or lines which might interfere with the cylinder head cover removal.

3. On the 4K-E engine, remove the air intake chamber and its two brackets. Remove the air intake pipes. These steps are detailed in the Manifold Removal and Installation section.

4. Unscrew the retaining screws/bolts and then lift off the cylinder head cover.

NOTE: *If the cylinder head cover is stuck, tap it lightly with a rubber mallet to loosen it. DO NOT attempt to pry it off.*

5. Using a new gasket and silicone sealant, replace the cylinder head cover and tighten the bolts down until they are snug—not too tight!

6. Installation of the remaining components is in the reverse order of removal.

Rocker Arms

REMOVAL AND INSTALLATION

NOTE: *The diesel engine (1C-L) uses no rocker arms as the valves are operated directly off of the camshaft.*

A-Series and K-Series Engines

1. Remove the cylinder head cover as previously detailed.

2. Loosen the valve rocker support bolts lit-

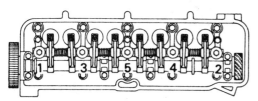

Rocker support bolt loosening sequence—A-series engines

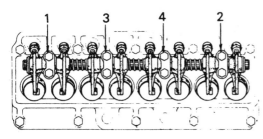

Rocker support bolt loosening sequence—K-series engines

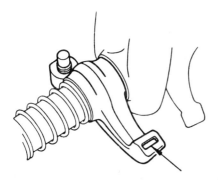

Inspect the valve contacting surface of each rocker arm

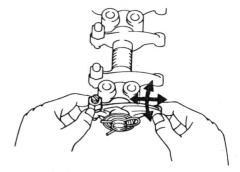

Checking the rocker arm-to-shaft clearance

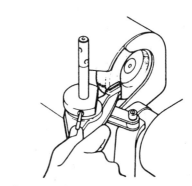

Resurfacing the rocker arm contact face

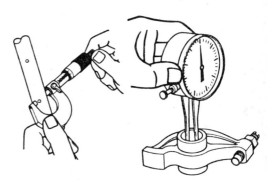

Checking oil clearance

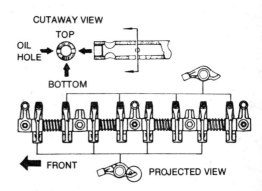

Oil hole positioning—A-series engines

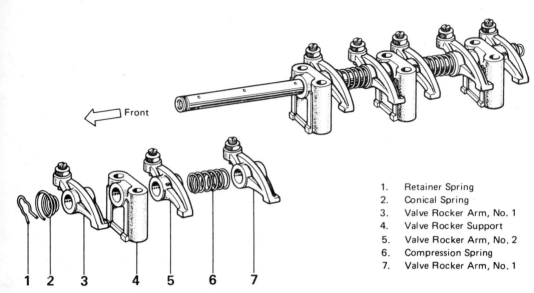

1. Retainer Spring
2. Conical Spring
3. Valve Rocker Arm, No. 1
4. Valve Rocker Support
5. Valve Rocker Arm, No. 2
6. Compression Spring
7. Valve Rocker Arm, No. 1

Disassemble the rocker shafts in this order (K-series shown)

tle-by-little, in 3 steps, in the proper sequence. Remove the rocker arm assembly.

3. Inspect the valve contacting surface of each rocker arm for wear. Inspect the rocker arm. If movement is felt, disassemble and inspect.

4. Disassemble the rocker shaft assembly as shown in the illustration.

5. If the valve contacting surface of the rocker arm is worn, resurface it with a valve refacer or an oil stone.

6. Measure the oil clearance between the

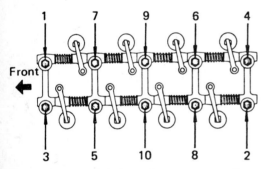

Rocker support bolt loosening sequence—T-series engines

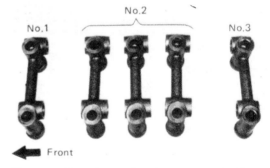

There are three types of rocker arms on the T-series engine

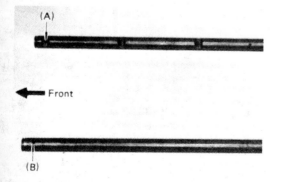

Face the oil holes toward the front

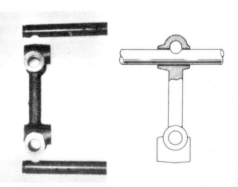

Oil hole alignment—T-series engines

rocker arms and the shaft.It should be no more than 0.0024″, if the clearance is greater, replace the rocker arms.

7. Assembly and installation of the rocker arms and shaft assembly are in the reverse order. When assembling the rocker shaft assembly on the 4A-C engine, face the oil holes in the rocker shaft to the right, left and bottom.

NOTE: *Tighten the rocker support bolts to 14-17 ft.*

lbs.in the reverse order of loosening.

2T-C and 3T-C Engines

1. Follow Steps 1-3 of the previous procedure.

2. To disassemble the rocker shaft assembly, remove the retaining clips from the ends of each shaft and then carefully slide the supports, springs and rocker arms off of each shaft.

3. Follow Steps 5-6 of the previous procedure.

4. When assembling the rocker arms and shafts:

   a. Face the holes in the intake and exhaust shafts toward the front.

   b. There are three (3) types of rocker supports, install them on the shafts in the order illustrated.

   c. Face the side of the rocker support with an **F** toward the front.

   d. The short rocker arms are for the intake (right) side and the long ones are for the exhaust (left) side.

   e. Align the hole in the rocker support with the groove in the rocker shaft and then install the bolt to keep the shaft from turning.

5. Installation is in the reverse order of removal.

NOTE: *As the rocker support bolts are the cylinder head bolts, make sure that they are properly torqued.*

Intake Manifold

REMOVAL AND INSTALLATION

1C-L

1. Disconnect the negative battery cable.

2. Drain the coolant.

CAUTION: *When draining the coolant, keep in mind that cats and dogs are attracted by the ethylene glycol antifreeze, and are quite likely to drink any that is left in an uncovered container or in puddles on the ground. This will prove fatal in sufficient quantity. Always drain the coolant into a sealable container. Coolant should be reused unless it is contaminated or several years old.*

3. Remove the air cleaner.

4. Tag and disconnect all wires, hoses and cables which are in the way of manifold removal.

5. Remove the coolant bypass pipe.

6. Unbolt and remove the manifold.

7. Installation is in the reverse order of removal.

2T-C, 3T-C and 3E

1. Drain the cooling system.

CAUTION: *When draining the coolant, keep in mind that cats and dogs are attracted by the ethylene glycol antifreeze, and are quite likely to drink any that is left in an uncovered container or in puddles on the ground. This will prove fatal in sufficient quantity. Always drain the coolant into a sealable container. Coolant should be reused unless it is contaminated or several years old.*

2. Remove the air cleaner assembly, complete with hoses, from its bracket.

3. Remove the choke stove hoses, fuel lines, and vacuum lines from the carburetor. Unfasten the emission control system wiring, hoses, and the accelerator linkage from it.

4. Unfasten the four nuts which secure the carburetor to the manifold and remove the carburetor.

5. Remove the mixture control valve line from its intake manifold fitting (1971-74).

6. Disconnect the PCV hose.

7. Disconnect the water by-pass hose from the intake manifold.

8. Unbolt and remove the manifold.

9. Installation is performed in the reverse order of removal. Remember to use new gaskets. Tighten the intake manifold bolts to the specifications given in the Torque Specification chart.

NOTE: *Tighten the bolts, in several stages, working from the inside out.*

4A-GE
3E

Note: *Refer to cylinder head removal and installation.*

1. Disconnect the negative battery cable. Drain the coolant. Remove the air cleaner assembly.

CAUTION: *When draining the coolant, keep in mind that cats and dogs are attracted by the ethylene glycol antifreeze, and are quite likely to drink any that is left in an uncovered container or in puddles on the ground. This will prove fatal in sufficient quantity. Always drain the coolant into a sealable container. Coolant should be reused unless it is contaminated or several years old.*

2. Tag (for identification) and disconnect wires, hoses and cables that will interfere with manifold removal.

3. Remove the necessary components in or-

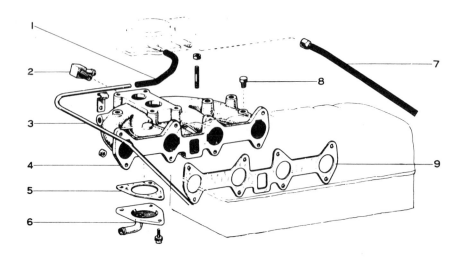

1. Choke stove intake hose
2. Elbow
3. Choke stove intake
4. Intake manifold
5. Gasket
6. Water by-pass outlet
7. Choke stove outlet
8. Plug
9. Intake manifold gasket

2T-C and 3T-C intake manifold assembly

der to gain access to the intake manifold mounting bolts.

4. Remove the carburetor assembly. Remove the water hose from the intake manifold.

5. Remove the intake manifold, starting with the outside mounting bolts, and working your way to the center. Clean all gasket mounting surfaces. Install in the reverse order of removal using a new intake manifold mounting gasket. Tighten the mounting bolts from the center outward to 18 ft.lb.

Exhaust Manifold

REMOVAL AND INSTALLATION

1C-L

1. Disconnect the negative battery cable.
2. Raise and support the vehicle on jackstands.
3. Remove the gravel shield from underneath the engine.
4. Remove the downpipe support bracket.
5. Unscrew the bolts from the exhaust flange

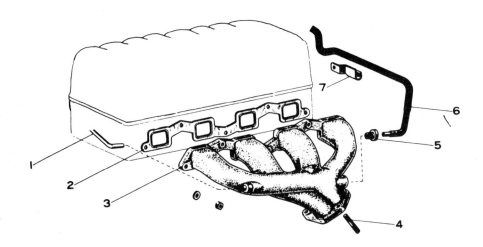

1. Automatic choke stove intake pipe
2. Exhaust manifold gasket
3. Exhaust manifold
4. Stud
5. Union
6. Automatic choke stove outlet
7. Clamp

2T-C and 3T-C exhaust manifold assembly

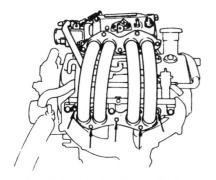

Remove the air intake chamber and pipes as an assembly

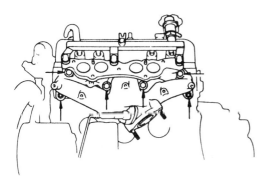

The combination manifold is mounted with six bolts

and then detach the downpipe from the manifold.

6. Loosen the manifold retaining bolts.

CAUTION: *Always remove and tighten the manifold bolts in two or three stages, starting from the inside and working out.*

7. Installation is in the reverse order of removal. Always use a new gasket and tighten the retaining bolts to the proper specifications.

2T-C and 3T-C

CAUTION: *Do not perform this operation on a warm or hot engine!*

1. Detach the manifold heat stove intake pipe.

2. Unfasten the nut on the stove outlet pipe union.

3. Remove the wiring from the emission control system thermosensor.

4. Unfasten the U-bolt from the downpipe bracket.

5. Unfasten the downpipe flange from the manifold.

6. In order to remove the manifold, unfasten the manifold retaining bolts.

NOTE: *Remove the bolts in two or three stages and starting from the inside working out.*

7. Installation of the manifold is performed in the reverse order of removal. Remember to

use a new gasket. See the Torque Specifications chart for the proper tightening torque.

4A-GE Series

1. Disconnect the negative battery cable. Raise and safely support the vehicle. Remove the right side gravel shield.

2. Disconnect the exhaust pipe from the manifold after removing the support bracket. Disconnect the oxygen sensor connector.

3. Lower the vehicle and remove the mounting bolts and exhaust manifold. Install in the reverse order of removal. Torque the manifold mounting (from center outwards) to 18 ft.lb.

Combination Manifold

REMOVAL AND INSTALLATION

CAUTION: *Do not perform this procedure on a warm engine!*

3K-C and 4K-C

1. Remove the air cleaner assembly, complete with hoses.

2. Disconnect the accelerator and choke linkages from the carburetor, as well as the fuel and vacuum lines.

3. Remove, or move aside, any of the emission control system components which are in the way.

4. Unfasten the retaining bolts and remove the carburetor from the manifold.

5. Loosen the manifold retaining nuts, working form the inside out, in two or three stages.

6. Remove the intake/exhaust manifold assembly from the cylinder head as a complete unit.

7. Installation is performed in the reverse order of removal. Always use new gaskets. Tighten the bolts, working from the inside out, to the specifications given in the Torque Specifications chart.

NOTE: *Tighten the bolts in two or three stages.*

4K-E

1. Loosen the two hose clamps and remove the air cleaner hose.

2. Disconnect the throttle cable from its two attachment points on the air intake chamber and the throttle body. Position the cable out of the way.

3. Tag and disconnect all vacuum hoses leading from the air intake chamber.

4. Tag and disconnect the three electrical leads attached to the air intake chamber.

5. Unscrew and remove the two air intake chamber support brackets. Remove the air intake pipe-to-manifold retaining bolts and lift off

the air intake chamber and pipes as an assembly.

CAUTION: *The air intake assembly must be supported while removing the pipe retaining bolts!*

6. Tag and disconnect the four injector wires. Remove the two wiring harness clamps and then remove the EFI solenoid wiring harness from the delivery pipe.

7. Disconnect the heater outlet hoses. Remove the two bracket set bolts and remove the pipe.

8. Disconnect the exhaust pipe from the exhaust manifold.

9. Remove the six mounting bolts and then remove the combination manifold.

10. Installation is in the reverse order of removal.

1A-C, 3A, 3A-C, 4A-C and 4A-LC

1. Disconnect the negative battery terminal.

2. Remove the air cleaner and all necessary hoses.

3. Remove all the carburetor linkages.

4. Remove the carburetor.

NOTE: *Cover the carburetor with a clean towel to prevent dirt from entering it.*

5. Remove the exhaust manifold pipe.

6. Remove the manifold.

7. Installation is the reverse of removal. Tighten the manifold bolts to 15-21 ft.lb.

Cylinder Head

REMOVAL AND INSTALLATION

3K-C and 4K-C

CAUTION: *Do not perform this operation on a warm engine!*

1. Disconnect the battery and drain the cooling system.

CAUTION: *When draining the coolant, keep in mind that cats and dogs are attracted by the ethylene glycol antifreeze, and are quite likely to drink any that is left in an uncovered container or in puddles on the ground. This will prove fatal in sufficient quantity. Always drain the coolant into a sealable container. Coolant should be reused unless it is contaminated or several years old.*

2. Remove the air cleaner assembly from its bracket, complete with its attendant hoses.

3. Disconnect the hoses from the air injection system (1970-71) or the vacuum switching valve lines (1972-74).

4. Detach the accelerator cable from its support on the cylinder head cover and also from the carburetor throttle arm.

5. Remove the choke cable and fuel lines from the carburetor.

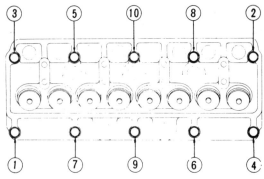

Cylinder head loosening sequence—K-series engines

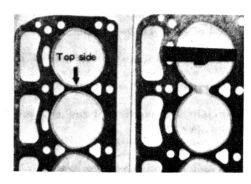

Identification of the 3K-C, 4K-C head gasket top side

6. Remove the water hose bracket from the cylinder head cover.

7. Unfasten the water hose clamps and remove the hoses from the water pump and the water valve. Detach the heater temperature control cable from the water valve.

8. Disconnect the PCV line from the cylinder head cover.

9. Unbolt and remove the valve cover.

10. Remove the valve rocker support securing bolts and nuts. Lift out the valve rocker assembly.

11. Withdraw the pushrods from their bores.

CAUTION: *Keep the pushrods in their original order.*

12. Unfasten the hose clamps and remove the upper radiator hose from the water outlet.

13. Tag and disconnect the wires from the spark plugs.

14. Disconnect the wiring and the fluid line from the windshield washer assembly. Remove the assembly.

NOTE: *Use a clean container to catch the fluid from the windshield washer reservoir when disconnect its fluid line.*

15. Unfasten the exhaust pipe flange from the exhaust manifold.

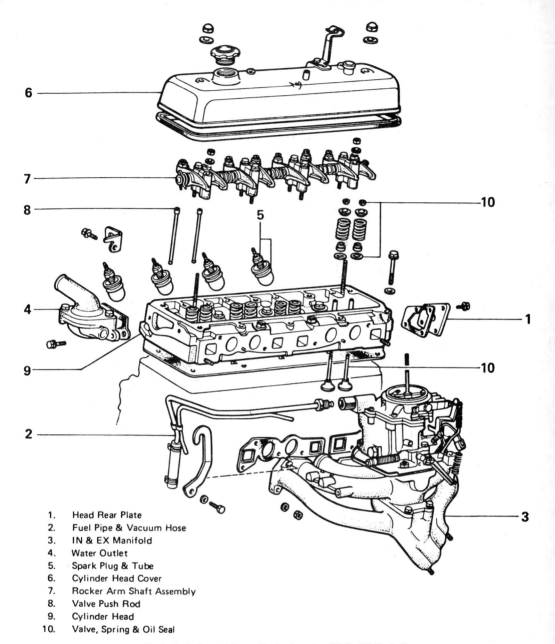

1. Head Rear Plate
2. Fuel Pipe & Vacuum Hose
3. IN & EX Manifold
4. Water Outlet
5. Spark Plug & Tube
6. Cylinder Head Cover
7. Rocker Arm Shaft Assembly
8. Valve Push Rod
9. Cylinder Head
10. Valve, Spring & Oil Seal

Exploded view of the cylinder head—4K-C; 3K-C similar

16. Remove the head assembly retaining bolts and remove the head from the engine.

NOTE: *Remove the head bolts in the sequence illustrated and in two or three stages.*

17. Place the cylinder head on wooden blocks to prevent damage to it.

18. Installation is essentially the reverse order of removal. Clean both the cylinder head and block gasket mounting surfaces. Always use a new head gasket.

NOTE: *Be sure that the top side of the gasket is facing upward (see the illustration). When installing the head on the block, be sure to*

tighten the bolts in the sequence shown (see *Torque Sequences*), in several stages, to the torque specified in the *Torque Specifications* chart. The valve clearance should be adjusted to specification with each piston at top dead center (TDC) of its compression stroke.

4K-E

1. Disconnect the negative battery cable.

2. Drain the engine coolant into a suitable container.

CAUTION: *When draining the coolant, keep in mind that cats and dogs are attracted by*

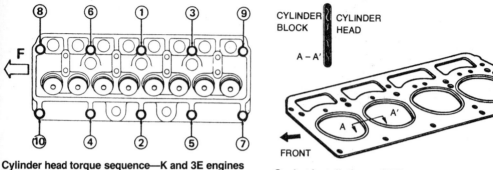

Cylinder head torque sequence—K and 3E engines

Gasket installation—4K-E

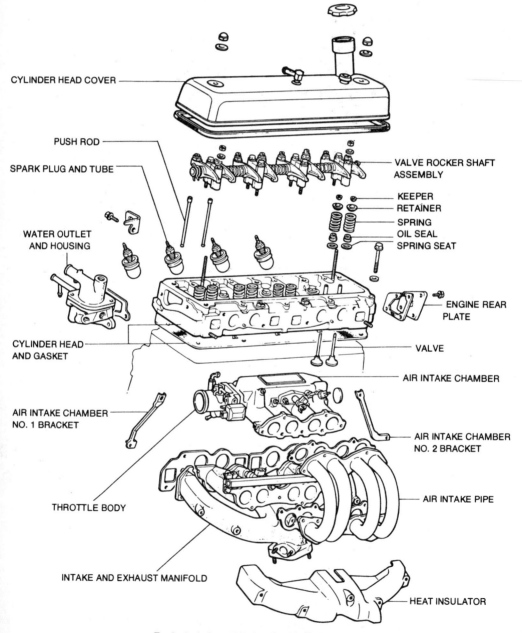

Exploded view of the cylinder head—4K-E

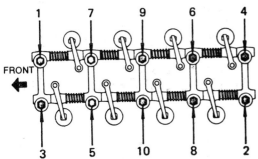

Cylinder head loosening sequence—T-series engines

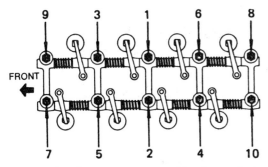

Cylinder head torque sequence—T-series engines

the ethylene glycol antifreeze, and are quite likely to drink any that is left in an uncovered container or in puddles on the ground. This will prove fatal in sufficient quantity. Always drain the coolant into a sealable container. Coolant should be reused unless it is contaminated or several years old.

3. Loosen the two hose clamps and remove the air cleaner hose.

4. Disconnect the throttle cable from the two places it attaches to the air intake chamber and the throttle body.

5. Tag and disconnect the four vacuum hoses connected to the air intake chamber. Do the same for the spark plug wires, the temperature detect switch wire and the water temperature sender gauge wire.

6. Tag and disconnect all remaining wires, hoses and leads attached to the cylinder head or which might interfere with its removal.

7. Remove the spark plugs and tube.

8. Remove the intake and exhaust manifolds as detailed in the appropriate section.

9. Remove the cylinder head cover and then remove the rocker shaft assembly as detailed in the appropriate section.

10. Lift out the pushrods.

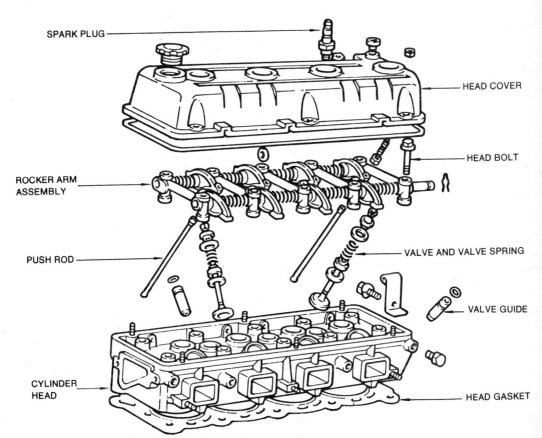

Exploded view of the cylinder head—3T-C; 2T-C similar

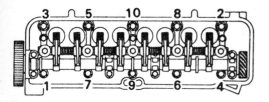

Cylinder head loosening sequence—A-series engines

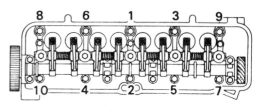

Cylinder head torque sequence—A-series engines

NOTE: *Make sure that the pushrods remain in the correct order.*

11. Little-by-little, in the proper sequence, loosen the cylinder head bolts (see illustration under 4K-C procedure).

CAUTION: *Head warpage or cracking could result from removing the bolts in the wrong order!*

12. Lift the cylinder head from the dowels on the block and place it on wooden blocks.

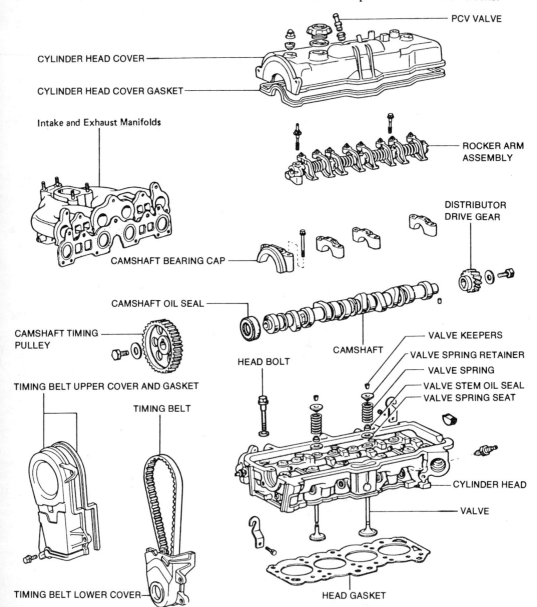

Exploded view of the cylinder head—A-series engines

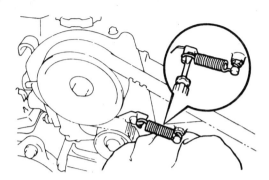

Use a small screwdriver to remove the tension spring

NOTE: *If the head is difficult to remove, carefully pry with a small prybar between the head and the block. Be very careful not to damage the cylinder head and/or block surfaces.*

13. Installation is in the reverse order of removal. Clean the cylinder head and block gasket mounting surfaces.

NOTE: *Install the cylinder head gasket as illustrated. The cylinder head bolts should be torqued in the proper sequence (see 4K-C procedure), to the proper specifications. Adjust the valves.*

2T-C, 3T-C Engine

CAUTION: *Do not perform this operation on a warm engine!*

1. Perform Steps 1-2 of the 3K-C Head Removal procedure.

2. Disconnect the vacuum lines which run from the vacuum switching valve to the various emission control devices mounted on the cylinder head. Disconnect the air injection system lines on engines so equipped.

3. Disconnect the mixture control valve hose which runs to the intake manifold and remove the valve from its mounting bracket (1971-74).

4. Perform Step 7 of the 3K-C Engine Removal procedure.

5. Detach the water temperature sender wiring.

6. Remove the choke stove pipe and its intake pipe.

7. Remove the PCV hose from the intake manifold.

8. Disconnect the fuel and vacuum lines from the carburetor.

9. Remove the clutch hydraulic line bracket from the cylinder head.

10. Raise the car and support it with jackstands. Unfasten the exhaust pipe clamp. Remove the exhaust manifold from the cylinder head (see below).

11. Label and disconnect the spark plug leads. Remove the valve cover.

12. Remove the cylinder head bolts in the sequence illustrated.

CAUTION: *Remove the bolts in stages; not one at a time.*

13. Perform Steps 10-11 of the 3K-C, 4K-C Engine Removal procedure.

14. Remove the cylinder head, complete with the intake manifold.

15. Separate the intake manifold from the cylinder head.

Install the cylinder head in the following order:

1. Clean the gasket mounting surfaces of the cylinder head and the block completely.

NOTE: *Remove oil from the cylinder head bolt holes, if present.*

2. Place a new gasket on the block and install the head assembly.

CAUTION: *Do not slide the cylinder head across the block, as there are locating pins on the block!*

3. Install the pushrods and the valve rocker assembly.

4. Tighten the cylinder head bolts evenly, in stages, as illustrated in the Torque Sequence diagrams. See the Torque Specifications chart for the proper tightening torque.

5. Install the intake manifold, using a new gasket and tighten it to specifications.

6. The rest of the installation procedure is the reversal of removal. Remember to adjust the valve clearances.

1A-C, 3A, 3A-C, 4A-C and 4A-LC

1. Disconnect the negative battery terminal.

2. Remove the exhaust pipe from the manifold.

3. Drain the cooling system. Save the coolant as it can be reused.

CAUTION: *When draining the coolant, keep in mind that cats and dogs are attracted by the ethylene glycol antifreeze, and are quite likely to drink any that is left in an uncovered container or in puddles on the ground. This will prove fatal in sufficient quantity. Always drain the coolant into a sealable container. Coolant should be reused unless it is contaminated or several years old.*

4. Remove the air cleaner and all necessary hoses.

5. Mark all vacuum lines for easy installation and then remove them.

6. Remove all linkage from the carburetor, fuel lines, etc., from the head and manifold.

7. Remove the fuel pump.

NOTE: *Before removing the carburetor cover it with a clean rag to prevent dirt from entering it.*

8. Remove the carburetor.

9. Remove the manifold.

10. Remove the valve cover.

11. Note the position of the spark plug wires and remove them.

12. Remove the spark plugs.

13. Set the engine on No. 1 cylinder top dead center. This is accomplished by removing the No.1 spark plug, placing your finger over the hole and then turning the crankshaft pulley until you feel pressure exerted against your finger.

CAUTION: *Do not put your finger into the spark plug hole!*

14. Remove the crankshaft pulley with an appropriate puller.

15. Remove the water pump pulley.

16. Remove the top and bottom timing chain cover.

17. Matchmark the camshaft pulley and timing belt for reassembly (see Timing Belt Removal procedure).

18. Loosen the belt tensioner.

19. Remove the water pump.

20. Remove the timing belt. Do not bend, twist, or turn the belt inside out.

NOTE: *Check the belt for wear, cracks, or glazing. Once the belt is removed it is a good idea to replace it with a new one even though it is not necessary.*

21. Remove the rocker arm bolts and remove the rocker arms.

22. Remove the camshaft as detailed later in this chapter.

23. Loosen the head bolts in the proper order to prevent warping of the head.

24. Lift the head directly up. Do not attempt to slide it off.

25. Installation is the reverse of removal.

NOTE: *When replacing the head, always use a new gasket. Also replace the camshaft seal, making sure to grease the lip before installation. The following torques are needed for installation: cam bearing caps 8-10 ft.lb., cam sprocket 29-39 ft.lb., crankshaft pulley 55-61 ft.lb., manifold bolts 15-21 ft.lb., rocker arm bolts 17-19 ft.lb., timing gear idler bolt 22-32 ft.lb., belt tension 0.24-0.28". Adjust the valves to the proper clearances.*

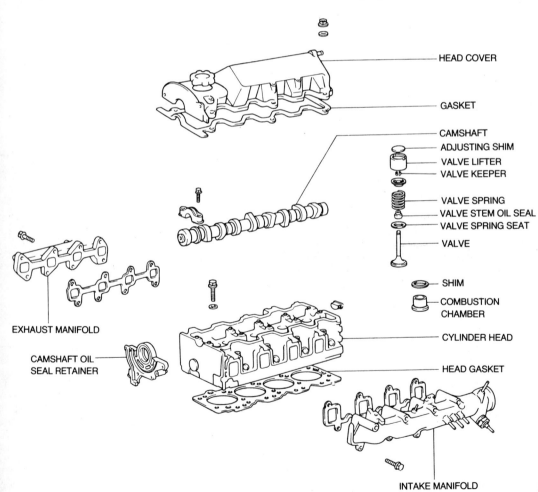

HEAD COVER

GASKET

CAMSHAFT

ADJUSTING SHIM

VALVE LIFTER

VALVE KEEPER

VALVE SPRING

VALVE STEM OIL SEAL

VALVE SPRING SEAT

VALVE

SHIM

COMBUSTION CHAMBER

CYLINDER HEAD

HEAD GASKET

EXHAUST MANIFOLD

CAMSHAFT OIL SEAL RETAINER

INTAKE MANIFOLD

Exploded view of the cylinder head—1C-L diesel engine

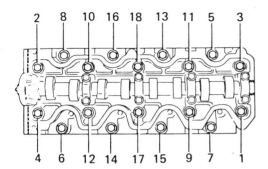

Cylinder head bolt loosening sequence—1C-L diesel engine

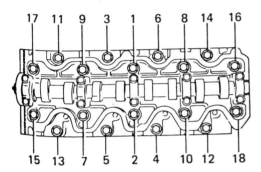

Cylinder head torque sequence—1C-L diesel engine

1C-L Diesel Engine

1. Disconnect the negative battery cable.
2. Drain the coolant. If you are on a tight budget, you'll probably want to save and reuse the old coolant.

CAUTION: *When draining the coolant, keep in mind that cats and dogs are attracted by the ethylene glycol antifreeze, and are quite likely to drink any that is left in an uncovered container or in puddles on the ground. This will prove fatal in sufficient quantity. Always drain the coolant into a sealable container. Coolant should be reused unless it is contaminated or several years old.*

3. Remove the engine undercover and then drain the oil-you can't save this no matter how tight your budget is.
4. Disconnect the exhaust pipe from the manifold.
5. Disconnect the air inlet hose.
6. On models equipped with an automatic transmission, disconnect the accelerator and throttle cables from the injection pump.
7. Disconnect the water inlet hose and then remove the inlet pipe.
8. Disconnect the two heater hoses.
9. Remove the EGR valve and its pipe.
10. Tag and disconnect all wires and cables

which might interfere with cylinder head removal.
11. Disconnect the water bypass hose from the cylinder head union.
12. Disconnect the fuel hoses from the fuel pipe.
13. Remove the clamp and then disconnect the injection pipe.
14. Disconnect the fuel return hose at the injection pump. Remove the four locknuts and then remove the return pipe.
15. Remove the current sensor and then remove the glow plugs.
16. Use special tool 09268064010 to remove the injectors. Don't lose the injection seats and gaskets.

NOTE: *Arrange the injector holders in the proper order.*

17. Remove the No. 2 timing belt cover and its gasket.
18. Turn the crankshaft clockwise and set the No. 1 cylinder at TDC of the compression stroke. Place matchmarks on the camshaft timing pulley, the injection pump pulley and the timing belt.
19. Remove the tension spring. Loosen the No. 1 idler pulley mounting bolt and push it aside. Remove the timing belt from the gear.

CAUTION: *DO NOT pinch the tension spring with pliers or the like!*

20. Loosen the mounting bolt and remove the camshaft gear.
21. Support the timing belt so it doesn't slip a tooth.

CAUTION: *Be very careful not to drop anything into the timing cover. Make sure that the timing belt does not touch oil, water or dust!*

22. Remove the cylinder head cover and the oil level gauge guide clamp.
23. Loosen the remove the cylinder head bolts in two or three stages, in the order shown in the illustration.
24. The cylinder head is positioned by means of dowels—lift it straight upward when removing it. Never attempt to slide it off the block.
25. Installation is in the reverse order of removal. Tighten the cylinder head bolts in two or three stages, in the sequence illustrated. Refer to the Timing Belt Removal and Installation procedure when installing the belt.

NOTE: *When replacing the cylinder head, always use a new gasket. It's also a good idea to replace the camshaft oil seal, making sure to grease the lip before installation.*

26. Note the following tightening torques: Cylinder head bolts: 64 ft.lb. Cylinder head cover nuts: 65 in.lb. Camshaft gear bolt: 22 ft.lb. Idler pulley set bolt: 27 ft.lb. Injectors: 47 ft.lb. Glow plugs: 9 ft. lbs.

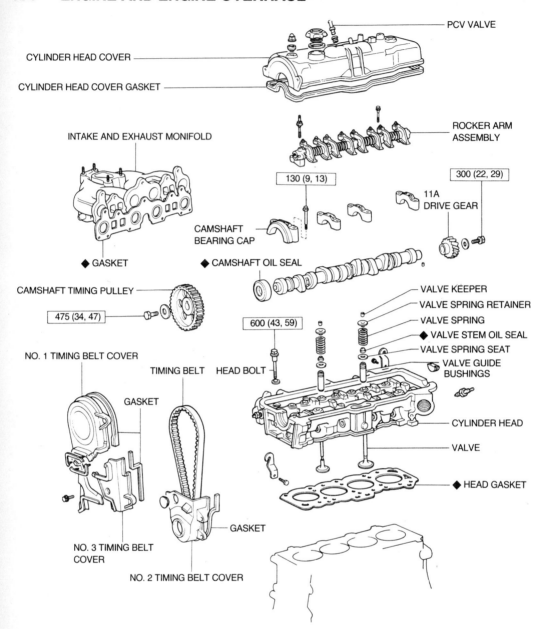

PCV VALVE

CYLINDER HEAD COVER

CYLINDER HEAD COVER GASKET

INTAKE AND EXHAUST MONIFOLD

ROCKER ARM ASSEMBLY

130 (9, 13)

300 (22, 29)

11A DRIVE GEAR

CAMSHAFT BEARING CAP

◆ GASKET

◆ CAMSHAFT OIL SEAL

CAMSHAFT TIMING PULLEY

475 (34, 47)

600 (43, 59)

VALVE KEEPER

VALVE SPRING RETAINER

VALVE SPRING

◆ VALVE STEM OIL SEAL

VALVE SPRING SEAT

VALVE GUIDE BUSHINGS

NO. 1 TIMING BELT COVER

TIMING BELT   HEAD BOLT

GASKET

CYLINDER HEAD

VALVE

◆ HEAD GASKET

NO. 3 TIMING BELT COVER

GASKET

NO. 2 TIMING BELT COVER

KG-CM (FT-LB, N·M) : SPECIFIED TORQUE

◆ NON-REUSABLE PART

Cylinder head assembly—4A-C

3E

1. Disconnect the negative battery cable. Remove the right side under engine splash shield.
2. Drain the engine coolant from the radiator.

CAUTION: *When draining the coolant, keep in mind that cats and dogs are attracted by the ethylene glycol antifreeze, and are quite likely to drink any that is left in an uncovered container or in puddles on the ground. This will prove fatal in sufficient quantity. Always drain the coolant into a sealable container. Coolant should be reused unless it is contaminated or several years old.*

3. Remove the power steering pump and bracket (if equipped).
4. If equipped with AC, but not power steering, remove the idler pulley/bracket.

5. Disconnect the radiator hoses. Disconnect the accelerator and throttle valve cable linkage from the carburetor.

6. Remove the timing belt and camshaft timing pulley.

7. Disconnect the heater inlet hose. Disconnect and plug the fuel lines.

8. Disconnect the power brake booster vacuum line from the intake manifold.

9. Disconnect the water inlet hose. Disconnect the intake manifold water hose from the intake manifold.

10. Tag (for identification) all vacuum lines, hoses and wires or harnesses to the intake manifold and cylinder head and disconnect them.

11. Remove the evaporative valve and cold enrichment valve.

12. Disconnect the water by-pass hoses from the carburetor.

13. Disconnect the exhaust pipe from the exhaust manifold.

14. Remove the intake manifold stay bracket and ground strap. Remove the engine wire harness bracket clamp from the intake manifold.

15. Remove the cylinder head cover.

16. Loosen and remove the head mounting bolts gradually in three passes working from the ends of the cylinder head inward.

17. Lift the head straight up from the engine block.

18. Clean all gasket surfaces.

19. Service as necessary. Install in the reverse order of removal. Install a new cylinder head gasket. Torque the cylinder head mounting bolts in three progressive steps. Torque to 22 ft.lb. in the first pass. 36 ft. lb. in the second pass, and finally for the third pass, tighten the head bolts an additional 90° from the second pass. Tighten the bolts in sequence from the center of the head outwards.

20. Adjust the valves by turning the crankshaft pulley until the groove in the pulley is aligned with the 0 mark on the timing belt cover. Check that No. 1 cylinder rocker arms are loose and No. 4 rocker arms are tight. If not, turn the engine one complete revolution and align the marks again. Adjust cold to 0.007". Turn one complete revolution and adjust the remaining valves (see illustrations). Complete installation, start the engine and check ignition timing and carburetor adjustments.

4A-GE Series

1. Disconnect the negative battery cable. Remove the engine undercover. Drain the coolant and engine oil.

CAUTION: *When draining the coolant, keep in mind that cats and dogs are attracted by the ethylene glycol antifreeze, and are quite likely to drink any that is left in an uncovered*

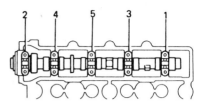

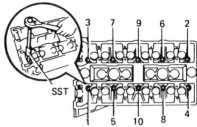

(upper)Loosen the camshaft bearing caps in this order—4A-GE (lower) Cylinder head bolt removal sequence—4A-GE

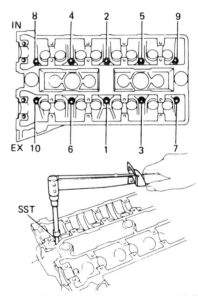

Cylinder head bolt tightening sequence—4A-GE

container or in puddles on the ground. This will prove fatal in sufficient quantity. Always drain the coolant into a sealable container. Coolant should be reused unless it is contaminated or several years old.

2. Loosen the retaining clamp and then disconnect the No. 1 air cleaner hose from the throttle body. Disconnect the actuator and accelerator cables from the mounting bracket on the throttle body.

3. If the vehicle is equipped with power steering, remove the pump (with hoses attached) and the mounting bracket and position to the side.

4. Loosen the water pump pulley set nuts.

Remove the drive belt adjusting bolt and remove the drive belt. Remove the pulley set nuts and remove the fluid coupling with the fan and water pump pulley.

5. Disconnect the upper radiator hose at the water outlet on the cylinder head. Disconnect the two heater hoses at the water bypass pipe and at the cylinder head rear plate.

6. Remove the distributor. Remove the cold start injector pipe and the PCV hose from the cylinder head.

7. Remove the pulsation damper from the delivery pipe. Disconnect the fuel return hose from the pressure regulator.

8. Tag (for identification) and disconnect all vacuum hoses which may interfere with cylinder head removal. Remove the wiring harness and the vacuum pipe from the No. 3 timing cover. Tag (for identification) and disconnect all wires which might interfere with cylinder head removal. Position the wiring harness to one side.

9. Disconnect the exhaust bracket from the exhaust pipe, and disconnect the exhaust pipe from the manifold.

10. Remove the vacuum tank and the VCV valve. Remove the exhaust manifold.

11. Remove the water outlet housing from the cylinder head with the No. 1 bypass pipe and gasket. Pull the bypass pipe out of the housing.

12. Remove the fuel delivery pipe along with the fuel injectors. When removing the delivery pipe, be very careful not to drop or bump the fuel injector nozzles. Do not remove the injector cover.

13. Remove the intake manifold stay bracket. Remove the intake manifold along with the air control valve.

14. Remove the cylinder head covers and gaskets. Remove the spark plugs.

15. Rotate the crankshaft until the groove on the crank pulley is aligned with the timing mark (0) on the N0. 1 timing cover. Check that the valve lifters on No. 1 cylinder are loose. If not, rotate the engine, once again aligning the marks and checking the lifters. Remove the timing covers and gaskets.

16. Place matchmarks on the timing belt and two timing pulleys. Loosen the idler pulley bolts and move the pulley to the left as far as it will go. Tighten a pulley bolt to keep it in position.

17. Remove the timing belt from the camshaft pulleys. Support the belt during removal so that it does not turn the pulleys out of position. Take care not to drop anything in to the timing cases. Do not allow the timing belt to come into contact with dirt or grease.

18. Lock the camshafts in position (a flat in the center of each shaft is provided for holding it in position with a suitable wrench) and remove the pulleys. Remove the No.4 timing belt cover.

19. It is now possible to check camshaft end play , if desired. Mount a dial indicator so that the probe is zeroed and resting against the nose of the camshaft. Move the camshaft back and forth and measure play. Maximum play allowed is 0.0118". Replace the thrust bearing if necessary.

20. Loosen each camshaft bearing cap a little at a time starting from each end and working toward the center. Remove the caps, oil seal and camshafts.

21. Use a suitable socket tool (SST 09205-16010 or equivalent), and loosen the head bolts in stages, starting from the ends and working toward the center.

22. Remove the cylinder head from the vehicle. Clean all block and head gasket mounting surfaces. Service the head as required.

23. Position the cylinder head a new gasket in position. Lightly coat the mounting bolts with engine oil. Install the short bolts on the intake side, and the long bolts on the exhaust side. Starting at the center of the cylinder head and working outward, tighten the cylinder head bolts gradually in three stages. The final torque value should be 45 ft.lb.

24. Position the camshafts on the head. Position the bearing caps over the camshaft (arrows pointing forward).

25. Tighten each bearing cap bolt in stages, starting from the center outwards. Tighten to 9 ft.lb. Recheck endplay.

26. Use a suitable driver tool and carefully drive new oil seals into position. Install the No. 4 timing cover.

27. Install the timing pulleys onto the camshafts. Make sure the pins and matchmarks are in the correct position. Lock the camshafts in position and tighten the pulley mounting bolts to 34 ft.lb.

28. Align the matchmarks made during removal and install the timing belt. Loosen the bolt that is holding the idler pulley in position. Be sure that the pulleys have not been moved when installing the belt.

29. Rotate the engine two complete revolutions (from TDC to TDC; 0 to 0). Make sure that the matchmarks align. If not, the timing is wrong. If necessary, shift the belt to pulley meshing to correct mark misalignment. Repeat Step 28.

30. Tighten the idler pulley bolts to 27 ft.lb. Measure the timing belt deflection at the top span between the two camshaft pulleys. Deflection should be no more that 0.16" at 4.4 lbs. of pressure. If deflection is not correct, adjust by

increasing or decreasing idler pulley pressure. Install the remaining components in the reverse order of removal.

CHECKING ENGINE COMPRESSION

A noticeable lack of engine power, excessive oil consumption and/or poor fuel mileage measured over an extended period are all indicators of internal engine wear. Worn piston rings, scored and worn cylinder bores, blown head gaskets, sticking or burnt valves and worn valve seats are all possible culprits here. A check of each cylinder's compression will help you locate the problems.

As mentioned in the Tools and Equipment section of Chapter 1, a screw-in compression gauge is more accurate than the type you simply hold against the spark plug hole, although it takes slightly longer to use (it's worth it). To check compression:

1. Warm the engine up to operating temperature.

2. Disconnect the fuel-cut solenoid wire on the 1C-L.

3. Remove all four spark plugs (gasoline engines). Remove all four glow plugs (diesel engines).

4. Disconnect the high tension wire from the ignition coil (gasoline engines only).

5. Screw the compression gauge into the No. 1 spark plug hole (or glow plug hole) until the fitting is snug. Be very careful not to cross-thread the hole, as the head is aluminum.

6. Fully open the throttle either by operating the carburetor throttle linkage by hand, or on fuel injected cars having an assistant floor the accelerator pedal (gasoline engines only).

7. Ask your assistant to crank the engine a few times using the ignition switch.

8. Record the highest reading on the gauge, and compare it to the compression specifications in the Tune-Up Specifications chart in this chapter. The specs listed are maximum, and a cylinder is usually acceptable if its compression is within about 20 pounds of maximum.

9. Repeat the procedure for the remaining cylinders, recording each cylinder's compression. The difference between each cylinder should be no more than 14 pounds on gasoline engines, 71 pounds on the diesel engine. If a cylinder is unusually low, pour a tablespoon of clear engine oil into the cylinder through the spark plug (glow plug) hole and repeat the compression test. If the compression comes up after adding the oil, it appears that cylinder's piston rings or bore are damaged or worn. If the pressure remains low, the valves may not be seating

properly (a valve job is needed) or the head gasket may be blown near that cylinder.

CLEANING AND INSPECTION

When the rocker assembly and valve train have been removed from the cylinder head (see Valves and Springs below), set the head on two wooden blocks on the bench, combustion chamber side up. Use a scraper or putty knife, and carefully scrape away any gasket material that may have stuck to the head-to-block mating surface when the head was removed. Make sure you DO NOT gouge the mating surface with the tool.

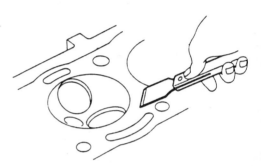

Do not scratch the head mating surface when removing old gasket material

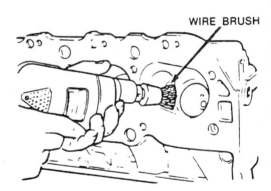

Removing combustion chamber carbon; make sure it is removed and not merely burnished

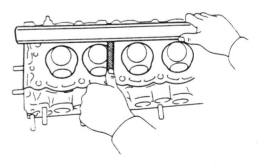

Check head mating surface straightness with a precision straight-edge and a feeler gauge

Use a wire brush chucked into your electric drill, remove the carbon in each combustion chamber. Make sure the brush is actually removing the carbon and not merely burnishing it.

Clean all the valve guides using a valve guide brush (available at most auto parts or auto tool shops) and solvent. A fine-bristled rifle bore cleaning brush also works here.

Inspect the threads of each spark plug hole by screwing a plug into each, making sure it screws down completely. Heli-coil® any plug hole that is damaged.

CAUTION: *DO NOT hot tank the cylinder head! The head material on most engines is aluminum, which is ruined if subjected to the hot tank solution!*

NOTE: *Before hot-tanking any overhead cam head, check with the machine shop doing the work. Some cam bearings are easily damaged by the hot tank solution.*

Finally, go over the entire head with a clean shop rag soaked in solvent to remove any grit, old gasket particles, etc. Blow out the bolt holes, coolant galleys, intake and exhaust ports, valve guides and plug holes with compressed air.

RESURFACING

While the head is removed, check the head-to-block mating surface for straightness. If the

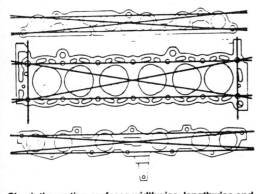

Check the mating surfaces widthwise, lengthwise and diagonally

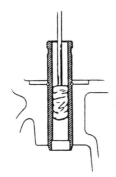

Cleaning the valve guides

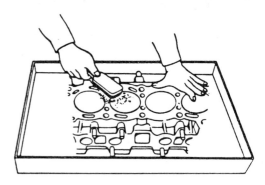

Wire brush the top of the block

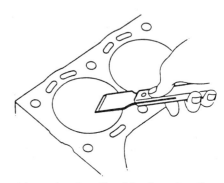

Removing carbon from the piston tops; do not scratch the pistons

engine has overheated and blown a head gasket, this must be done as a matter of course. A warped mating surface must be resurfaced (milled); this is done on a milling machine and is quite similar to planing a piece of wood.

Use a precision steel straightedge and a blade-type feeler gauge, and check the surface of the head across its length, width and diagonal length as shown in the illustrations. Check the intake and exhaust manifold mating surfaces. If head warpage exceeds 0.003″, in a 6″ span, or 0.006″, over the total length, the head must be milled. If warpage is highly excessive, the head must be replaced. Again, consult the machine shop operator on head milling limitations.

CYLINDER BLOCK CLEANING

When the cylinder head is removed, the top of the cylinder block and pistons must be cleaned. Before you begin, rotate the crankshaft until one or more pistons are flush with the top of the block (on the four cylinder engines, you will either have Nos. 1 and 4 up, or Nos. 2 and 3 up). Carefully stuff clean rags into the cylinders in which the pistons are down. This will help keep grit and carbon chips out during cleaning. Use care not to gouge or scratch the block-to-head mating surface and the piston top(s), clean away any old gasket material with a wire brush and/or scraper. On the piston tops, make sure you are actually removing the carbon and not merely burnishing it.

Remove the rags from the down cylinders after you have wiped the top of the block with a solvent soaked rag. Rotate the crankshaft until the other pistons come up flush with the top of the block, and clean those pistons.

NOTE: *Because you have rotated the crankshaft, you will have to re-time the engine following the procedure listed under the Timing Chain/Timing Belt removal.*

Make sure you wipe out each cylinder thoroughly with a solvent soaked rag, to remove all traces of grit, before the head is reassembled to the block.

Valves and Springs

REMOVAL AND INSTALLATION

1. Remove the cylinder head and rocker arm shafts (gasoline engines only) as detailed previously in this chapter. On the diesel engine, remove the camshaft as detailed later in this chapter. Lift out the valve lifter and any accompanying shims.

NOTE: *Always be sure to keep the diesel valve lifters and shims in the proper order.*

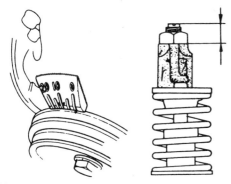

Make sure that each adjustment screw has the same reserve height—4K-E engines

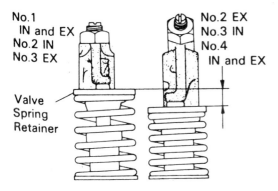

No.1
 IN and EX
No.2 IN
No.3 EX

No.2 EX
No.3 IN
No.4
 IN and EX

Valve
Spring
Retainer

Half the valves should be positioned lower than the others—4K-E engines

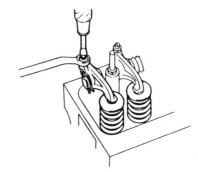

Tighten the locknut while holding the adjusting screw—4K-E engines

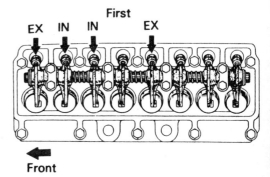

First

EX IN IN EX

Front

Adjust these valves first on the 4K-E engine

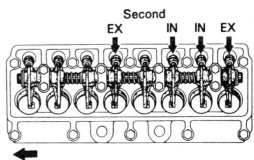

Second

EX IN IN EX

Front

Adjust these valves second on the 4K-E engine

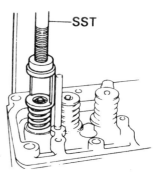

SST

Use a valve spring compressor to remove the keepers—gasoline engines

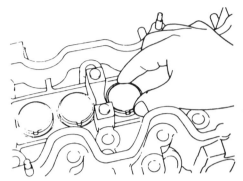

Removing the valve lifter—1C-L diesel engine

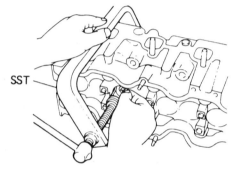

SST

Removing the valve spring—1C-L diesel engine

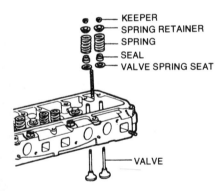

KEEPER
SPRING RETAINER
SPRING
SEAL
VALVE SPRING SEAT

VALVE

Typical valve and related components

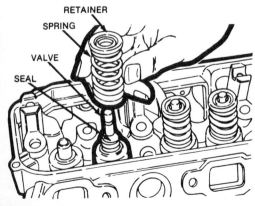

RETAINER
SPRING
VALVE
SEAL

Installing the valve

2. Using a valve spring compressor, compress the spring and remove the keeper.

3. Lift off the spring retainer and the spring.

4. Pull off the valve oil seal and the lower spring seat. Remove the valve through the bottom of the cylinder head.

NOTE: *When removing the valve seal and the lower spring seat, a small screwdriver and a magnet may come in handy.*

5. Inspect the valve and spring. Clean the valve guide with a cotton swab and solvent. Inspect the valve guide and seat and check the valve guide-to-stem clearance.

6. Lubricate the valve stem and guide with engine oil. Install the valve in the cylinder head through the bottom and position the lower spring seat.

7. Lubricate the valve seal with engine oil and then install it into position over the lower spring seat.

NOTE: *When installing seals, ensure that a small amount of oil is able to pass the seal to lubricate the valve guides; otherwise, excessive wear may result.*

8. Install the valve spring and the upper spring retainer, compress the spring as in Step 2 and install the two valve keepers.

NOTE: *Tap the installed valve stem lightly with a rubber mallet to ensure proper fit.*

9. Don't forget the valve lifter and shims on the diesel engine. Make sure the lifters rotate smoothly in the cylinder head.

INSPECTION

Inspect the valve faces and seats (in the cylinder head) for pits, burned spots and other evidence of poor seating. If the valve face is in such bad shape that the head of the valve must be ground in order to true up the face, discard the valve because the sharp edge will run too hot. The correct angle for valve faces is given in the specification section at the front of this chapter. It is recommended that any reaming or resurfacing (grinding) be performed by a reputable machine shop.

Check the valve stem for scoring and/or burned spots. If not noticeably scored or damaged, clean the valve stem with a suitable solvent to remove all gum and varnish. Clean the valve guides using a suitable solvent and an expanding wire-type valve guide cleaner (generally available at a local automotive supply store). If you have access to a dial indicator for measuring valve stem-to-guide clearance, mount it so that the stem of the indicator is at a 90° angle to the valve stem and as close to the valve guide as possible. Move the valve off its seat lightly and measure the valve guide-to-stem clearance by rocking the valve back and forth so that the stem actuates the dial indicator. Measure the

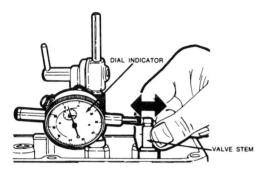

Check the valve stem-to-guide clearance

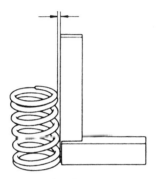

Checking the valve spring for squareness

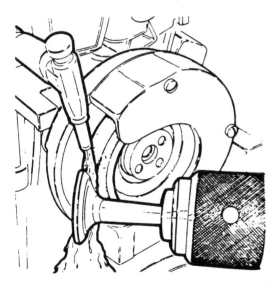

Valve refacings should be handled by a reputable machine shop

Lapping a valve in by hand

0.063"; A-series engines: 0.079"; T-series engines: 0.075"), it will require replacement. Check that the spring free height is up to specifications. Measure the distance between the spring pad and the lower edge of the spring retainer, and compare to specifications. If the installed height is incorrect, add shim washers between the spring pad and the spring.

NOTE: *Use only washers designed for this purpose.*

REFACING

Valve refacing should only be handled by a reputable machine shop, as the experience and equipment needed to do the job are beyond that of the average owner/mechanic. During the course of a normal valve job, refacing is necessary when simply lapping the valves into their seats will not correct the seat and face wear. When the valves are reground (resurfaced), the valve seats must also be recut, again requiring special equipment and experience.

VALVE LAPPING

The valves must be lapped into their seats after resurfacing, to ensure proper sealing. Even if the valves have not been refaced, they should be lapped into the head before reassembly.

Set the cylinder head on the workbench, combustion chamber side up. Rest the head on wooden blocks on either end, so there are 2-3" between the tops of the valve guides and the bench.

1. Lightly lube the valve stem with clean engine oil. Coat the valve seat completely with valve grinding compound. Use just enough compound that the full width and circumference of the seat are covered.

2. Install the valve in its proper location in the head. Attach the suction cup end of the valve lapping tool to the valve head. It usually

valve stem using a micrometer, and compare to specifications in order to determine whether the stem or the guide is responsible for the excess clearance. If a dial indicator and a micrometer are not available, take the cylinder head and valves to a reputable machine shop.

Use a steel square to check the squareness of the valve spring. If the spring is out of square more than the maximum allowable (K-series:

helps to put a small amount of saliva into the suction cup to aid it sticking to the valve.

3. Rotate the tool between the palms, changing position and lifting the tool often to prevent grooving. Lap the valve in until a smooth, evenly polished seat and valve face are evident.

4. Remove the valve from the head. Wipe away all traces of grinding compound from the valve face and seat. Wipe out the port with a solvent soaked rag, and swab out the valve guide with a piece of solvent soaked rag to make sure there are no traces of compound grit inside the guide. This cleaning is important.

5. Proceed through the remaining valves, one at a time. Make sure the valve faces, seats, cylinder ports and valve guides are clean before reassembling the valve train.

Valve Seats

The valve seats in the engines covered in this guide are all non-replaceable, and must be recut when service is required. Seat recutting requires a special tool and experience, and should be handled at a reputable machine shop. Seat concentricity should also be checked by a machinist.

Valve Guides

INSPECTION

Valve guides should be cleaned as outlined earlier, and checked when valve stem diameter and stem-to-guide clearance is checked. Generally, if the engine is using oil through the guides (assuming the valve seals are OK) and the valve stem diameter is within specification, it is the guides that are worn and need replacing.

Valve guides which are not excessively worn or distorted may, in some cases, be knurled rather than replaced. Knurling is a process in which metal inside the valve guide bore is displaced and raised (forming a very fine cross-hatch pattern), thereby reducing clearance. Knurling also provides for excellent oil control. The possibility of knurling rather than replacing the guides should be discussed with a machinist.

REMOVAL AND INSTALLATION

Except T-Series

1. Heat the cylinder head to 176-212°F, evenly, before beginning the replacement procedure.

2. On models equipped with a snapring retainer: Use a brass rod to break the valve guide off above its snapring.

NOTE: *On the diesel, insert an old valve wrapped with tape into the guide. Break off*

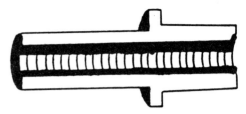

Cross-section of a knurled valve guide

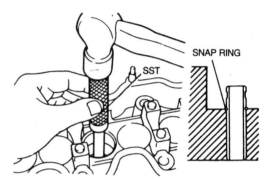

SNAP RING

SST

The snap ring must be removed before driving out the valve guide on the diesel engine

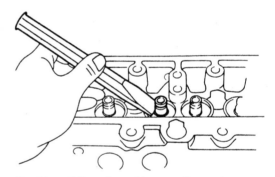

Breaking off the valve guide—gasoline engines

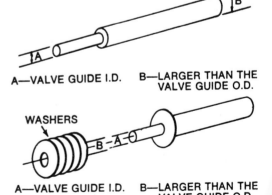

A—VALVE GUIDE I.D.   B—LARGER THAN THE VALVE GUIDE O.D.

WASHERS

A—VALVE GUIDE I.D.   B—LARGER THAN THE VALVE GUIDE O.D.

Valve guide installation tool using washers for installation

the guide by rapping in sharply with a hammer. Remove the guide bushing snapring.

3. Drive out the valve guide, toward the combustion chamber. Use a tool fabricated as in the illustration.

The guides are replaced using a stepped drift. Determine the height above the boss that the guide must extend, and obtain a stack of washers, their inner diameter similar to the guide's outer diameter, of that height. Place the stack of washers on the guide, and insert the guide into the boss.

NOTE: *Valve guides are often tapered or beveled for installation.*

4. Use the stepped installation tool and press or tap the guides into position. Ream the guides according to the size of the valve stem. Install a snapring on the new valve guide.

Front Cover

REMOVAL AND INSTALLATION

Except 1C-L and A-Series Engines

1. Drain the cooling system and the crankcase.

CAUTION: *When draining the coolant, keep in mind that cats and dogs are attracted by the ethylene glycol antifreeze, and are quite likely to drink any that is left in an uncovered container or in puddles on the ground. This will prove fatal in sufficient quantity. Always drain the coolant into a sealable container. Coolant should be reused unless it is contaminated or several years old.*

2. Disconnect the battery.

3. Remove the air cleaner assembly, complete with hoses, from its bracket.

4. Remove the hood latch as well as its brace and support.

5. Remove the headlight bezels and grille assembly.

6. Unfasten the upper and lower radiator hose clamps and remove both of the hoses from the engine.

7. Unfasten the radiator securing bolts and remove the radiator.

NOTE: *Take off the shroud first, if so equipped.*

8. Loosen the drive belt adjusting link and remove the drive belt. Unfasten the alternator multi-connector, withdraw the retaining bolts, and remove the alternator.

9. Perform Step 8 to the air injection pump, if so equipped. Disconnect the hoses from the pump before removing it.

10. Unfasten the crankshaft pulley retaining bolt. Remove the crankshaft pulley with a gear puller.

11. Remove the gravel shield from underneath the engine.

12. The following steps apply to the 3K-C engine only: Remove the nuts and washers from both the right and left front engine mounts. Detach the exhaust pipe flange from the exhaust manifold. Slightly raise the front of the engine.

13. On 2T-C engines, remove the right hand brace plate.

14. Remove the front oil pan bolts, to gain access to the bottom of the timing chain cover.

NOTE; *It may be necessary to insert a thin knife between the pan and the gasket in order to break the pan loose. Use care not to damage the gasket.*

Installation is basically the reverse order of removal. There are, however, several points to

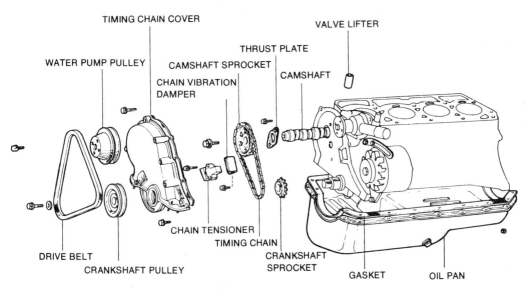

Front cover and related components—K-series engines

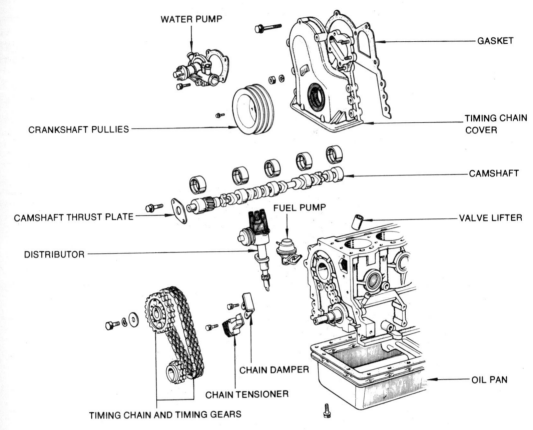

Front cover and related components—T-series engines

remember: Apply sealer to the two front corners of the 2T-C engine's oil pan gasket. Tighten the crankshaft pulley to the figure given in the Torque Specifications chart. Adjust the drive belts as outlined in Chapter 1.

1A-C, 3A, 3A-C and 4A-C RWD

1. Disconnect the negative battery terminal.
2. Remove all the drive belts.
3. Bring the engine to the top dead center

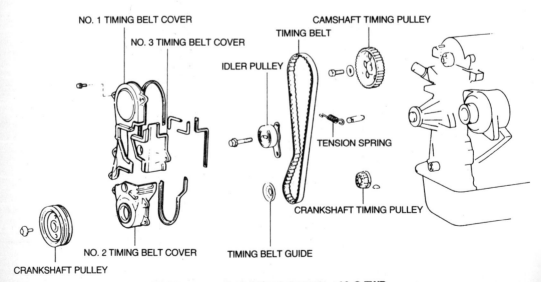

Front cover and related components—4A-C FWD

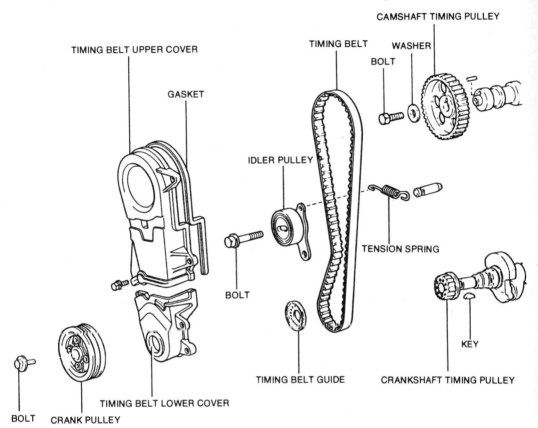

CAMSHAFT TIMING PULLEY

TIMING BELT UPPER COVER

TIMING BELT   WASHER

BOLT

GASKET

IDLER PULLEY

TENSION SPRING

BOLT

KEY

TIMING BELT GUIDE   CRANKSHAFT TIMING PULLEY

TIMING BELT LOWER COVER

BOLT   CRANK PULLEY

Front cover and related parts—A-series and 3E engines (except 4A-C FWD)

timing position. See the cylinder head removal section.

4. Remove the crankshaft pulley with a suitable pulley.

5. Remove the water pump pulley.

6. Remove the upper and lower timing case covers.

7. Installation is the reverse of removal. Tighten the timing belt cover to 61-99 in.lb.

4A-C, 4A-LC FWD

1. Disconnect the negative battery terminal.

2. Remove the right side cover under the engine.

3. Loosen the water pump pulley bolts and then remove the alternator belt. Remove the power steering pump drive belt (if so equipped).

4. Remove the bolts and then disconnect the water pump pulley from the water pump.

5. Loosen the idler pulley mounting bolt. Loosen the adjusting nut and then remove the A/C drive belt. Remove the idler pulley.

6. Set the No. 1 piston to TDC of its compression stroke. Loosen the crankshaft pulley mounting bolt and then remove the pulley.

NOTE: *Before removing the pulley, check that the rockers on the No. 1 cylinder are*

loose, if not, turn the engine one complete revolution.

7. Remove the mounting bolts and then remove the No. 1 (lower) timing belt cover.

8. Remove the four bolts and then remove the center engine mount.

9. Place a block of wood on a floor jack and then raise the engine slightly. Remove the two bolts and then remove the right engine mount.

10. Lower the engine and then remove the No. 2 (upper) timing cover and its gasket.

11. Remove the No. 3 (center) timing cover and its gasket.

12. Installation is in the reverse order of removal. Tighten the crankshaft pulley bolt to 80-94 ft.lb. (108-127 Nm) and the center engine mount bolts to 29 ft.lb. (39 Nm).

1C-L Diesel Engine

1. Disconnect the negative battery terminal.

2. Remove the cover under the engine.

3. Remove the power steering pump drive belt and pulley.

4. Remove the mounting bolts and then remove the power steering pump.

5. Remove the three clips and five bolts and

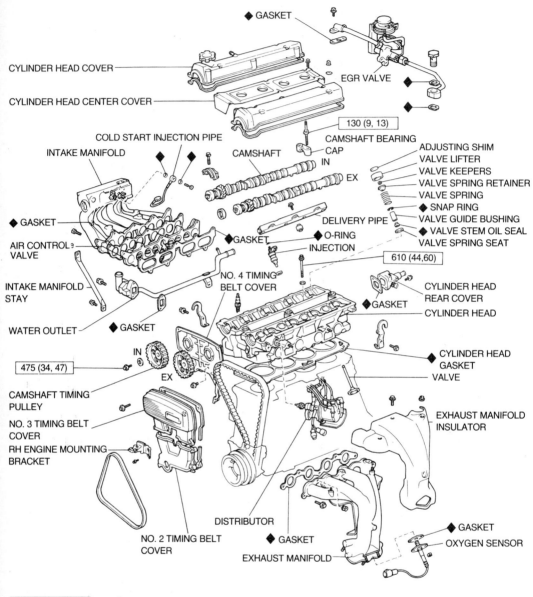

◆ GASKET

CYLINDER HEAD COVER

EGR VALVE

CYLINDER HEAD CENTER COVER

130 (9, 13)

CAMSHAFT BEARING CAP

COLD START INJECTION PIPE

INTAKE MANIFOLD

CAMSHAFT

IN

EX

ADJUSTING SHIM
VALVE LIFTER
VALVE KEEPERS
VALVE SPRING RETAINER
VALVE SPRING
◆ SNAP RING
VALVE GUIDE BUSHING
◆ VALVE STEM OIL SEAL
VALVE SPRING SEAT

◆ GASKET

DELIVERY PIPE

◆ GASKET

◆ O-RING
INJECTION

610 (44,60)

AIR CONTROL
VALVE

INTAKE MANIFOLD
STAY

NO. 4 TIMING
BELT COVER

CYLINDER HEAD
REAR COVER

◆ GASKET

CYLINDER HEAD

WATER OUTLET

◆ GASKET

IN

475 (34, 47)

EX

CYLINDER HEAD
GASKET

VALVE

CAMSHAFT TIMING
PULLEY

NO. 3 TIMING BELT
COVER

RH ENGINE MOUNTING
BRACKET

EXHAUST MANIFOLD
INSULATOR

DISTRIBUTOR

NO. 2 TIMING BELT
COVER

◆ GASKET

EXHAUST MANIFOLD

◆ GASKET

OXYGEN SENSOR

KG-CM (FT-LB, N·M) : SPECIFIED TORQUE

◆ NON-REUSABLE PART

Cylinder head assembly—4A-GE

then remove the No. 2 (upper) timing belt cover along with its gasket.

6. Remove the alternator drive belt.

7. Set the No. 1 piston to TDC of the compression stroke. Loosen the set bolt and remove the crankshaft pulley.

8. Remove the mounting bolts and then remove the No. 1 (lower) timing belt cover along with the gasket and belt guide.

9. Remove the four bolts and then disconnect the center engine mount.

10. Installation is in the reverse order of re-

moval. Tighten the center engine mount bolts to 29 ft.lb. (39Nm) and the crankshaft pulley bolt to 72 ft.lb. (98 Nm). Tighten the power steering pump bolts and the idler pulley nut to 29 ft.lb. (39 Nm).

4A-GE
3E

Note: *Refer to the Timing Belt removal and installation section.*

1. Disconnect the negative battery cable. Re-

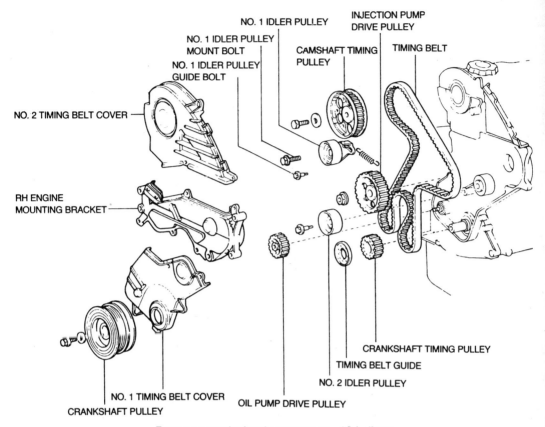

Front cover and related components—1C-L diesel

move the air cleaner assembly. Rmove all drive belts.

2. If the vehicle is equipped with cruise control, remove the actuator and bracket assembly.

3. Raise and support the vehicle safely. Remove the right side front tire and wheel. Remove the right side engine splash shield. Remove the right side mount insulator.

4. Remove the valve cover. Remove the crankshaft pulley and remove the timing cover mounting bolts and cover.

5. Install in the reverse order.

Front Cover Oil Seal

REPLACEMENT

1. Remove the timing cover, as previously detailed.

2. Inspect the oil seal for signs of wear, leakage, or damage.

3. If worn, pry the oil seal out, using a suitable flat bladed tool. Remove it toward the front of the cover.

NOTE: *Once the oil seal has been removed, it must be replaced with a new one.*

4. Use a socket, pipe, or block of wood and a hammer to drift the oil seal into place. Work from the front of the cover.

CAUTION: *Be extremely careful not to damage the seal or else it will leak!*

5. Install the timing cover as previously outlined or else it will leak.

Timing Chain and Tensioner

REMOVAL AND INSTALLATION

K-Series and T-Series Engines

1. Remove the drive belts.

2. Remove the crankshaft set bolt and then, using a puller, remove the crankshaft pulley.

3. Remove the front cover as previously detailed.

4. Using a spring scale, measure the timing chain slack. If the slack is more than 0.531" at 22 lbs. of tension, replace the chain and sprockets (K-series only).

5. Remove the timing chain tensioner and vibration damper.

6. On K-series engines, remove the camshaft sprocket set bolt and then remove the timing chain and sprocket together. Use a gear puller to remove the crankshaft sprocket. On T-series engines remove the chain and both sprockets at the same time.

7. Measure the timing chain length with the

chain fully stretched. It should be no more than 10.7″ for K-series engines or 11.472″ for T-series engines in any three positions. Wrap the chain around a sprocket. Using a vernier caliper, measure the outer sides of the chain rollers. If the measurement is less than 2.339″ on the crankshaft sprocket or 4.480″ around the camshaft sprocket, replace the chain and sprocket.

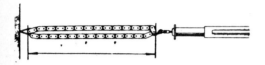

Measure the timing chain stretch with a spring scale

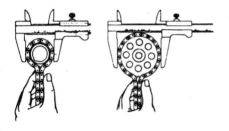

Measure the outer sides of the chain rollers with a vernier caliper

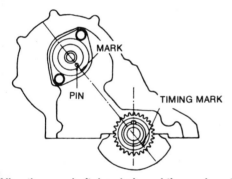

Align the camshaft dowel pin and the mark on the thrust plate

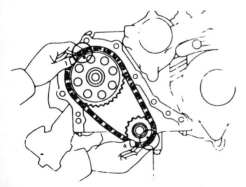

Align the marks on the two sprockets with the bright links on the timing chain

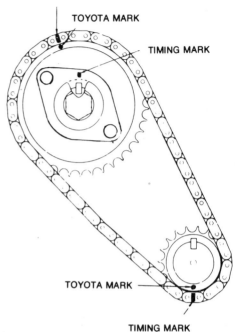

Aligning the timing marks on the 2T-C and 3T-C timing chain and sprocket

8. **Installation for the K-series engines is performed in the following order:**

9. Install the camshaft sprocket.

10. Set the No. 1 piston to TDC and align the camshaft dowel pin with the mark on the thrust plate.

11. Install the timing chain around the two sprockets. Make sure that the marks on the sprockets are aligned with the marks (usually bright links) on the timing chain.

12. Install the timing chain and the two sprockets on to the shafts. Make sure the timing marks are aligned with the camshaft dowel pin and the mark on the thrust plate.

13. Install the timing chain tensioner and the vibration damper.

14. Installation of the remaining components is in the reverse order of removal.

15. **Installation for the T-series engines is performed in the following order:**

16. Align the key in the camshaft with the mark on the thrust plate. Face the key in the crankshaft straight up.

17. Install the timing chain around the two sprockets so that the bright links line up with the timing marks on the sprockets.

18. Install the chain and gears on to the shafts.

19. Squirt oil into the cylinder in the chain tensioner and then install it to the cylinder block.

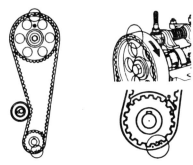

Mark the timing belt before removal—A-series engines

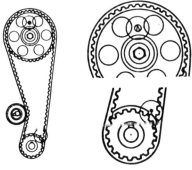

When checking the valve timing, turn the crankshaft two (2) complete revolutions clockwise from TDC to TDC and make sure that each pulley aligns with the marks shown—A-series engines

20. Install the chain damper parallel to the chain so that there is a 0.020″ space in between.

21. Installation of the remaining components is in the reverse order of removal.

Timing Belt

REMOVAL AND INSTALLATION

A-Series Engines (SOHC)

1. Remove the timing belt upper and lower dust covers and gaskets as previously detailed.

2. If the timing belt is to be reused, mark an arrow in the direction of engine revolution on its surface. Matchmark the belt to the pulleys as shown in the illustration.

3. Loosen the idler pulley bolt, push it to the left as far as it will go and then temporarily tighten it.

4. Remove the timing belt, idler pulley bolt, idler pulley and the return spring.

NOTE: *Do not bend, twist, or turn the belt inside out. Do not allow grease or water to come in contact with it.*

5. Inspect the timing belt for cracks, missing teeth or overall wear. Replace as necessary.

6. Install the return spring and idler pulley.

7. Install the timing belt. Align the marks made earlier if reusing the old belt.

8. Adjust the idler pulley so that the belt deflection is 0.24-0.28″ at 4.5 lbs.

9. Check the valve timing.

10. Installation of the remaining components is in the reverse order of removal.

4A-GE Series (DOHC)

1. Disconnect the negative battery cable. Disconnect the air cleaner hose from the throttle intake.

2. If the vehicle is equipped with power steering, remove the pump (with hoses attached) and position it out of the way..

3. Loosen the water pump pulley set nuts, remove the drive belt adjusting bolt and then remove the drive belt. Remove the set nuts, fluid coupling, fan and water pump pulley.

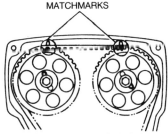

Place matchmarks on the camshaft timing pulleys and belt—4A-GE

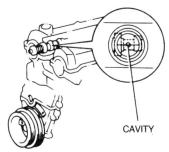

When setting the No. 1 cylinder at TDC on the 4A-GE, remove the oil filler cap and check that the cavity in the camshaft is visible

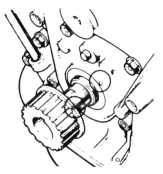

When installing the crankshaft pulley, make sure the TDC marks on the oil pump body and the pulley are in alignment—4A-GE

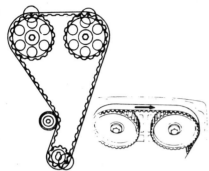

If the timing belt is to be reused, draw a directional arrow and matchmark the belt to the pulleys as shown—4A-GE

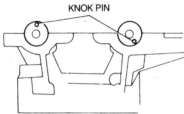

Position the camshafts into the cylinder head as shown—4A-GE

4. Remove the spark plugs. Rotate the crankshaft so that the timing groove on the pulley is in alignment with the timing mark (0) on the timing cover. Remove the oil filler cap and check to see that the cavity in the camshaft is visible. If the cavity is not visible, turn the crankshaft until the timing marks are lined up again, and recheck.

5. Lock the crankshaft pulley and remove the pulley mounting bolt. Use a suitable puller and remove the crank pulley. Remove the three timing covers and their gaskets. Remove the timing belt guide.

6. Matchmark the camshaft pulleys to the inner case and timing belt (if the old belt is to be reused. Also mark the old belt for rotation direction).

7. Loosen the idler pulley mounting bolts and move the idler pulley as far to the left as possible. Secure the pulley in the far left position. Remove the timing belt. Remove the idler pulley and the tensioner spring if servicing is required.

8. Service the engine as required. Install the timing belt making sure all matchmarks, and timing marks are aligned. Use care when installing the belt so that the camshaft pulleys are not moved out of position. Set the idler pulley in to position so that belt deflection is 0.16" at 4.4 lbs. Apply more or less tension as required. Turn the engine, clockwise, two complete revolutions and recheck timing mark

alignment. Readjust if necessary. The idler pulley mounting bolts should be torqued to 27 ft.lb. Install the remaining components in the reverse order of removal.

3E

1. Disconnect the negative battery cable. Remove the right side engine splash shield.

2. Remove all of the drive belts. Remove the alternator and mounting bracket. Remove the air cleaner assembly. Remove the spark plugs.

3. Raise the engine slightly and remove the right side engine mounting insulator assembly.

4. Remove the top engine cover. Align the timing marks so that the engine is at TDC on the compression stroke of No. 1 cylinder. Remove the crankshaft pulley with a suitable puller.

5. Remove both timing belt covers and the belt guide. Loosen the idler pulley and move it as far to the left as possible, secure it in position. Remove the timing belt.

6. Service the components as required. To install a new timing belt, make sure that the that the front bearing cap mark is aligned with the center of the hole in the camshaft sprocket and that the TDC marks on the oil pump body and crank pulley are aligned. Install the timing belt taking care not to move the sprockets out of position. Release the idler pulley to apply pressure on the belt. Secure the pulley. Rotate the engine clockwise two complete revolutions and recheck timing mark alignment. Adjust as required. Timing belt deflection should be 0.24" at 4.4 lbs. Idler pulley mounting bolts should be torqued to 27 ft.lb.

1C-L Diesel Engines

1. Remove the front covers as previously detailed.

2. Raise the engine slightly with a jack and a block of wood. Disconnect the right engine mount from its bracket.

3. Lower the engine and then remove the right engine mount.

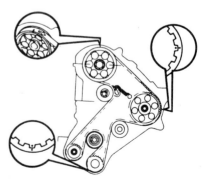

If the timing belt is to be reused, mark it as shown— 1C-L diesel engine

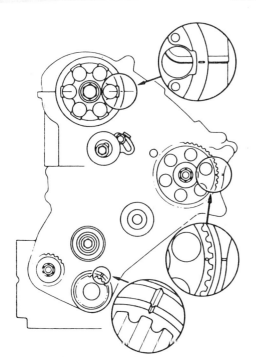

When installing a new timing belt, align it as shown—
1C-L diesel engine

4. If the timing belt is to be reused, mark an arrow in the direction of engine rotation on its surface. Matchmark the belt to the pulleys as shown in the illustration.

5. Use a screwdriver and remove the idler pulley tension spring.

CAUTION: *Don't pinch the spring with pliers!*

6. Loosen the idler pulley bolt, push it to the left as far as it will go and then temporarily tighten it.

7. Remove the timing belt.

CAUTION: *Do not bend, twist or turn the belt inside out. Do not allow grease or water to come in contact with it!*

8. Inspect the belt for cracks, missing teeth or overall wear. Replace as necessary.

9. Install the idler pulley and then install the timing belt. Make sure that the belt is aligned at all positions (as illustrated) if new, or at all previously marked points are being reused.

CAUTION: *Be sure that the timing belt is securely meshed with the gear teeth; it should never be loose!*

10. Install the tension spring and then turn the engine two complete revolutions (from TDC to TDC). Always turn the engine clockwise, using the crankshaft pulley bolt. All alignment marks should still be in alignment; if not, remove the belt and try again.

11. Further installation is in the reverse order of removal.

Camshaft

REMOVAL AND INSTALLATION

K-Series and T-Series Engines

1. Remove the cylinder head as detailed previously in this chapter.

2. Remove the distributor. Remove the radiator.

3. Remove the timing chain as detailed previously.

4. Remove the valve lifters in the proper sequence. Be sure to keep them in order.

NOTE: *The 4K-E engine used in the 1983-84 Starlet utilizes a new type of hydraulic lifter.*

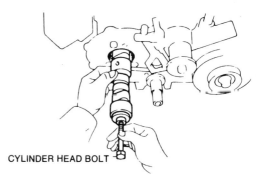

CYLINDER HEAD BOLT

Use a cylinder head bolt to remove and install the camshaft

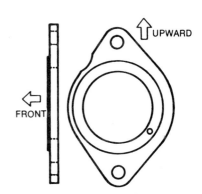

Proper positioning of the thrust plate—K-series engines

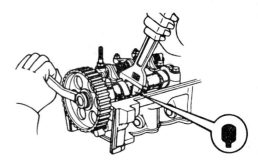

Removing the camshaft timing pulley—A-series engines

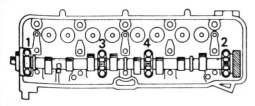

Loosen the bearing cap, little by little, in this order—A-series engines

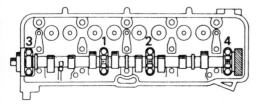

Tighten the bearing caps in this order—A-series engines

Although similar in size and appearance to a conventional hydraulic lifter, the new design has no oil inlet holes in the lifter body. Instead, the lifter is completely sealed and contains a special silicone oil for lubrication. If the new lifter is disassembled, and the special lubricant is lost, replacement will be required.

5. Remove the fuel pump on carburetor equipped engines.

6. Remove the two thrust plate set bolts.

7. Screw a cylinder head bolt into the end of the camshaft. Slowly turn the camshaft and pull it out being careful not to damage the bearing.

8. Inspect the camshaft and bearings.

9. Coat the camshaft bearings and journals lightly with oil and then carefully install it into the cylinder block.

10. Install the thrust plate in the proper position and torque the two bolts to 4-6 ft.lb. on the K-series engines and 7-11 ft.lb. on the T-series engines.

11. Installation of the remaining components is in the reverse order of removal.

A-Series Engines (SOHC)

1. Perform Steps 1-21 of the Cylinder Head Removal procedure for this engine.

2. Remove the camshaft timing pulley by holding the camshaft with a pair of channel lock pliers and removing the bolt in the pulley end of the shaft.

NOTE: *Never hold the camshaft on the lobes, as damage will result.*

3. Secure the camshaft with channel locks once again and loosen the distributor drive gear bolt.

4. Loosen each bearing cap bolt a little at a

time in the proper sequence. Make sure that you keep the bearing caps in the proper order.

5. Remove the camshaft oil seal and then the camshaft itself.

6. Install the distributor drive gear and the plate washer with the bolt onto the camshaft.

7. Coat all bearing journals lightly with oil and then place the camshaft into position in the head.

8. Place the bearing caps Nos. 2, 3 and 4 on each journal with the arrows pointing toward the front of the engine.

9. Apply grease to the inside edge of the oil seal and liquid sealant to the outside edge and then slip the seal onto the camshaft.

NOTE: *Be careful not to install the oil seal onto the camshaft crooked.*

10. Apply liquid sealant to the two bottom edges of the No. 1 bearing cap then install it into position.

11. Torque each bearing cap bolt a little at a time and in the proper sequence. Tighten to 8-10 ft.lb.

12. Recheck the thrust clearance and then tighten the distributor drive gear bolt to 20-23 ft.lb.

13. Installation of the remaining components is in the reverse order of removal.

1C-L Diesel

1. Perform Steps 1-22 of the 1C-L Cylinder Head Removal and Installation procedure.

2. Remove the exhaust manifold.

3. Remove the camshaft oil seal retainer.

4. Loosen each bearing cap bolt a little at a time and in the proper sequence; start at the ends and work in. Make sure that the bearing caps are kept in the proper order.

5. Remove the camshaft and the half-circle plug at the rear of the head.

6. Coat the half-circle plug with adhesive and position it in the cylinder head.

7. Coat all bearing journals lightly with oil and then place the camshaft into position on the cylinder head.

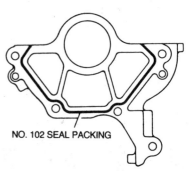

NO. 102 SEAL PACKING

Use sealant when installing the oil seal retainer—1C-L diesel engine

8. Install the bearing caps in order. Tighten the cap bolts in two or three stages until they reach a final torque of 13 ft.lb. (18 Nm).

9. Check the thrust and oil clearances.

10. Apply adhesive to the oil seal retainer as shown and then install it onto the cylinder head.

11. Installation of the remaining components is in the reverse order of removal.

All Other Engines

NOTE: *Refer to Cylinder Head removal and installation for details on camshaft replacement.*

CHECKING

1. Using a micrometer, check that the camshaft journal diameter is within the specifica-

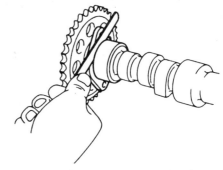

Checking the camshaft end play—K-series and T-series engines

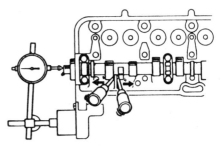

Checking the camshaft endplay—1C-L diesel and all A-series engines

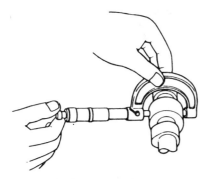

Use a micrometer to check the camshaft journal diameter

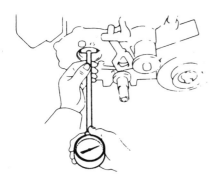

Use a cylinder micrometer to check the bearing bore—K-series and T-series engines

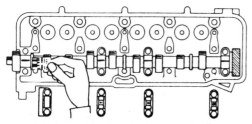

Compare the Plastigage® to the scale provided—1C-L diesel and all A-series engines

tions given in the Camshaft Specifications chart.

2. Check the bearing oil clearance:

a. On K-series and T-series engines, check the bearing bore with a cylinder micrometer. Subtract the journal diameter measurement taken in Step 1 from the bearing bore measurement. If the clearance is greater than that given in the Camshaft Specifications chart, replace the bearing and/or camshaft.

b. On the 1C-L and all A-series engines, clean the bearing caps and camshaft journals. Lay a strip of Plastigage® across each journal and then install the bearing caps and torque them down in the proper sequence.

NOTE: *Never turn the camshaft with the Plastigage® in place. Remove the bearing caps and compare the Plastigage® to the scale included in the package. If the clearance at the widest point of any strip is greater than that which is specified in the Camshaft Specifications chart, replacement of the camshaft or the cylinder head is required.*

3. Check the camshaft end play:

a. On chain driven engines, install the thrust plate and camshaft sprocket to the camshaft. Tighten to 40-47 ft.lb. Using a feeler gauge, measure the clearance between the camshaft and the thrust plate. If the clearance is greater than listed in the Camshaft Specifications chart, replace the thrust plate and/or sprocket.

b. On belt driven engines, attach a dial indicator to the cylinder head so that its tip is touching the end of the installed camshaft. Lever the camshaft back and forth. If the measurement is greater than that listed in the Camshaft Specifications chart, replace the cylinder head or , if equipped, the thrust bearing.

Pistons and Connecting Rods
REMOVAL

Before removing the pistons, the top of the cylinder bore must be examined for a ridge. A ridge at the top of the bore is the result of normal cylinder wear; caused by the piston rings only traveling so far up the bore in the course of the piston stroke. If the ridge can be felt by hand, it must be removed before the pistons are removed.

A ridge reamer is necessary for this operation. Place the piston at the bottom of its stroke and cover it with a rag. Cut the ridge away with the ridge reamer, using extreme care to avoid cutting too deeply. Remove the rag, and remove the cuttings that remain on the piston with a magnet and a rag soaked in clean oil. Make sure the piston top and cylinder bore are absolutely clean before moving the piston.

1. Remove the engine and cylinder head as detailed previously.

2. Remove the oil pan.

3. Remove the oil pump assembly if necessary.

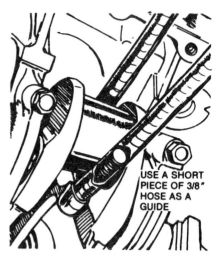

USE A SHORT PIECE OF 3/8″ HOSE AS A GUIDE

Use lengths of vacuum hose or rubber tubing to protect the crankshaft journals and cylinder walls during piston installation

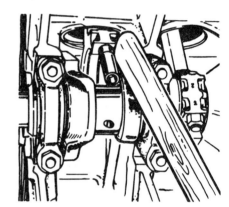

Push the piston out with a hammer handle

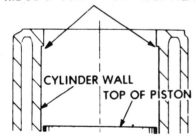

Cylinder ridge

RIDGE CAUSED BY CYLINDER WEAR

CYLINDER WALL

TOP OF PISTON

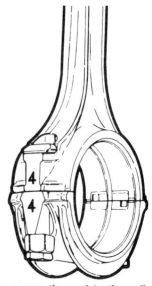

Match the connecting rod to the cylinder with a number stamp

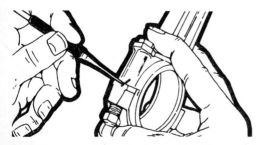

Match the connecting rod and cap with scribe marks

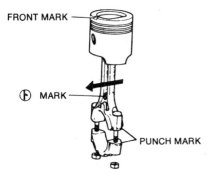

FRONT MARK

Ⓕ MARK

PUNCH MARK

Piston positioning

4. Matchmark the connecting rod cap to the connecting rod with a scribe; each cap must be reinstalled on its proper rod in the proper direction. Remove the connecting rod bearing cap and the rod bearing. Number the top of each piston with silver paint or a felt-tip pen for later assembly.

5. Cut lengths of ⅜" diameter rubber hose to use as rod bolt guides. Install the hose over the threads of the rod bolts, to prevent the bolt threads from damaging the crankshaft journals and cylinder walls when the piston is removed.

6. Squirt some clean engine oil onto the cylinder wall from above until the wall is coated. Carefully push the piston and rod assembly up and out of the cylinder by tapping on the bottom of the connecting rod with a wooden hammer handle.

7. Place the rod bearing and cap back on the connecting rod, and install the nuts temporarily. Using a number stamp or punch, stamp the cylinder number on the side of the connecting rod and cap; this will help keep the proper piston and rod assembly on the proper cylinder.

NOTE: *On all Toyota engines, the cylinders are numbered 1-4 from front to back.*

8. Remove the remaining pistons in a similar manner. When ready for reassembly, please note the following:

a. Connecting rods/caps must be reinstalled in the same cylinder and are so marked. Make sure that the markings on the rod and cap are on the same side when reassembling.

b. The piston pins are matched to the pistons and are not interchangeable.

c. The arrow notch top of the piston must face forward (toward the timing chain). The oil hole in the connecting rod faces the same direction as the arrow on top of the piston.

d. Rings are installed with the code markings upward, plain ring at the top, taper face second, and beveled oil control ring at the bottom. Offset each ring gap as illustrated.

PISTON RING AND WRIST PIN REMOVAL

Pistons are mounted onto the connecting rods by wrist pins. The wrist pins are retained either by circlips, or are pressed through the rod. Servicing press fitted wrist pins should be done by a machine shop. Circlip retained wrist pins are serviced by removing the circlip with a pair of circlip pliers and pushing out the pin.

A piston ring expander is necessary for removing piston rings without damaging them; any other method (screwdriver blades, pliers, etc.) usually results in the rings being bent, scratched or distorted, or the piston itself being damaged. When the rings are removed, clean the ring grooves using an appropriate ring groove cleaning tool, using care not to cut too deeply. Thoroughly clean all carbon and varnish from the piston with solvent.

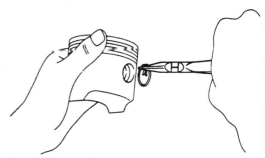

Remove the circlip

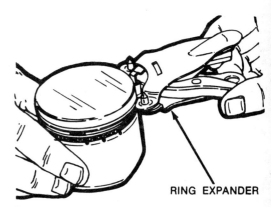

RING EXPANDER

Removing the piston rings

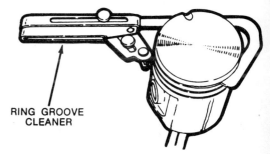

RING GROOVE CLEANER

Clean the piston ring grooves

CAUTION: *Do not use a wire brush or caustic solvent (acids, etc.) on pistons!*

Inspect the pistons for scuffing, scoring, cracks, pitting, or excessive ring groove wear. If they are evident, the pistons must be replaced.

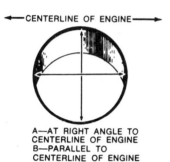

A—AT RIGHT ANGLE TO CENTERLINE OF ENGINE
B—PARALLEL TO CENTERLINE OF ENGINE

Cylinder bore measuring points

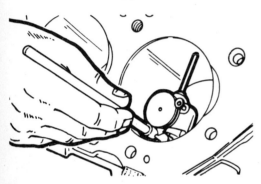

Measure the cylinder bore with a dial gauge

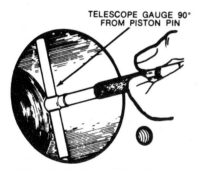

TELESCOPE GAUGE 90° FROM PISTON PIN

Measure the cylinder bore with a telescope gauge

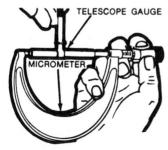

TELESCOPE GAUGE

MICROMETER

Measure the telescope gauge with a micrometer to determine the cylinder bore

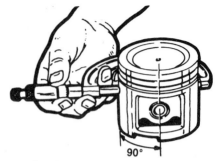

Measure the piston prior to fitting

The piston should also be checked in relation to the cylinder diameter. Using a telescoping gauge and micrometer, or a dial gauge, measure the cylinder bore diameter perpendicular (90°) to the piston pin, 2½″ below the cylinder block deck (surface where the block mates with the heads). Then, with the micrometer, measure the piston perpendicular to its wrist pin on the skirt. The difference between the two measurements is the piston clearance. If the clearance is within specifications or slightly below (after the cylinders have been bored or honed), finish honing is all that is necessary. If the clearance is excessive, try to obtain a slightly larger piston to bring clearance within specifications. If this is not possible, obtain the first oversize piston and hone (or if necessary, bore) the cylinder to size. Generally, if the cylinder bore is tapered 0.005″ or more, or is out-of-round 0.003″ or more, it is advisable to rebore for the smallest possible oversize piston and rings. After measuring, mark the pistons with a felt-tip pen for reference and assembly.

NOTE: *Cylinder honing and/or boring should be performed by an authorized service technician with the proper equipment. In some cases, clean-up honing can be done with the cylinder block in the car, but most excessive honing and all cylinder boring must be done with the block stripped and removed from the car.*

PISTON RING END GAP

Piston ring end gap should be checked while the rings are removed from the pistons. Incorrect end gap indicates that the wrong size rings are being used: ring breakage could occur.

Compress the piston rings to be used in a cylinder, one at a time, into that cylinder. Squirt clean oil into the cylinder, so that the rings and the top 2″ of cylinder wall are coated. Using an inverted piston, press the rings approximately 1″ below the deck of the block. Measure the ring end gap with a feeler gauge, and compare to the specifications chart in this chapter. Carefully pull the ring out of the cylinder and file the

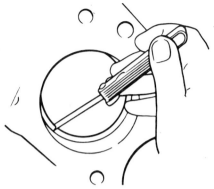

Checking the piston ring end gap

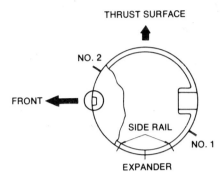

Piston ring positioning—T-series engines

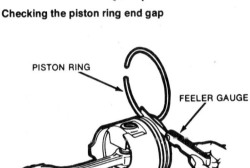

Checking the piston ring side clearance

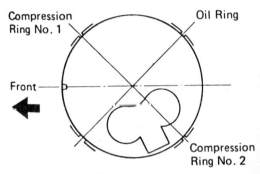

Piston ring positioning—1C-L diesel engine

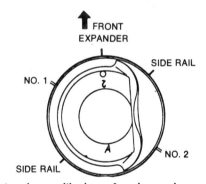

Piston ring positioning—A-series engines

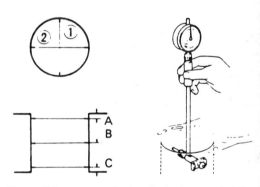

Use a dial gauge to check cylinder bore and piston clearance

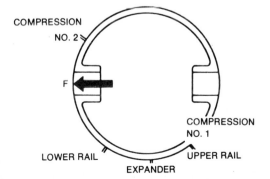

Piston ring positioning—K-series engines

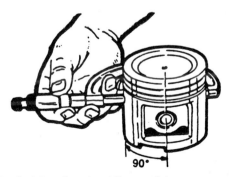

Check piston diameter at these points

ends squarely with a fine file to obtain the proper clearance.

PISTON RING SIDE CLEARANCE CHECK AND INSTALLATION

Check the pistons to see that the ring grooves and oil return holes have been properly cleaned. Slide a piston ring into its groove, and check the side clearance with a feeler gauge. Make sure that you insert the gauge between the ring and its lower land (lower edge of the groove), because any wear that occurs forms a step at the inner portion of the lower land. If the piston grooves have worn to the extent that relatively high steps exist on the lower land, the piston should be replaced, because these will interfere with the operation of the new rings and ring clearances will be excessive. Piston rings are not furnished in oversize widths to compensate for ring groove wear.

Install the rings on the piston, lowest ring first, using a piston ring expander. There is a high risk of breaking or distorting the rings, or scratching the piston, if the rings are installed by hand or other means.

Position the rings on the piston as illustrated; spacing of the various piston ring gaps is crucial to proper oil retention and even cylinder wear. When installing new rings, refer to the installation diagram furnished with the new parts.

NOTE: *For piston positioning information, please refer to Step 8 of the Piston and Connecting Rod Removal section in this chapter.*

CYLINDER BORE INSPECTION

Place a rag over the crankshaft journals. Wipe out each cylinder with a clean, solvent-soaked rag. Visually inspect the cylinder bores for roughness, scoring or scuffing; also check the bores by feel. Measure the cylinder bore diameter with an inside micrometer, or a telescope gauge and micrometer. Measure the bore at points parallel and perpendicular to the engine centerline at the top (below the ridge) and bottom of the bore. Subtract the bottom measurements from the top to determine cylinder taper.

Measure the piston diameter with a micrometer; since this micrometer may not be part of your tool kit as it is necessarily large, you may have to have the pistons miked at a machine shop. Take the measurements at right angles to the wrist pin center line, about an inch down the piston skirt from the top. Compare this measurement to the bore diameter of each cylinder; the difference is the piston clearance. If the clearance is greater than that specified in the Piston and Ring Specifications chart, have the cylinders honed or rebored and replace the pistons with an oversize set. Piston clearance can also be checked by inverting a piston into an oiled cylinder, and sliding in a feeler gauge between the two.

CONNECTING ROD BEARINGS

Connecting rod bearings for the engines covered in this guide consist of two halves or shells which are interchangeable in the rod and cap. When the shells are placed in position, the ends extend slightly beyond the rod and cap surfaces so that when the rod bolts are torqued, the shells will be clamped tightly in place to insure positive seating and to prevent turning. A tang holds the shells in place.

NOTE: *The ends of the bearing shells must never be filed flush with the mating surface of the rod and cap.*

If a rod bearing becomes noisy or is worn so that its clearance on the crank journal is sloppy, a new bearing of the correct undersize must be selected and installed since there is no provision for adjustment.

CAUTION: *Under no circumstances should the rod end or cap be filed to adjust the bearing clearance, nor should shims of any kind be used!*

Inspect the rod bearings while the rod assemblies are out of the engine. If the shells are scored or show flaking, they should be replaced. If they are in good shape check for proper clearance on the crank journal (see below). Any scoring or ridges on the crank journal means the crankshaft must be replaced, or reground and fitted with undersized bearings.

Checking Bearing Clearance and Replacing Bearings

Replacement bearings are available in standard size, and in oversizes for reground crankshafts. Connecting rod-to-crankshaft bearing clearance is checked using Plastigage® at either the top or bottom of each crank journal. Plastigage has a range of 0.001–0.003″.

1. Remove the rod cap with the bearing shell. Completely clean the bearing shell and the crank journal, and blow any oil from the oil hole in the crankshaft; Plastigage® is soluble in oil.

2. Place a piece of Plastigage® lengthwise along the bottom center of the lower bearing shell, then install the cap with shell and torque the bolt or nuts to specification. DO NOT turn the crankshaft with Plastigage® in the bearing.

3. Remove the bearing cap with the shell. The flattened Plastigage® will be found sticking to either the bearing shell or crank journal. Do not remove it yet.

4. Use the scale printed on the Plastigage® envelope to measure the flattened material at its widest point. The number within the scale

which most closely corresponds to the width of the Plastigage® indicates bearing clearance in thousandths of an inch.

5. Check the specifications chart in this chapter for the desired clearance. It is advisable to install a new bearing if clearance exceeds 0.003"; however, if the bearing is in good condition and is not being checked because of bearing noise, bearing replacement is not necessary.

6. If you are installing new bearings, try a standard size, then each undersize in order until one is found that is within the specified limits when checked for clearance with Plastigage®. Each undersize shell has its size stamped on it.

7. When the proper size shell is found, clean off the Plastigage®, oil the bearing thoroughly, reinstall the cap with its shell and torque the rod bolt nuts to the proper specifications.

NOTE: *With the proper bearing selected and the nuts torqued, it should be possible to move the connecting rod back and forth freely on the crank journal as allowed by the specified connecting rod end clearance. If the rod cannot be moved, either the rod bearing is too far undersize or the rod is misaligned.*

PISTON AND CONNECTING ROD ASSEMBLY AND INSTALLATION

Install the connecting rod to the piston, making sure piston installation notches and any marks on the rod are in proper relation to one another. Lubricate the wrist pin with clean engine oil, and install the pin into the rod and piston assembly, either by hand or by using a wrist pin press as required. Install snap rings if equipped, and rotate them in their grooves to make sure they are seated. To install the piston and connecting rod assembly:

1. Make sure that the connecting rod big-end bearings (including end cap) are of the correct size and properly installed.

2. Fit rubber hoses over the connecting rod bolts to protect the crankshaft journals, as in

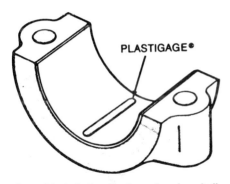

Plastigage® installed on the lower bearing shell

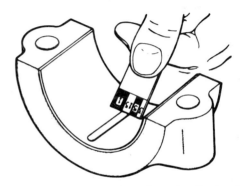

Measure the Plastigage® to determine the bearing clearance

Install the piston using a ring compresser

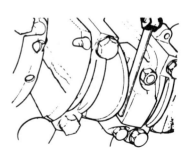

Check the connecting rod side clearance with a feeler gauge

the Piston Removal procedure. Coat the rod bearings with clean oil.

3. Using the proper ring compressor, insert the piston assembly into the cylinder so that the word TOP faces the front of the engine (this assumes that the dimple(s) or other markings on the connecting rods are in the correct relationship.

4. From beneath the engine, coat each crank journal with clean oil. Pull the connecting rod, with the bearing shell in place, into position against the crank journal.

5. Remove the rubber hoses. Install the bearing cap and cap nuts and torque to the proper specifications.

Chilton Tip: *When more than one rod and piston assembly is being installed, the connecting rod cap attaching nuts should only be tightened enough to keep each rod in position until all have been installed. This will ease the installation of the remaining piston assemblies.*

6. Check the clearance between the sides of the connecting rods and the crankshaft using a feeler gauge. Spread the rods slightly with a screwdriver to insert the gauge. If clearance is below the minimum tolerance, the rod may be machined to provide adequate clearance. If clearance is excessive, substitute an unworn rod, and recheck. If clearance is still outside specifications, the crankshaft must be welded and reground, or replaced.

7. Replace the oil pump if removed and the oil pan.

Crankshaft and Main Bearings

CRANKSHAFT REMOVAL

1. Drain the engine oil and remove the engine from the car. Mount the engine on a work stand in a suitable working area. Invert the engine, so the oil pan is facing up.

2. Remove the engine front (timing) cover.

3. Remove the timing chain/belt and gears.

4. Remove the oil pan.

5. Remove the oil pump.

6. Stamp the cylinder number on the machined surfaces of the bolt bosses of the connecting rods and caps for identification when reinstalling. If the pistons are to be removed eventually from the connecting rod, mark the cylinder number on the pistons with silver paint or felt-tip pen for proper cylinder identification and cap-to-rod location.

7. Remove the connecting rod caps. Install lengths of rubber hose on each of the connecting rod bolts, to protect the crank journals when the crank is removed.

8. Mark the main bearing caps with a number punch or punch so that they can be reinstalled in their original positions.

9. Remove all main bearing caps.

10. Note the position of the keyway in the crankshaft so it can be installed in the same position.

Chilton Tip: *To keep the connecting rods from banging against the side of the cylinders while removing the crankshaft, screw four oil pan bolts loosely into the block and then stretch a rubber band between a connecting rod bolt and oil pan bolt.*

11. Carefully lift the crankshaft out of the block. The rods will pivot to the center of the engine when the crank is removed.

MAIN BEARING INSPECTION

Like connecting rod big-end bearings, the crankshaft main bearings are shell-type inserts that do not utilize shims and cannot be adjusted. The bearings are available in various standard and oversizes; if main bearing clearance is found to be too sloppy, a new bearing (both upper and lower halves) is required.

Generally, the lower half of the bearing shell (except No. 1 bearing) shows greater wear and fatigue. If the lower half only shows the effects of normal wear (no heavy scoring or discoloration), it can usually be assumed that the upper half is also in good shape; conversely, if the lower half is heavily worn or damaged, both halves should be replaced. Never replace one bearing half without replacing the other.

CHECKING CLEARANCE

Main bearing clearance can be checked both with the engine in the car and with the engine out of the car. If the engine block is still in the car, the crankshaft should be supported both front and rear (by the damper and to remove clearance from the upper bearing). Total clearance can then be measured between the lower bearing and journal. If the block has been removed from the car, and is inverted, the crank will rest on the upper bearings and the total clearance can be measured between the lower bearing and journal. Clearance is checked in the same manner as the connecting rod bearings, with Plastigage®.

NOTE: *Crankshaft bearing caps and bearing shells should NEVER be filed flush with the cap-to-block mating surface to adjust for wear in the old bearings. Always install new bearings.*

1. If the crankshaft has been removed, install it (block removed from car). If the block is still in the car, remove the oil pan and oil pump. Starting with the rear bearing cap, remove the cap and wipe all oil from the crank journal and bearing cap.

2. Place a strip of Plastigage® the full width of the bearing, (parallel to the crankshaft), on the journal.

CAUTION: *Do not rotate the crankshaft while the gauging material is between the bearing and the journal!*

3. Install the bearing cap and evenly torque the cap bolts to specification.

4. Remove the bearing cap. The flattened Plastigage® will be sticking to either the bearing or the crankshaft journal.

5. Use the graduated scale on the Plastigage® envelope to measure the material at its widest point.

NOTE: *If the flattened Plastigage® tapers toward the middle or ends, there is a difference in clearance indicating the bearing or journal has a taper, low spot, or other irregularity. If this is indicated, measure the crank journal with a micrometer.*

6. If bearing clearance is within specifications, the bearing insert is in good shape. Replace the insert if the clearance is not within specifications. Always replace both upper and lower inserts as a unit.

7. Standard, 0.001″ or 0.002″ undersize bearings should produce the proper clearance. If these sizes still produce too sloppy a fit, the crankshaft must be reground for use with the next undersize bearing. Recheck all clearances after installing new bearings.

8. Replace the rest of the bearings in the same manner. After all bearings have been checked, rotate the crankshaft to make sure there is no excessive drag. When checking the No. 1 main bearing, loosen the accessory drive belts (engine in car) to prevent a tapered reading with the Plastigage®.

MAIN BEARING REPLACEMENT

Engine Out of Car

1. Remove and inspect the crankshaft.

2. Remove the main bearings from the bearing saddles in the cylinder block and main bearing caps.

3. Coat the bearing surfaces of the new, correct size main bearings with clean engine oil and install them in the bearing saddles in the block and in the main bearing caps.

4. Install the crankshaft. See Crankshaft Installation.

Engine in Car

1. With the oil pan, oil pump and spark plugs removed, remove the cap from the main bearing needing replacement and remove the bearing from the cap.

2. Make a bearing roll-out pin, (using a bent cotter pin) as shown in the illustration. Install the end of the pin in the oil hole in the crankshaft journal.

3. Rotate the crankshaft clockwise as viewed from the front of the engine. This will roll the upper bearing out of the block.

4. Lube the new upper bearing with clean engine oil and insert the plain (unnotched) end between the crankshaft and the indented or notched side of the block. Roll the bearing into place, making sure that the oil holes are aligned. Remove the roll pin from the oil pin.

5. Lube the new lower bearing and install the main bearing cap. Install the main bearing cap, making sure it is positioned in the proper direction with the matchmarks in alignment.

6. Torque the main bearing cap bolts to the proper specification.

NOTE: *See Crankshaft Installation for thrust bearing alignment.*

CRANKSHAFT END PLAY AND INSTALLATION

When main bearing clearance has been checked, bearings examined and/or replaced, the crankshaft can be installed. Thoroughly

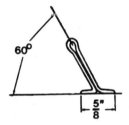

Home-made bearing roll-out pin

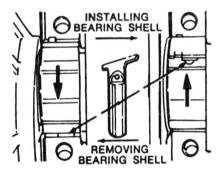

Remove or install the upper bearing insert using a roll-out pin

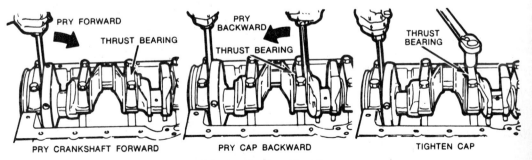

Aligning the thrust bearing

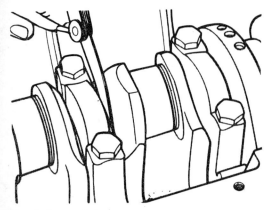

Check the crankshaft end play with a feeler gauge

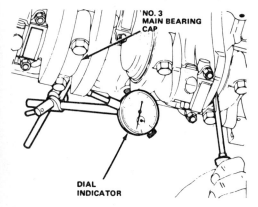

Check the crankshaft end play with a dial indicator

clean the upper and lower bearing surfaces, and lube them with clean engine oil. Install the crankshaft and main bearing caps.

Dip all main bearing cap bolts in clean oil, and torque all main bearing caps, excluding the thrust bearing cap, to specifications (see the Crankshaft and Connecting Rod chart in this chapter to determine which bearing is the thrust bearing). Tighten the thrust bearing bolts finger tight. To align the thrust bearing, pry the crankshaft the extent of its axial travel several times, holding the last movement toward the front of the engine. Add thrust washers, if required for proper alignment. Torque the thrust bearing cap to specifications.

To check crankshaft end-play, pry the crankshaft to the extreme rear of its axial travel, then to the extreme front of its travel. Using a feeler gauge or a dial indicator, measure the end-play at the front of the rear main bearing. End play may also be measured at the thrust bearing. Install a new rear main bearing oil seal in the cylinder block and main bearing cap. Continue to reassemble the engine.

Cylinder Block

Most inspection and service work on the cylinder block should be handled by a machinist or professional engine rebuilding shop. Included in this work are bearing alignment checks, line boring, deck resurfacing, hot-tanking and cylinder honing or boring. A block that has been checked and properly serviced will last much longer than one which has not had the proper attention when the opportunity was there for it.

Cylinder de-glazing (honing) can, however, be performed by the owner/mechanic who is careful and takes his or her time. The cylinder bores become glazed during normal operation as the rings continually ride up and down against them. This shiny glaze must be removed in order for a new set of piston rings to be able to properly seat themselves.

Cylinder hones are available at most auto tool stores and parts jobbers. With the piston and rod assemblies removed from the block, cover the crankshaft completely with a rag or cover to keep grit from the hone and cylinder material off of it. Chuck a hone into a variable-speed power drill (preferable here to a constant speed drill), and insert it into the cylinder.

NOTE: *Make sure the drill and hone are kept square to the cylinder bore throughout the entire honing operation.*

Start the hone and move it up and down in the cylinder at a rate which will produce approximately a 60° crosshatch pattern. DO NOT extend the hone below the cylinder bore! After developing the pattern, remove the hone and recheck piston fit. Wash the cylinders with a detergent and water solution to remove the hone

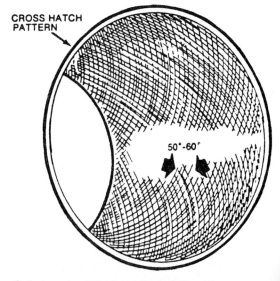

Cylinders should be hones to look like this

and cylinder grit. Wipe the bores out several times with a clean rag soaked in clean engine oil. Remove the cover from the crankshaft, and check closely to see that no grit has found its way onto the crankshaft.

Oil Pan

REMOVAL AND INSTALLATION

1971-82 Corolla and Starlet

1. Open the engine compartment hood.
NOTE: *Leave it open for the duration of this procedure.*
2. Raise the front end of the car and support it with jackstands.
CAUTION: *Be sure that the car is securely supported. Remember, you will be working underneath it.*
3. Remove the splash shield from underneath the engine.
4. Place a jack under the transmission to support it.
5. Unfasten the bolts which secure the engine rear supporting crossmember to the chassis.
6. Raise the jack under the transmission, slightly.
7. Unbolt the oil pan and work it out from underneath the engine.
NOTE: *If the oil pan does not come out easily, it may be necessary to unfasten the rear engine mounts from the crossmember.*
8. Installation is performed in the reverse order of removal. On Corolla models equipped with the 2T-C engine, apply liquid sealer to the four corners of the oil pan. Tighten the oil pan securing bolts to the following specifications: 3K-C, 4K-C and 4K-E engine: 1.8-2.5 ft.lb. 2T-C and 3K-C engine: 3.6-5.8 ft.lb.

Carina

1. Drain the oil.
2. Raise the front end of the car with jacks and support it with jackstands.
CAUTION: *Be sure that the car is supported*

securely. Remember, you will be working underneath it.
3. Detach the steering relay rod and the tie rods from the idler arm, pitman arm, and steering knuckles.
4. Remove the engine stiffening plates.
5. Remove the splash shields from underneath the engine.
6. Support the front of the engine with a jack and remove the front engine mount attaching bolts.
7. Raise the front of the engine slightly with the jack.
CAUTION: *Be sure that the hood is open before raising the front of the engine.*
8. Unbolt and withdraw the oil pan. Installation is performed in the reverse order of removal. Apply liquid sealer to the four corners of the oil pan gasket used on 2T-C or 20R engines. Torque the oil pan securing bolts to the following specifications: 2T-C engine: 3.6-5.8 ft.lb.

Tercel and 1983-87 Corolla

1. Disconnect the negative battery terminal.
2. Jack up the vehicle and support it with jackstands.
3. Drain the oil.
4. Remove the sway bar and any other necessary steering linkage parts.
5. Disconnect the exhaust pipe from the manifold.
6. Jack up the engine enough to take the weight off it.
7. Remove the engine mounts and engine shock absorber.
8. Continue to jack up the engine enough to remove the pan.
9. Remove the pan bolts and remove the pan.
10. Installation is the reverse of removal. Always use a new pan gasket when reinstalling the pan.

Rear Main Oil Seal

REPLACEMENT

All Engines

NOTE: *This procedure applies only to those models with manual transmissions. If your car has an automatic transmission, leave removal of the oil seal to your dealer. On models equipped with the 1A-C, 3A or 3A-C engines, engine removal is required.*
1. Remove the transmission.
2. Remove the clutch cover assembly and flywheel.
3. Remove the oil seal retaining plate, complete with the oil seal.
4. Use a suitable pry bar to pry the old seal from the retaining plate. Be careful not to damage the plate.

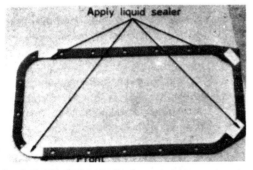
Apply liquid sealant to the four corners

5. Install the new seal, carefully, by using a block of wood to drift it into place.

CAUTION: *Do not damage the seal; a leak will result.*

6. Lubricate the lips of the seal with multi-purpose grease. Install the components in the reverse order from removal.

Oil Pump

REMOVAL AND INSTALLATION

Except Models Listed Below

1. Remove the oil pan, as outlined in the appropriate preceding section.

2. Unbolt the oil pump securing bolts and remove it as an assembly. Installation is the reverse of removal.

1A-3C, 3A, 3A-C, 4A-C RWD and 4A-GE Series

1. Remove the fan shroud and then raise the front of the vehicle and support it on safety stands.

2. Drain the engine oil. On the Tercel, drain the coolant and then remove the radiator.

CAUTION: *When draining the coolant, keep in mind that cats and dogs are attracted by the ethylene glycol antifreeze, and are quite*

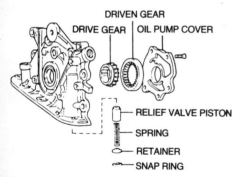

Exploded view of the oil pump—typical A-series and 1C-L

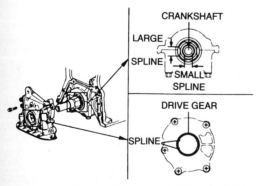

Aligning the oil pump drive gear with the crankshaft gear—A-series engines except 4A-C FWD

likely to drink any that is left in an uncovered container or in puddles on the ground. This will prove fatal in sufficient quantity. Always drain the coolant into a sealable container. Coolant should be reused unless it is contaminated or several years old.

3. Remove the oil pan and the oil strainer.

4. Remove the crankshaft pulley and the timing belt as detailed earlier in the chapter.

5. Remove the oil level gauge guide and then the gauge.

6. Remove the mounting bolts and then use a rubber mallet to carefully tap the oil pump body from the cylinder block.

7. Position a new gasket on the cylinder block.

8. Position the oil pump on the block so that the teeth on the pump drive gear are engaged with the teeth of the crankshaft gear.

9. Installation of the remaining components is in the reverse order of removal.

4A-C FWD and 1C-L Diesel

1. Remove the engine cover under the car and then drain the oil.

2. Remove the hood.

3. Disconnect the center engine mount.

4. Remove the oil pan and oil strainer.

5. Attach an engine hoist to the two engine lifting brackets and suspend the engine.

6. Remove all drive belts; remove the water pump pulley. A/C idler pulley and the crankshaft pulley.

7. Remove the timing belt.

8. Perform Steps 5-9 of the previous procedure.

3E

1. Remove the right hand engine splash shield. Disconnect the exhaust pipe from the manifold. Remove the timing belt.

2. Drain the engine oil. Remove the oil pan, the oil strainer and the dipstick.

3. Remove the oil pump mounting bolts and the tensioner spring bracket. Remove the oil pump. Service as necessary and install in the reverse order of removal.

Radiator

REMOVAL AND INSTALLATION

All Models

1. Drain the cooling system.

CAUTION: *When draining the coolant, keep in mind that cats and dogs are attracted by the ethylene glycol antifreeze, and are quite likely to drink any that is left in an uncovered container or in puddles on the ground. This will prove fatal in sufficient quantity. Always drain the coolant into a sealable container.*

Coolant should be reused unless it is contaminated or several years old.

2. Unfasten the clamps and remove the radiator upper and lower hoses. If equipped with an automatic transmission, remove the oil cooler lines.

3. Detach the hood lock cable and remove the hood lock from the radiator upper support.

NOTE: *It may be necessary to remove the grille in order to gain access to the hood lock/radiator support assembly.*

4. Remove the fan shroud, if so equipped.

5. On models equipped with a coolant recovery system, disconnect the hose from the thermal expansion tank from its bracket.

6. Unbolt and remove the radiator upper support.

7. Unfasten the bolts and remove the radiator.

CAUTION: *Use care not to damage the radiator fins on the cooling fan!*

8. Installation is performed in the reverse order of removal. Remember to check the transmission fluid level on cars with automatic transmissions.

9. Fill the radiator to the specified level.

10. Certain models are equipped with an electric, rather than a belt-driven, cooling fan. Using a radiator-mounted thermoswitch, the fan operates when the coolant temperatures reach 203°F and stops when it lowers to 190°F. It is attached to the radiator by the four radiator retaining bolts. Radiator removal is the same for this engine as all others, except for disconnecting the wiring harness and thermoswitch connector.

Water Pump

REMOVAL AND INSTALLATION

Except 1C-L and A-Series

1. Drain the cooling system.

CAUTION: *When draining the coolant, keep in mind that cats and dogs are attracted by the ethylene glycol antifreeze, and are quite likely to drink any that is left in an uncovered container or in puddles on the ground. This will prove fatal in sufficient quantity. Always drain the coolant into a sealable container. Coolant should be reused unless it is contaminated or several years old.*

2. Unfasten the fan shroud securing bolts and remove the fan shroud, if so equipped.

3. Loosen the alternator adjusting link bolt and remove the drive belt.

4. Repeat Step 3 for the air and/or power steering pump drive belt, if so equipped.

5. Detach the by-pass hose from the water pump.

6. Unfasten the water pump retaining bolts

and remove the water pump and fan assembly, using care not to damage the radiator with the fan.

CAUTION: *If the fan is equipped with a fluid coupling, do not tip the fan/pump assembly on its side, as the fluid will run out!*

7. Installation is performed in the reverse order of removal. Always use a new gasket between the pump body and its mounting. Remember to check for leaks after installation is completed.

A-Series

1. Drain the radiator; save the coolant as it can be reused.

CAUTION: *When draining the coolant, keep in mind that cats and dogs are attracted by the ethylene glycol antifreeze, and are quite likely to drink any that is left in an uncovered container or in puddles on the ground. This will prove fatal in sufficient quantity. Always drain the coolant into a sealable container. Coolant should be reused unless it is contaminated or several years old.*

2. Remove the fan shroud (4A-C RWD only).

3. Remove the fluid coupling (4A-C RWD only), water pump pulley and the drive belt.

4. Remove the water outlet housing and by-pass pipe.

5. Remove the water inlet housing and thermostat.

6. Remove the upper front cover (3A-C only).

7. Disconnect the heater outlet hose from the outlet pipe and then remove the outlet pipe mounting bolt (3A-C only).

8. Remove the heater outlet pipe (4A-C RWD only).

9. Remove the oil level gauge guide and gauge.

10. Remove the lower front cover (4A-C only).

11. Remove the water pump.

12. Installation is in the reverse order of removal.

1C-L

1. Drain the radiator; save the coolant as it can be reused.

CAUTION: *When draining the coolant, keep in mind that cats and dogs are attracted by the ethylene glycol antifreeze, and are quite likely to drink any that is left in an uncovered container or in puddles on the ground. This will prove fatal in sufficient quantity. Always drain the coolant into a sealable container. Coolant should be reused unless it is contaminated or several years old.*

2. Remove the injection pump pulley as detailed in Chapter 4.

3. Remove the water pump.

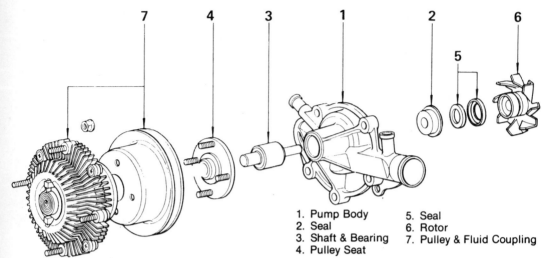

1. Pump Body
2. Seal
3. Shaft & Bearing
4. Pulley Seat
5. Seal
6. Rotor
7. Pulley & Fluid Coupling

Typical water pump components

4. Installation is in the reverse order of removal.

Thermostat

REMOVAL AND INSTALLATION

All Engines

1. Drain the cooling system.

CAUTION: *When draining the coolant, keep in mind that cats and dogs are attracted by the ethylene glycol antifreeze, and are quite likely to drink any that is left in an uncovered container or in puddles on the ground. This will prove fatal in sufficient quantity. Always drain the coolant into a sealable container. Coolant should be reused unless it is contaminated or several years old.*

2. Unfasten the clamp and remove the upper radiator hose from the water outlet elbow.

3. Unbolt and remove the water outlet (thermostat housing).

4. Withdraw the thermostat.

5. Installation is performed in the reverse order of the removal procedure. Use a new gasket on the water outlet.

CAUTION: *Be sure that the thermostat is installed with the spring pointing down!*

Troubleshooting Basic Charging System Problems

Problem	Cause	Solution
Noisy alternator	• Loose mountings • Loose drive pulley • Worn bearings • Brush noise • Internal circuits shorted (High pitched whine)	• Tighten mounting bolts • Tighten pulley • Replace alternator • Replace alternator • Replace alternator
Squeal when starting engine or accelerating	• Glazed or loose belt	• Replace or adjust belt
Indicator light remains on or ammeter indicates discharge (engine running)	• Broken fan belt • Broken or disconnected wires • Internal alternator problems • Defective voltage regulator	• Install belt • Repair or connect wiring • Replace alternator • Replace voltage regulator
Car light bulbs continually burn out—battery needs water continually	• Alternator/regulator overcharging	• Replace voltage regulator/alternator
Car lights flare on acceleration	• Battery low • Internal alternator/regulator problems	• Charge or replace battery • Replace alternator/regulator
Low voltage output (alternator light flickers continually or ammeter needle wanders)	• Loose or worn belt • Dirty or corroded connections • Internal alternator/regulator problems	• Replace or adjust belt • Clean or replace connections • Replace alternator or regulator

Troubleshooting Basic Starting System Problems

Problem	Cause	Solution
Starter motor rotates engine slowly	• Battery charge low or battery defective	• Charge or replace battery
	• Defective circuit between battery and starter motor	• Clean and tighten, or replace cables
	• Low load current	• Bench-test starter motor. Inspect for worn brushes and weak brush springs.
	• High load current	• Bench-test starter motor. Check engine for friction, drag or coolant in cylinders. Check ring gear-to-pinion gear clearance.
Starter motor will not rotate engine	• Battery charge low or battery defective	• Charge or replace battery
	• Faulty solenoid	• Check solenoid ground. Repair or replace as necessary.
	• Damage drive pinion gear or ring gear	• Replace damaged gear(s)
	• Starter motor engagement weak	• Bench-test starter motor
	• Starter motor rotates slowly with high load current	• Inspect drive yoke pull-down and point gap, check for worn end bushings, check ring gear clearance
	• Engine seized	• Repair engine
Starter motor drive will not engage (solenoid known to be good)	• Defective contact point assembly	• Repair or replace contact point assembly
	• Inadequate contact point assembly ground	• Repair connection at ground screw
	• Defective hold-in coil	• Replace field winding assembly
Starter motor drive will not disengage	• Starter motor loose on flywheel housing	• Tighten mounting bolts
	• Worn drive end busing	• Replace bushing
	• Damaged ring gear teeth	• Replace ring gear or driveplate
	• Drive yoke return spring broken or missing	• Replace spring
Starter motor drive disengages prematurely	• Weak drive assembly thrust spring	• Replace drive mechanism
	• Hold-in coil defective	• Replace field winding assembly
Low load current	• Worn brushes	• Replace brushes
	• Weak brush springs	• Replace springs

Troubleshooting Engine Mechanical Problems

Problem	Cause	Solution
External oil leaks	• Fuel pump gasket broken or improperly seated	• Replace gasket
	• Cylinder head cover RTV sealant broken or improperly seated	• Replace sealant; inspect cylinder head cover sealant flange and cylinder head sealant surface for distortion and cracks
	• Oil filler cap leaking or missing	• Replace cap
	• Oil filter gasket broken or improperly seated	• Replace oil filter
	• Oil pan side gasket broken, improperly seated or opening in RTV sealant	• Replace gasket or repair opening in sealant; inspect oil pan gasket flange for distortion
	• Oil pan front oil seal broken or improperly seated	• Replace seal; inspect timing case cover and oil pan seal flange for distortion

Troubleshooting Engine Mechanical Problems (cont.)

Problem	Cause	Solution
External oil leaks (cont.)	• Oil pan rear oil seal broken or improperly seated	• Replace seal; inspect oil pan rear oil seal flange; inspect rear main bearing cap for cracks, plugged oil return channels, or distortion in seal groove
	• Timing case cover oil seal broken or improperly seated	• Replace seal
	• Excess oil pressure because of restricted PCV valve	• Replace PCV valve
	• Oil pan drain plug loose or has stripped threads	• Repair as necessary and tighten
	• Rear oil gallery plug loose	• Use appropriate sealant on gallery plug and tighten
	• Rear camshaft plug loose or improperly seated	• Seat camshaft plug or replace and seal, as necessary
	• Distributor base gasket damaged	• Replace gasket
Excessive oil consumption	• Oil level too high	• Drain oil to specified level
	• Oil with wrong viscosity being used	• Replace with specified oil
	• PCV valve stuck closed	• Replace PCV valve
	• Valve stem oil deflectors (or seals) are damaged, missing, or incorrect type	• Replace valve stem oil deflectors
	• Valve stems or valve guides worn	• Measure stem-to-guide clearance and repair as necessary
	• Poorly fitted or missing valve cover baffles	• Replace valve cover
	• Piston rings broken or missing	• Replace broken or missing rings
	• Scuffed piston	• Replace piston
	• Incorrect piston ring gap	• Measure ring gap, repair as necessary
	• Piston rings sticking or excessively loose in grooves	• Measure ring side clearance, repair as necessary
	• Compression rings installed upside down	• Repair as necessary
	• Cylinder walls worn, scored, or glazed	• Repair as necessary
	• Piston ring gaps not properly staggered	• Repair as necessary
	• Excessive main or connecting rod bearing clearance	• Measure bearing clearance, repair as necessary
No oil pressure	• Low oil level	• Add oil to correct level
	• Oil pressure gauge, warning lamp or sending unit inaccurate	• Replace oil pressure gauge or warning lamp
	• Oil pump malfunction	• Replace oil pump
	• Oil pressure relief valve sticking	• Remove and inspect oil pressure relief valve assembly
	• Oil passages on pressure side of pump obstructed	• Inspect oil passages for obstruction
	• Oil pickup screen or tube obstructed	• Inspect oil pickup for obstruction
	• Loose oil inlet tube	• Tighten or seal inlet tube
Low oil pressure	• Low oil level	• Add oil to correct level
	• Inaccurate gauge, warning lamp or sending unit	• Replace oil pressure gauge or warning lamp
	• Oil excessively thin because of dilution, poor quality, or improper grade	• Drain and refill crankcase with recommended oil
	• Excessive oil temperature	• Correct cause of overheating engine
	• Oil pressure relief spring weak or sticking	• Remove and inspect oil pressure relief valve assembly
	• Oil inlet tube and screen assembly has restriction or air leak	• Remove and inspect oil inlet tube and screen assembly. (Fill inlet tube with lacquer thinner to locate leaks.)

Troubleshooting Engine Mechanical Problems (cont.)

Problem	Cause	Solution
Low oil pressure (cont.)	• Excessive oil pump clearance • Excessive main, rod, or camshaft bearing clearance	• Measure clearances • Measure bearing clearances, repair as necessary
High oil pressure	• Improper oil viscosity • Oil pressure gauge or sending unit inaccurate • Oil pressure relief valve sticking closed	• Drain and refill crankcase with correct viscosity oil • Replace oil pressure gauge • Remove and inspect oil pressure relief valve assembly
Main bearing noise	• Insufficient oil supply • Main bearing clearance excessive • Bearing insert missing • Crankshaft end play excessive • Improperly tightened main bearing cap bolts • Loose flywheel or drive plate • Loose or damaged vibration damper	• Inspect for low oil level and low oil pressure • Measure main bearing clearance, repair as necessary • Replace missing insert • Measure end play, repair as necessary • Tighten bolts with specified torque • Tighten flywheel or drive plate attaching bolts • Repair as necessary
Connecting rod bearing noise	• Insufficient oil supply • Carbon build-up on piston • Bearing clearance excessive or bearing missing • Crankshaft connecting rod journal out-of-round • Misaligned connecting rod or cap • Connecting rod bolts tightened improperly	• Inspect for low oil level and low oil pressure • Remove carbon from piston crown • Measure clearance, repair as necessary • Measure journal dimensions, repair or replace as necessary • Repair as necessary • Tighten bolts with specified torque
Piston noise	• Piston-to-cylinder wall clearance excessive (scuffed piston) • Cylinder walls excessively tapered or out-of-round • Piston ring broken • Loose or seized piston pin • Connecting rods misaligned • Piston ring side clearance excessively loose or tight • Carbon build-up on piston is excessive	• Measure clearance and examine piston • Measure cylinder wall dimensions, rebore cylinder • Replace all rings on piston • Measure piston-to-pin clearance, repair as necessary • Measure rod alignment, straighten or replace • Measure ring side clearance, repair as necessary • Remove carbon from piston
Valve actuating component noise	• Insufficient oil supply • Push rods worn or bent • Rocker arms or pivots worn • Foreign objects or chips in hydraulic tappets • Excessive tappet leak-down • Tappet face worn • Broken or cocked valve springs	• Check for: (a) Low oil level (b) Low oil pressure (c) Plugged push rods (d) Wrong hydraulic tappets (e) Restricted oil gallery (f) Excessive tappet to bore clearance • Replace worn or bent push rods • Replace worn rocker arms or pivots • Clean tappets • Replace valve tappet • Replace tappet; inspect corresponding cam lobe for wear • Properly seat cocked springs; replace broken springs

Troubleshooting Engine Mechanical Problems (cont.)

Problem	Cause	Solution
Value actuating component noise (cont.)	• Stem-to-guide clearance excessive	• Measure stem-to-guide clearance, repair as required
	• Valve bent	• Replace valve
	• Loose rocker arms	• Tighten bolts with specified torque
	• Valve seat runout excessive	• Regrind valve seat/valves
	• Missing valve lock	• Install valve lock
	• Push rod rubbing or contacting cylinder head	• Remove cylinder head and remove obstruction in head
	• Excessive engine oil (four-cylinder engine)	• Correct oil level

Emission Controls and Fuel System

EMISSION CONTROLS

There are three sources of automotive pollutants; crankcase fumes, exhaust gases, and gasoline evaporation. The pollutants formed from these substances fall into three categories. unburned hydrocarbons (HV), carbon monoxide (CO), and oxides of nitrogen (NOx). The equipment used to limit these pollutants is called emission control equipment.

Due to varying state, federal, and provincial regulations, specific emission control equipment have been devised for each. The U.S. emission equipment is divided into two categories: California and 49 State. In this section, the term California applies only to cars originally built to be sold in California. California emissions equipment is generally not shared with equipment installed on cars built to be sold in the other 49 States. Models built to be sold in Canada also have specific emissions equipment, although in most years 49 State and Canadian equipment is the same.

NOTE: *Due to the complex nature of modern electronic engine control systems, comprehensive diagnosis and testing procedures fall outside the confines of this repair manual. For complete information on diagnosis, testing and repair procedures concerning all modern engine and emissions control systems, please refer to Chilton's Guide to Electronic Engine Controls.*

Positive Crankcase Ventilation

A closed, positive crankcase ventilation system is employed on most models. This system cycles incompletely burned fuel which works its way past the piston rings back into the intake manifold for reburning with the fuel/air mixture. The oil filler cap is sealed and the air is drawn from the top of the crankcase into the intake manifold through a valve with a variable orifice.

This valve (commonly known as the PCV valve) regulates the flow of air into the manifold according to the amount of manifold vacuum. When the throttle plates are open fairly wide, the valve opens to maximize the flow. However, at idle speed, when manifold vacuum is at a maximum, the PCS valve throttles the flow in order not to unnecessarily affect the small volume of mixture passing into the engine.

During most driving conditions, manifold vacuum is high and all of the vapor from the crankcase, plus a small amount of excess air, is drawn into the manifold via the PCV valve. However, at full throttle, the increase in the volume of blow-by and the decrease in manifold vacuum make the flow via the PCV valve inadequate. Under these conditions, excess vapors are drawn into the air cleaner and pass into the engine.

REMOVAL AND INSTALLATION

Remove the PCV valve from the cylinder head cover on most engines. Remove the hose from the valve.

On the remainder of the engines, remove the valve from the manifold-to-crankcase hose.

Installation is the reverse of removal.

TESTING

Check the PCV system hoses and connections, to ensure that there are no leaks; then replace or tighten, as necessary.

To check the valve, remove it and blow through both of its ends. When blowing from the side which goes toward the intake manifold, very little air should pass through it. When blowing from the crankcase (valve cover) side, air should pass through freely.

Replace the valve with a new one, if the valve fails to function as outlined.

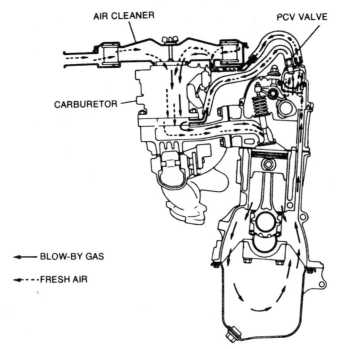

Typical positive crankcase ventilation system on a carbureted engine—4A-C shown

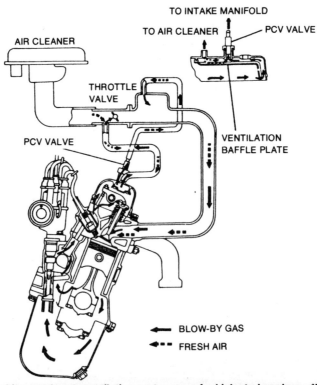

Typical positive crankcase ventilation system on a fuel injected engine—4K-E shown

Replace the valve with a new one, if the valve fails to function as outlined.

NOTE: *Do not attempt to clean or adjust the valve; replace it with a new one.*

Evaporative Emission Control System

To prevent hydrocarbon emissions from entering the atmosphere, Toyota vehicles use evaporative emission control (EEC or EVAP) systems. Models produced between 1970 and 1971 use a case storage system, while later models use a charcoal canister storage system.

The major components of the case storage system are a purge control or vacuum switching valve, a fuel vapor storage case, an air filter, a thermal expansion tank, and a special fuel tank.

When the vehicle is stopped or the engine is running at a low speed, the purge control or vacuum switching valve is closed; fuel vapor travels only as far as the case where it is stored.

When the engine is running at a high speed (cruising speed), the purge control valve is opened by pressure from the air pump or else the vacuum switching valve opens, depending upon the type of emission control system used. This allows the vapor stored in the case to be drawn into the intake manifold along with fresh air which is drawn in from the filter.

The charcoal canister storage system functions in a similar manner to the case system, except that the fuel vapors are stored in a canister filled with activated charcoal, rather than in a case, and that all models use a vacuum switching valve to purge the system. The air filter is not external as it is on the case system; rather it is an integral part of the charcoal canister.

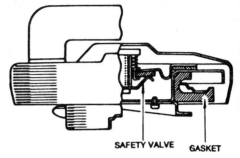

The fuel filler cap with a safety valve

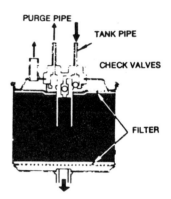

Testing the charcoal canister check valves

REMOVAL AND INSTALLATION

Removal and installation of the various evaporative emission control system components consists of unfastening hoses, loosening securing screws, and removing the part which is to be replaced from its mounting bracket. Installation is the reverse of removal.

NOTE: *When replacing any EEC system hoses, always use hoses that are fuel-resistant or are marked EVAP.*

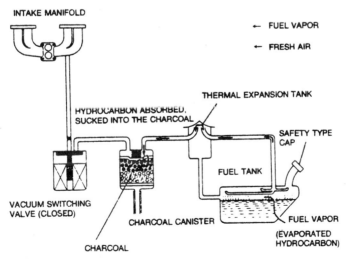

Schematic of a typical charcoal canister vapor storage system

CHECKING THE FILLER CAP

Check that the filler cap seals effectively. Remove the filler cap and pull the safety valve outward to check for smooth operation. Replace the filler cap if the seal is defective or if it is not operating properly.

CHECKING THE PURGE CONTROL VALVE

1970-71

NOTE: *This valve is used only on 1970-71 engines which are also equipped with an air injection system.*

1. Disconnect the line which runs from the storage case to the valve, at the valve end.
2. Connect a tachometer to the engine in accordance with the manufacturer's instructions.
3. Start the engine and slowly increase its speed until the tachometer reads 2,500 rpm (transmission in Neutral).
4. Place a finger over the hose fitting (storage case-to-valve) on the valve.
5. If there is no suction, check the air pump for a malfunction. (See above). If the air pump is not defective, replace the valve.

CHECKING THE CHARCOAL CANISTER AND CHECK VALVES

Remove the charcoal canister from the engine compartment and visually inspect it for cracks or other damage.

Check for stuck check valves. All models from 1971-78 have one check valve in the line between the fuel tank and the charcoal canister. It is located in the trunk. To check:

1. Remove the check valve from the line.
NOTE: *Mark which end goes toward the fuel tank and which end goes toward the charcoal canister.*
2. Blow into the fuel tank end. A slight resistance should be felt at first.
3. Blow through the other end. No resistance should be felt at all.
4. If your results differ from those above, the check valve will require replacement.

1979 and later models have two or three check valves, all are located in the charcoal canister. To check:
1. Using low pressure compressed air, blow into the tank pipe. The air should flow from the other pipes without resistance.
2. If the air flow is incorrect, the check valve will require replacement. Before installing the canister, clean the filter. Blow compressed air into the purge pipe while keeping the others blocked with your fingers.
NOTE: *Do not attempt to wash the charcoal canister. While cleaning the canister, under no circumstances should any activated charcoal be removed.*

TESTING

EEC System Troubleshooting

There are several things which may be checked if a malfunction of the evaporative emission control system is suspected.

1. Leaks may be traced by using a hydrocarbon tester. Run the test probe along the lines and connections. The meter will indicate the presence of a leak by a high hydrocarbon (HC) reading. This method is much more accurate than visual inspection which would only indicate the presence of a leak large enough to pass liquid.
2. Leaks may be caused by any of the following: Defective or worn hoses; Disconnected or pinched hoses; Improperly routed hoses; A defective filler cap or safety valve (sealed cap system).
NOTE: *If it becomes necessary to replace any of the hoses used in the evaporative emission control system, use only hoses which are fuel-resistant or are marked EVAP.*
3. If the fuel tank, storage case, or thermal expansion tank collapse, it may be the fault of clogged or pinches vent lines, a defective vapor separator, or a plugged or incorrect filler cap.
4. To test the filler cap (if it is the safety valve type), clean it and place it against the mount. Blow into the relief valve house. If the cap passes pressure with light blowing or if it fails to release with hard blowing, it is defective and must be replaced.
NOTE: *Use the proper cap for the type of system used; either a sealed cap or safety valve cap, as required. See the chart at the end of this section for proper cap usage.*

Outer Vent Control Valve

1. Disconnect the hoses from the valve.
2. Check that the valve is open when the ignition switch is turned OFF.
3. Check that the valve is closed when the ignition switch is in the ON position.
4. If the valve doesn't operate properly, check the fuse and wiring, if ok, replace the valve.

Thermoswitch (Except Canada 4A-C FWD)

1. Drain the radiator and save the coolant.
2. Remove the thermoswitch from the intake manifold. Cool the switch to below 109°F (43°C).
3. Use an ohmmeter and check for continuity; it should exist.
4. Heat the switch with hot water to a temperature above 131°F (55°C). There should be no continuity.

5. Apply liquid sealer to the threads of the switch and then reinstall it in the manifold.

6. Refill the coolant.

Dual Diaphragm Distributor

Some Toyota models are equipped with a dual diaphragm distributor unit. This distributor has a retard diaphragm, as well as a diaphragm for advance.

Retarding the timing helps to reduce exhaust emissions, as well as making up for the lack of engine braking on models equipped with a throttle positioner.

TESTING

1. Connect a timing light to the engine. Check the ignition timing.

NOTE: *Before proceeding with the tests, disconnect any spark control devices, distributor vacuum valves, etc. If these are left connected, inaccurate results may be obtained.*

2. Remove the retard hose from the distributor and plug it. Increase the engine speed. The

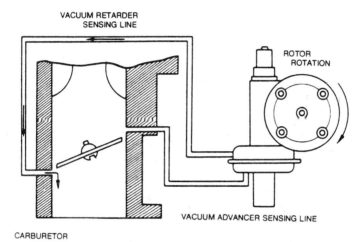

Dual-diaphragm distributor with vacuum switching valve

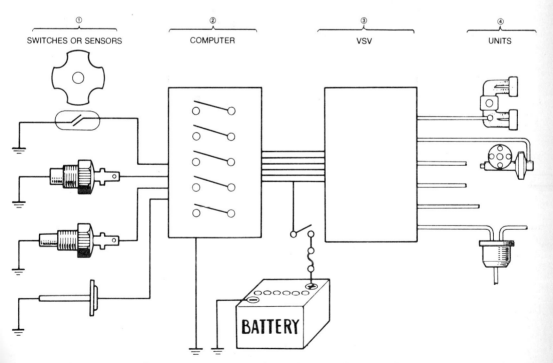

Block diagram of a typical engine modification system

timing should advance. If it fails to do so, then the vacuum unit is faulty and must be replaced.

3. Check the timing with the engine at normal idle speed. Unplug the retard hose and connect it to the vacuum unit. The timing should instantly be retarded from 4 to 10°. If this does not occur, the retard diaphragm has a leak and the vacuum unit must be replaced.

Dual Vacuum Advance Distributor

This system is available on non-California Corollas as an option starting 1976. It replaces the old dual point distributor and its function is basically the same.

SYSTEM CHECKS

1. Check all the hoses for proper connections and tightness.

2. With the engine cold, disconnect hose **D**, idle the engine and see if the octane selector is drawn in. If not, check for vacuum at sub-diaphragm **B**. If there is vacuum, replace the distributor diaphragm. If not, pinch hose **A** with your finger. If the octane selector is drawn in, replace TVSV 3. If it's still not drawn in, check the check valve. If the check valve is OK, replace the thermostatic valve or the choke breaker diaphragm.

3. If the octane selector is drawn in (at the beginning of Step 2), you should then disconnect hose **C** from the check valve. If the octane selector isn't drawn in, replace the check valve.

4. If the octane selector is drawn in, disconnect hose **B** from the distributor and open and close the throttle valve. The octane selector should move. If not, see that TVSV 1 is open. If not, replace it. If it is open, replace the distributor diaphragm.

5. If the octane selector moves in the previous step with the engine temperature around 104°F, check that the ignition timing is approximately 10°B at idle. If the timing is off, adjust it. If the ignition timing is OK, replace TVSV 3.

6. Pinch hose **A** closed and check ignition timing. The timing should change to a figure in the range of 18-22°B. If the timing doesn't change, replace the distributor. If the timing does change, rev the engine to 2,000 rpm. Check to see if the octane selector is pulled in after about four seconds. If not, replace the vacuum transmitting valve (VTV). If the octane selector is pulled in, the system is OK.

Engine Modifications System

Toyota also uses an assortment of engine modifications to regulate exhaust emissions. Most of these devices fall into the category of engine vacuum controls. There are three principal components used on the engine modifications system, as well as a number of smaller parts. The three major components are: a speed sensor; a computer (speed marker); and a vacuum switching valve.

The vacuum switching valve and computer circuit operates most of the emission control components. Depending upon year and engine usage, the vacuum switching valve and computer may operate the pure control for the evaporative emission control system; the transmission controlled spark (TCS) or speed controlled spark (SCS); the dual diaphragm distributor, the throttle positioner systems, the EGR system, the catalyst protection system, etc.

The functions of the evaporative emissions control system, the throttle positioner, and the dual diaphragm distributor are described in detail in the preceding sections. However, a word is necessary about the functions of the TCS and SCS systems before discussing the operation of the vacuum switching valve/computer circuit.

The major difference between the transmission controlled spark and speed controlled spark systems is the manner in which system operation is determined. Toyota TCS systems use a mechanical switch to determine which gear is selected; SCS systems use a speed sensor built into the speedometer cable.

Below a predetermined speed, or any gear other than Fourth, the vacuum advance unit on the distributor is rendered inoperative or the timing retarded. By changing the distributor advance curve in this manner, it is possible to reduce emissions of oxides of nitrogen (NOx).

NOTE: *Some engines are equipped with a thermo-sensor so that the TCS or SCS system only operates when the coolant temperature is 140-212°F.*

Aside from determining the preceding conditions, the vacuum switching valve computer circuit operates other devices in the emission control system (EGR, Catalytic converter, etc.).

The computer acts as a speed market; at certain speeds it sends a signal to the vacuum switching valve which acts as a gate, opening and closing the emission control system vacuum circuits.

The vacuum switching valve on all 1970 and some 1971 engines is a simple affair; a single solenoid operates a valve which uncovers certain vacuum ports at the same time others are covered.

The valve used on all 1972-81 and some 1971 engines contains several solenoid and valve assemblies so that different combinations of opened and closed vacuum ports are possible. This allows greater flexibility of operation for the emission control system.

CHILTON'S
FUEL ECONOMY
& TUNE-UP TIPS

Tune-up • Spark Plug Diagnosis • Emission Controls

Fuel System • Cooling System • Tires and Wheels

General Maintenance

CHILTON'S FUEL ECONOMY & TUNE-UP TIPS

Fuel economy is important to everyone, no matter what kind of vehicle you drive. The maintenance-minded motorist can save both money and fuel using these tips and the periodic maintenance and tune-up procedures in this Repair and Tune-Up Guide.

There are more than 130,000,000 cars and trucks registered for private use in the United States. Each travels an average of 10-12,000 miles per year, and, and in total they consume close to 70 billion gallons of fuel each year. This represents nearly ⅔ of the oil imported by the United States each year. The Federal government's goal is to reduce consumption 10% by 1985. A variety of methods are either already in use or under serious consideration, and they all affect you driving and the cars you will drive. In addition to "down-sizing", the auto industry is using or investigating the use of electronic fuel delivery, electronic engine controls and alternative engines for use in smaller and lighter vehicles, among other alternatives to meet the federally mandated Corporate Average Fuel Economy (CAFE) of 27.5 mpg by 1985. The government, for its part, is considering rationing, mandatory driving curtailments and tax increases on motor vehicle fuel in an effort to reduce consumption. The government's goal of a 10% reduction could be realized — and further government regulation avoided — if every private vehicle could use just 1 less gallon of fuel per week.

How Much Can You Save?

Tests have proven that almost anyone can make at least a 10% reduction in fuel consumption through regular maintenance and tune-ups. When a major manufacturer of spark plugs sur-

TUNE-UP

1. Check the cylinder compression to be sure the engine will really benefit from a tune-up and that it is capable of producing good fuel economy. A tune-up will be wasted on an engine in poor mechanical condition.

2. Replace spark plugs regularly. New spark plugs alone can increase fuel economy 3%.

3. Be sure the spark plugs are the correct type (heat range) for your vehicle. See the Tune-Up Specifications.

Heat range refers to the spark plug's ability to conduct heat away from the firing end. It must conduct the heat away in an even pattern to avoid becoming a source of pre-ignition, yet it must also operate hot enough to burn off conductive deposits that could cause misfiring.

The heat range is usually indicated by a number on the spark plug, part of the manufacturer's designation for each individual spark plug. The numbers in bold-face indicate the heat range in each manufacturer's identification system.

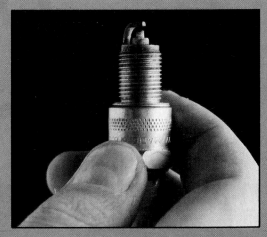

Periodically, check the spark plugs to be sure they are firing efficiently. They are excellent indicators of the internal condition of your engine.

Manufacturer	Typical Designation
AC	R **45** TS
Bosch (old)	WA **145** T30
Bosch (new)	HR **8** Y
Champion	RBL **15** Y
Fram/Autolite	4**15**
Mopar	P-**62** PR
Motorcraft	BRF-**42**
NGK	BP **5** ES-15
Nippondenso	W **16** EP
Prestolite	14GR **5** 2A

On AC, Bosch (new), Champion, Fram/Autolite, Mopar, Motorcraft and Prestolite, a higher number indicates a hotter plug. On Bosch (old), NGK and Nippondenso, a higher number indicates a colder plug.

4. Make sure the spark plugs are properly gapped. See the Tune-Up Specifications in this book.

5. Be sure the spark plugs are firing efficiently. The illustrations on the next 2 pages show you how to "read" the firing end of the spark plug.

6. Check the ignition timing and set it to specifications. Tests show that almost all cars have incorrect ignition timing by more than 2°.

veyed over 6,000 cars nationwide, they found that a tune-up, on cars that needed one, increased fuel economy over 11%. Replacing worn plugs alone, accounted for a 3% increase. The same test also revealed that 8 out of every 10 vehicles will have some maintenance deficiency that will directly affect fuel economy, emissions or performance. Most of this mileage-robbing neglect could be prevented with regular maintenance.

Modern engines require that all of the functioning systems operate properly for maximum efficiency. A malfunction anywhere wastes fuel. You can keep your vehicle running as efficiently and economically as possible, by being aware of your vehicle's operating and performance characteristics. If your vehicle suddenly develops performance or fuel economy problems it could be due to one or more of the following:

PROBLEM	POSSIBLE CAUSE
Engine Idles Rough	Ignition timing, idle mixture, vacuum leak or something amiss in the emission control system.
Hesitates on Acceleration	Dirty carburetor or fuel filter, improper accelerator pump setting, ignition timing or fouled spark plugs.
Starts Hard or Fails to Start	Worn spark plugs, improperly set automatic choke, ice (or water) in fuel system.
Stalls Frequently	Automatic choke improperly adjusted and possible dirty air filter or fuel filter.
Performs Sluggishly	Worn spark plugs, dirty fuel or air filter, ignition timing or automatic choke out of adjustment.

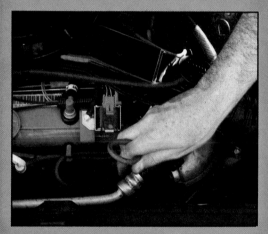

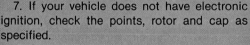

Check spark plug wires on conventional point type ignition for cracks by bending them in a loop around your finger.

Be sure that spark plug wires leading to adjacent cylinders do not run too close together. (Photo courtesy Champion Spark Plug Co.)

7. If your vehicle does not have electronic ignition, check the points, rotor and cap as specified.

8. Check the spark plug wires (used with conventional point-type ignitions) for cracks and burned or broken insulation by bending them in a loop around your finger. Cracked wires decrease fuel efficiency by failing to deliver full voltage to the spark plugs. One misfiring spark plug can cost you as much as 2 mpg.

9. Check the routing of the plug wires. Misfiring can be the result of spark plug leads to adjacent cylinders running parallel to each other and too close together. One wire tends to

pick up voltage from the other causing it to fire "out of time".

10. Check all electrical and ignition circuits for voltage drop and resistance.

11. Check the distributor mechanical and/or vacuum advance mechanisms for proper functioning. The vacuum advance can be checked by twisting the distributor plate in the opposite direction of rotation. It should spring back when released.

12. Check and adjust the valve clearance on engines with mechanical lifters. The clearance should be slightly loose rather than too tight.

SPARK PLUG DIAGNOSIS

Normal

APPEARANCE: This plug is typical of one operating normally. The insulator nose varies from a light tan to grayish color with slight electrode wear. The presence of slight deposits is normal on used plugs and will have no adverse effect on engine performance. The spark plug heat range is correct for the engine and the engine is running normally.

CAUSE: Properly running engine.

RECOMMENDATION: Before reinstalling this plug, the electrodes should be cleaned and filed square. Set the gap to specifications. If the plug has been in service for more than 10-12,000 miles, the entire set should probably be replaced with a fresh set of the same heat range.

Oil Deposits

APPEARANCE: The firing end of the plug is covered with a wet, oily coating.

CAUSE: The problem is poor oil control. On high mileage engines, oil is leaking past the rings or valve guides into the combustion chamber. A common cause is also a plugged PCV valve, and a ruptured fuel pump diaphragm can also cause this condition. Oil fouled plugs such as these are often found in new or recently overhauled engines, before normal oil control is achieved, and can be cleaned and reinstalled.

RECOMMENDATION: A hotter spark plug may temporarily relieve the problem, but the engine is probably in need of work.

Incorrect Heat Range

APPEARANCE: The effects of high temperature on a spark plug are indicated by clean white, often blistered insulator. This can also be accompanied by excessive wear of the electrode, and the absence of deposits.

CAUSE: Check for the correct spark plug heat range. A plug which is too hot for the engine can result in overheating. A car operated mostly at high speeds can require a colder plug. Also check ignition timing, cooling system level, fuel mixture and leaking intake manifold.

RECOMMENDATION: If all ignition and engine adjustments are known to be correct, and no other malfunction exists, install spark plugs one heat range colder.

Photos Courtesy Fram Corporation

Carbon Deposits

APPEARANCE: Carbon fouling is easily identified by the presence of dry, soft, black, sooty deposits.

CAUSE: Changing the heat range can often lead to carbon fouling, as can prolonged slow, stop-and-start driving. If the heat range is correct, carbon fouling can be attributed to a rich fuel mixture, sticking choke, clogged air cleaner, worn breaker points, retarded timing or low compression. If only one or two plugs are carbon fouled, check for corroded or cracked wires on the affected plugs. Also look for cracks in the distributor cap between the towers of affected cylinders.

RECOMMENDATION: After the problem is corrected, these plugs can be cleaned and reinstalled if not worn severely.

MMT Fouled

APPEARANCE: Spark plugs fouled by MMT (Methycyclopentadienyl Maganese Tricarbonyl) have reddish, rusty appearance on the insulator and side electrode.

CAUSE: MMT is an anti-knock additive in gasoline used to replace lead. During the combustion process, the MMT leaves a reddish deposit on the insulator and side electrode.

RECOMMENDATION: No engine malfunction is indicated and the deposits will not affect plug performance any more than lead deposits (see Ash Deposits). MMT fouled plugs can be cleaned, regapped and reinstalled.

High Speed Glazing

APPEARANCE: Glazing appears as shiny coating on the plug, either yellow or tan in color.

CAUSE: During hard, fast acceleration, plug temperatures rise suddenly. Deposits from normal combustion have no chance to fluff-off; instead, they melt on the insulator forming an electrically conductive coating which causes misfiring.

RECOMMENDATION: Glazed plugs are not easily cleaned. They should be replaced with a fresh set of plugs of the correct heat range. If the condition recurs, using plugs with a heat range one step colder may cure the problem.

Ash (Lead) Deposits

APPEARANCE: Ash deposits are characterized by light brown or white colored deposits crusted on the side or center electrodes. In some cases it may give the plug a rusty appearance.

CAUSE: Ash deposits are normally derived from oil or fuel additives burned during normal combustion. Normally they are harmless, though excessive amounts can cause misfiring. If deposits are excessive in short mileage, the valve guides may be worn.

RECOMMENDATION: Ash-fouled plugs can be cleaned, gapped and reinstalled.

Detonation

APPEARANCE: Detonation is usually characterized by a broken plug insulator.

CAUSE: A portion of the fuel charge will begin to burn spontaneously, from the increased heat following ignition. The explosion that results applies extreme pressure to engine components, frequently damaging spark plugs and pistons.

Detonation can result by over-advanced ignition timing, inferior gasoline (low octane) lean air/fuel mixture, poor carburetion, engine lugging or an increase in compression ratio due to combustion chamber deposits or engine modification.

RECOMMENDATION: Replace the plugs after correcting the problem.

Photos Courtesy Champion Spark Plug Co.

EMISSION CONTROLS

13. Be aware of the general condition of the emission control system. It contributes to reduced pollution and should be serviced regularly to maintain efficient engine operation.

14. Check all vacuum lines for dried, cracked or brittle conditions. Something as simple as a leaking vacuum hose can cause poor performance and loss of economy.

15. Avoid tampering with the emission control system. Attempting to improve fuel econ-

FUEL SYSTEM

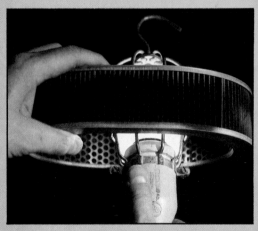

Check the air filter with a light behind it. If you can see light through the filter it can be reused.

Extremely clogged filters should be discarded and replaced with a new one.

18. Replace the air filter regularly. A dirty air filter richens the air/fuel mixture and can increase fuel consumption as much as 10%. Tests show that 1/3 of all vehicles have air filters in need of replacement.

19. Replace the fuel filter at least as often as recommended.

20. Set the idle speed and carburetor mixture to specifications.

21. Check the automatic choke. A sticking or malfunctioning choke wastes gas.

22. During the summer months, adjust the automatic choke for a leaner mixture which will produce faster engine warm-ups.

COOLING SYSTEM

29. Be sure all accessory drive belts are in good condition. Check for cracks or wear.

30. Adjust all accessory drive belts to proper tension.

31. Check all hoses for swollen areas, worn spots, or loose clamps.

32. Check coolant level in the radiator or ex-pansion tank.

33. Be sure the thermostat is operating properly. A stuck thermostat delays engine warm-up and a cold engine uses nearly twice as much fuel as a warm engine.

34. Drain and replace the engine coolant at least as often as recommended. Rust and scale

TIRES & WHEELS

38. Check the tire pressure often with a pencil type gauge. Tests by a major tire manufacturer show that 90% of all vehicles have at least 1 tire improperly inflated. Better mileage can be achieved by over-inflating tires, but never exceed the maximum inflation pressure on the side of the tire.

39. If possible, install radial tires. Radial tires deliver as much as 1/2 mpg more than bias belted tires.

40. Avoid installing super-wide tires. They only create extra rolling resistance and decrease fuel mileage. Stick to the manufacturer's recommendations.

41. Have the wheels properly balanced.

omy by tampering with emission controls is more likely to worsen fuel economy than improve it. Emission control changes on modern engines are not readily reversible.

16. Clean (or replace) the EGR valve and lines as recommended.

17. Be sure that all vacuum lines and hoses are reconnected properly after working under the hood. An unconnected or misrouted vacuum line can wreak havoc with engine performance.

23. Check for fuel leaks at the carburetor, fuel pump, fuel lines and fuel tank. Be sure all lines and connections are tight.

24. Periodically check the tightness of the carburetor and intake manifold attaching nuts and bolts. These are a common place for vacuum leaks to occur.

25. Clean the carburetor periodically and lubricate the linkage.

26. The condition of the tailpipe can be an excellent indicator of proper engine combustion. After a long drive at highway speeds, the inside of the tailpipe should be a light grey in color. Black or soot on the insides indicates an overly rich mixture.

27. Check the fuel pump pressure. The fuel pump may be supplying more fuel than the engine needs.

28. Use the proper grade of gasoline for your engine. Don't try to compensate for knocking or "pinging" by advancing the ignition timing. This practice will only increase plug temperature and the chances of detonation or pre-ignition with relatively little performance gain.

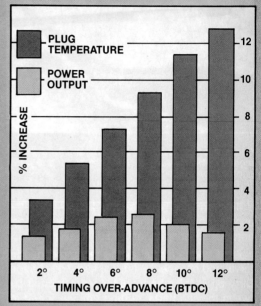

Increasing ignition timing past the specified setting results in a drastic increase in spark plug temperature with increased chance of detonation or preignition. Performance increase is considerably less. (Photo courtesy Champion Spark Plug Co.)

that form in the engine should be flushed out to allow the engine to operate at peak efficiency.

35. Clean the radiator of debris that can decrease cooling efficiency.

36. Install a flex-type or electric cooling fan, if you don't have a clutch type fan. Flex fans use curved plastic blades to push more air at low speeds when more cooling is needed; at high speeds the blades flatten out for less resistance. Electric fans only run when the engine temperature reaches a predetermined level.

37. Check the radiator cap for a worn or cracked gasket. If the cap does not seal properly, the cooling system will not function properly.

42. Be sure the front end is correctly aligned. A misaligned front end actually has wheels going in differed directions. The increased drag can reduce fuel economy by .3 mpg.

43. Correctly adjust the wheel bearings. Wheel bearings that are adjusted too tight increase rolling resistance.

Check tire pressures regularly with a reliable pocket type gauge. Be sure to check the pressure on a cold tire.

GENERAL MAINTENANCE

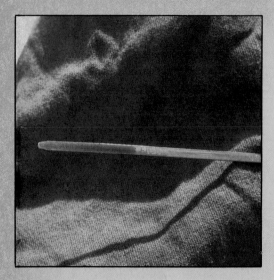

Check the fluid levels (particularly engine oil) on a regular basis. Be sure to check the oil for grit, water or other contamination.

A vacuum gauge is another excellent indicator of internal engine condition and can also be installed in the dash as a mileage indicator.

44. Periodically check the fluid levels in the engine, power steering pump, master cylinder, automatic transmission and drive axle.

45. Change the oil at the recommended interval and change the filter at every oil change. Dirty oil is thick and causes extra friction between moving parts, cutting efficiency and increasing wear. A worn engine requires more frequent tune-ups and gets progressively worse fuel economy. In general, use the lightest viscosity oil for the driving conditions you will encounter.

46. Use the recommended viscosity fluids in the transmission and axle.

47. Be sure the battery is fully charged for fast starts. A slow starting engine wastes fuel.

48. Be sure battery terminals are clean and tight.

49. Check the battery electrolyte level and add distilled water if necessary.

50. Check the exhaust system for crushed pipes, blockages and leaks.

51. Adjust the brakes. Dragging brakes or brakes that are not releasing create increased drag on the engine.

52. Install a vacuum gauge or miles-per-gallon gauge. These gauges visually indicate engine vacuum in the intake manifold. High vacuum = good mileage and low vacuum = poorer mileage. The gauge can also be an excellent indicator of internal engine conditions.

53. Be sure the clutch is properly adjusted. A slipping clutch wastes fuel.

54. Check and periodically lubricate the heat control valve in the exhaust manifold. A sticking or inoperative valve prevents engine warm-up and wastes gas.

55. Keep accurate records to check fuel economy over a period of time. A sudden drop in fuel economy may signal a need for tune-up or other maintenance.

SYSTEM CHECKS

Due to the complexity of the components involved, about the only engine modification system checks which can be made, are the following:

1. Examine the vacuum lines to ensure that they are not clogged, pinched, or loose.
2. Check the electrical connections for tightness and corrosion.
3. Be sure that the vacuum sources for the vacuum switching valve are not plugged.
4. On models equipped with speed controlled spark, a broken speedometer cable could also render the system inoperative. Beyond these checks, servicing the engine modifications system is best left to an authorized service facility.

NOTE: *A faulty vacuum switching valve or computer could cause more than one of the emission control systems to fail. Therefore, if several systems are out, these two units (and the speedometer cable) would be the first things to check.*

Throttle Positioner

On Toyotas with an engine modification system, a throttle positioner is included to reduce exhaust emissions during deceleration. The positioner prevents the throttle from closing completely. Vacuum is reduced under the throttle valve which, in turn, acts on the retard chamber of the distributor vacuum unit. This compensates for the loss of engine braking caused by the partially opened throttle.

NOTE: *For a description of the operation of the dual diaphragm distributor, see Dual Diaphragm Distributor.*

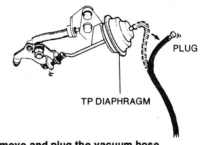

Remove and plug the vacuum hose

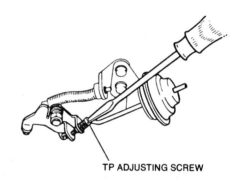

Adjusting the throttle positioner

Once the vehicle drops below a predetermined speed, the vacuum switching valve provides vacuum to the throttle positioner diaphragm; the throttle positioner retracts allowing the throttle valve to close completely, The distributor also is returned to normal operation.

ADJUSTMENT

1. Start the engine and allow it to reach normal operating temperature.

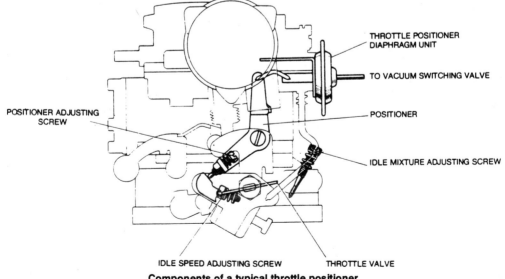

Components of a typical throttle positioner

Throttle Positioner Setting
(rpm)

Year	Engine	Engine rpm (Positioner Set)
1975–77 ①	2T-C	1500 MT 1400 AT ①
	3K-C	1500 (Canada)
1978–82	2T-C	1400 MT 1200 AT
	3T-C	1600 MT 1300 AT ②
1980–82	1A-C, 3A 3A-C	1700 MT 1400 AT
1983–84	3A-C, 4A-C	1400 ③
1981–82	4K-C	2000

① 1977: 1200
② Calif.: 1400
③ Canadian 3A/MT: 1700
AT Automatic transmission
MT Manual transmission

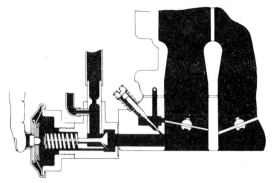

Inspecting the auxiliary slow system diaphgram

2. Adjust the idle speed as detailed in Chapter 1.

NOTE: *Leave the tachometer connected after completing the idle adjustments, as it will be needed in Step 5.*

3. Detach the vacuum line from the positioner diaphragm unit and plug the line up.

4. Accelerate the engine slightly to set the throttle positioner in place.

5. Check the engine speed with a tachometer when the throttle positioner is set.

6. If necessary, adjust the engine speed, with the throttle positioner adjusting screw.

7. Connect the vacuum hose to the positioner diaphragm.

8. The throttle lever should be freed from the positioner as soon as the vacuum hose is connected. Engine idle should return to normal.

9. If the throttle positioner fails to function properly, check its linkage, and vacuum diaphragm. If there are no defects in either of these, the fault probably lies in the vacuum switching valve or the speed marker unit.

NOTE: *Due to the complexity of these two components, and also because they require special test equipment, their service is best left to an authorized facility.*

Carburetor Auxiliary Slow System

A carburetor auxiliary slow system is used on 1970-71 3K-C engines. It provides uniform combination during deceleration. The components of the auxiliary slow system consist of a

vacuum operated valve, a fresh air intake, and a fuel line which is connected to the carburetor float chamber.

During deceleration, manifold vacuum acts on the valve which opens it, causing additional air/fuel mixture to flow into the intake manifold. The additional mixture aids in more complete combustion.

REMOVAL AND INSTALLATION

1. Remove the hoses from the auxiliary slow system unit.

2. Unfasten the recessed screws and withdraw the system as a complete unit. Installation is performed in the reverse order.

TESTING

1. Start the engine, allow it to reach normal operating temperature, and run it at normal idle speed.

2. Remove the rubber cap from the diaphragm assembly and place your finger over the opening. There should be no suction at idle speed. If there is, the diaphragm is defective and the unit must be replaced.

3. Pinch the air intake hose which runs from the air cleaner to the auxiliary slow system. There should be no change in engine idle with the hose pinched.

4. Disconnect the air intake hose at the auxiliary slow system. Race the engine. Place your finger over the air intake. Release the throttle; suction should be felt at the air intake.

5. If any of the tests indicate a defective auxiliary slow system, replace it as a unit.

Mixture Control (MC) System

The mixture control valve, used on certain engines, aids in combustion of unburned fuel during periods of deceleration. The mixture control valve is operated by the vacuum switching valve during periods of deceleration to admit additional fresh air into the intake manifold. The extra air allows more complete com-

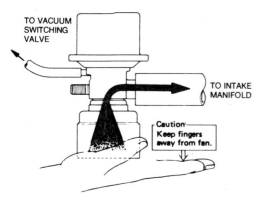

Testing the mixture control valve

bustion of the fuel, thus reducing hydrocarbon emissions.

REMOVAL AND INSTALLATION

1. Unfasten the vacuum switching valve line from the mixture control valve.
2. Remove the intake manifold hose from the valve.
3. Remove the valve from its engine mounting. Installation is performed in the reverse order of removal.

TESTING

1. Start the engine and allow it idle (warmed up).
2. Place your hand over the air intake at the bottom of the valve.
CAUTION: *Keep your fingers clear of the engine fan.*
3. Increase the engine speed and then release the throttle.
4. Suction should be felt at the air intake only while the engine is decelerating. Once the engine has returned to idle, no suction should be felt. If the above test indicates a malfunction, proceed with the next step; if not, the mixture control valve is functioning properly and requires no further adjustment.

5. Disconnect the vacuum line from the mixture control valve. If suction can be felt underneath the valve with the engine at idle, the valve seat is defective and must be replaced.
6. Reconnect the vacuum line to the valve. Disconnect the other end of the line from the vacuum switching valve and place it in your mouth.
7. With the engine idling, suck on the end of the vacuum line to duplicate the action of the vacuum switching valve.
8. Suction at the valve air intake should only be felt for an instant. If air cannot be drawn into the valve at all, or if it is continually drawn in, replace the mixture control valve. If the mixture control valve is functioning properly, and all of the hose and connections are in good working order, the vacuum switching valve is probably at fault.

Auxiliary Enrichment System

An auxiliary enrichment system, which Toyota calls an Auxiliary Accelerator Pump (AAP) System, is used on all models, starting in 1975.

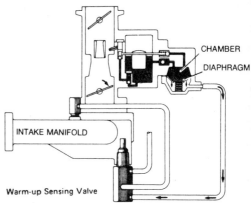

Components of the auxiliary enrichment system— 1974–77

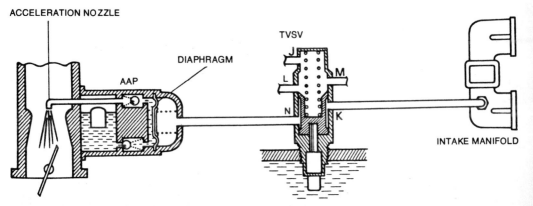

Auxiliary enrichment system—1978–83

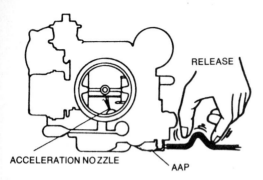

ACCELERATION NOZZLE

RELEASE

AAP

Checking the accelerator pump—1978–83

When the engine is cold, an auxiliary enrichment circuit in the carburetor is operated to squirt extra fuel into the acceleration circuit in order to prevent the mixture from becoming too lean.

A thermostatic vacuum valve (warmup valve), which is threaded into the intake manifold, controls the operation of the enrichment circuit. Below a specified temperature, the valve is opened and manifold vacuum is allowed to act on a diaphragm in the carburetor. The vacuum pulls the diaphragm down, allowing fuel to flow into a special chamber above it.

Under sudden acceleration manifold vacuum drops momentarily, allowing the diaphragm to be pushed up by spring tension. This in turn forces the fuel from the chamber through a passage and out the accelerator pump jet.

When the coolant temperature goes above specification, the thermostatic vacuum valve closes, preventing the vacuum from reaching the diaphragm which makes the enrichment system inoperative.

TESTS

1974-77

1. Check for clogged, pinched, disconnected, or misrouted vacuum lines.
2. With the engine cold (below 75°F), remove the top of the air cleaner, and allow the engine to idle.
3. Disconnect the vacuum line from the carburetor AAP unit. Gasoline should squirt out the accelerator pump jet.
4. If gas doesn't squirt out of the jet, check for vacuum at the AAP vacuum line with the engine idling. If there is no vacuum and the hose are in good shape, the thermostatic vacuum valve is defective and must be replaced.
5. If the gas doesn't squirt out and vacuum is present at the vacuum line in Step 4, the AAP unit is defective and must be replaced.
6. Repeat Step 3 with the engine at normal operating temperature. If gasoline squirts out

of the pump jet, the thermostatic vacuum valve is defective and must be replaced.

7. Reconnect all of the vacuum lines and install the top of the air cleaner.

1978-83

This system is used on some engines to improve driveability. It cuts air supplied to the main nozzle of the carburetor under certain conditions to improve performance.

If the system is suspected to be operating improperly, test the VCV valve as described below. If any of the tests are failed, replace the valve.

1. The engine must be completely cold for this test.
2. Remove the air cleaner cover and start the engine.
3. Pinch the AAP hose and then have a helper turn off the engine while you continue pinching the hose.
4. With the engine off, release the hose. Gasoline should squirt out of the accelerator nozzle inside the carburetor.
5. Run the engine until it reaches normal operating temperature. Repeat Steps 3-4 and check that gasoline does not squirt out of the nozzle.

Inspect the AAP diaphragm.

1. Start the engine and disconnect the hose from the diaphragm.
2. Apply and release the vacuum directly to the diaphragm at idle.

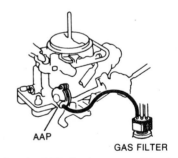

AAP

GAS FILTER

Checking the AAP diaphragm—1978–83

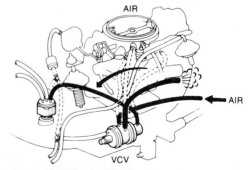

AIR

AIR

VCV

Connect hoses as shown

3. Check that the engine rpm changes when you release vacuum.

4. Reconnect the APP hose. If a problem is found, replace the diaphragm.

Spark Delay Valve

Starting 1975, non-California Corolla models have a spark delay valve (SDV) in the distributor vacuum line. The valve has a small orifice in it, which slows down the vacuum flow to the vacuum advance unit on the distributor. By delaying the vacuum to the distributor, a reduction in HC and CO emissions is possible.

When the coolant temperature is below 95°F, a coolant temperature operated vacuum control valve is opened, allowing the distributor to receive undelayed, ported vacuum through a separate vacuum line. Above 95°F, this line is blocked and all ported vacuum must go through the spark delay valve.

TESTING

1. Allow the engine to cool, so that the coolant temperature is below 95°F.

2. Disconnect the vacuum line which runs from the coolant temperature operated vacuum valve to the vacuum advance unit at the advance unit end. Connect a vacuum gauge to this line.

3. Start the engine. Increase the engine speed; the gauge should indicate a vacuum.

4. Allow the engine to warm-up to normal operating temperature. Increase the engine speed; this time the vacuum gauge should read zero.

5. Replace the coolant temperature operated vacuum valve, if it fails either of these tests. Disconnect the vacuum gauge and reconnect the vacuum lines.

6. Remove the spark delay valve from the vacuum lines, noting which side faces the distributor.

7. Connect a hand operated vacuum pump which has a built-in vacuum gauge to the carburetor side of the spark delay valve.

8. Connect a vacuum gauge to the distributor side of the valve.

9. Operate the hand pump to create a vacuum. The vacuum gauge on the distributor side should show a hesitation before registering.

10. The gauge reading on the pump side should drop slightly, taking several seconds for it to balance with the reading on the other gauge.

11. If Steps 9 and 10 are negative, replace the spark delay valve.

12. Remove the vacuum gauge from the distributor side of the valve. Cover the distributor

side of the valve with your finger and operate the pump to create a vacuum of 15 in.Hg.

13. The reading on the pump gauge should remain steady. If the gauge reading drops, replace the valve.

14. Remove your finger; the reading of the gauge should drop slowly. If the reading goes to zero rapidly, replace the valve.

Exhaust Gas Recirculation (EGR)

Most engines, except for early 2T-C engines and the 4K-E, use EGR.

In all cases, the EGR valve is controlled by the same computer and vacuum switching valve which is used to operate other emission control system components.

On all engines there are several conditions, determined by the computer which permit exhaust gas recirculation to take place:

1. Vehicle speed.
2. Engine coolant temperature.
3. EGR valve temperature.
4. Carburetor flange temperature.

EGR VALVE CHECK

1974-78

1. Allow the engine to warm up and remove the top from the air cleaner.

NOTE: *Do not remove the entire air cleaner assembly.*

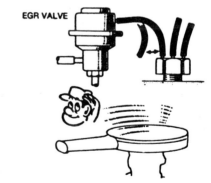

Checking the EGR valve—1974–78

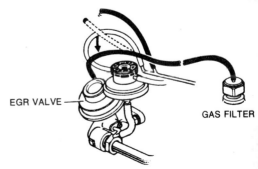

Checking the EGR valve— typical from 1979

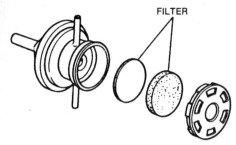

FILTER

EGR vacuum modulator

2. Disconnect the hose (white tape coded), which runs from the vacuum switching valve to the EGR valve, at its EGR valve end.

3. Remove the intake manifold hose (red coded) from the vacuum switching valve and connect it to the EGR valve. When the engine is at idle, a hollow sound should be heard coming from the air cleaner.

4. Disconnect the hose from the EGR valve; the hollow sound should disappear.

5. If the sound doesn't vary, the EGR valve is defective and must be replaced.

6. Reconnect the vacuum hoses as they were originally found. Install the top on the air cleaner.

After 1979

1. Start the engine.

2. Disconnect the vacuum hose leading from the EGR valve.

3. Disconnect the hose coming from the intake manifold and connect it to the empty pipe on the EGR valve.

4. When applying vacuum directly to the EGR valve, the engine should stall, if not, the EGR valve will probably require replacement.

EGR VALVE THERMO-SENSOR

1. Disconnect the electrical lead which runs to the EGR valve thermo-sensor.

2. Remove the thermo-sensor from the side of the EGR valve.

3. Heat the thermo-sensor in a pan of water to the following temperature: 260°F.

4. Connect an ohmmeter, in series with a 10Ω resistor, between the thermo-sensor terminal and case.

5. With the ohmmeter set on the k-ohm scale, the following reading should be obtained: 2.55 kΩ.

6. Replace the thermo-sensor if the ohmmeter readings vary considerably from those specified.

7. To install the thermo-sensor on the EGR valve, tighten it to 15-21 ft.lb.

CAUTION: *Do not tighten the thermo-sensor with an impact wrench.*

CHECKING THE EGR VACUUM MODULATOR

1. Tag and disconnect all hoses leading from the vacuum modulator.

2. Remove the vacuum modulator.

3. Unscrew the vented top plate and remove the filter.

4. Check the filter for any contamination or other damage.

5. Clean the filter using compressed air.

6. Installation is in the reverse order of removal.

SYSTEM CHECK

If, after having completed the above tests, the EGR system still doesn't work right and everything else checks out OK, the fault probably lies in the computer. If this is the case, it is best to have the car checked out by a test facility which has the necessary Toyota emission system test equipment.

NOTE: *A good indication that the fault doesn't lie in the EGR system, but rather in the vacuum supply system, would be if several emission control systems were not working properly.*

Air Injection System

A belt driven air pump supplies air to an injection manifold which has nozzles in each exhaust port. Injection of air at this point causes combustion of unburned hydrocarbons in the exhaust manifold rather than allowing them to escape into the atmosphere. An anti-backfire valve controls the flow of air from the pump to prevent backfiring which results from an overly rich mixture under closed throttle conditions. There are two types of anti-backfire valve used on Toyota models: 1970-71 models use gulp valves; Later models use air by-pass valves.

A check valve prevents hot exhaust gas backflow into the pump and hoses, in case of a pump failure, or when the anti-backfire valve is not working.

In addition late model engines have an air switching valve (ASV). On engines without catalytic converters, the ASV is used to stop air injection under a constant heavy engine load condition.

On engines with catalytic converters, the ASV is also used to protect the catalyst from overheating, by blocking the injected air necessary for the operation of the converter.

On late model passenger car engines, the pump relief valve is built into the ASV.

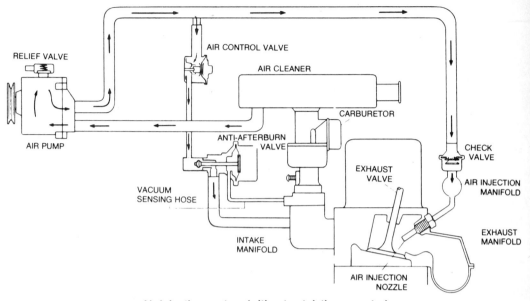

Air injection system (without catalytic converter)

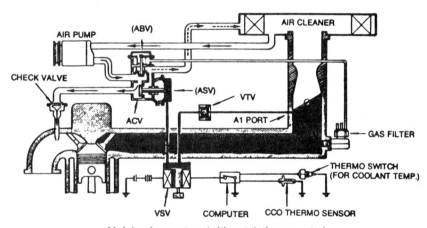

Air injection system (with catalytic converter)

REMOVAL AND INSTALLATION

Air Pump

1. Disconnect air hoses from the pump.
2. Loosen the bolt on the adjusting link and remove the drive belt.

3. Remove the mounting bolts and withdraw the pump.

CAUTION: *Do not pry on the pump housing; it may be distorted.*

4. Installation is in the reverse order of re-

Removing the check valve

Removing the pump-mounted relief valve

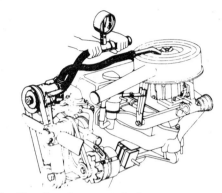

Checking the air pump output

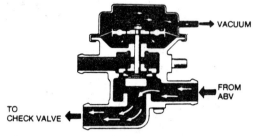

Checking the 2T-C ASV

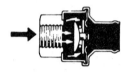

A1 MANIFOLD SIDE   ASV SIDE

Testing the 1979–82 check valve

moval. Adjust the drive belt tension after installation. Belt deflection should be ½-¾″ with 22 lbs. pressure.

Anti-backfire Valve and Air Switching Valve

1. Detach the air hoses from the valve, and electrical leads (4M, ASV 1975).
2. Remove the valve securing bolt.

3. Withdraw the valve. Installation is performed in the reverse order of removal.

Check Valve

1. Detach the intake hose from the valve.
2. Use an open-end wrench to remove the valve from its mounting. Installation is the reverse of removal.

Relief Valve

1. Remove the air pump from the car.
2. Support the pump so that it cannot rotate. CAUTION: *Never clamp the pump in a vise; the aluminum case will be distorted.*
3. Use a bridge to remove the relief valve from the top of the pump.
4. Position the new relief valve over the opening in the pump.
NOTE: *The air outlet should be pointing toward the left.*
5. Gently tap the relief valve home, using a block of wood and a hammer.
6. Install the pump on the engine, as outlined above.
NOTE: *For 1975-77 models with ASV-*

Air Injection System Diagnosis Chart

Problem	Cause		Cure	
1. Noisy drive belt	1a	Loose belt	1a	Tighten belt
	1b	Seized pump	1b	Replace
2. Noisy pump	2a	Leaking hose	2a	Trace and fix leak
	2b	Loose hose	2b	Tighten hose clamp
	2c	Hose contacting other parts	2c	Reposition hose
	2d	diverter or check valve failure	2d	Replace
	2e	Pump mounting loose	2e	Tighten securing bolts
	2f	Defective pump	2f	Replace
3. No air supply	3a	Loose belt	3a	Tighten belt
	3b	Leak in hose or at fitting	3b	Trace and fix leak
	3c	Defective antibackfire valve	3c	Replace
	3d	Defective check valve	3d	Replace
	3e	Defective pump	3e	Replace
	3f	Defective ASV	3f	Replace
4. Exhaust backfire	4a	Vacuum or air leaks	4a	Trace and fix leak
	4b	Defective antibackfire valve	4b	Replace
	4c	Sticking choke	4c	Service choke
	4d	Choke setting rich	4d	Adjust choke

mounted relief valves, replace the entire ASV/relief valve as an assembly.

Air Injection Manifold

1. Remove the check valve, as previously outlined.
2. Loosen the air injection manifold attachment nuts and withdraw the manifold. Installation is in the reverse order of removal.

Air Injection Nozzles

1. Remove the air injection manifold as previously outlined.
2. Remove the cylinder head, as detailed in Chapter 3.
3. Place a new nozzle on the cylinder head.
4. Install the air injection manifold over it.
5. Install the cylinder head on the engine block.

Air Control Valve — 3K-C, 4K-C Engine

The air control valve is used only on the 3K-C and 4K-C engines. It is removed by simply unfastening the hoses from it.

TESTING

Air Pump

CAUTION: *Do not hammer, pry, or bend the pump housing while tightening the drive belt or testing the pump.*

BELT TENSION AND AIR LEAKS

1. Before proceeding with the tests, check the pump drive belt tension to ensure that it is within specifications.
2. Turn the pump by hand. If it has seized, the belt will slip, making a noise. Disregard any chirping, squealing, or rolling sounds from inside the pump; these are normal when it is turned by hand.
3. Check the hoses and connections for leaks. Hissing or a blast of air is indicative of a leak. Soapy water, applied lightly around the area in question, is a good method for detecting leaks.

AIR OUTPUT

1. Disconnect the air supply hose at the anti-backfire valve.
2. Connect a vacuum gauge, using a suitable adaptor, to the air supply hose.
NOTE: *If there are two hoses, plug the second one.*
3. With the engine at normal operating temperature, increase the idle speed and watch the vacuum gauge.
4. The airflow from the pump should be steady and fall between 2 and 6 psi. If it is unsteady or falls below this, the pump is defective and must be replaced.

PUMP NOISE DIAGNOSIS

The air pump is normally noisy; as engine speed increases, the noise of the pump will rise in pitch. The rolling sound the pump bearings make is normal. But if this sound becomes objectionable at certain speeds, the pump is defective and will have to be replaced.

A continual hissing sound from the air pump pressure relief valve at idle, indicates a defective valve. Replace the relief valve.

If the pump rear bearing fails, a continual knocking sound will be heard. Since the rear bearing is not separately replaceable, the pump will have to be replaced as an assembly.

Anti-backfire Valve Tests

There are two different types of anti-backfire valve used with air injection systems. A bypass valve is used on 1972 and later engines, while 1970-71 engines use a gulp type of anti-backfire valve. Test procedures for both types are given below.

GULP VALVE

1. Detach the air supply hose which runs between the pump and the gulp valve.
2. Connect a tachometer and run the engine to 1,500-2,000 rpm.
3. Allow the throttle to snap shut. This should produce a loud sucking sound from the gulp valve.
4. Repeat this operation several times. If no sound is present, the valve is not working or else the vacuum connections are loose.
5. Check the vacuum connections. If they are secure, replace the gulp valve.

BY-PASS VALVE

1. Detach the hose, which runs from the by-pass valve to the check valve, at the by-pass valve hose connection.
2. Connect a tachometer to the engine. With the engine running at normal idle speed, check to see that air is flowing from the by-pass valve hose connection.
3. Speed up the engine so that it is running at 1,5000-2,000 rpm. Allow the throttle to snap shut. The flow of air from the by-pass valve at the check valve hose connection should stop momentarily and air should then flow from the exhaust port on the valve body or the silencer assembly.
4. Repeat Step 3 several times. If the flow of air is not diverted into the atmosphere from the valve exhaust port or if it fails to stop flowing from the hose connection, check the vacuum lines and connections. If these are tight, the valve is defective and requires replacement.
5. A leaking diaphragm will cause the air to flow out both the hose connection and the ex-

haust port at the same time. If this happens, replace the valve.

Check Valve Test — 1974-78

1. Before starting the test, check all of the hoses and connections for leaks.
2. Detach the air supply hose from the check valve.
3. Insert a suitable probe into the check valve and depress the plate. Release it; the plate should return to its original position against the valve seat. If binding is evident, replace the valve.
4. With the engine running at normal operating temperature, gradually increase its speed to 1,500 rpm. Check for exhaust gas leakage. If any is present, replace the valve assembly.

NOTE: *Vibration and flutter of the check valve at idle speed is a normal condition and does not mean that the valve should be replaced.*

Check Valve Test — 1979-82

1. Remove the check valve from the air injection manifold.
2. Blow into the manifold side (large side) and check that the valve is closed.
3. Blow into the ASV side (small side) and check that the valve is open.
4. If the valve is not operating properly it will probably require treatment.

Air Switching Valve (ASV) Tests

1975-81 2T-C ENGINES

1. Start the engine and allow it to reach normal operating temperature and speed.
2. At curb idle, the air from the by-pass valve should be discharged through the hose which runs to the ASV.

3. When the vacuum line to the ASV is disconnected, the air from the by-pass valve should be diverted out through the ASV-to-air cleaner hose. Reconnect the vacuum line.
4. Disconnect the ASV-to-check valve hose and connect a pressure gauge to it.
5. Increase the engine speed. The relief valve should open when the pressure gauge registers 2.7-6.5 psi.
6. If the ASV fails any of the above tests, replace it. Reconnect all hoses.

Vacuum Delay Valve Test

1975-81 2T-C ENGINES

The vacuum delay valve is located in the line which runs from the intake manifold to either the vacuum surge tank (20R) or to the ASV (2T-C). To check it, proceed as follows:

1. Remove the vacuum delay valve from the vacuum line. Be sure to note which end points toward the intake manifold.
2. When air is blown in from the ASV (surge tank) side, it should pass through the valve freely.
3. When air is blown in from the intake manifold side, a resistance should be felt.
4. Replace the valve if it fails either of the above tests.
5. Install the valve in the vacuum line, being careful not to install it backward.

Air Suction System

This system is used only on 1983 and later model Corollas and Tercels. Air is drawn from the air filter, through the Air Suction filter and valve, and into the catalytic converter on all Federal vehicles and the Canadian Tercel with a 3A-C engine and a four speed transmission; or into the exhaust manifold on all other vehicles.

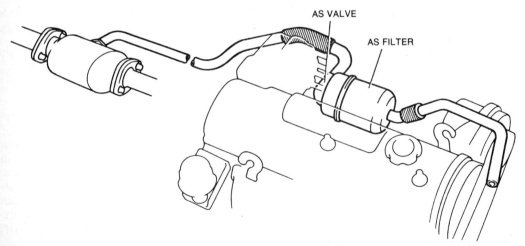

AS VALVE

AS FILTER

Air Suction System on all Federal models and the Canadian Tercel with a 3A-C engine and a four speed transmission

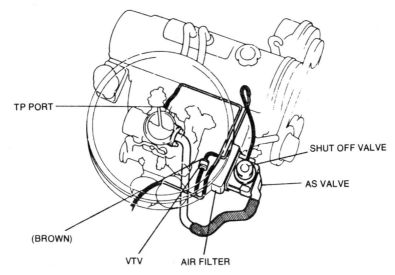

TP PORT

SHUT OFF VALVE

AS VALVE

(BROWN)

VTV   AIR FILTER

Air Suction System on all California models—Canadian models similar

AS VALVE

Checking the AS valve—Federal and Canada

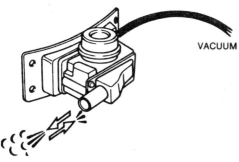

VACUUM

Checking the AS valve—California

INSPECTING THE AS SYSTEM

1. Visually check all hoses and tubes for cracks, kinks, loose connections or other damage.

2. Check the AS valve:

a. On all Federal models and Canada models with the 3A-C and 4 spd, start the engine and check that air is being drawn into the inlet pipe while idling.

b. On California models, disconnect and plug the vacuum hose from the AS valve. Remove the air cleaner cover and start the engine. Reconnect the vacuum hose and check that a bubbling noise is heard from the AS valve inlet within 6 sec.

c. On all other Canadian models, remove the air cleaner cover and with the engine idling, check that a bubbling noise is heard from the AS valve inlet.

INSPECTION OF THE AS VALVE

Federal and Canada

1. Remove the valve from the air cleaner on Canadian models.

2. Disconnect the valve from the AS filter on Federal models.

3. Blow into the valve. There should be no passage of air through the valve.

4. Suck out of the valve. There should be passage of air.

5. Reinstall the valve.

California

1. Remove the AS filter and valve from the air cleaner. Clean the filter.

2. Apply vacuum to the diaphragm and check that air flows from the filter side but not from the outlet pipe side.

3. Release the vacuum and check that hardly any air flows from the filter side to the outlet pipe side.

4. Reinstall the AS valve and filter.

Catalytic Converter

The catalytic converter is a muffler-like container built into the exhaust system to aid in the reduction of exhaust emissions. The catalytic element consists of individual pellets coated with a noble metal such as platinum, palladium, rhodium or a combination. When the exhaust gases come into contact with the catalyst, a chemical reaction occurs which will reduce the pollutants into harmless substances like water and carbon dioxide.

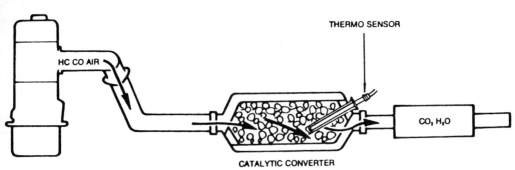

Typical oxidizing catalytic converter system

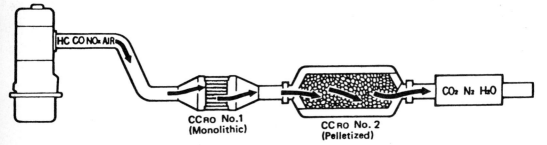

Typical three-way catalytic converter system

There are essentially two types of catalytic converters: an oxidizing type and a three-way type. The oxidizing catalytic converter is used on most late model Toyotas. It requires the addition of oxygen to spur the catalyst into reducing the engine's HC and CO emissions into H_2O and CO_2.

An air injection system is used to supply air to the exhaust system to aid in the reaction. A thermo-sensor, inserted into the converter, shuts off the air supply if the temperature of the catalyst becomes excessive.

The same sensor circuit will also cause an instrument panel warning light labeled **EXH TEMP** to come on when the catalyst temperature gets too high.

NOTE: *It is normal for the light to come on temporarily if the car is being driven downhill for long periods of time (such as descending a mountain).*

The light will come on and stay on if the air injection system is malfunctioning or if the engine is misfiring.

The oxidizing catalytic converter, while effectively reducing HC and CO emissions, does little, if anything, in the way of reducing NOx emissions. Thus, the three-way catalytic converter.

The three-way converter, unlike the oxidizing type, is capable of reducing HC, CO and NOx emissions; all at the same time. In theory, it seems impossible to reduce all three pollutants in one system since the reduction of HC and CO requires the addition of oxygen, while

the reduction of NOx calls for the removal of oxygen. In actuality, the three-way system really can reduce all three pollutants, but only if the amount of oxygen in the exhaust system is precisely controlled. Due to this precise oxygen control requirement, the three-way converter system is used only in cars equipped with an oxygen sensing system.

PRECAUTIONS

1. Use only unleaded fuel.
2. Avoid prolonged idling; the engine should run no longer than 20 minutes at curb idle, nor longer than 10 minutes at fast idle.
3. Reduce the fast idle speed, by quickly depressing and releasing the accelerator pedal, as soon as the coolant temperature reaches 120°F.
4. Do not disconnect any spark plug leads while the engine is running.
5. Make engine compression checks as quickly as possible.
6. Do not dispose of the catalyst in a place where anything coated with grease, gas or oil is present; spontaneous combustion could result.

CATALYST TESTING

At the present time there is no known way to reliably test catalytic converter operation in the field. The only reliable test is a 12 hour and 40 min. soak test (CVS) which must be done in a laboratory.

An infrared HC/CO tester is not sensitive enough to measure the higher tailpipe emissions from a failing converter. Thus, a bad converter may allow enough emissions to escape so that the car is no longer in compliance with Federal or state standards, but will still not cause the needle on a tester to move off zero.

The chemical reactions which occur inside a catalytic converter generate a great deal of heat. Most converter problems can be traced to fuel or ignition system problems which cause unusually high emissions. As a result of the increased intensity of the chemical reactions, the converter literally burns itself up.

A completely failed converter might cause a tester to show a slight reading. As a result, it is occasionally possible to detect one of these.

As long as you avoid severe overheating and the use of leaded fuels it is reasonably safe to assume that the converter is working properly. If you are in doubt, take the car to a diagnostic center that has a tester.

WARNING LIGHT CHECKS

NOTE: *The warning light comes on while the engine is being cranked, to test its operation, just like any of the other warning light.*

1. If the warning light comes on and stays on, check the components of the air injection system as previously outlined. If these are not defective, check the ignition system for faulty leads, plugs, points, or control box.
2. If no problems can be found in Step 1, check the wiring for the light for shorts or opened circuits.
3. If nothing else can be found wrong in Steps 1 and 2, check the operation of the emission control system vacuum switching valve or computer, either by substitution of new unit, or by taking it to a service facility which has Toyota's special emission control system checker.

Oxygen Sensor System

The three way catalytic converter, which is capable of reducing HC, CO and NOx into CO_2, H_2O, O_2 and N_2, can only function as long as the fuel/air mixture is kept within a critically precise range. The oxygen sensor system is what keeps the oxygen range in control.

Basically, the oxygen sensor system works like this: As soon as the engine warms up, the computer begins to work. The oxygen sensor, located in the exhaust manifold, senses the oxygen content of the exhaust gases. The amount of oxygen in the exhaust varies according to the fuel/air mixture. The O_2 sensor produces a small voltage that varies depending on the amount of oxygen in the exhaust at the time. This voltage is picked up by the computer. The computer works together with the fuel distributor and together and together they will vary the

amount of fuel which is delivered to the engine at any given time.

If the amount of oxygen in the exhaust system is low, which indicates a rich mixture, the sensor voltage will be high. The higher the voltage signal sent to the computer, the more it will reduce the amount of fuel supplied to the engine. The amount of fuel is reduced until the amount of oxygen in the exhaust system increases, indicating a lean mixture. When the mixture is lean, the sensor will send a low voltage signal to the computer. The computer will then increase the quantity of fuel until the sensor voltage increases again and then the cycle will start all over.

OXYGEN SENSOR REPLACEMENT

1. Disconnect the negative battery cable.
2. Unplug the wiring connector leading from the O_2 sensor.

NOTE: *Be careful not to bend the waterproof hose as the oxygen sensor will not function properly if the air passage is blocked.*

3. Unscrew the two nuts and carefully pull out the sensor.
4. Installation is in the reverse order of removal. Please note the following: Always use a new gasket; Tighten the nuts to 13-16 ft.lb.

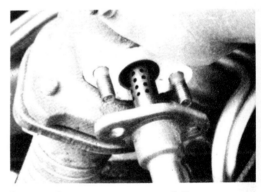

Remove the oxygen sensor carefully

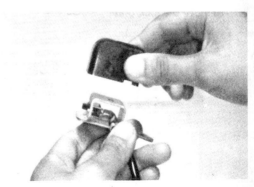

In order to reset the counter, you must first remove the cover

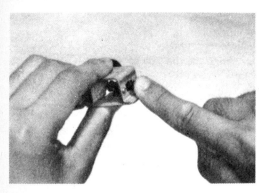

To reset the counter, push the switch

OXYGEN SENSOR WARNING LIGHT

Many models are equipped with an oxygen sensor warning light on the instrument panel. The light may go on when the car is started, then it should go out. If the light stays on, check your odometer. The light is hooked up to an elapsed mileage counter which goes off every 30,000 miles. This is your signal that it is time to replace the oxygen sensor and have the entire system checked out. After replacement of the sensor, the elapsed mileage counter must be reset. To rest:

1. Locate the counter. If can be found under the left side of the instrument panel, on the brake pedal bracket.
2. Unscrew the mounting bolt, disconnect the wiring connector and remove the counter.
3. Remove the bolt on top of the counter.
4. Lift off the counter cover and push the reset switch.
NOTE: *The warning light on the instrument panel must go out at this time.*
5. Installation is in the reverse order of removal.

FUEL SYSTEM

Understanding the Fuel System

An automotive fuel system consists of everything between the fuel tank and the carburetor or fuel injection unit. This includes the tank, itself, all the lines, one or more fuel filters, a fuel pump (mechanical or electric, or both), and the carburetor or fuel injection unit.

With the exception of the carburetor or fuel injection unit, the fuel system is quite simple in operation. Fuel is drawn from the tank through the fuel line by the fuel pump, which forces it through the fuel filter, and from there to the carburetor/injection unit where it is distributed to the cylinders.

Fuel Filters
REMOVAL AND INSTALLATION
Carbureted Engines

All engines employ a disposable, in-line filter; when dirty, or at recommended intervals, remove from line and replace.

Fuel Injected Engines
IN-LINE FILTERS

1. Unbolt the retaining screws and remove the protective shield for the fuel filter.
2. Place a pan under the delivery pipe (large connection) to catch the dripping fuel and SLOWLY loosen the union bolt to bleed off the fuel pressure.
3. Remove the union bolt and drain the remaining fuel.
4. Disconnect and the plug the inlet line.
5. Unbolt and remove the fuel filter.
NOTE: *When tightening the fuel line bolts to the fuel filter, you must use a torque wrench. The tightening torque is very important as under or over tightening may cause fuel leakage. Insure that there is no fuel line interference and that there is sufficient clearance between it and any other parts.*
6. Coat the flare nut, union nut and bolt threads with engine oil.
7. Hand tighten the inlet line to the fuel filter.
8. Install the fuel filter and then tighten the inlet bolt to 23-33 ft.lb.
9. Reconnect the delivery pipe using new gaskets and then tighten the union bolt to 18-25 ft.lb.
10. Run the engine for a few minutes and check for any fuel leaks.
11. Install the protective shield.

IN-TANK FILTERS

1. Disconnect the negative battery cable. Drain the gasoline from the fuel tank.
2. Remove the fuel tank from the vehicle.
3. Remove the fuel pump bracket retaining bolts and remove the fuel pump bracket.
4. Remove the retaining clip from the fuel filter hose and remove the fuel filter.
5. Install a new fuel filter and reverse the removal procedure to complete the installation procedure.

Mechanical Fuel Pump
REMOVAL AND INSTALLATION

1. Disconnect the negative battery cable.
2. Disconnect and plug both of the fuel lines form the fuel pump (some models have 3 lines).
3. Unscrew and remove the two fuel pump mounting bolts.

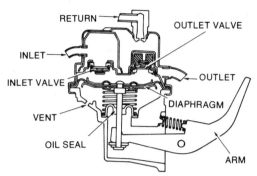

Cross-section of a typical mechanical fuel pump

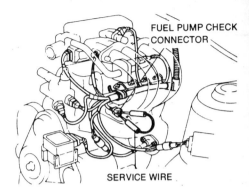

Shorting the fuel pump check connector

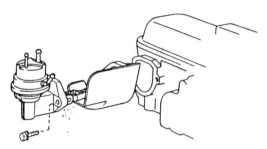

Removing the mechanical fuel pump

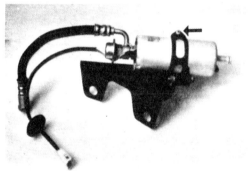

On the 1983 and later Starlet, the electric fuel pump is located on the outside of the fuel tank

4. Withdraw the fuel pump assembly from the engine block.

5. Installation is in the reverse order of removal.

NOTE: *Always use a new gasket when installing the fuel pump.*

6. Start the engine and check the pump for any leaks.

TESTING

Fuel pumps should always be tested on the vehicle. The larger line between the pump and tank is the suction side of the system and the smaller line, between the pump and carburetor, is the pressure side. A leak in the pressure side would be apparent because of dripping fuel. A leak in the suction side is usually only apparent because of a reduced volume of fuel delivered to the pressure side.

1. Tighten any loose line connections and look for any kinks or restrictions.

2. Disconnect the fuel line at the carburetor. Disconnect the distributor-to-coil primary wire. Place a container at the end of the fuel line and crank the engine a few revolutions. If little or no fuel flows from the line, either the fuel pump is inoperative or the line is plugged. Blow through the lines with compressed air and try the test again. Reconnect the line.

3. If fuel flows in good volume, check the fuel pump pressure to be sure.

4. Attach a pressure gauge to the pressure side of the fuel line. On cars equipped with a vapor return system, squeeze off the return hose.

5. Run the engine at idle and note the reading on the gauge. Stop the engine and compare the reading with the specifications listed in the Tune-Up Specifications chart. If the pump is operating properly, the pressure will be as specified and will be constant at idle speed. If pressure varies sporadically or is too high or low, the pump should be replaced.

6. Remove the pressure gauge.

The following flow test can also be performed:

1. Disconnect the fuel line from the carburetor or the fuel injection pump. Run the fuel line into a suitable measuring container.

2. Run the engine at idle until there is one pint of fuel in the container. One pint should be pumped in 30 seconds or less.

3. If the flow is below minimum, check for a restriction in the line. The only way to check fuel pump pressure is by connecting an accurate pressure gauge to the fuel line at the carburetor level. Never replace a fuel pump without performing this simple test. If the engine seems to be starting out, check the ignition system first. Also check for a plugged fuel filter or a restricted fuel line before replacing the pump.

Electric Fuel Pump

REMOVAL AND INSTALLATION

1. Disconnect the negative battery cable.
2. Unplug the fuel pump wiring connector inside the trunk.
3. Unscrew the four bolts and remove the service hole cover.
4. Disconnect and plug the fuel pump inlet hose.
5. Remove the bolt at the fuel pump bracket.
6. Raise the rear of the car and support it with jackstands.
7. Remove the fuel pipe bracket. Slowly loosen and then disconnect the fuel pump outlet hose.
8. Unscrew the two remaining fuel pump bracket bolts and then remove the pump.
9. Installation is in the reverse order of removal.
10. Start the engine and check for any leaks.

TESTING

1. Turn the ignition switch to the **ON** position, but don't start the engine.
2. Remove the rubber cap from the fuel pump check connector and short both terminals.
3. Check that there is pressure in the hose to the cold start injector.
NOTE: *At this time you should be able to hear the fuel return noise from the pressure regulator.*
4. If no pressure can be felt in the line, check the fuses and all other related electrical connections. If everything is alright, the fuel pump will probably require replacement.
5. Remove the service wire, reinstall the rubber cap and turn off the ignition switch.

Carburetor

The carburetor is the most complex part of the entire fuel system. Carburetors vary greatly in construction, but they all operate basically the same way; their job is to supply the correct mixture of fuel and air to the engine in response to varying conditions.

Despite their complexity in operation, carburetors function because of a simple physical principle (the venturi principle). Air is drawn into the engine by the pumping action of the pistons. As the air enters the top of the carburetor, it passes through a venturi, which is nothing more than a restriction in the throttle bore. The air speeds up as it passes through the venturi, causing a slight drop in pressure. This pressure drop pulls fuel from the float bowl through a nozzle into the throttle bore, where it mixes with the air and forms a fine mist, which is distributed to the cylinders through the intake manifold.

There are six different systems (fuel/air circuits) in a carburetor that make it work; the Float system, Main Metering system, Idle and Low-Speed system, Accelerator Pump system, Power system, and the Choke system. The way these systems are arranged in the carburetor determines the carburetor's size and shape.

It's hard to believe that the little single-barrel carburetor used on 4 or 6 cylinder engines have all the same basic systems as the enormous 4-barrels used on V8 engines. Of course, the 4-barrels have more throttle bores (barrels) and a lot of other hardware you won't find on the little single-barrels. But, basically, all carburetors are similar, and if you understand a simple single-barrel, you can use that knowledge to understand a 4-barrel. If you'll study the explanations of the various systems on this stage, you'll discover that carburetors aren't as tricky as you thought they were. In fact, they're fairly simple, considering the job they have to do.

It's important to remember that carburetors seldom give trouble during normal operation. Other than changing the fuel and air filters and making sure the idle speed and mixture are ok at every tune-up, there's not much maintenance you can perform on the average carburetor.

The carburetors used on Toyota models are conventional two-barrel, down-draft types similar to domestic carburetors. The main circuits are: primary, for normal operational requirements; secondary, to supply high-speed fuel needs; float, to supply fuel to the primary and secondary circuits; accelerator, to supply fuel for quick and safe acceleration; choke, for reliable starting in cold weather; and power valve, for fuel economy. Although slight differences in appearance may be noted, these carburetors are basically alike. Of course, different jets and settings are demanded by the different engines to which they are fitted.

REMOVAL AND INSTALLATION

1. Disconnect the negative battery cable.
2. Loosen the radiator drain plug and drain the coolant into a suitable container.
3. Unscrew the mounting screws and remove the air filter housing. Disconnect all hoses and lines leading from the air cleaner.
4. Tag and disconnect all fuel, vacuum, coolant and electrical lines or hoses leading from the carburetor.
5. Disconnect the accelerator linkage from the carburetor. On cars equipped with an automatic transmission, disconnect the throttle cable linkage running from the transmission.

6. Remove the four carburetor mounting bolts and lift off the carburetor and its gasket.

NOTE: *Cover the manifold opening with a clean rag to prevent anything from falling into the engine.*

7. Installation is in the reverse order of removal.

8. Start the engine and check for any leaks. Check the float level.

FLOAT LEVEL ADJUSTMENT

Float level adjustments are unnecessary on models equipped with a carburetor sight glass, if the fuel level falls within the lines when the engine is running.

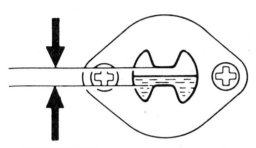

CORRECT LEVEL

No float level adjustment is necessary when the fuel level falls between the line on the carburetor sight glass

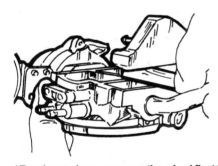

A and T-series engines—measure the raised float level as shown

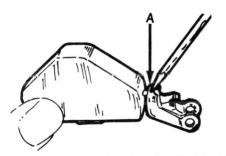

A and T- series engines—adjust the raised float level at (A)

A and T-series engines—measure the lowered float level as shown

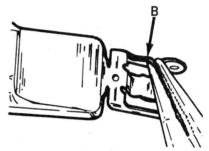

A and T-series engines—adjust the lowered float level at (B)

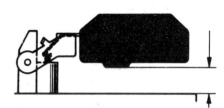

K-series engine—measure the raised float level as indicated

K-series engines—adjust the raised float level at (A)

There are two float level adjustments which may be made on Toyota carburetors. One if with the air horn inverted, so that the float is in a fully raised position; the other is with the air horn in an upright position, so that the float falls to the bottom of its travel.

The float level is either measured with a special carburetor float level gauge, which comes

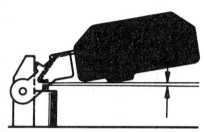

K-series engines—measure the lowered float level as indicated

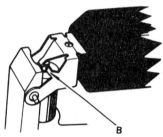

K-series engines—adjust the lowered float level at (B)

1978–84

Engine	Speed (rpm)
2T-C (US)	3,200
2T-C (Calif)	3,000
4K-C	3,500
3A-C, 4A-C '81–'82 '83	3,600 3,000
3A	3,000
3T-C	3,000 Canada 3,400 U.S.A.

US—United States
Calif—California
Not available for 3K-C engine

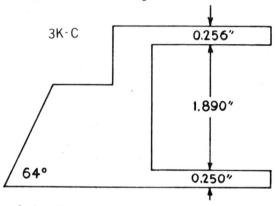

Carburetor gauge

with a rebuilding kit, or with a standard wire gauge.

1. Turn the air horn upside down and let the float hang down by its own weight.

2. Using a special float gauge (available at your local dealer), check the clearance between the tip of the float and the flat surface of the air horn.

NOTE: *This measurement should be made without the gasket on the air horn.*

3. If the float clearance is not within specifications, adjust it by bending the upper (center) float tab.

4. Lift up the float and check the clearance between the needle valve plunger and the flat lip. Clearance may be checked with a special float gauge. The clearance should be as specified in the accompanying chart.

5. If the clearance is not within specifications, adjust it by bending the lower float tabs (2).

FAST IDLE ADJUSTMENT

Off-Vehicle

The fast idle adjustment is performed with the choke valve fully closed, except on the 2T-C

Fast Idle Speed
1975–77

Engine	Speed (rpm)
2T-C (US)	3000
2T-C (Calif)	2700

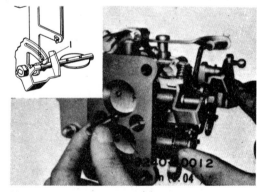

Make fast idle adjustments by bending the linkage

Screw-type fast idle adjustment (1)

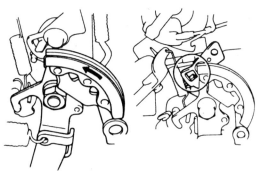

Set the throttle lever to the first step of the fast idle cam—1983 and later

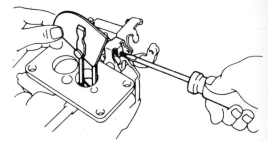

Adjust the fast idle with the adjusting screw—1983 and later

and 3T-C engine which should have the choke valve fully opened.

Adjust the gap between the throttle valve edge and bore to the specifications, where giv-en, in the Fast Idle Adjustment chart. Use a wire gauge to determine the gap.

The chart also gives the proper primary throttle valve opening angle, where necessary, and the proper means of fast idle adjustment.

NOTE: *The throttle valve opening angle is*

Float Level Adjustments

	Float Raised			Float Lowered		
Engine	Gauge Type	Machine Distance Between:	Gap (in.)	Gauge Type	Measure Distance Between:	Gap (in.)
3K-C	Special	Float end and air horn	0.056 ① ③	Special	Lowest point of float and upper side of gauge	1.89 ②
2T-C, 3TC	Block	Float tip and air horn	0.138 ④	Wire	Needle valve bushing pin and float lip	0.047
1A-C, 3A, 3A-C, 4A-C	Special	Float tip and air horn	0.158 ⑤	Special	Needle valve plunger and float tab	0.047 ⑥
4K-C	Special	Float tip and air horn	0.030	Special	Needle valve plunger and float tip	0.02

① 1977—0.26
② 1977—from float lip 0.035
   1978–79—float lip gap .024
   1980–81—float tip gap 0.020
③ 1978–81—0.30
④ 1978–81—0.236
⑤ 1983 and later—0.283
⑥ 1983 and later—0.0657–0.0783

Fast Idle Linkage Adjustment

Engine	Throttle Valve to Bore Clearance (in.)	Primary Throttle Angle (deg)	To Adjust Fast Idle:
3K-C through 1980	0.040 ①	9 ②	Bend the fast idle lever
4K-C and 1981 3K-C	0.040	90	Bend the fast idle lever
2T-C, 3T-C	0.032 ③	7	Turn the fast idle adjusting screw
3A (1981–83)	—	24	Turn the fast idle screw
(1984)	—	21	Turn the fast idle screw
3A-C (1981–82)	—	24 ④	Turn the fast idle screw
(1983–84)	—	20 ⑤	Turn the fast idle screw
4A-C	—	20 ⑥	Turn the fast idle screw

① 0.051 in 1976; 0.056 in 1977; 0.037 in 1978–79
② 20° open
③ 1976–79: 0.043
④ Canada: 25°
⑤ Canadian wagon w/3A-C: 21°
⑥ Canada: 21°

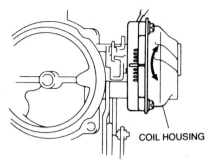

Align the marks and then turn the housing when adjusting the automatic choke

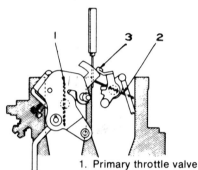

1. Primary throttle valve
2. Secondary throttle valve
3. Secondary throttle lever

Kick-up adjustment

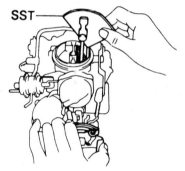

Checking the primary throttle valve angle before adjusting the choke unloader

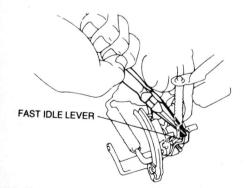

Adjust the choke unloader by bending the fast idle lever

measured with a gauge supplied in the carburetor rebuilding kit. It is also possible to make one out of cardboard by using a protractor to obtain the correct angle.

On-Vehicle — 1975-82 (exc. 1982 Corolla)

1. Perform the idle speed/mixture adjustments as outlined in Chapter 2. Leave the tachometer connected.
2. Remove the top of the air cleaner.
3. Open the throttle valve slightly and close the choke valve. Next, hold the choke valve with your finger and close the throttle valve. The choke valve is now fully closed.
4. Without depressing the accelerator pedal, start the engine.
5. Check the engine fast idle speed against the following chart.
6. If the reading on the tachometer is not within specifications, adjust the fast idle speed by turning the fast idle screw.
7. Disconnect the tachometer, install the air cleaner cover, and connect the EGR valve vacuum line if it was disconnected.

1983 and Later (inc. Corolla)

1. Set the throttle shaft lever to the first step of the fast idle cam.
2. With the choke valve fully closed, check the primary throttle valve with the appropriate gauge.
3. Adjust by turning the fast idle adjusting screw.

AUTOMATIC CHOKE ADJUSTMENT

NOTE: *Not all models utilize an automatic choke.*

The automatic choke should be adjusted with the carburetor installed and the engine running.

1. Check to ensure that the choke valve will close from fully opened when the coil housing is turned counterclockwise.
2. Align the mark on the coil housing with the center line on the thermostat case. In this position, the choke valve should be fully closed when the ambient temperature is 77°F.
3. If necessary, adjust the mixture by turning the coil housing. If the mixture is too rich, rotate the housing clockwise; if too lean, rotate the housing counterclockwise.

NOTE: *Each graduation on the thermostat case is equivalent to 9°F.*

CHOKE UNLOADER ADJUSTMENT

Make the unloader adjustment with the primary valve fully opened. Adjust by performing the procedure indicated on the Choke Unloader Adjustment chart. The total angle of choke valve opening, in the chart, is measured with either a special gauge, supplied in the carburetor rebuilding kit, or a gauge of the proper angle fabricated from cardboard.

KICK-UP ADJUSTMENT

1970-81

1. Open the primary throttle valve the amount specified in the Kick-Up Adjustment chart.
2. Measure the secondary throttle valve-to-bore clearance with a 0.008″ gauge.
3. Adjust the clearance by bending the secondary throttle lever.

1983 and Later

1. With the primary throttle valve fully open, check the clearance between the secondary throttle valve and the bore.
2. Clearance should be 0.0043-0.0087″ (0.11-0.22mm) on U.S. models and 0.0063-0.0106″ (0.16-0.27mm) on Canadian models.
3. Adjust by bending the secondary throttle lever.

INITIAL IDLE MIXTURE SCREW ADJUSTMENT

When assembling the carburetor, turn the idle mixture screw the number of turns specified below. After the carburetor is installed, perform the appropriate idle speed/mixture adjustment as outlined in Chapter 2.

- 3K-C 1978-79 – 3 turns from seating
- 3K-C 1977 – 1¾ turns from seating
- 4K-C 1981-82 – 1½ turns from seating
- 3K-C through 1976 – 2 turns from seating
- 1977 3K-C – 1¾ turns from seating
- 1977 and later 2T-C 3T-C – 2⅝ turns out
- 1A-C – 2¼ turns
- 1980-82 3A, 3A-C – 2¾ turns

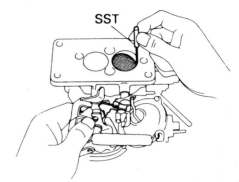

Check the clearance between the secondary throttle valve and the bore—1982 and later kick-up adjustment

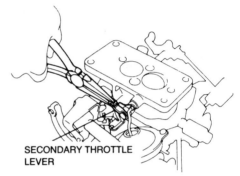

SECONDARY THROTTLE LEVER

Adjust the kick-up by bending the secondary throttle lever—1982 and later

Kick-Up Adjustment

Engine	Primary Throttle Valve Open Angle (deg)
3K-C	81 from closed
2T-C	55 from closed ①

① 1977–79—64–90°

Choke Unloader Adjustment

Engine	Choke Valve Angle (deg)			To Adjust Bend
	Throttle Valve Fully Closed (deg)	From Closed to Fully Open (deg)	Throttle Valve Open (total) (deg)	
1970–75 2T-C, 3K-C	20	27	47	Fast idle cam follower or choke shaft lip
1976–81 3K-C	9	20	90	Fast idle cam follower or choke shaft tab
4K-C	8.5	52	90	Connecting link
2T-C	7	38	90	Fast idle lever, follower or choke shaft tab
3T-C, 1A-C 3A, 3A-C, 4A-C	20	—	47 ①	Fast idle lever

—Not available   ① 1983–84: 41°—U.S.
                             47°—Canada

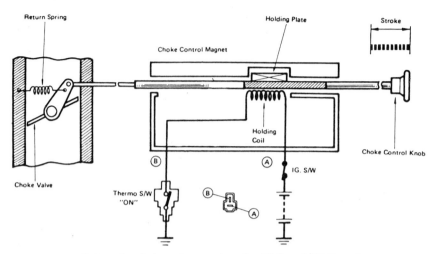

Automatic choke return system for 3K-C and 4K-C engine

- 1983 and later 3E, 3A-C, 3A — 2⅝ turns (US) 2½ turns (Can.)
- 4A-C — 3¼ turns (US) 2½ turns (Can.)

CAUTION: *Seat the idle mixture screw lightly; overtightening will damage its tip.*

CHOKE RETURN SYSTEM

1977 and later 3K-C engines and all 4K-C engines have a choke return system to protect the catalytic converter. Because of the chance of overheating the exhaust system and damaging the catalytic converter by running with the choke out, a thermoswitch and return spring system automatically close the choke when the coolant temperature reaches 104°F.

A holding coil and holding plate surround the choke cable and retain it when the temperature is low enough. When the temperature reaches 104°F the thermoswitch opens, freeing the return spring to pull in the choke. There are no adjustments on the system. If a malfunction occurs, trace the loss and replace that segment of the unit.

GENERAL OVERHAUL NOTES

Efficient carburetion depends greatly on careful cleaning and inspection during overhaul since dirt, gum, water, or varnish in or on the carburetor parts are often responsible for poor performance.

Overhaul your carburetor in a clean, dust-free area. Carefully disassemble the carburetor, referring often to the exploded views. Keep all similar and look-alike parts segregated during disassembly and cleaning to avoid accidental interchange during assembly. Make a note of all jet sizes.

When the carburetor is disassembled, wash all parts (except diaphragms, electric choke units, pump plunger, and any other plastic,

leather, fiber, or rubber parts) in clean carburetor solvent. Do not leave parts in the solvent any longer than is necessary to sufficiently loosen the deposits. Excessive cleaning may remove the special finish from the float bowl and choke valve bodies, leaving these parts unfit for service. Rinse all parts in clean solvent and blow them dry with compressed air or allow them to air dry. Wipe clean all cork, plastic, leather, and fiber parts with a clean, lint-free cloth.

Blow out all passages and jets with compressed air and be sure that there are no restrictions or blockages. Never use wire or similar tools to clean jets. Never use wire or similar tools to clean jets, fuel passages, or air bleeds. Clean all jets and valves separately to avoid accidental interchange.

Check all parts for wear or damage. If wear or damage is found, replace the defective parts. Especially check the following:

1. Check the float needle and seat for wear. If wear is found, replace the complete assembly.

2. Check the float hinge pin for wear and the float(s) for dents or distortion. Replace the float if fuel has leaked into it.

3. Check the throttle and choke shaft bores for wear or an out-of-round condition. Damage or wear to the throttle arm, shaft, or shaft bore will often require replacement of the throttle body. These parts require a close tolerance of fit; wear may allow air leakage, which could affect starting and idling.

NOTE: *Throttle shafts and bushings are not included in overhaul kits. They can be purchased separately.*

4. Inspect the idle mixture adjusting needles for burrs or grooves. Any such condition requires replacement of the needle, since you will not be able to obtain a satisfactory idle.

5. Test the accelerator pump check valves.

They should pass air one way but not the other. Test for proper seating by blowing and sucking on the valve. Replace the valve if necessary. If the valve is satisfactory, wash the valve again to remove breath moisture.

6. Check the bowl cover for warped surfaces with a straightedge.

7. Closely inspect the valves and seats for wear and damage, replacing as necessary.

8. After the carburetor is assembled, check the choke valve for freedom of operation.

Carburetor overhaul kits are recommended for each overhaul. These kits contain all gaskets and new parts to replace those that deteriorate most rapidly. Failure to replace all parts supplied with the kit (especially gaskets) can result in poor performance later.

Some carburetor manufacturers supply overhaul kits of 3 basic types: minor repair; major repair; and gasket kits. Basically, they contain the following:

Minor Repair Kits:
- All gaskets
- Float needle valve
- Volume control screw
- All diaphragms
- Spring for the pump diaphragm

Major Repair Kits:
- All jets and gaskets
- All diaphragms
- Float needle valve
- Volume control screw
- Pump ball valve
- Float
- Complete intermediate rod
- Intermediate pump lever
- Some cover holddown screws and washers

Gasket Kits:
- All gaskets

After cleaning and checking all components, reassemble the carburetor, using new parts and referring to the exploded view. When reassembling, make sure that all screws and jets are tight in their seats, but do not over tighten, as the tips will be distorted. Tighten all screws gradually, in rotation. Do not tighten needle valves into their seats; uneven jetting will result. Always use new gaskets. Be sure to adjust the float level when reassembling.

Fuel Injection

NOTE: *Due to the complex nature of modern fuel injection systems, comprehensive*

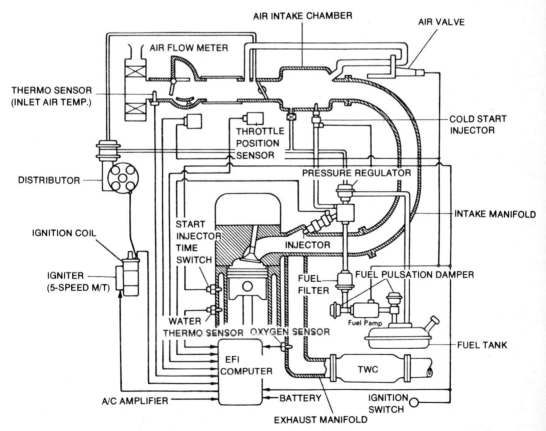

Main components of the typical EFI system

diagnosis and testing procedures fall outside the confines of this repair manual. For complete information on fuel injection diagnosis, testing and repair procedures please refer to Chilton's Guide to Fuel Injection and Feedback Carburetors.

EFI

One style of fuel injection used is known as the EFI (electronic fuel injection) system. The EFI system can be broken down into three basic systems; the fuel system, the air induction system, and the electronic control system.

The main components of the fuel system are the fuel tank, the fuel pump and the fuel injectors. The electric fuel pump supplies sufficient fuel from the fuel tank, under a constant pressure, to the EFI fuel injectors. These injectors in turn inject a metered quantity of fuel into the intake manifold in accordance with signals given by the EFI computer. Each injector injects, at the same time, one half of the fuel required for ideal combustion with each engine revolution.

The air induction system consists of the air cleaner, an air flow meter, an air valve and an air intake chamber. All of these components contribute to the supply of the proper amount of air to the intake manifold as controlled by the EFI computer.

The main component of the electronic control system is the EFI computer. The computer receives signals from various sensors indicating changing engine operating conditions such as:
- Intake air volume
- Intake air temperature
- Coolant temperature
- Engine load
- Acceleration/deceleration
- Exhaust oxygen content, etc.

These signals are utilized by the computer to determine the injection duration necessary for an optimum air/fuel ratio.

TROUBLESHOOTING

Engine troubles are not usually caused by the EFI system. When troubleshooting, always check first the condition of all other related systems.

Many times the most frequent cause of problems is a bad contact in a wiring connector, so always make sure that the connections are secure. When inspecting the connector, pay particular attention to the following points:

1. Check to see that the terminals are not bent.

2. Check to see that the connector is pushed in all the way and locked.

3. Check that there is no change in signal when the connector is tapped or wiggled.

Actual troubleshooting of the EFI system and the EFI computer is a complex process which requires the use of a few expensive and hard to find tools. Other than checking the operation of the main components individually, we suggest that you leave any further troubleshooting to an authorized service facility.

Cold Start Injector

During cold engine starting, the cold start injector is used to supply additional fuel to the intake manifold to aid in initial start-up. The opening and closing of the injector is determined by the Start Injector Time Switch. When the engine coolant temperature falls below a certain point, the switch is tripped and then opens the cold start injector. As the engine coolant warms up, the switch will eventually close the injector.

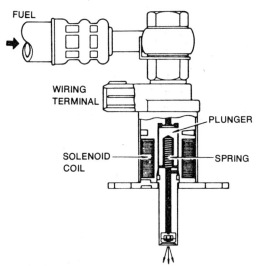

Cold start injector

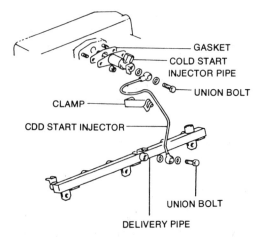

Removing the cold start injector

REMOVAL AND INSTALLATION

1. Disconnect the negative battery cable.

2. Remove the cold start injector union bolt on the delivery pipe.

NOTE: *Before removing the union bolt, place a suitable container under it to catch any escaping fuel.*

3. Disconnect the wiring connector at the injector.

4. Unscrew the two mounting bolts and then remove the cold start injector from the air intake chamber.

5. Installation is in the reverse order of removal.

NOTE: *Always use new gaskets when reinstalling the injector.*

6. Start the engine and check for any leaks.

CHECKING

1. Unplug the wiring connector and remove the cold start injector from the air intake chamber.

NOTE: *Do not disconnect the fuel line.*

2. Using Special Tool 09843-30011, connect one end to the injector and the other to the battery.

3. Remove the rubber cap from the Fuel Pump Check terminal and short both terminals with a wire.

4. Hold the injector over a suitable container and then turn the ignition switch to the 'ON' position. Do not start the engine.

5. Check that the fuel splash pattern is an even, V-shaped one.

6. Disconnect the test probes from the battery and check that the fuel does not leak from the injector tip any more than one drop per minute.

7. Remove the Special Tool and install the cold start injector.

8. Check the resistance of the injector. It should be 3-5Ω.

9. If the cold start injector did not operate properly in any of these tests, it will require replacement.

Pressure Regulator

The pressure regulator maintains correct fuel pressure throughout the system. The regulator is vacuum controlled to provide a relatively constant pressure differential.

The regulator is open during most engine op-

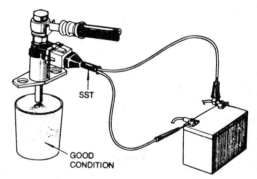

The fuel spray pattern should be an even, V-shaped one

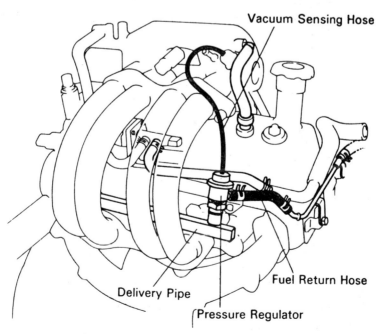

Pressure regulator

erating conditions. This provides for better re-circulation of the fuel to lower the temperature of the fuel supply.

REMOVAL AND INSTALLATION

1. Disconnect the negative battery cable.
2. Place a suitable container under the union and pipe support.
3. Disconnect the vacuum sensing hose from the top of the regulator.
4. Disconnect the fuel return hose and plug the pipe of the hose support.
5. Remove the union bolt from the regulator.
6. Unscrew the two regulator mounting bolts and lift out the regulator.
7. Installation is in the reverse order of removal.
8. Start the engine and check for any leaks.

CHECKING

1. Disconnect the negative battery cable.
2. Unplug the wiring connector from the cold start injector.
3. Place a suitable container under the front end of the delivery pipe and slowly remove the union bolt for the cold start injector. Drain all of the fuel in the delivery pipe.
4. Install a fuel pressure gauge in the union bolt's place, connect the battery cable and start the engine.
5. Disconnect the vacuum sensing hose from the pressure regulator and block it off.
6. Measure the fuel pressure at idle. It should be 33-38 psi. If the pressure is high, replace the regulator.
7. Installation is in the reverse order of removal.

Fuel Injectors

There is one fuel injector for each cylinder. They spray fuel in front of the intake valve. When the injector is energized, the coil pulls the plunger up, opening the needle valve and allowing the fuel to pass through the injector. Opening of the injectors is controlled by the EFI computer. The injectors operate at low pressure and are open for only a fraction of a second at a time.

REMOVAL AND INSTALLATION

1. Disconnect the negative battery cable.
2. Remove the cold start injector pipe.
NOTE: *Be sure to have a suitable container on hand to catch any dripping fluid.*
3. Remove the air intake pipes as detailed in Cylinder Head Removal in Chapter 3.
4. Disconnect the fuel inlet line from the delivery pipe. Tag and disconnect the vacuum sensing hose and the fuel return line from the pressure regulator.

5. Remove the two plastic EFI solenoid wiring harness clamps and then tag and disconnect the wiring connectors from the tops of the fuel injectors.
6. Unscrew the three nuts and then remove the delivery pipe with the injectors attached.
NOTE: *Be careful not to drop the injectors when removing the delivery pipe. Do not remove the cover.*
7. Insert four new insulators into the injector holes on the intake manifold.
8. Install the grommet and a new O-ring to the delivery pipe end of each injector.
9. Apply a thin coat of gasoline to the O-ring on each injector and then press them into the delivery pipe.
10. Install the injectors together with the delivery pipe to the intake manifold. Tighten the mounting bolts to 11-15 ft.lb.
11. Installation of the remaining components is in the reverse order of removal.

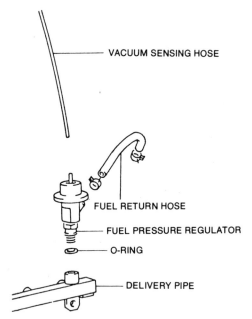

Pressure regulator and its components

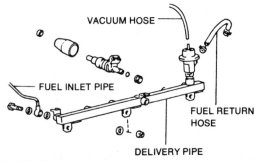

Removing the injector

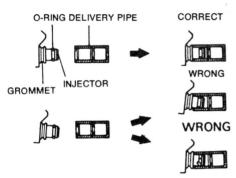

Be sure to insert the injector into the fuel delivery pipe properly

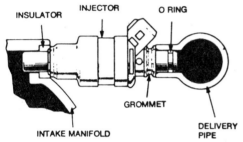

A cut-away view of how it should look upon reinstallation

12. Start the engine and check for any fuel leaks.

CHECKING

We recommend that any checking or testing of the injectors be left to an authorized service facility.

Air Flow Meter

Air is drawn in through the air filter to the air flow meter. The volume of air being drawn in depends on the throttle plate opening as controlled by the accelerator pedal. The volume of air and the temperature of the air is measured by the air flow meter which then converts the measurement to a voltage signal that is sent to the EFI computer.

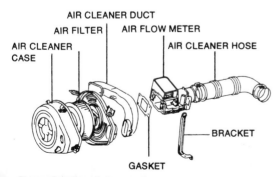

Removing the air flow meter

REMOVAL AND INSTALLATION

1. Unscrew the mounting bolts and remove the air cleaner inlet.
2. Remove the air cleaner element.
3. Unplug the electrical connector from the top of the meter and remove the oxygen sensor wire from the clamp on the side of the meter.

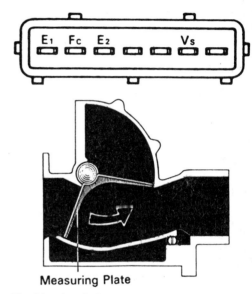

Checking the air flow meter

Resistance

Between Terminals	Resistance Ω	Measuring Plate Opening
$E_1 - F_c$	Infinity	Fully closed
	Zero	Other than closed position
$E_2 - zs$	20 – 400	Fully closed
	20 – 1000	Fully closed to Fully open position

NOTE: Resistance between E_2 and V_s will change in accordance with the measuring plate opening.

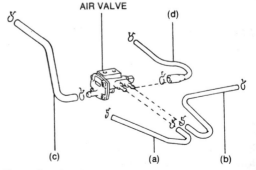

Removing the air valve

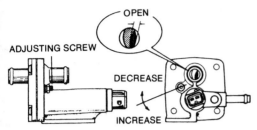

Check that the air valve opens slightly when room temperature is about 68° F

4. Loosen the hose clamp and pull off the intake air connector.

5. Unscrew the meter support bracket bolt.

6. Unscrew the four air flow meter mounting bolts from inside the air cleaner housing and remove the meter.

7. Installation is in the reverse order of removal.

CHECKING

NOTE: *Check the air flow meter with the unit out of the car.*

Using an ohmmeter, check the resistance between each terminal of the electrical connector by moving the measuring plate.

NOTE: *Resistance between E2 and Vs will be changed in accordance with the measuring plate opening.*

Air Valve

During cold engine operation, the air valve is open, providing a bypass circuit past the throttle plate opening. This causes the volume of air being drawn in to increase, the increased volume is sensed by the air flow meter which in turn signals the EFI Computer to increase the fuel flow. This provides a higher idle speed during cold engine operation. As the valve gradually closes, the air volume is reduced, thereby reducing the fuel flow.

REMOVAL AND INSTALLATION

1. Drain the engine coolant.

2. Squeeze the hose clamps and remove the two air hoses from the valve.

3. Unplug the electrical connector.

4. Unscrew the hose clamps and remove the two water hoses from the valve.

5. Unscrew the mounting bolts and remove the air valve.

6. Installation is in the reverse order of removal.

CHECKING

1. Start the engine and pinch the hose between the air valve and the intake air chamber. The engine rpm should drop noticeable.

2. Run the engine until it reaches normal operating temperature and pinch the hose again. This time the engine speed should not drop more than 150 rpm.

3. After the engine has cooled off, restart it and remove the above hose from the air valve. You should be able to see that the valve is slightly open. If it is not, turn the adjusting screw until it is open slightly.

4. Check the heat coil resistance by removing the electrical connector and measuring across the two terminals with an ohmmeter. The resistance should be 40-60Ω.

Throttle Body
CHECKING

1. Check that the throttle linkage moves smoothly.

2. Start the engine and remove the hose from the vacuum port.

3. With your finger, check that there is no

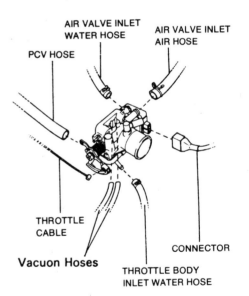

Removing the throttle body

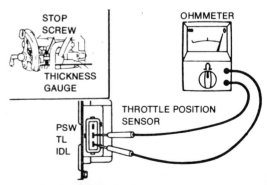

Checking the throttle body

Clearance between lever and stop screw		Continuity between terminals		
		IDL – TL	Psw – TL	IDL – Psw
0.34 mm	(0.0134 in.)	Continuity	No continuity	No continuity
0.70 mm	(0.0276 in.)	No continuity	No continuity	No continuity
Throttle valve fully opened position		No continuity	Continuity	No continuity

vacuum at idle and that there is vacuum at anything other than idle.

4. Unplug the electrical connector from the throttle position sensor.

5. Insert a flat feeler gauge between the throttle stop screw and the stop lever.

6. Using an ohmmeter, check the continuity between each terminal on the sensor.

7. Check the dash pot as detailed in Chapter 2.

REMOVAL AND INSTALLATION

1. Drain the engine coolant.

2. Tag and disconnect all lines, hoses or wires that lead from the throttle body. Position them out of the way.

3. Unscrew the mounting bolts and remove the throttle body and gasket.

4. Installation is in the reverse order of removal.

DIESEL ENGINE FUEL SYSTEM

Injection Nozzle

REMOVAL AND INSTALLATION

1. Loosen the clamps and remove the injection hoses from between the injection pump and pipe.

2. Disconnect both ends of the injection pipes from the pump and nozzle holders.

3. Disconnect the fuel cut off wire from the connector clamp.

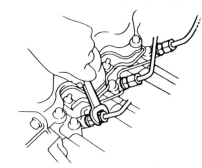

Removing the injection nozzle

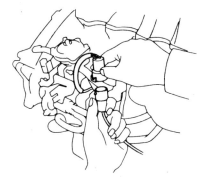

Disconnect the fuel cut solenoid connector

4. Remove the nut, connector clamp and bond cable.

5. Unbolt and remove the injector pipes.

6. Disconnect the fuel hoses from the leakage pipes.

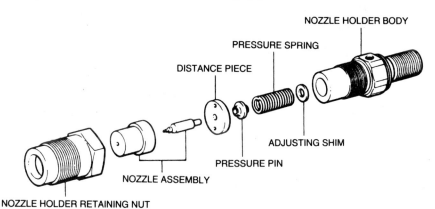

NOZZLE HOLDER BODY

PRESSURE SPRING

DISTANCE PIECE

ADJUSTING SHIM

PRESSURE PIN

NOZZLE ASSEMBLY

NOZZLE HOLDER RETAINING NUT

Exploded view of the diesel injection nozzle

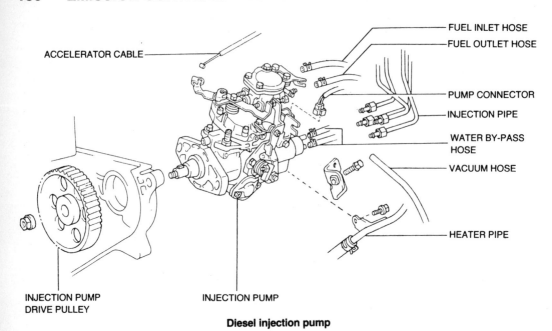

ACCELERATOR CABLE

FUEL INLET HOSE
FUEL OUTLET HOSE
PUMP CONNECTOR
INJECTION PIPE
WATER BY-PASS HOSE
VACUUM HOSE
HEATER PIPE

INJECTION PUMP DRIVE PULLEY

INJECTION PUMP

Diesel injection pump

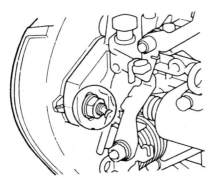

Matchmark the timing mark on the pump flange with the block

7. Remove the four nuts, leakage pipe and four washers.

8. Unscrew and remove the nozzles.

9. Installation is the reverse of removal. Torque the nozzles to 47 ft. lb. Always use new nozzle seat gaskets and seats. Bleed the system by loosening the pipes at the nozzles and crank-ing the engine until all air is expelled and fuel sprays.

Injection Pump

REMOVAL AND INSTALLATION

1. Drain the cooling system.

2. Disconnect the accelerator and cruise control cables from the pump.

3. Disconnect the fuel cut off wire at the pump.

4. Disconnect the fuel inlet and outlet hoses, the water by-pass hoses, the boost compensator hoses, the A/C or heater idle-up vacuum hoses and the heater hose.

5. Remove the injector pipes at the pump.

6. Remove the pump pulley.

7. Matchmark the raised timing mark on the pump flange with the block. Unbolt and remove the pump.

8. Installation is the reverse of removal. There must be no clearance between the pump bracket and stay.

Troubleshooting Basic Fuel System Problems

Problem	Cause	Solution
Engine cranks, but won't start (or is hard to start) when cold	• Empty fuel tank • Incorrect starting procedure • Defective fuel pump • No fuel in carburetor • Clogged fuel filter • Engine flooded • Defective choke	• Check for fuel in tank • Follow correct procedure • Check pump output • Check for fuel in the carburetor • Replace fuel filter • Wait 15 minutes; try again • Check choke plate
Engine cranks, but is hard to start (or does not start) when hot—(presence of fuel is assumed)	• Defective choke	• Check choke plate

Troubleshooting Basic Fuel System Problems (cont.)

Problem	Cause	Solution
Rough idle or engine runs rough	• Dirt or moisture in fuel • Clogged air filter • Faulty fuel pump	• Replace fuel filter • Replace air filter • Check fuel pump output
Engine stalls or hesitates on acceleration	• Dirt or moisture in the fuel • Dirty carburetor • Defective fuel pump • Incorrect float level, defective accelerator pump	• Replace fuel filter • Clean the carburetor • Check fuel pump output • Check carburetor
Poor gas mileage	• Clogged air filter • Dirty carburetor • Defective choke, faulty carburetor adjustment	• Replace air filter • Clean carburetor • Check carburetor
Engine is flooded (won't start accompanied by smell of raw fuel)	• Improperly adjusted choke or carburetor	• Wait 15 minutes and try again, without pumping gas pedal • If it won't start, check carburetor

Chassis Electrical

UNDERSTANDING BASIC ELECTRICITY

Understanding the basic theory of electricity makes electrical troubleshooting much easier. Several gauges are used in electrical trouble-shooting to see inside the circuit being tested. Without a basic understanding, it will be difficult to understand testing procedures.

Electricity is the flow of electrons, hypothetical particles thought to constitute the basic stuff of electricity. In a comparison with water flowing in a pipe, the electrons would be the water. As the flow of water can be measured, the flow of electricity can be measured. The unit of measurement is amperes, frequently abbreviated amps. An ammeter will measure the actual amount of current flowing in the circuit.

Just as the water pressure is measured in units such as pounds per square inch, electrical pressure is measured in volts. When a voltmeter's two probes are placed on two live portions of an electrical circuit with different electrical pressures, current will flow through the voltmeter and produce a reading which indicates the difference in electrical pressure between the two parts of the circuit.

While increasing the voltage in a circuit will increase the flow of current, the actual flow depends not only on voltage, but on the resistance of the circuit. The standard unit for measuring circuit resistance is an ohm, measured by an ohmmeter. The ohmmeter is somewhat similar to an ammeter, but incorporates its own source of power so that a standard voltage is always present.

An actual electric circuit consists of four basic parts. These are: the power source, such as a generator or battery; a hot wire, which conducts the electricity under a relatively high voltage to the component supplied by the circuit; the load, such as a lamp, motor, resistor, or relay coil; and the ground wire, which carries the current back to the source under very low voltage. In such a circuit the bulk of the resistance exists between the point where the hot wire is connected to the load, and the point where the load is grounded. In an automobile, the vehicle's frame, which is made of steel, is used as a part of the ground circuit for many of the electrical devices.

Remember that, in electrical testing, the voltmeter is connected in parallel with the circuit being tested (without disconnecting any wires) and measures the difference in voltage between the locations of the two probes; that the ammeter is connected in series with the load (the circuit is separated at one point and the ammeter inserted so it becomes a part of the circuit); and the ohmmeter is self-powered, so that all the power in the circuit should be off and the portion of the circuit to be measured contacted at either end by one of the probes of the meter.

For any electrical system to operate, it must make a complete circuit. This simply means that the power flow from the battery must make a complete circle. When an electrical component is operating, power flows from the battery to the component, passes through the component causing it to perform its function (lighting a light bulb) and then returns to the battery through the ground of the circuit. This ground is usually (but not always) the metal part of the car on which the electrical component is mounted.

Perhaps the easiest way to visualize this is to think of connecting a light bulb with two wires attached to it to your car battery. The battery in your car has two posts (negative and positive). If one of the two wires attached to the light bulb was attached to the negative post of the battery and the other wire was attached to the positive post of the battery, you would have a complete circuit. Current from the battery would flow out one post, through the wire attached to it and then to the light bulb, where it would pass through causing it to light. It would then leave the light bulb, travel through the other wire, and return to the other post of the battery.

The normal automotive circuit differs from this simple example in two ways. First, instead of having a return wire from the bulb to the battery, the light bulb returns the current to the battery through the chassis of the vehicle. Since the negative battery cable is attached to the chassis and the chassis is made of electrically conductive metal, the chassis of the vehicle can serve as a ground wire to complete the circuit. Secondly, most automotive circuits contain switches to turn components on and off when it is turned off.

Some electrical components which require a large amount of current to operate also have a relay in their circuit. Since these circuits carry a large amount of current, the thickness of the wire in the circuit (gauge size) is also greater. If this large wire were connected from the component to the control switch on the instrument panel, and then back to the component, a voltage drop would occur in the circuit. To prevent this potential drop in voltage, an electromagnetic switch (relay) is used. The large wires in the circuit are connected from the car battery to one side of the relay, and from the opposite side of the relay to the component. The relay is normally open, preventing current from passing through the circuit. When the control switch is turned on, it grounds the smaller wire from the relay. If you were to disconnect the light bulb (from the previous example of a light bulb being connected to the battery by two wires) from the wires and touch the two wires together (please take our word for this; don't try it), the result will be a shower of sparks. A similar thing happens (on a smaller scale) when the power supply wire to a component or the electrical component itself becomes grounded before the normal ground connection for the circuit. To prevent damage to the system, the fuse for the circuit blows to interrupts the circuit-protecting the components from damage. Because grounding a wire from a power source makes a complete circuit, less the required component to use the power, the phenomenon is called a short circuit. The most common causes of short circuits are: the rubber insulation on a wire breaking or rubbing through to expose the current carrying core of the wire to a metal part of the car, or a shorted switch.

Some electrical systems on the car are protected by a circuit breaker which is, basically, a self-repairing fuse. When either of the above-described events takes place in a system which is protected by a circuit breaker, the circuit breaker opens the circuit the same way a fuse does. However, when either the short is removed from the circuit or the surge subsides, the circuit breaker resets itself and does not have to be replaced as a fuse does.

The final protective device in the chassis electrical system is a fuse link. A fuse link is a wire that acts as a fuse. It is connected between the starter relay and the main wiring harness for the car. This connection is under the hood, very near a similar fuse link which protects the engine electrical system. Since the fuse link protects all the chassis electrical components, it is the probable cause of trouble when none of the electrical components function, unless the battery is disconnected or dead.

Electrical problems generally fall into one of three areas:

1. The component that is not functioning is not receiving current.

2. The component itself is not functioning.

3. The component is not properly grounded.

Problems that fall into the first category are by far the most complicated. It is the current supply system to the component which contains all the switches, relays, fuses, etc.

The electrical system can be checked with a test light and a jumper wire. A test light is a device that looks like a pointed screwdriver with a wire attached to it. It has a light bulb in its handle. A jumper wire is a piece of insulated wire with an alligator clip attached to each end.

If a light bulb is not working, you must follow a systematic plan to determine which of the three causes is the villain.

1. Turn on the switch that controls the inoperable bulb.

2. Disconnect the power supply wire from the bulb.

3. Attach the ground wire on the test light to a good metal ground.

4. Touch the probe end of the test light to the end of the power supply wire that was disconnected from the bulb. If the bulb is receiving current, the test light will go on.

NOTE: *If the bulb is one which works only when the ignition key is turned on (turn signal), make sure the key is turned on.*

If the test light does not go on, then the problem is in the circuit between the battery and the bulb. As mentioned before, this includes all the switches, fuses, and relays in the system. Turn to the wiring diagram and find the bulb on the diagram. Follow the wire that runs back to the battery. The problem is an open circuit between the battery and the bulb. If the fuse is blown and, when replaced, immediately blows again, there is a short circuit in the system which must be located and repaired. If there is a switch in the system, bypass it with a jumper wire to the wire coming out of the switch.

Again, consult the wiring diagram. If the test light lights with the jumper wire installed, the switch or whatever was bypassed is defective.

NOTE: *Never substitute the jumper wire for the bulb, as the bulb is the component required to use the power from the power source.*

5. If the bulb in the test light goes on, then the current is getting to the bulb that is not working in the car. This eliminates the first of the three possible causes. Connect the power supply wire and connect a jumper wire from the bulb to a good metal ground. Do this with the switch which controls the bulb turned on, and also the ignition switch turned on if it is required for the light to work. If the bulb works with jumper wire installed, then it has a bad ground. This is usually caused by the metal area on which the bulb mounts to the car being coated with some type of foreign matter.

6. If neither test located the source of the trouble, then the light bulb itself is defective.

The above test procedure can be applied to any of the components of the chassis electrical system by substituting the component that is not working for the light bulb. Remember that for any electrical system to work, all connections must be clean and tight.

HEATER AND AIR CONDITIONING

On some models the air conditioner, if so equipped, is integral with the heater, and therefore, heater removal may differ from the procedures detailed below. In some cases it may be necessary to remove the AC/Heater housing and assembly to remove the blower motor. If ant A.C. lines must be disconnected, use CAUTION and the correct discharge procedure to bleed the system of freon.

Blower

REMOVAL AND INSTALLATION

Carina

1. Working from under the instrument panel, unfasten the defroster hoses from the heater box.
2. Unplug the multiconnector.
3. Loosen the mounting screws and withdraw the blower assembly. Installation is the reverse of removal.

Corolla — 1970-74

1. Drain the cooling system.
CAUTION: *When draining the coolant, keep in mind that cats and dogs are attracted by the ethylene glycol antifreeze, and are quite likely to drink any that is left in an uncovered container or in puddles on the ground. This will prove fatal in sufficient quantity. Always drain the coolant into a sealable container. Coolant should be reused unless it is contaminated or several years old.*

2. Remove the package tray from beneath the dashboard.
3. Unfasten the two water hoses from the heater.
NOTE: *Have a container ready to catch any water which remains in the system.*
4. Unfasten the clamp and remove the defroster hose.
5. Unfasten the three heater control cables from the heater box.
6. Remove the fresh air duct.
7. Unfasten the electrical connections.
8. Unfasten the four heater box attachment bolts and withdraw the heater box.
9. Loosen the fan attachment nut by tapping it lightly and then withdraw the fan from the shaft.
CAUTION: *Do not remove the balancing weight from the fan.*
10. Unfasten the blower motor securing screws and remove the motor.
11. Installation is the reverse of removal. Be sure that the fan does not contact the blower housing when it is assembled. Hold the fan adaptor in place on the armature shaft while tightening the fan locknut to 43 ft.lb.

Corolla — 1975-81

1. Disconnect the negative battery cable and drain the cooling system.
CAUTION: *When draining the coolant, keep in mind that cats and dogs are attracted by the ethylene glycol antifreeze, and are quite likely to drink any that is left in an uncovered container or in puddles on the ground. This will prove fatal in sufficient quantity. Always drain the coolant into a sealable container. Coolant should be reused unless it is contaminated or several years old.*

2. Remove the glove compartment.
3. Loosen the screws and then remove the blower duct.
4. Disconnect the blower motor electrical connection.
5. Remove the two screws, the nut and then lift out the blower motor assembly.
6. Installation is in the reverse order of removal.

Corolla — 1982 and Later

1. Disconnect the negative battery cable and then drain the cooling system.
CAUTION: *When draining the coolant, keep*

in mind that cats and dogs are attracted by the ethylene glycol antifreeze, and are quite likely to drink any that is left in an uncovered container or in puddles on the ground. This will prove fatal in sufficient quantity. Always drain the coolant into a sealable container. Coolant should be reused unless it is contaminated or several years old.

2. Remove the following components:

  a. Center console box

  b. Scuff plate and the front seat

  c. Front carpeting

  d. Rear heater duct

  e. Glove compartment

  f. Left side blower duct and then the instrument cluster brace

  g. Ash tray and its bracket.

3. Remove the heater control assembly as detailed later.

4. On the sedan and station wagon, remove the radio, the No. 2 air duct and then the No. 1 air duct.

5. On all other models, remove the upper console box and then the radio. Unbolt the instrument cluster finish panel, pull the top toward you, raise it up and then remove it. Remove the combination meter and the No. 1 air duct.

6. Disconnect the two heater hoses at the heater core.

7. Remove the two retaining bolts, the nut and the screw and then slide the heater unit out the passenger side.

8. Installation is in the reverse order of removal.

HEATER CONTROL ASSEMBLY REMOVAL

1. Working under the instrument panel, disconnect the four control cables from their clamps.

On the sedan and wagon:

2. Remove the instrument cluster finish panel.

3. Remove the knobs and heater control lens. CAUTION: *Don't bend the clips on either end of the heater control lens.*

4. Disconnect and remove the A/C switch.

5. Remove the cluster finish lower center panel.

6. Disconnect the electrical connector at the blower switch.

7. Pull out the heater control assembly and then remove the blower switch from the control assembly.

8. Disconnect the control cables.

On all other models:

1. Remove the knobs and the heater control panel.

2. Remove the ashtray and its mounting bracket.

3. Disconnect and remove the A/C switch.

Carina blower assembly

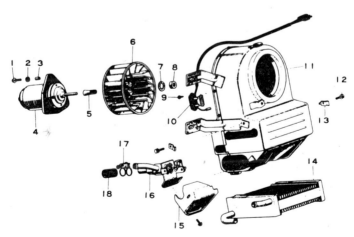

1. Screw and washer	7. Serrated washer	13. Clamp
2. Bushing	8. Nut	14. Core
3. Bushing	9. Screw and washer	15. Water valve cover
4. Blower motor	10. Resistor	16. Water valve
5. Fan adapter	11. Blower housing	17. Clamp
6. Fan	12. Bolt and washer	18. Hose

1970–74 Corolla heater assembly

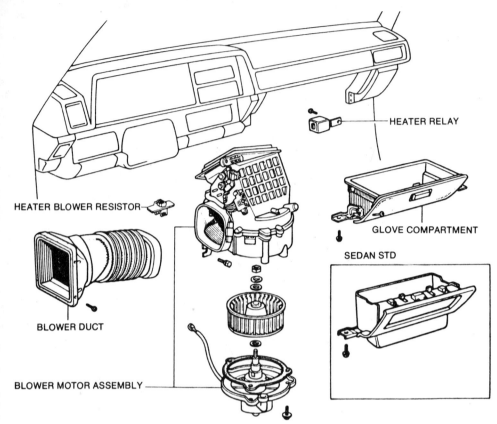

HEATER RELAY

HEATER BLOWER RESISTOR

GLOVE COMPARTMENT

SEDAN STD

BLOWER DUCT

BLOWER MOTOR ASSEMBLY

Heater blower assembly—1975–81 Corolla

4. Repeat Steps 6-8 of the sedan and wagon procedure.

To install, reverse the order of removal and note the following:

1. Install the heater control knob and position all levers toward the outside edges of the panel.

2. Install the air inlet damper and position the blower lever against the stopped as shown in the illustration.

Tercel

1. Disconnect the negative battery cable and drain the cooling system.

CAUTION: *When draining the coolant, keep in mind that cats and dogs are attracted by the ethylene glycol antifreeze, and are quite likely to drink any that is left in an uncovered container or in puddles on the ground. This will prove fatal in sufficient quantity. Always drain the coolant into a sealable container. Coolant should be reused unless it is contaminated or several years old.*

2. Remove the ash tray and its retaining bracket.

3. Remove the heater rear duct work if so equipped.

4. Remove the left and right side duct piping.

Removing the heater assembly—1975 Corolla

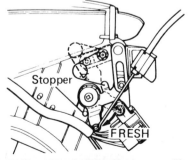

When installing the air inlet damper, position the blower lever against the stopper

SEDAN AND WAGON

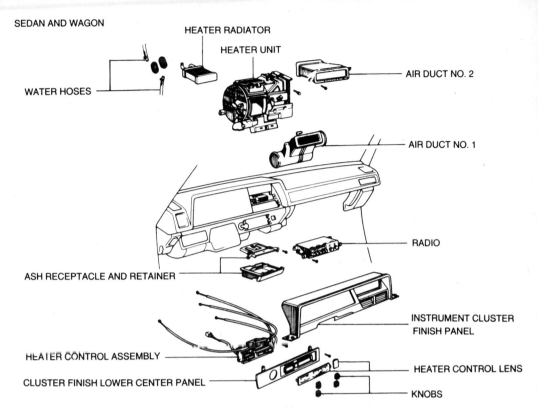

HEATER RADIATOR

HEATER UNIT

WATER HOSES

AIR DUCT NO. 2

AIR DUCT NO. 1

RADIO

ASH RECEPTACLE AND RETAINER

INSTRUMENT CLUSTER
FINISH PANEL

HEATER CONTROL ASSEMBLY

HEATER CONTROL LENS

CLUSTER FINISH LOWER CENTER PANEL

KNOBS

HARDTOP, COUPE AND LIFTBACK

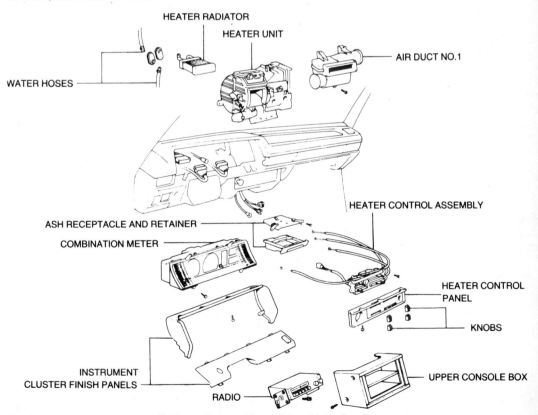

HEATER RADIATOR

HEATER UNIT

WATER HOSES

AIR DUCT NO.1

HEATER CONTROL ASSEMBLY

ASH RECEPTACLE AND RETAINER

COMBINATION METER

HEATER CONTROL
PANEL

KNOBS

INSTRUMENT
CLUSTER FINISH PANELS

UPPER CONSOLE BOX

RADIO

Heater unit assembly—1982 and later Corolla

5. Remove the under tray if so equipped. Remove the glove compartment.

6. Remove the air duct.

7. Remove the radio. Remove the heater control panel and assembly and then remove the blower switch.

8. Loosen the two hose clamps and slide the two heater hoses off the heater duct fittings.

9. Remove the two air duct fittings.

10. Remove the heater retaining bolts and clips and then remove the heater blower assembly from the passenger side.

11. Installation is in the reverse order of removal.

Starlet

1. Disconnect the negative battery cable and drain the cooling system.

CAUTION: *When draining the coolant, keep in mind that cats and dogs are attracted by the ethylene glycol antifreeze, and are quite likely to drink any that is left in an uncovered container or in puddles on the ground. This will prove fatal in sufficient quantity. Always drain the coolant into a sealable container. Coolant should be reused unless it is contaminated or several years old.*

2. Remove the rear seat duct work if so equipped.

3. Remove the heater under tray, the right side kick panel and the glove compartment.

4. Remove the air duct and the damper assembly from the right side.

5. Remove the defroster hoses and the attached duct work.

6. Remove the radio, clock and the ash tray.

7. Remove the heater control panel and assembly. Remove the blower switch.

8. Remove the ignition coil and then disconnect the two heater hoses from the back of the blower assembly.

9. Remove the heater retaining screws and lift the heater assembly out through the passenger side.

10. Installation is in the reverse order of removal.

Heater Core
REMOVAL AND INSTALLATION
Except Later Models (Following)

1. Remove the heater blower assembly as previously detailed.

2. On the Carina, unclip the heater box halves and remove the core.

3. On all other models, carefully pull the heater core out of the heater case.

4. Installation is in the reverse order of removal.

Corolla (FWD)

1. Disconnect the negative battery cable. Drain the engine coolant.

CAUTION: *When draining the coolant, keep in mind that cats and dogs are attracted by the ethylene glycol antifreeze, and are quite likely to drink any that is left in an uncovered container or in puddles on the ground. This will prove fatal in sufficient quantity. Always drain the coolant into a sealable container. Coolant should be reused unless it is contaminated or several years old.*

2. Remove the center console, plate and front seats.

3. Position the floor carpet out of the way and remove the heater duct.

4. Remove the under tray, glove box and blower duct.

5. On the Corolla station wagon and sedan models, remove the following components: Heater control knobs and lens; Cluster lower center panel finish; Ashtray and heater control assembly. Instrument cluster finish panel; Radio; and Air ducts.

6. On Corolla coupe and liftback models, remove the following components: Instrument cluster finish panel; Instrument cluster; Radio trim panel and Radio; Ashtray; Heater control knobs; Heater control panel; Heater control assembly; and the Air duct.

7. Disconnect the heater hoses from the heater core assembly. Remove the hose mounting grommet.

8. Remove the heater core assembly mounting bolts and remove the assembly.

9. Remove the heater core from the assembly. Service as required and install in the reverse order. Refill the cooling system. Start the engine and check for coolant leaks.

Corolla (RWD)

1. Disconnect the negative battery cable. Drain the cooling system.

CAUTION: *When draining the coolant, keep in mind that cats and dogs are attracted by the ethylene glycol antifreeze, and are quite likely to drink any that is left in an uncovered container or in puddles on the ground. This will prove fatal in sufficient quantity. Always drain the coolant into a sealable container. Coolant should be reused unless it is contaminated or several years old.*

2. Disconnect the heater hoses from the heater core on the engine side of the firewall.

3. Remove the knobs from the heater and fan controls.

4. Remove the two securing screws, and take off the heater control panel.

5. Remove the heater control and cable assembly.

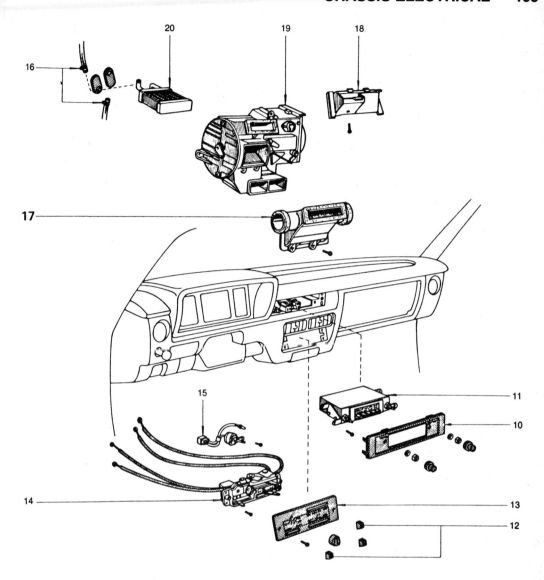

10.	Knob & Radio Tuner Finish Plate		16.	Heater Hose & Grommet
11.	Radio Tuner		17.	Air Duct
12.	Knob		18.	Air Duct
13.	Heater Control Panel		19.	Radiator Unit Assembly
14.	Heater Control Assembly		20.	Radiator Unit
15.	Heater Blower Switch & Heater			
	Control Indicator Light			

Tercel heater blower assembly

6. Disconnect the wiring harness.

7. Remove the three heater assembly mounting bolts and remove the assembly.

8. Separate the core from the heater assembly. Install in the reverse order. Fill the cooling system, start the engine, and check for coolant leaks.

Starlet

1. Disconnect the negative battery cable. Drain the cooling system.

CAUTION: *When draining the coolant, keep in mind that cats and dogs are attracted by the ethylene glycol antifreeze, and are quite likely to drink any that is left in an uncovered*

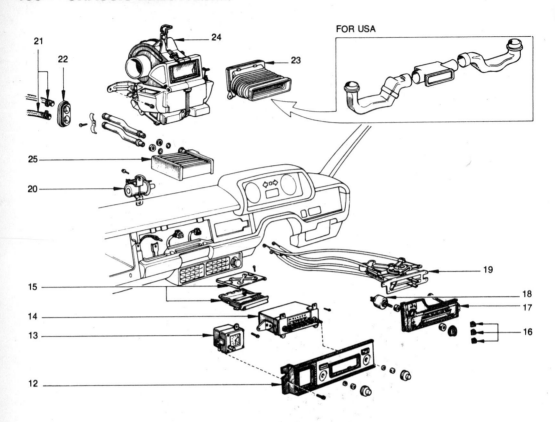

FOR USA

12. Radio Tuner Finish Plate	19. Heater Control Assembly
13. Clock (OPT)	20. Ignition Coil
14. Radio Tuner (OPT)	21. Water Hose
15. Ash Receptacle & Retainer	22. Grommet
16. Knob	23. Air Duct
17. Heater Control Panel	24. Radiator Unit Assembly
18. Heater Blower Switch	25. Radiator Unit

Starlet heater blower assembly

container or in puddles on the ground. This will prove fatal in sufficient quantity. Always drain the coolant into a sealable container. Coolant should be reused unless it is contaminated or several years old.

2. Remove the rear heater duct and dash under tray.

3. Remove the cowl side trim, glove box, and air damper assembly. Remove the air duct, defroster hoses and inside air duct.

4. Remove the radio finish panel plate, and the clock and radio. Remove the ashtray, heater control knobs and the heater control front panel.

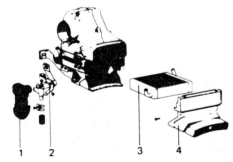

1. Water valve cover
2. Water valve
3. Core
4. Duct/cover assembly

Carina core removal

On most models, the heater core will just slide right out of the blower assembly

5. Remove the heater blower switch and heater control assembly. Remove the ignition coil, then disconnect the heater hoses from the heater core.

6. Remove the grommet that mounts the heater hoses. Remove the screws that mount the heater core assembly. and remove the assembly from the car.

7. Remove the heater core from the assembly. Service as require. Install the heater core in the reverse order. Fill the cooling system, start the engine and check for coolant leaks.

Tercel

1. Disconnect the negative battery cable. Drain the engine coolant.

CAUTION: *When draining the coolant, keep in mind that cats and dogs are attracted by the ethylene glycol antifreeze, and are quite likely to drink any that is left in an uncovered container or in puddles on the ground. This will prove fatal in sufficient quantity. Always drain the coolant into a sealable container. Coolant should be reused unless it is contaminated or several years old.*

2. Remove the ashtray and retainer.

3. Remove the rear heater duct (optional equipment).

4. Remove the left and right defroster ducts.

5. Remove the dash undertray.

6. Remove the glove box.

7. Remove the main duct.

8. Remove the radio.

9. Disconnect the heater control cables and remove the controls.

10. Disconnect the heater hoses.

11. Remove the front and rear air ducts. Disconnect the electrical connector.

12. Remove the heater assembly mounting bolts and remove the assembly from the right side of the vehicle.

13. Remove the heater core from the assembly.

14. Service as required. Install in the reverse order. Fill the cooling system, start the engine and check for coolant leaks.

Radio

Never operate the radio without a speaker; severe damage to the output transistors will result. If the speaker must be replaced, use a speaker of the correct impedance (ohms) or else the output transistors will be damaged and require replacement.

REMOVAL AND INSTALLATION

Carina

1. Remove the center air outlet from under the dash.

2. Unfasten the radio control mounting bracket.

3. Remove the radio control knobs and then the retaining nuts from the control shafts.

4. Detach the speaker, and the power and antenna leads from the radio.

5. Withdraw the radio from underneath the dashboard.

6. Unfasten the speaker retaining nuts and remove the speaker. Installation is performed in the reverse order of removal.

Corolla (1970-74)

1. Remove the knobs from the radio.

2. Remove the nuts from the radio control shafts.

3. Detach the antenna lead from the jack on the radio case.

4. Remove the cowl air intake duct.

5. Detach the power and speaker leads.

6. Remove the radio support nuts and bolts.

7. Withdraw the radio from beneath the dashboard

8. Remove the nuts which secure the speaker through the service hole in the top of the glovebox.

9. Remove remainder of the speaker securing nuts from above the radio mounting location.

10. Withdraw the speaker.

11. Installation is performed in the reverse order of removal.

Corolla — 1975 and Later, Starlet, and Tercel

1. Remove the two screws from the top of the dashboard center trim panel.

2. Lift the center panel out far enough to gain access to the cigarette lighter wiring and disconnect the wiring. Remove the trim panel.

3. Unfasten the screws which secure the radio to the instrument panel braces.

4. Lift the radio and disconnect the leads from it. Remove the radio.

5. Installation is the reverse of removal.

WINDSHIELD WIPERS

Blade and Arm

REPLACEMENT

1. To remove the wiper blades lift up on the spring release tab on the wiper blade-to-wiper arm connector.

2. Pull the blade assembly off the wiper arm.

3. There are two types of replacements for Toyotas:

a. Pre-1973 — replace the entire wiper blade as an assembly. Simply snap the replacement into place on the arm.

b. Post-1973 — press the old wiper blade insert down, away from the blade assembly, to free it from the retaining clips on the blade ends. Slide the insert out of the blade. Slide the new insert into the blade assembly and bend the insert upward slightly to engage the retaining clips.

4. To replace a wiper arm, unscrew the acorn nut which secures it to the pivot and carefully pull the arm upward and off the pivot. Install the arm by reversing this procedure.

Motor

REMOVAL AND INSTALLATION

Corolla — 1970-74

1. Disconnect the car battery.
2. Unfasten the wiper motor connection.
3. Detach the wiper motor from the linkage by prying it with a small prybar.
4. Remove the package tray.
5. Unfasten the three wiper motor securing nuts and withdraw the motor from inside the cars.
6. Installation is performed in the reverse order of removal.

Corolla (1975 and Later RWD), Carina and Starlet

1. Disconnect the wiper motor multiconnector.
2. Remove the service cover and loosen the wiper motor securing bolts.
3. Use a small prybar to separate the wiper link-to-motor connection.
CAUTION: *Be careful not to bend the linkage.*
4. Withdraw the wiper motor assembly.

5. Installation is performed in the reverse order of removal.

Tercel and Corolla FWD

1. Disconnect the negative battery terminal.
2. Insert a small prybar between the linkage and the motor.
3. Pry up to separate the linkage from the motor.
4. Disconnect the electrical connector from the motor.
5. Remove the mounting bolts and remove the motor.
6. Installation is the reverse of removal.

Rear Wiper Motor

Disconnect the negative battery cable. Remove the windshield wiper arm and blade assembly. Remove the rear trim trim panel and cover from the gate. Disconnect the wiring connector to the motor. Remove the motor bracket mounting bolts and remove the motor and bracket assembly. Install the motor and bracket assembly in the reverse order.

Linkage

REMOVAL AND INSTALLATION

1970-74 Corolla

1. Disconnect the battery.
2. Remove the wiper arms and the pivot caps.
3. Remove the instrument cluster.
4. Unfasten the heater's defroster hose, loosen the two screws, and then remove right hand defroster nozzle.

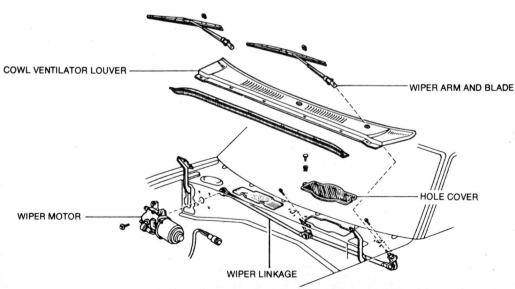

Windshield wiper motor and linkage—late model Corolla (Starlet similar)

COWL VENTILATOR LOUVER

WIPER ARM AND BLADE

HOLE COVER

WIPER MOTOR

WIPER LINKAGE

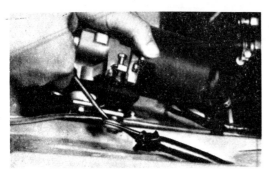

On Carina and 1975–76 Corolla, separate the wiper link from the motor with a screwdriver

5. Disconnect the wiper motor and link by prying on the link with a small prybar.

6. Loosen the three bolts which attach the pivots. Remove both pivots.

7. Remove the wiper linkage assembly.

8. Installation is performed in the reverse order of removal. Tighten the pivot to 0.9-1.9 ft.lbs.

CAUTION: *If the pivot is overtightened, the linkage will be damaged.*

Before installing the wiper arms, operate the motor once by turning it on and off at the wiper switch so that the wipers may be easily installed in the park position.

All Others

1. Perform the wiper motor removal procedure.

2. Loosen the wiper arm retaining nuts and remove the arms.

3. Unfasten the wiper pivot nuts and remove the linkage assembly through the access hole.

4. Installation is the reverse of removal.

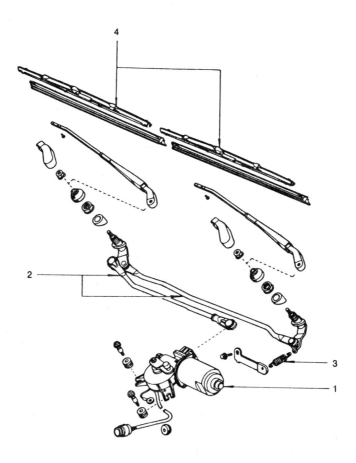

1.   Wiper Motor
2.   Wiper Link
3.   Spring
4.   Wiper Arm & Blade

Windshield wiper motor and linkage—Tercel

INSTRUMENT CLUSTER

REMOVAL AND INSTALLATION

1970-74 Corolla

1. Disconnect the negative battery cable.
2. Detach the speedometer cable from the speedometer.
3. Remove the center and right hand trim moldings from the instrument panel.
4. Unfasten the instrument cluster and panel molding retainer screw.
5. Remove the two nuts which secure the instrument cluster from behind.

6. Pull the cluster out slightly and disconnect the wiring.
7. Remove the cluster assembly completely. CAUTION: *Be careful not to scratch the steering column cover.*
8. Installation is performed in the reverse order of removal.

Starlet, 1975 and Later Corolla (RWD)

1. Disconnect the negative battery cable.
2. Remove the screws which secure the instrument cluster surround (two at the top and one next to the fresh air vent).

Sedan and Wagon

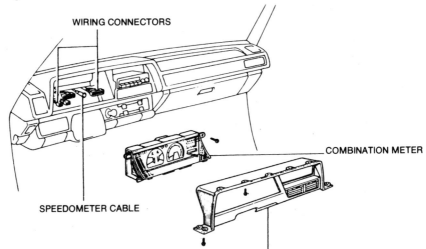

Hardtop, Coupe and Liftback

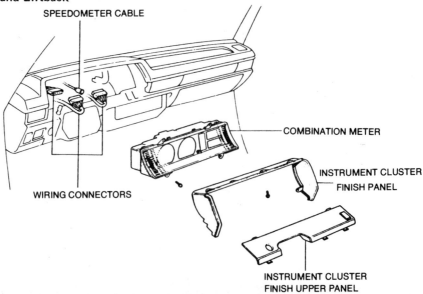

Late model Corolla instrument cluster

3. Remove the center trim panel by unfastening its two retaining screws. Disconnect the cigarette lighter wiring before completely removing the panel.

4. Withdraw the speedometer cable and disconnect it.

5. Pull the instrument cluster out just far enough so that its wiring harness may be disconnected.

6. Remove the cluster.

7. Installation is performed in the reverse order of removal.

Carina

1. Remove the glove box door and withdraw the glove box slightly.

2. Disconnect the inspection lamp socket and glove box light wiring.

3. Remove the glove box completely.

4. Unfasten the cigarette lighter wiring and remove the ash tray.

5. Unfasten the lower crash pad screws and remove the crash pad.

NOTE: *It may be necessary to unfasten the attachment screws and lower the steering column. Be careful, the column is the collapsible type.*

6. Loosen the car rear attaching screws and detach the heater cable at the heater.

7. Unfasten the instrument retaining screws and tilt the panel toward the rear.

8. Detach the speedometer cable and the wir-

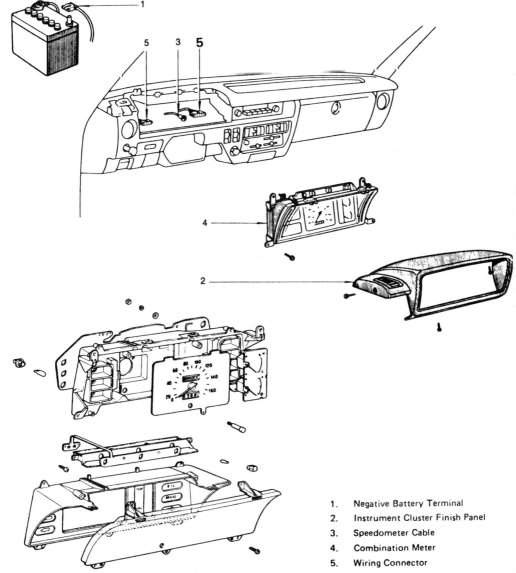

1.	Negative Battery Terminal
2.	Instrument Cluster Finish Panel
3.	Speedometer Cable
4.	Combination Meter
5.	Wiring Connector

Tercel instrument cluster—Starlet similar

ing multiconnectors. Remove the cluster assembly.

9. Installation is performed in the reverse order of removal.

Tercel and Corolla (FWD)

1. Disconnect the negative battery terminal.
2. Remove the steering column cover.
NOTE: *Be careful not to damage the collapsible steer column mechanism.*
3. Remove the screws from the instrument panel.
4. Gently pull the panel out approximately half way.
5. Disconnect the speedometer and any other electrical connections that are necessary.
6. Remove the panel at this time.
7. Installation is the reverse of removal.

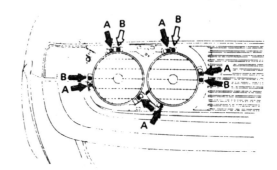

To remove the headlights, remove the retaining screws "A"; but do not loosen adjusting screws "B"

LIGHTING

Headlights

REMOVAL AND INSTALLATION

Corolla, Tercel and Starlet

NOTE: *The following procedure is for early models, or models without retractable headlamps or semi-sealed beam units. Refer to the next procedure paragraph for the afore mentioned models.*
1. Unfasten the two headlight bezel (1970-74) or grille (1975-77) securing screws. Remove the bezel or grille.
2. Loosen (do not remove) the three headlight retaining ring screws and rotate the ring counterclockwise in order to remove it.
CAUTION: *Be careful not to disturb the two headlight aiming screws.*
3. Detach the connector from the back of the sealed beam unit and remove the unit from the car.
4. Installation is performed in the reverse order of removal.

Carina

1. Remove the headlight bezel and/or radiator grille, as necessary.
2. Repeat Steps 2-3 of the Corolla Headlight Removal procedure for each lamp unit to be replaced.
NOTE: *On some models, the headlight retainer must be rotated clockwise in order to remove the headlight unit.*
3. Installation is performed in the reverse order of removal.
CAUTION: *Do not interchange inner and outer headlight units.*

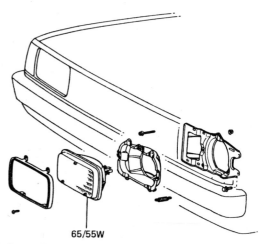

65/55W

Removing the headlight—late model Corolla shown

Retractable Headlamps/Semi-Sealed Beam Bulbs

On models equipped with retractable headlamps: Push the headlamp switch in and twist it to the third clickstop (the headlamps raised with the lights off). Pull out the RTR fusible link that is located by the battery. Pull out the fusible link will insure that the headlamps will not retract will you are servicing the unit. Loosen the headlight ornament screws and remove the headlamp retaining ornament retainer. Remove the headlamp retaining ring screws, take out the bulb out and disconnect the wiring plug. Install the new beam in the reverse order.

On models equipped with semi-sealed beams (replace filament units): Make sure the light switch is in the off position. Open the hood of the vehicle and disconnect the wiring connector while depressing the lock release. Turn the bulb retaining ring counterclockwise and take out the bulb. Install the bulb by reversing the removal sequence.

CIRCUIT PROTECTION

Turn Signal and Hazard Flasher Locations

1970-74

These models' turn signals and hazard warning flashers are combined in a single unit. It is located on the left hand side, underneath the dashboard, next to the fuse block.

NOTE: *On some models it may be necessary to remove the fuse block bracket in order to gain access to the flasher.*

1975 and Later

The combination turn signal/hazard flasher is located behind the kick panel on the driver's side. In order to remove the flasher, first remove the panel retaining screw and lift out the kick panel.

WIRING DIAGRAMS

Wiring diagrams have been left out of this book. As cars have become more complex, and available with longer and longer option lists, wiring diagrams have grown in size and complexity also. It has become virtually impossible to provide a readable reproduction in a reasonable number of pages. Information on ordering wiring diagrams from the vehicle manufacturer can be found in the owners manual.

Troubleshooting Basic Air Conditioning Problems

Problem	Cause	Solution
There's little or no air coming from the vents (and you're sure it's on)	• The A/C fuse is blown • Broken or loose wires or connections • The on/off switch is defective	• Check and/or replace fuse • Check and/or repair connections • Replace switch
The air coming from the vents is not cool enough	• Windows and air vent wings open • The compressor belt is slipping • Heater is on • Condenser is clogged with debris • Refrigerant has escaped through a leak in the system • Receiver/drier is plugged	• Close windows and vent wings • Tighten or replace compressor belt • Shut heater off • Clean the condenser • Check system • Service system
The air has an odor	• Vacuum system is disrupted • Odor producing substances on the evaporator case • Condensation has collected in the bottom of the evaporator housing	• Have the system checked/repaired • Clean the evaporator case • Clean the evaporator housing drains
System is noisy or vibrating	• Compressor belt or mountings loose • Air in the system	• Tighten or replace belt; tighten mounting bolts • Have the system serviced
Sight glass condition Constant bubbles, foam or oil streaks Clear sight glass, but no cold air Clear sight glass, but air is cold Clouded with milky fluid	• Undercharged system • No refrigerant at all • System is OK • Receiver drier is leaking dessicant	• Charge the system • Check and charge the system • Have system checked
Large difference in temperature of lines	• System undercharged	• Charge and leak test the system
Compressor noise	• Broken valves • Overcharged • Incorrect oil level • Piston slap • Broken rings • Drive belt pulley bolts are loose	• Replace the valve plate • Discharge, evacuate and install the correct charge • Isolate the compressor and check the oil level. Correct as necessary. • Replace the compressor • Replace the compressor • Tighten with the correct torque specification

Troubleshooting Basic Air Conditioning Problems (cont.)

Problem	Cause	Solution
Excessive vibration	· Incorrect belt tension · Clutch loose · Overcharged · Pulley is misaligned	· Adjust the belt tension · Tighten the clutch · Discharge, evacuate and install the correct charge · Align the pulley
Condensation dripping in the passenger compartment	· Drain hose plugged or improperly positioned · Insulation removed or improperly installed	· Clean the drain hose and check for proper installation · Replace the insulation on the expansion valve and hoses
Frozen evaporator coil	· Faulty thermostat · Thermostat capillary tube improperly installed · Thermostat not adjusted properly	· Replace the thermostat · Install the capillary tube correctly · Adjust the thermostat
Low side low—high side low	· System refrigerant is low · Expansion valve is restricted	· Evacuate, leak test and charge the system · Replace the expansion valve
Low side high—high side low	· Internal leak in the compressor—worn	· Remove the compressor cylinder head and inspect the compressor. Replace the valve plate assembly if necessary. If the compressor pistons, rings or
Low side high—high side low (cont.)	 · Cylinder head gasket is leaking · Expansion valve is defective · Drive belt slipping	cylinders are excessively worn or scored replace the compressor · Install a replacement cylinder head gasket · Replace the expansion valve · Adjust the belt tension
Low side high—high side high	· Condenser fins obstructed · Air in the system · Expansion valve is defective · Loose or worn fan belts	· Clean the condenser fins · Evacuate, leak test and charge the system · Replace the expansion valve · Adjust or replace the belts as necessary
Low side low—high side high	· Expansion valve is defective · Restriction in the refrigerant hose · Restriction in the receiver/drier · Restriction in the condenser	· Replace the expansion valve · Check the hose for kinks—replace if necessary · Replace the receiver/drier · Replace the condenser
Low side and high side normal (inadequate cooling)	· Air in the system · Moisture in the system	· Evacuate, leak test and charge the system · Evacuate, leak test and charge the system

Troubleshooting the Heater

Problem	Cause	Solution
Blower motor will not turn at any speed	· Blown fuse · Loose connection · Defective ground · Faulty switch · Faulty motor · Faulty resistor	· Replace fuse · Inspect and tighten · Clean and tighten · Replace switch · Replace motor · Replace resistor
Blower motor turns at one speed only	· Faulty switch · Faulty resistor	· Replace switch · Replace resistor
Blower motor turns but does not circulate air	· Intake blocked · Fan not secured to the motor shaft	· Clean intake · Tighten security

Troubleshooting the Heater (cont.)

Problem	Cause	Solution
Heater will not heat	• Coolant does not reach proper temperature • Heater core blocked internally • Heater core air-bound • Blend-air door not in proper position	• Check and replace thermostat if necessary • Flush or replace core if necessary • Purge air from core • Adjust cable
Heater will not defrost	• Control cable adjustment incorrect • Defroster hose damaged	• Adjust control cable • Replace defroster hose

Troubleshooting Basic Lighting Problems

Problem	Cause	Solution
Lights		
One or more lights don't work, but others do	• Defective bulb(s) • Blown fuse(s) • Dirty fuse clips or light sockets • Poor ground circuit	• Replace bulb(s) • Replace fuse(s) • Clean connections • Run ground wire from light socket housing to car frame
Lights burn out quickly	• Incorrect voltage regulator setting or defective regulator • Poor battery/alternator connections	• Replace voltage regulator • Check battery/alternator connections
Lights go dim	• Low/discharged battery • Alternator not charging • Corroded sockets or connections • Low voltage output	• Check battery • Check drive belt tension; repair or replace alternator • Clean bulb and socket contacts and connections • Replace voltage regulator
Lights flicker	• Loose connection • Poor ground • Circuit breaker operating (short circuit)	• Tighten all connections • Run ground wire from light housing to car frame • Check connections and look for bare wires
Lights "flare"—Some flare is normal on acceleration—if excessive, see "Lights Burn Out Quickly"	• High voltage setting	• Replace voltage regulator
Lights glare—approaching drivers are blinded	• Lights adjusted too high • Rear springs or shocks sagging • Rear tires soft	• Have headlights aimed • Check rear springs/shocks • Check/correct rear tire pressure
Turn Signals		
Turn signals don't work in either direction	• Blown fuse • Defective flasher • Loose connection	• Replace fuse • Replace flasher • Check/tighten all connections
Right (or left) turn signal only won't work	• Bulb burned out • Right (or left) indicator bulb burned out • Short circuit	• Replace bulb • Check/replace indicator bulb • Check/repair wiring
Flasher rate too slow or too fast	• Incorrect wattage bulb • Incorrect flasher	• Flasher bulb • Replace flasher (use a variable load flasher if you pull a trailer)
Indicator lights do not flash (burn steadily)	• Burned out bulb • Defective flasher	• Replace bulb • Replace flasher
Indicator lights do not light at all	• Burned out indicator bulb • Defective flasher	• Replace indicator bulb • Replace flasher

Troubleshooting Basic Turn Signal and Flasher Problems

Most problems in the turn signals or flasher system, can be reduced to defective flashers or bulbs, which are easily replaced. Occasionally, problems in the turn signals are traced to the switch in the steering column, which will require professional service.

F = Front   R = Rear   • = Lights off   o = Lights on

Problem		Solution
Turn signals light, but do not flash		• Replace the flasher
No turn signals light on either side		• Check the fuse. Replace if defective. • Check the flasher by substitution • Check for open circuit, short circuit or poor ground
Both turn signals on one side don't work		• Check for bad bulbs • Check for bad ground in both housings
One turn signal light on one side doesn't work		• Check and/or replace bulb • Check for corrosion in socket. Clean contacts. • Check for poor ground at socket
Turn signal flashes too fast or too slow		• Check any bulb on the side flashing too fast. A heavy-duty bulb is probably installed in place of a regular bulb. • Check the bulb flashing too slow. A standard bulb was probably installed in place of a heavy-duty bulb. • Check for loose connections or corrosion at the bulb socket
Indicator lights don't work in either direction		• Check if the turn signals are working • Check the dash indicator lights • Check the flasher by substitution
One indicator light doesn't light		• On systems with 1 dash indicator: See if the lights work on the same side. Often the filaments have been reversed in systems combining stoplights with taillights and turn signals. Check the flasher by substitution • On systems with 2 indicators: Check the bulbs on the same side Check the indicator light bulb Check the flasher by substitution

Troubleshooting Basic Dash Gauge Problems

Problem	Cause	Solution
Coolant Temperature Gauge		
Gauge reads erratically or not at all	• Loose or dirty connections • Defective sending unit • Defective gauge	• Clean/tighten connections • Bi-metal gauge: remove the wire from the sending unit. Ground the wire for an instant. If the gauge registers, replace the sending unit. • Magnetic gauge: disconnect the wire at the sending unit. With ignition ON gauge should register COLD. Ground the wire; gauge should register HOT.
Ammeter Gauge—Turn Headlights ON (do not start engine). Note reaction		
Ammeter shows charge Ammeter shows discharge Ammeter does not move	• Connections reversed on gauge • Ammeter is OK • Loose connections or faulty wiring • Defective gauge	• Reinstall connections • Nothing • Check/correct wiring • Replace gauge
Oil Pressure Gauge		
Gauge does not register or is inaccurate	• On mechanical gauge, Bourdon tube may be bent or kinked • Low oil pressure • Defective gauge • Defective wiring • Defective sending unit	• Check tube for kinks or bends preventing oil from reaching the gauge • Remove sending unit. Idle the engine briefly. If no oil flows from sending unit hole, problem is in engine. • Remove the wire from the sending unit and ground it for an instant with the ignition ON. A good gauge will go to the top of the scale. • Check the wiring to the gauge. If it's OK and the gauge doesn't register when grounded, replace the gauge. • If the wiring is OK and the gauge functions when grounded, replace the sending unit
All Gauges		
All gauges do not operate All gauges read low or erratically All gauges pegged	• Blown fuse • Defective instrument regulator • Defective or dirty instrument voltage regulator • Loss of ground between instrument voltage regulator and car • Defective instrument regulator	• Replace fuse • Replace instrument voltage regulator • Clean contacts or replace • Check ground • Replace regulator
Warning Lights		
Light(s) do not come on when ignition is ON, but engine is not started Light comes on with engine running	• Defective bulb • Defective wire • Defective sending unit • Problem in individual system • Defective sending unit	• Replace bulb • Check wire from light to sending unit • Disconnect the wire from the sending unit and ground it. Replace the sending unit if the light comes on with the ignition ON. • Check system • Check sending unit (see above)

Troubleshooting Basic Windshield Wiper Problems

Problem	Cause	Solution
Electric Wipers		

Wipers do not operate—
Wiper motor heats up or hums
	• Internal motor defect
	• Bent or damaged linkage
	• Arms improperly installed on link-
	  ing pivots
		• Replace motor
		• Repair or replace linkage
		• Position linkage in park and rein-
		  stall wiper arms

Wipers do not operate— No current to motor	• Fuse or circuit breaker blown • Loose, open or broken wiring • Defective switch • Defective or corroded terminals • No ground circuit for motor or switch	• Replace fuse or circuit breaker • Repair wiring and connections • Replace switch • Replace or clean terminals • Repair ground circuits
Wipers do not operate— Motor runs	• Linkage disconnected or broken	• Connect wiper linkage or replace broken linkage
Vacuum Wipers		

Wipers do not operate	• Control switch or cable inoperative
	• Loss of engine vacuum to wiper
	  motor (broken hoses, low
	  engine vacuum, defective
	  vacuum/fuel pump)
	• Linkage broken or disconnected
	• Defective wiper motor
		• Repair or replace switch or cable
		• Check vacuum lines, engine
		  vacuum and fuel pump
		
		• Repair linkage
		• Replace wiper motor

Wipers stop on engine acceleration	• Leaking vacuum hoses • Dry windshield • Oversize wiper blades • Defective vacuum/fuel pump	• Repair or replace hoses • Wet windshield with washers • Replace with proper size wiper blades • Replace pump

MANUAL TRANSMISSION

LINKAGE ADJUSTMENT

Most late model passenger cars sold in the US have floor mounted shifters, and internally mounted shift linkages. On some older models, the linkage is contained in the side cover which is bolted on the transmission case. All of the other models have the linkage mounted inside the top of the transmission case itself. No external adjustments are needed or possible.

REMOVAL AND INSTALLATION

Carina, 1970-83 Corolla RWD and Starlet

Working from inside of the car, perform the following:

1. Place the gear selector in neutral. Remove the center console, if so equipped.
2. Remove the trim boot at the base of the shift lever and the boot underneath it on the shift tower.
3. On all Corolla (except 1600) and Starlet models:
   a. Unfasten the snapring from the base of the shift lever.
   b. Withdraw the council spring and the shift lever itself.
4. On Corolla 1600 and Carina models only:
   a. Unfasten the four shift lever plate retaining screws.
   b. Withdraw the shift lever assembly.
   c. Remove the gasket.
NOTE: *Cover the hole with a clean cloth to prevent anything from falling into the transmission case.*

Working in the engine compartment perform the following:

5. Drain the cooling system and disconnect the cable from the negative side of the battery.
6. Remove the radiator hoses.
7. On Corolla 1200 models, only:
   a. Unfasten the back-up lamp switch connector.
   b. Remove the engine fan.
8. On Corolla 1600, 1800 and Carina models, only:
   a. Remove the air cleaner, complete with hoses.
   b. Unfasten the accelerator torque rod at the carburetor.
   c. Remove the clutch hydraulic line support bracket.
   d. Remove the starter assembly from the left side of the engine.
   e. Remove the upper left hand clutch housing bolt, from the flat at the top of the clutch housing.
9. On the Starlet:
   a. Remove the water outlet hose.
   b. Remove the air cleaner.
   c. Disconnect the accelerator pump lever.
   d. Disconnect the wiring harness connector.
   e. Wrap the steering rack boot with a rag.
   f. Remove the starter.
Be sure that the car is securely supported with jackstands. Remember, you will be working underneath it.

10. Drain the transmission oil.
11. Detach the exhaust pipe from the manifold and remove the exhaust pipe support bracket.
12. Remove the driveshaft.
NOTE: *It will be necessary to plug the opening in the end of the transmission with an old yoke or if none is available, cover it with a plastic bag secured by a rubber band.*
13. Unfasten the speedometer cable from the right side of the transmission.
14. On Corolla 1600, 1800 and Carina models, only:
   a. Remove the clutch release cylinder assembly from the transmission and tie it aside, so that it is out of the way.
   b. Unplug the back-up lamp switch connector.

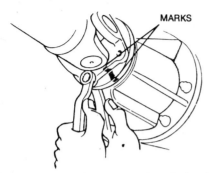

MARKS

It's always a good idea to matchmark the drive-shaft flange to the transmission yoke before removal

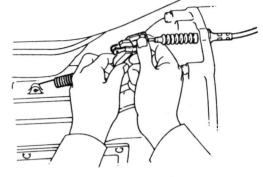

Disconnecting the clutch cable from the release fork

15. Support the front of the transmission with a jack.

16. Unfasten the engine rear mounts. Remove the rear crossmember.

17. Remove the jack from under the transmission.

18. On Corolla 1600, 1800 and Carina models, unbolt the clutch housing from the engine and withdraw the transmission assembly.

NOTE: *Remove the brace, if so equipped.*

19. Perform the following on Corolla 120 and Starlet models, before removing the transmission:

a. Remove the cotter pin from the clutch release linkage.

b. Remove the clutch release cable.

c. Separate the clutch housing from the engine by removing the bolts which secure it.

Installation is performed in the reverse order of removal, but remember to perform the following during installation.

Apply a light coating of multipurpose grease

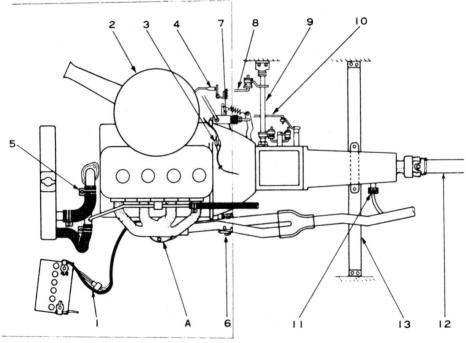

A. Exhaust pipe flange
1. Positive battery cable (+)
2. Air cleaner
3. Back-up lamp connector
4. Torque rod
5. Radiator hose
6. Exhaust pipe clamp
7. Master cylinder w/line support bracket
8. Accelerator linkage
9. Pivot—not applicable in USA
10. Bellcrank—not applicable in the USA
11. Speedometer cable
12. Driveshaft
13. Rear supporting crossmember

Removing the transmission from the Corolla and Carina

to the input shaft end, input shaft spline, clutch release bearing, and driveshaft end. On Corolla 1200 and Starlet models, apply multipurpose grease to the ball on the end of the gearshaft lever assembly and clutch release cable end.

On Corolla 1200 and Starlet models, install the clutch housing-to-engine bolts in two or three stages. After installation: Fill the transmission and cooling system. Adjust the clutch. Check to ensure that the back-up lamps come on when Reverse is selected.

1984 and Later Corolla RWD

1. Disconnect the negative battery terminal.
2. Loosen the distributor pinch bolt and turn the distributor body so it doesn't come in contact with the dash panel.
3. Remove the center console box.
4. Remove the trim boot at the base of the shift lever and the boot underneath it on the shift tower.
5. Unfasten the four shift lever plate retaining screws, withdraw the shift lever and remove the gasket.
CAUTION: *Cover the hole with a clean cloth to prevent anything from falling into the transmission case.*
6. Raise the front of the vehicle and drain the transmission fluid.
7. Disconnect and remove the front exhaust pipe at the manifold.
8. Matchmark the two flanges, remove the four bolts and nuts and then disconnect the driveshaft from the differential.
9. Remove the center support bearing and its heat shield from the vehicle underbody.
10. Remove the driveshaft.
CAUTION: *It will be necessary to plug the opening in the end of the transmission with an old yoke or, if none is available to cover it with a plastic bag secured by a rubber bag.*
11. Disconnect the speedometer cable and position it out of the way.
12. Disconnect the back-up light switch connector at the switch.
13. Remove the clutch release cylinder.
14. Disconnect the two electrical leads and remove the starter.
15. Raise the transmission slightly so as to remove the weight from the rear support.
16. Remove the rear engine mount. Remove the stiffener plate and then remove the transmission mounting bolts.
17. Remove the transmission down and toward the rear.
18. Installation is in the reverse order of removal. Please note the following:
    a. Align the input shaft spline with the clutch disc and then push the transmission

fully into position. Install the two upper set bolts and tighten them to 53 ft.lb. (72 Nm).
    b. Tighten the rear engine mount to 38 ft.lb. (52 Nm).
    c. Tighten the transmission and stiffener plate mounting bolts to 27 ft.lb. (37 Nm).
    d. When reconnecting the driveshaft to the differential, be sure that the matchmarks made earlier align and then tighten the mounting bolts to 31 ft.lb. (42 Nm).

1981-84 Tercel

NOTE: *Manual transmission removal does not require removal of the transaxle.*
1. Disconnect the negative battery cable.
2. Drain the coolant from the radiator tank and remove the top radiator hose.
3. Remove the air cleaner intake duct.
4. Remove the intermediate steering shaft.
5. Drain the gear oil from the transmission.
NOTE: *Remove all three drain plugs.*
6. Remove the exhaust pipe.
7. Remove the No. 1 gear shift rod and shift lever housing rod.
8. Remove the speedometer cable and back-up light switch connector.
9. Remove the rear engine support crossmember.
NOTE: *Support the transaxle with a jack and a block of wood.*
10. Loosen the nine transmission-to-transaxle bolts.
11. Remove 4 bolts and install them on the transaxle side to an equal depth.
NOTE: *Install the bolts into holes which still contain a bolt on the transmission side.*
12. Separate the transmission by tightening the bolts a little at a time on the transmission side.
13. Remove the remaining bolts and then remove the transmission from the transaxle.
14. Installation is the reverse of removal. Tighten the transmission bolts 8-11 ft.lb. Fill the transmission with 6.5 pints of gear oil.

Transaxle

REMOVAL AND INSTALLATION

Tercel

1. Disconnect the negative battery cable and then drain the cooling system. Remove the upper radiator hose.
2. Remove the air cleaner inlet duct.
3. Disconnect the clutch cable from the release fork. Remove the upper transaxle set bolts.
4. On 4X4 models, remove the center console box and then remove the shift lever with snapring pliers.

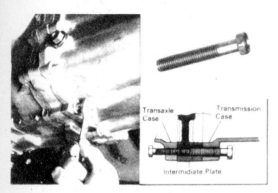

Split the transmission from the transaxle like this

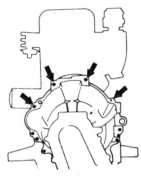

Remove the upper transaxle set bolts

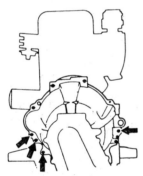

Remove the lower transaxle set bolts

5. Remove both halfshafts.

6. Raise the vehicle and support it with safety stands.

7. On 4X4 models, remove the driveshaft.
NOTE: *It will be necessary to plug the end of the extension housing with an old yoke, if none is available, cover it with a plastic bag secured by a rubber band.*

8. Disconnect and remove the front exhaust pipe. Remove the stiffener plate.
NOTE: *It may be necessary to remove the catalytic converter to gain working clearance.*

9. On 4X4 models, disconnect the 4X4 link.

10. On front wheel drive models, remove the No. 1 gear shift rod and the lever housing rod.

11. Disconnect the back-up light switch wire and the 4X4 switch wire (if so equipped). Disconnect the speedometer cable.

12. Remove all three drain plugs and drain the gear oil.

13. Remove the four lower transaxle set bolts. Disconnect the rear bond cable.

14. Position a block of wood between the engine and the dash panel, support the transaxle with a jack and then remove the engine rear support member.

15. Remove the transaxle.

16. Installation is in the reverse order of removal. Please note the following:

   a. Coat the end of the input shaft with clutch grease.

   b. Tighten the lower transaxle set bolts to 37-54 ft.lb.

   c. Tighten the engine rear support members to 70 ft.lb.

   d. Tighten the driveshaft bolts to 25 ft.lb.

Corolla FWD

1. Disconnect the negative battery cable.

2. Drain the cooling system. Remove the air cleaner along with the air hose.

3. Disconnect the back-up light switch connector at the connector. Disconnect the speedometer cable and position it out of the way.

4. Remove the clip and washers from the control cable, remove the retainer from the cable and then remove the control cable.

5. Remove the water inlet from the transaxle.

6. Remove the clutch release cylinder.

7. Remove the engine under cover. Disconnect and remove the front and rear mounting brackets.

8. Remove the center engine mount.

9. Remove the protractor from the transaxle and then disconnect the right side halfshaft.

10. Disconnect the steering knuckle from the lower arm. Pull it outward and then remove the left side halfshaft.

11. Disconnect the electrical leads and then remove the starter.

12. Disconnect the bond cable. Remove the engine rear plate No. 2.

13. Using a jack and a block of wood, raise the transaxle slightly and then disconnect the left engine mount.

14. Disconnect the transaxle mounting bolts, lower the left side of the engine and then remove the transaxle.

15. Installation is in the reverse order of removal. Please note the following:

   a. Always make sure that the input shaft spline and the clutch disc align properly upon installation. Tighten all 12mm mounting bolts to 47 ft.lb. (64 Nm) and all 10mm bolts to 34 ft.lb. (46 Nm) type C51 and 52; or 29 ft.lb. (39 Nm) types S41 and S50.

b. Tighten the left side engine mount to 38 ft.lb. (52 Nm).

c. Tighten the halfshaft retaining nuts to 27 ft.lb. (36 Nm).

d. Tighten the front, center and rear engine mounts to 29 ft.lb. (39 Nm).

Halfshafts

REMOVAL AND INSTALLATION

Tercel

1. Raise the front of the vehicle and support it with jackstands. Remove the tires.

2. Remove the cotter pin and locknut cap.

3. Have an assistant step on the brake pedal and at the same time, loosen the bearing locknut.

4. Remove the brake caliper and then position it out of the way. Remove the brake disc.

5. Remove the cotter pin and nut from the tie rod end and then, using a tie rod end puller, disconnect the tie rod end from the steering knuckle.

6. Matchmark the lower strut mounting bracket where it attaches to the steering knuckle, remove the mounting bolts and then disconnect the steering knuckle from the strut bracket.

7. Pull the axle hub off of the outer halfshaft end.

8. Remove the stiffener plate from the left side of the transaxle assembly.

9. Using a special tool available from Toyota, tap the halfshaft out of the transaxle casing.

NOTE: *Be sure to cover the halfshaft input hole.*

10. Installation is in the reverse order of removal. Please note the following:

a. Coat the oil seal in the transaxle input hold with MP grease before inserting the halfshaft.

b. Tighten the steering knuckle-to-strut bolts to 105 ft.lb.

c. Tighten the tie rod end nut to 29-43 ft.lb.

d. Tighten the bearing locknut to 137 ft.lb.

e. The length between the left and right halfshafts should be less than 7.626".

f. Check the front wheel alignment.

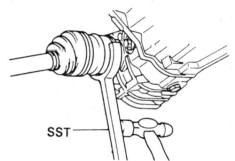

SST

Use the special tool to remove the halfshaft from the transaxle

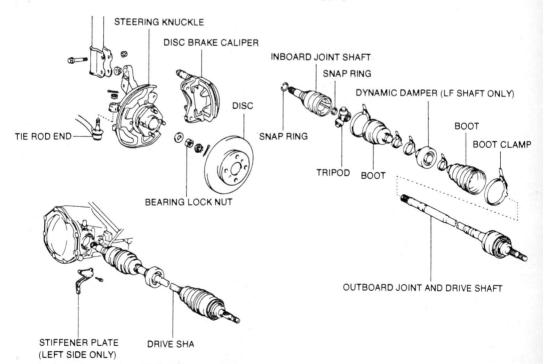

STEERING KNUCKLE

DISC BRAKE CALIPER

INBOARD JOINT SHAFT

SNAP RING

DYNAMIC DAMPER (LF SHAFT ONLY)

DISC

BOOT

TIE ROD END

SNAP RING

BOOT CLAMP

TRIPOD   BOOT

BEARING LOCK NUT

OUTBOARD JOINT AND DRIVE SHAFT

STIFFENER PLATE (LEFT SIDE ONLY)

DRIVE SHA

Halfshaft assembly and related components—Tercel

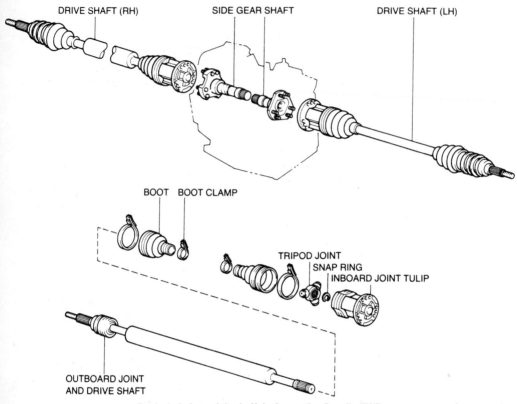

DRIVE SHAFT (RH)   SIDE GEAR SHAFT   DRIVE SHAFT (LH)

BOOT   BOOT CLAMP

TRIPOD JOINT
SNAP RING
INBOARD JOINT TULIP

OUTBOARD JOINT
AND DRIVE SHAFT

Exploded view of the halfshafts on the Corolla FWD

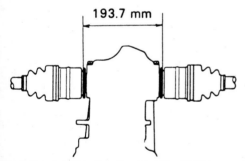

193.7 mm

The left and right halfshafts should be 7.626 in. apart

Corolla FWD

1. Raise the front of the vehicle and support it with jackstands. Remove the tires.
2. Remove the cotter pin and lock nut cap.
3. Have an assistant step on the brake pedal and at the same time, loosen and remove the bearing locknut.
4. Remove the engine under cover. Have an assistant depress the brake pedal, loosen and remove the six nuts which connect the halfshaft to the differential side gear shaft.
5. Remove the two retaining nuts and then disconnect the lower arm from the steering knuckle.

6. Remove the brake caliper and then position it out of the way. Remove the brake disc.
7. Use a two-armed puller and remove the axle hub from the outer end of the halfshaft.
8. Remove the halfshaft.
NOTE: *Be sure to cover the halfshaft input hole.*
9. Installation is in the reverse order of removal. Please note the following:
    a. Install the outboard side of the shaft into the axle hub and then insert the inner end into the differential. Finger tighten the six nuts. Be careful not to damage the boots during installation.
    b. Tighten the steering knuckle-to-lower arm bolts to 47 ft.lb. (64 Nm).
    c. Tighten the bearing locknut to 137 ft.lb. (186 Nm) and be sure to use a new cotter pin on the locknut cap.
    d. Depress the brake pedal and then tighten the six inner retaining nuts to 27 ft.lb. (36 Nm).

OVERHAUL

Tercel and Corolla FWD

1. Check to see that there is no play in the outboard joint.

2. Check to see that the inboard joint slides smoothly in the thrust direction.

3. Check to see that there is no abnormal play in the radial direction of the inboard joint.

4. Remove the CV-joint boot clamps.

5. Place matchmarks on the inboard joint tulip and on the tripod. Remove the tulip from the halfshaft (Corolla FWD only). When matchmarking the tulip to the tripod, never punch the marks.

6. Remove the snap ring on the tripod with snap ring pliers. Punch matchmarks on the shaft and the tripod and then gently tap the tripod off of the shaft. Never tap on the roller.

7. Remove both boots.

8. Tape the halfshaft splines and then install the boot and a new clamp to the outboard joint.

9. Repeat Step 1 for the inboard joint.

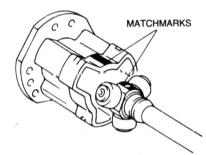

Place matchmarks on the inboard joint—Corolla FWD

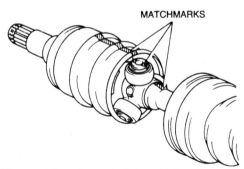

Place matchmarks on the inboard joint—Tercel

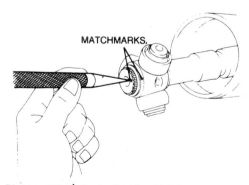

Place matchmarks on the tripod joint

10. Position the beveled side of the tripod axial spline toward the outboard joint. Align the matchmarks made previously and then using a brass drift or hammer, tap the tripod onto the halfshaft.

NOTE: *When replacing the inboard joint on the Tercel, always align the center of the inboard joint and the outboard joint first.*

11. Install a new snap ring.

12. Attach the boot to the outboard joint. Pack the boot with grease supplied in the boot kit; 165 grams for the Corolla and 240 grams for the Tercel.

13. On the Corolla, pack the tulip with 212 grams of grease, align the matchmarks and then install the tulip to the halfshaft.

14. On the Tercel, pack 90 grams of grease into the joint and 50 grams into the boot, align the matchmarks and then install the inboard joint shaft to the halfshaft.

15. Install the boots, making sure that the boot is in the shaft groove. Install new boot

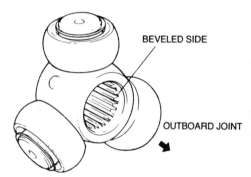

Make sure that the beveled side of the tripod faces the outboard joint

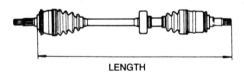

Measure the length of the halfshaft as shown—Tercel

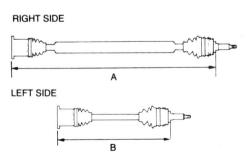

Measure the length of the halfshafts as shown—Corolla FWD

Halfshaft Lengths
in. (mm)

Model	Right Side	Left Side
Tercel	28.50 0.12 (724 3)	24.61 0.12 (625 3)
Corolla Gasoline Engine	27.48 0.20 (698 5)	16.54 0.20 (420 5)
Diesel Engine	27.76 0.20 (705 5)	16.46 0.20 (418 5)

Pedal Height Specifications

Model/Year	Height (in.)	Measure Between
Corolla 1200 1975–77	2.2 ①	Pedal pad and floor mat
Corolla 1200 1978–79	6.7	Pedal pad and floor mat
Tercel 1980–82 1983–84	6.65 7.55	Pedal pad and floor mat
Corolla 1600 & 1800 1975–84	6.5 ②	Pedal pad and floor mat
Starlet	6.93	Pedal pad and floor mat

① Pedal depressed
② FWD: 5.85

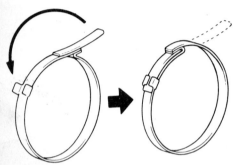

Lock the boot clamp as shown

clamps and lock them into position as shown in the illustration.

NOTE: *Make sure that the boot is not stretched or contracted when the halfshaft is at its standard length. Refer to chart for standard lengths.*

CLUTCH

The clutch is a single plate, dry disc type. Some early models use a coil spring pressure plate. Later models use a diaphragm spring pressure plate. Clutch release bearings are sealed ball bearing units which need no lubrication and should never be washed in any kind of solvent. All clutches, except those on the Tercel, Starlet and Corolla 1200 series, are hydraulically operated.

PEDAL HEIGHT ADJUSTMENT

Adjust the pedal height to the specifications given in the following chart, by rotating the pedal stop (nut).

FREE-PLAY ADJUSTMENT

Starlet and Tercel

1. Depress the pedal several times.
2. Depress the pedal by hand until resistance is felt. Free play should be as specified in the chart.
3. Check the clutch release sector pawl. Six

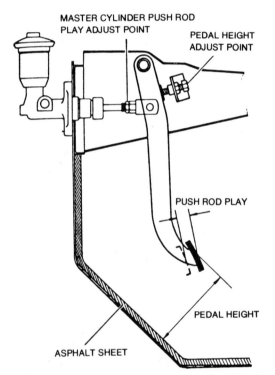

MASTER CYLINDER PUSH ROD PLAY ADJUST POINT
PEDAL HEIGHT ADJUST POINT
PUSH ROD PLAY
PEDAL HEIGHT
ASPHALT SHEET

Clutch pedal adjusting points—all Corollas except the 1200

notches should remain between the pawl and the end of the sector. If less than 6, replace the clutch disc. If the clutch disc has been replaced, the pawl should be between the 3rd and 10th notch.

4. To obtain either the used or new position on the 1981-82 Starlet, change the position of the E-ring.

Corolla 1200

1. Pull on the clutch release cable at the clutch support flange until a resistance is felt

when the release bearing contacts the clutch diaphragm spring.

2. Holding the cable in this position measure the distance between the E-ring and the end of the wire support flange. The distance should be 5-6 threads.

3. If adjustment is required, change the position of the E-ring.

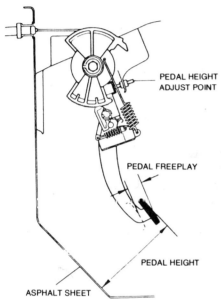

PEDAL HEIGHT ADJUST POINT

PEDAL FREEPLAY

PEDAL HEIGHT

ASPHALT SHEET

Clutch pedal adjusting points—Corolla 1200, Tercel and Starlet

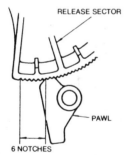

RELEASE SECTOR

PAWL

6 NOTCHES

Minimum pawl and sector position for a used clutch—Tercel and Starlet

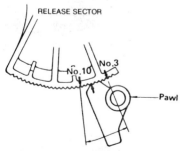

RELEASE SECTOR

No.10 No.3

Pawl

Pawl and sector position for a new clutch—Tercel and Starlet

4. After completing the adjustment, check the clutch pedal free-play which should be 0.8-1.4″ after the pedal is depressed several times.

Except Corolla 1200, Tercel and Starlet

NOTE: *The Tercel clutch is self-adjusting.*

1. Adjust the clearance between the master cylinder piston and the pushrod to the specifications given in the Clutch Pedal Free-Play Adjustment chart. Loosen the pushrod locknut and rotate the pushrod while depressing the clutch pedal lightly with your finger.

2. Tighten the locknut when finished with the adjustment.

3. Adjust the release cylinder free-play by loosening the release cylinder pushrod locknut and rotating the pushrod until the specification in the chart is obtained.

4. Measure the clutch pedal free-play after performing the above adjustments. If it fails to fall within specifications, repeat Steps 1-3 until it does.

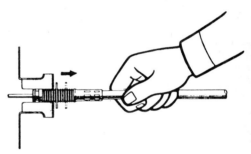

E-ring adjustment—1981–82 Starlet

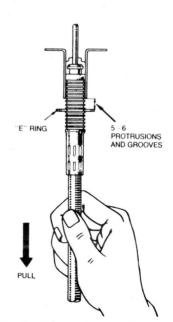

"E" RING

5 - 6 PROTRUSIONS AND GROOVES

PULL

Adjusting the clutch release cable on the Corolla 1200

Clutch Pedal Free-Play Specifications

Model	Year	Pedal Free-Play (in.)
Carina	'72–'73	1.00–1.75
Corolla 1200	'70–'77	1.00–1.80
	'78–'79	0.80–1.40
Corolla 1600	'71–'79	0.79–1.58
Corolla 1800	'80–'82	0.51–0.91
Corolla	'83–'87	0.51–0.91 ①
Tercel	'80–'87	0.08–1.10
Starlet	'81–'82	0.08–1.18
	'83–'84	0.08–1.38

① Diesel: 0.20–0.59

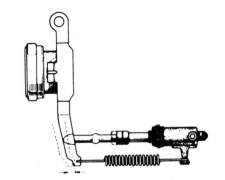

Release cylinder free-play is the distance between the arrows

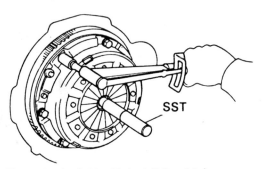

Use a clutch pilot tool to install the clutch

REMOVAL AND INSTALLATION

CAUTION: *Do not allow grease or oil to get on any of the disc, pressure plate, or flywheel surfaces.*

Except 1980-82 Tercel

1. Remove the transmission from the car as previously detailed.
2. Remove the clutch cover and disc from the bellhousing.
3. Unfasten the release fork bearing clips. Withdraw the release bearing hub, complete with the release bearing.
4. Remove the tension spring from the clutch linkage.
5. Remove the release fork and support.
6. Punch matchmarks on the clutch cover and the pressure plate so that the pressure plate can be returned to its original position during installation.
7. Slowly unfasten the screws which attach the retracting springs.

NOTE: *If the screws are released too fast, the clutch assembly will fly apart, causing possible injury or loss of parts.*

8. Separate the pressure plate from the clutch cover/spring assembly. Inspect the parts for wear or deterioration. Replace parts as required.

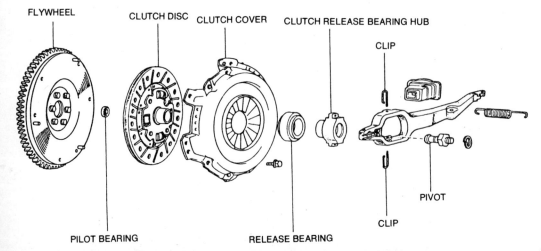

Exploded view of the clutch—Corolla shown; Starlet similar

FLYWHEEL CLUTCH DISC CLUTCH COVER CLUTCH RELEASE BEARING HUB CLIP PIVOT CLIP PILOT BEARING RELEASE BEARING

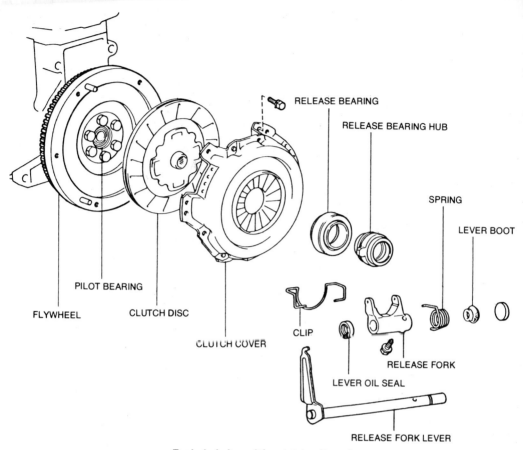

Exploded view of the clutch—Tercel

9. Installation is performed in the reverse order of removal. Several points should be noted, however: Be sure to align the matchmarks on the clutch cover and pressure plate which were made during disassembly. Apply a thin coating of multipurpose grease to the release bearing hub and release fork contact points. Also, pack the groove inside the clutch hub with multipurpose grease. Center the clutch disc by using a clutch pilot tool or an old input shaft. Insert the pilot into the end of the input shaft front bearing and bolt the clutch to the flywheel.

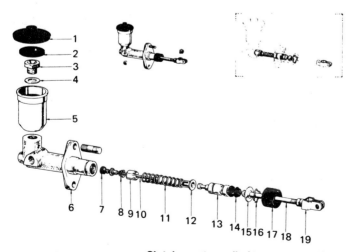

1. Filler cap
2. Float
3. Reservoir setbolt
4. Washer
5. Reservoir
6. Master cylinder body
7. Inlet valve
8. Spring
9. Inlet valve housing
10. Connecting rod
11. Spring
12. Spring retainer
13. Piston
14. Cylinder cup
15. Plate
16. Snap-ring
17. Boot
18. Pushrod
19. Clevis

Clutch master cylinder components

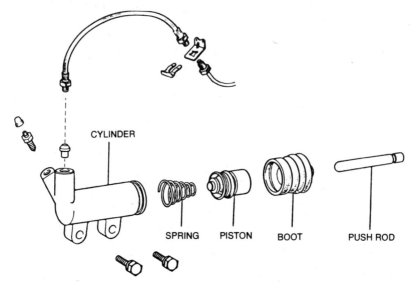

CYLINDER

SPRING   PISTON   BOOT   PUSH ROD

Exploded view of the clutch slave cylinder

NOTE: *Bolt the clutch assembly to the fly-wheel in two or three stages, evenly and to the torque specified.*

1980-82 Tercel

NOTE: *In order to replace the clutch, the engine must be removed.*
1. After the engine has been removed tie the bell housing to the cowl.
2. Place matchmarks on the clutch cover and flywheel.
3. Remove the clutch cover.
NOTE: *Loosen each bolt gradually to prevent distortion of the cover.*
4. Remove the disc.
5. Installation is the reverse of removal.
NOTE: *Do not allow grease to get on the disc lining, flywheel, or cover. When installing the clutch be sure to use a spline alignment tool or an old input shaft to properly align the clutch. Tighten the cover bolts to 11-15 ft.lb.*

Master Cylinder
REMOVAL AND INSTALLATION

1. Remove the clevis pin.
2. Detach the hydraulic line from the tub.
CAUTION: *Do not spill brake fluid on the painted surfaces of the vehicle.*
3. Unfasten the bolts which secure the master cylinder to the firewall. Withdraw the assembly.
4. Service as required. Installation is performed in the reverse order of removal. Bleed the system. Adjust the clutch pedal height and free-play.

OVERHAUL

1. Clamp the master cylinder body in a vise with soft jaws.
2. Separate the reservoir assembly from the master cylinder.
3. Remove the snapring and remove the pushrod/piston assembly.
4. Inspect all of the parts and replace any which are worn or defective.
5. Coat all parts with clean brake fluid, prior to assembly.
6. Install the piston assembly in the cylinder bore.
7. Fit the pushrod over the washer and secure them with the snapring.
8. Install the reservoir.

Clutch Slave Cylinder
REMOVAL AND INSTALLATION

CAUTION: *Do not spill brake fluid on the painted surface of the vehicle!*
1. Raise the front of the car and support it with jackstands. Be sure that it is supported securely.
2. If necessary, remove the rear gravel shield to gain access to the release cylinder.
3. Remove the clutch fork return spring.
4. Unfasten the hydraulic line from the release cylinder by removing its retaining nut.
5. Screw the threaded end of the pushrod in.
6. Remove the release cylinder retaining nuts and remove the cylinder.
7. Installation is performed in the reverse order of removal. Adjust the pushrod freeplay and bleed the hydraulic system.

OVERHAUL

1. Remove the pushrod assembly and the rubber boot.
2. Withdraw the piston, complete with its cup; don't remove the cup unless it is being replaced.
3. Wash all parts in brake fluid.
4. Replace any worn or damaged parts.
5. Replace the cylinder assembly if the piston-to-bore clearance is greater than 0.006".
6. Assembly is the reverse of disassembly. Coat all parts in clean brake fluid, prior to assembly.

Clutch Hydraulic System

BLEEDING

1. Fill the master cylinder reservoir with brake fluid.
   CAUTION: *Do not spill brake fluid on the painted surfaces of the vehicle.*
2. Remove the cap and loosen the bleeder plug. Block the outlet hole with your finger.
3. Pump the clutch pedal several times, then take your finger from the hole while depressing the clutch pedal. Allow the air to flow out. Place your finger back over the hole and release the pedal.
4. After fluid pressure can be felt (with your finger), tighten the bleeder plug.
5. Fit a bleeder tube over the plug and place the other end into a clean jar half filled with brake fluid.
6. Depress the clutch pedal, loosen the bleeder plug with a wrench, and allow the fluid to flow into the jar.
7. Tighten the plug and then release the clutch pedal.
8. Repeat Steps 6-7 until no air bubbles are visible in the bleeder tube.
9. When there are no more air bubbles, tighten the plug while keeping the clutch pedal fully depressed. Replace the cap.
10. Fill the master cylinder to the specified level.
11. Check the system for leaks.

AUTOMATIC TRANSMISSION

PAN REMOVAL

1. Unfasten the oil plug and drain the fluid from the transmission.
2. Unfasten the pan securing bolts.
3. Withdraw the pan.
4. Installation is performed in the reverse order of removal. Torque the pan securing bolts to 4-6 ft.lb. (17-20 ft.lb. A-40). Refill the transmission with fluid.

LOW SERVO AND BAND ADJUSTMENT

2-Speed (Corolla)

The low and band adjusting bolt is located on the outside of the transmission case, so that it is unnecessary to remove the oil pan in order to perform the adjustment.

1. Loosen the locknut on the adjusting bolt.
2. Tighten the bolt until it is bottomed.
3. Back off 3½ turns and hold the adjusting bolts securely while tightening the locknut.

FRONT BAND ADJUSTMENT

3-Speed Toyoglide

1. Remove the oil pan as previously outlined.
2. Pry the band engagement lever toward band with a small prybar.
3. The gap between end of the piston rod and the engagement bolts should be 0.138".
4. If the gap does not meet the specification, adjust it by turning the engagement bolt.
5. Install the oil pan and refill the transmission as previously outlined.

REAR BAND ADJUSTMENT

3-Speed Toyoglide

The rear band adjusting bolt is located on the outside of the case, so it is not necessary to remove the oil pan in order to adjust the band.

1. Loosen the adjusting bolt locknut and fully screw in the adjusting bolt.
2. Loosen the adjusting bolt one turn.
3. Tighten the locknut while holding the bolt so that it cannot turn.

BAND ADJUSTMENTS

A-40, A-40D, A-42DL, A-43D, A-55, A130L, A131L, A240L and A240E

No band adjustments are possible. The only external adjustments are throttle and shift linkages.

NEUTRAL SAFETY SWITCH ADJUSTMENT

2-Speed (Corolla)

The neutral safety switch used on Corolla models is not adjustable. If it malfunctions, it must be replaced. To do so proceed in the following manner:

1. Remove the center console.
2. Unfasten and remove the three screws securing the transmission selector assembly.
3. Disconnect the neutral safety switch multiconnector.
4. Slightly lift transmission selector assembly and unfasten the two neutral safety switch attaching screws.
5. Withdraw the switch.
6. Installation is performed in the reverse order of removal. Position the selector lever in

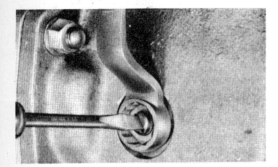

Adjusting the low servo and band on the two-speed Toyoglide

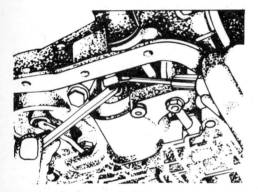

Adjusting the three-speed Toyoglide front band

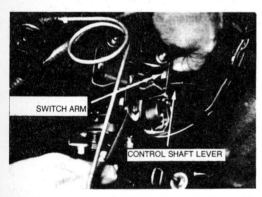

SWITCH ARM

CONTROL SHAFT LEVER

Adjusting the neutral safety switch on cars with column shift

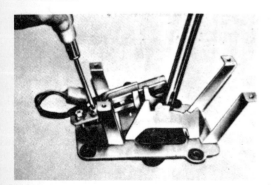

Adjusting the neutral safety switch on cars with three-speed automatic and floorshift

Neutral (N) and install the switch so that installation marks align with each other.

3 Speed (Column Selector)

The neutral safety switch/reverse lamp switch on the Toyoglide transmission with a column mounted selector is located under the hood on the shift linkage. If the switch is not functioning properly, adjust as follows:

1. Loosen the switch securing bolt.
2. Move the switch so that its arm just contacts the control shaft lever when the gear selector is in Drive (D) position.
3. Tighten the switch securing bolt.
4. Check the operation of the switch; the car should start only in Park (P) or Neutral (N) and the back-up lamps should come on only when Reverse (R) is selected.
5. If the switch cannot be adjusted so that it functions properly, replace it with a new one. Perform the adjustment as previously outlined.

Loosening the column shift swivel locknut

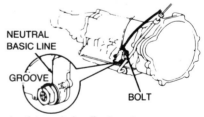

NEUTRAL BASIC LINE

GROOVE

BOLT

Neutral safety switch adjustment

	B	N	RB	RL
P	O	O		
R			O	O
N	O	O		

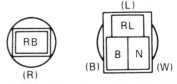

Checking the neutal safety switch for continuity between the connectors

3-Speed (Console Shift)

Models with a console mounted selector have the neutral safety switch on the linkage located beneath the console. To adjust it, proceed in the following manner:

1. Remove the screws securing the center console.

2. Unfasten the console multiconnector, if so equipped, and completely remove the console.

3. Adjust the switch in the manner outlined in the preceding column selector section.

4. Install the console in the reverse order of removal after completion of the switch adjustment.

A-40 and A-40D

If the engine will start in any range except Neutral or Park, the neutral safety switch will require adjustment.

1. Locate the neutral safety switch on the side of the transmission and loosen the switch bolt.

Connect an ohmmeter between terminals 2 and 3—Tercel (A-55)

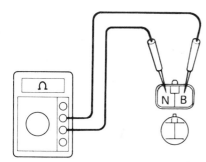

Connect an ohmmeter between terminals N and B—1984 Corolla RWD (A-42DL)

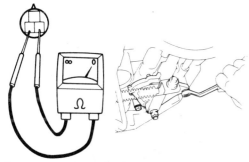

Connect an ohmmeter between the terminals as shown—Corolla FWD (A-130L, A-131L)

2. Move the gear selector to the Neutral position.

3. Align the groove on the safety switch shaft with the basic line which is scribed on the housing.

4. Tighten the switch bolt.

5. Using an ohmmeter, check the continuity between the switch terminals as shown in the accompanying illustration. If a continuity problem is found, replace the switch.

A-42DL, A-55, A-130L and A-131L

EXCEPT BELOW

If the engine will start in any range except Neutral or Park, the neutral safety switch will require adjustment.

1. Locate the neutral safety switch on the side of the transmission and loosen the switch bolt(s).

2. Move the gear selector to the Neutral position.

3. Disconnect the neutral safety switch connector and connect an ohmmeter between terminals 2 and 3 on the Tercel (A-55); terminals N and B on the 1984 Corolla RWD (A-42DL); and between the terminals shown in the illustration on the Corolla FWD (A-130L and A131L).

4. Adjust the switch to the point where there is continuity between the two terminals.

1986-87 COROLLA FWD

1. Loosen the neutral start switch bolt. Position the gear selector in the **N** position.

2. As required, disconnect the switch electrical connector. Align the switch shaft groove with the neutral base line which is located on the switch.

3. Tighten the bolt.

SHIFT LINKAGE ADJUSTMENT

2- and 3-Speed Toyoglide

The transmission should be engaged, in the gear selected as indicated on the shift quadrant. If it is not, then adjust the linkage as follows:

1. Check all of the shift linkage bushings for wear. Replace any worn bushings.

2. Loosen the connecting rod swivel locknut.

3. Move the selector lever and check movement of the pointer in the shift quadrant.

4. When the control shaft is set in the neutral position the quadrant pointer should indicate **N** as well.

NOTE: *Steps 5-7 apply only to cars equipped with column mounted gear selectors.*

5. If the pointer does not indicate Neutral (N), then check the drive cord adjustment.

6. Remove the steering column shroud.

7. Turn the drive cord adjuster with a phil-

lips screwdriver until the pointer indicates Neutral (N).

NOTE: *Steps 8-10 apply to both column mounted and floor mounted selectors:*

8. Position the manual valve lever on the transmission so that it is in the Neutral position.

9. Lock the connecting rod swivel with the locknut so that the pointer, selector, and manual valve lever are all positioned in Neutral.

10. Check the operation of the gear selector by moving it through all ranges.

A-40 and A-40D

1. Loosen the adjusting nut on the linkage and check the linkage for freedom of movement.

2. Push the manual valve lever toward the front of the car, as far as it will go.

3. Bring the lever back to its third notch (Neutral).

4. Have an assistant hold the shift lever in Neutral, while you tighten the linkage adjusting nut so that it can't slip.

A-42DL, A-55, A-130L and A-131L

1. Loosen the adjusting nut on the linkage and check the linkage for freedom of movement.

2. Push the manual lever fully rearward (right side on A-130L, A-131L, A240 L/E), as far as it will go.

3. Return the lever two (2) notches to the Neutral position.

4. Set the gear selector to **N**, while holding the selector slightly toward the **R**, have someone tighten the adjusting nut on the manual lever.

1987 Tercel

1. Loosen the swivel nut on the selector lever.

2. Push the lever fully toward the right side of the vehicle.

3. Return the lever two notches to the "N" position.

4. Hold the lever slightly toward the "R" position and tighten the swivel.

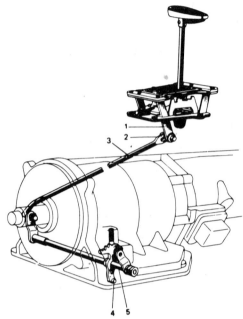

1. Gear selector lever
2. Intermediate rod
3. Control rod
4. Manual valve lever
5. Shaft

Toyoglide floorshift components

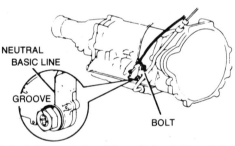

Adjust the neutral safety switch—A-40 and A-40D

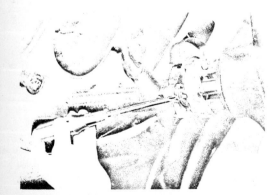

Adjusting the column shift indicator drive cord

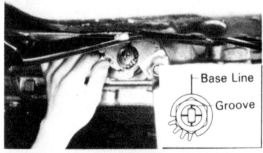

Adjusting the neutral safety switch—A55

Adjusting the shift linkage—A-40, A-40D, A-42DL and A-55

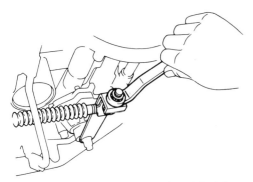

Adjusting the shift linkage—A-130L and A-131L

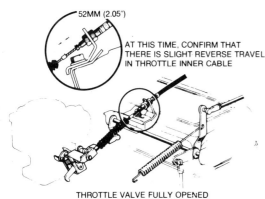

A-40 throttle linkage adjustment

THROTTLE LINKAGE ADJUSTMENT

2-Speed (Corolla)

1. Loosen the locknuts on the throttle linkage connecting rod turnbuckle.

2. Have an assistant depress the accelerator pedal fully.

3. Hold the throttle butterfly to the fully opened position.

4. Adjust the length of the rod so that the pointer lines up with the mark on the transmission case.

5. Tighten the locknut.

3-Speed Toyoglide

1. Loosen the locknut at each end of the linkage adjusting turnbuckle.

2. Detach the throttle linkage connecting rod from the carburetor.

3. Align the pointer on the throttle valve lever with the mark stamped on the transmission case.

4. Rotate the turnbuckle so that the end of the throttle linkage rod and the carburetor throttle lever are aligned.

NOTE: *The carburetor throttle valve must be fully opened during this adjustment.*

5. Tighten the turnbuckle locknuts and reconnect the throttle rod to the carburetor.

6. Open the throttle valve and check the

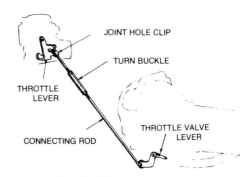

Toyoglide throttle linkage components

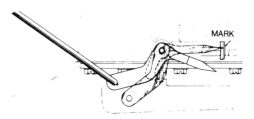

Toyoglide throttle linkage aligning marks

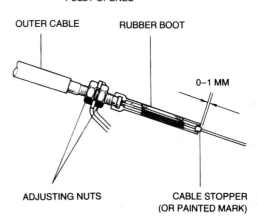

Throttle linkage adjustment—A-40, A-40D and A-42DL

Throttle linkage adjustment—A-55

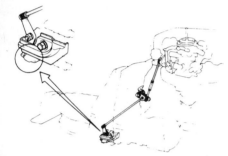

When the throttle valve is fully open, the throttle lever indicator should line up with the mark on the transmission case—A-55

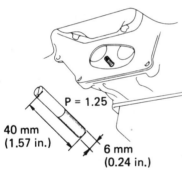

40 mm
(1.57 in.)

P = 1.25

6 mm
(0.24 in.)

Cut the head off a bolt to fabricate a guide pin—A-40, A-40D and A-42DL

pointer alignment with the mark on the transmission case.

7. Road test the car. If the transmission hunts, i.e., keeps shifting rapidly back and forth between gears at certain speeds or if it fails to downshift properly when going up hills, repeat the throttle linkage adjustment.

A-40, A-40D, A-42DL, A-130L and A-131L

1. Remove the air cleaner.

2. Confirm that the accelerator linkage opens the throttle fully. Adjust the link as necessary.

3. Peel the rubber dust boot back from the throttle cable.

4. Loosen the adjustment nuts on the throttle cable bracket (rocker cover) just enough to allow cable housing movement.

5. Have an assistant depress the accelerator pedal fully.

6. Adjust the cable housing so that the distance between its end and the cable stop collar is 2.05" (1980 and later: 0-0.4").

7. Tighen the adjustment nuts. Make sure that the adjustment hasn't changed. Install the dust boot and the air cleaner.

A-55

1. Remove the air cleaner.

2. Check that the carburetor throttle lever and the throttle link bracket are not bent.

3. Confirm that the accelerator linkage opens the throttle valve fully. Adjust the link as necessary.

4. Have an assistant hold the accelerator pedal to the floor so that it is depressed fully.

5. Loosen the turnbuckle locknut and adjust the linkage by turning the turnbuckle. When the throttle valve is fully open, the throttle valve lever indicator should line up with the mark on the transmission case.

6. Tighten the turnbuckle locknut and recheck the adjustment.

REMOVAL AND INSTALLATION

Tercel

1. Disconnect the negative battery cable.

2. Drain the coolant from the radiator tank and remove the top hose.

3. Remove the air cleaner inlet duct.

4. Remove the intermediate steering shaft.

5. Drain the fluid from the transmission.

6. Remove the exhaust pipe.

7. Remove the shift lever rod.

8. Remove the speedometer cable, backup light connector and any throttle linkage.

9. Remove the cooling lines from the transmission. Remove the converter cover. Remove the converter to flywheel mounting bolts.

10. Support the transaxle with a jack.

11. Remove the rear crossmember.

12. Separate the converter from the flywheel and the transmission from the transaxle.

13. Remove the transmission.

14. Installation is the reverse of removal.

3-Speed Toyoglide

1. Disconnect the battery.

2. Remove the air cleaner and disconnect the accelerator torque link or the cable.

3. Disconnect the throttle link rod at the carburetor side, then disconnect the backup light wiring at the firewall (on early models).

4. Jack up the car and support it on stands, then drain the transmission. Use a clean receptacle so that the fluid can be checked for color, smell and foreign matter.

5. Disconnect all shift linkage.

6. On early models, remove the cross shaft from the frame.

7. Disconnect the throttle link rod at the transmission side and remove the speedometer cable, cooler lines and parking brake equalizer bracket.

8. Loosen the exhaust flange nuts and remove the exhaust pipe clamp and bracket.

9. Remove the drive shaft and the rear mounting bracket, then lower the rear end of the transmission carefully.

10. Unbolt the torque converter from the drive plate. Support the engine with a suitable jack stand and remove the seven bolts that hold the transmission to the engine.

11. Reverse the order of the removal procedures with the following precautions:

12. Install the drive plate and ring gear, tighten the attaching bolts to 37-43 ft.lb.

13. After assembling the torque converter to the transmission, check the clearance, it should be about 0.59″.

14. Before installing the transmission, install the oil pump locator pin on the torque converter to facilitate installation.

15. While rotating the crankshaft, tighten the converter attaching bolts, a little at a time.

16. After installing the throttle connecting second rod, make sure the throttle valve lever indicator aligns with the mark on the transmission with the carburetor throttle fully opened. If required, adjust the rod.

17. To install the transmission control rod correctly, move the transmission lever to N (Neutral), and the selector lever to Neutral. Fill the transmission with automatic transmission fluid (Type F only), then start the engine. Run the engine at idle speed and apply the brakes while moving the selector lever through all positions, then return in to Neutral.

18. After warming the engine, move the selector lever through all positions, then back to Neutral, and check the fluid level. Fill as necessary.

19. Adjust the engine idle to 550-650 rpm with the selector lever at Drive. Road test the vehicle.

20. With the selector lever at 2 or Drive, check the point at which the transmission shifts. Check for shock, noise and slipping with the selector lever in all positions. Check for leaks from the transmission.

A-40, A-40D and A-42DL

1. Perform Steps 1 through 3 of the 3-speed Toyoglide removal procedure.

2. Remove the upper starter mounting nuts using a socket wrench with a long extension.

3. Raise the car and support it securely with jackstands. Drain the transmission.

4. Remove the lower starter mounting bolt and lay the starter alongside of the engine. Don't let it hang by the wires.

5. Unbolt the parking brake equalizer support.

6. Matchmark the driveshaft and the companion flange, to ensure correct installation. Remove the bolts securing the driveshaft to the companion flange.

7. Slide the driveshaft straight back and out of the transmission. Use a spare U-joint yoke or tie a plastic bag over the end of the transmission to keep any fluid from dripping out.

8. Remove the bolts from the cross-shaft body bracket, the cotter pin from the manual lever, and the cross-shaft socket from the transmission.

9. Remove the exhaust pipe bracket from the torque converter bell housing.

10. Disconnect the oil cooler lines from the transmission and remove the line bracket from the bell housing.

11. Disconnect the speedometer cable from the transmission.

12. Unbolt both support braces from the bell housing.

13. Use a transmission jack to raise the transmission slightly.

14. Unbolt the rear crossmember and lower the transmission about 3″.

15. Pry the two rubber torque converter access plugs out of their holes at the back of the engine.

16. Remove the six torque converter mounting bolts through the access hole. Rotate the engine with the crankshaft pulley.

17. Cut the head off a bolt to make a guide pin for the torque converter. Install the pin on the converter.

18. Remove the converter bell housing-to-engine bolts.

19. Push on the end of the guide pin in order to remove the converter with the transmission. Remove the transmission rearward and then bring it out from under the car. Don't catch the throttle cable during removal.

20. Installation is the reverse of removal. Be sure to note the following, however:

21. Install the two long bolts on the upper converter housing and tighten them to 36-58 ft.lb.

22. Tighten the converter-to-flex plate bolts finger tight, and then tighten them with a torque wrench to 11-16 ft.lb.

23. When installing the speedometer cable, make sure that the felt dust protector and washer are on the cable end.

24. Tighten the cooling line and exhaust pipe

bracket mounting bolts to 37-58 ft.lb. Tighten the cooling lines to 14-22 ft.lb.

25. Align the matchmarks made on the driveshaft and the companion flange during removal. Tighten the driveshaft mounting bolts to 11-16 ft.lb.

26. Be sure to install the oil pan drain plug. Tighten it to 11-14 ft.lb.

27. Adjust the throttle cable.

28. Fill the transmission to the proper capacity. Use only type **F** (ATF) fluid. Start the engine, run the selector through all gear ranges and place it in Park (P). Check the lever on the dipstick and add type F fluid, as necessary.

29. Road test the car and check for leaks.

Corolla FWD

1. Disconnect the negative battery cable.
2. Remove the air cleaner.
3. Disconnect the neutral start switch.
4. Disconnect the speedometer cable.
5. Remove the shift control cable.
6. Disconnect the oil cooler hose.
7. Remove the water inlet pipe.
8. Raise and support the vehicle on jackstands.
9. Drain the fluid.
10. Remove the engine undercover.
11. Remove the front and rear transaxle mounts.
12. Support the transaxle with a jack.
13. Remove the engine center support member.
14. Remove the halfshafts.
15. Remove the steering knuckles.
16. Remove the starter motor.
17. Remove the flywheel cover plate.
18. Remove the 6 torque converter bolts, through the opening covered by the cover plate.
19. Remove the left engine mount.
20. Remove the transaxle-to-engine bolts and

slowly and carefully back the transaxle away from the engine.

21. Installation is the reverse of removal. Observe the following torques: Transaxle-to-engine bolts: 12mm 47 ft. lb.: 10mm 25 ft. lb.: Left engine mount: 38 ft. lb.: Torque converter bolts: 13 ft. lb.: Support bolts: 28 ft. lb.

22. Fill the unit with Dexron II ATF.

DRIVELINE

Driveshaft and U-Joints

REMOVAL AND INSTALLATION

Rear Drive and 4x4 Vehicles

1. Raise the rear of the car with jacks and support the rear axle housing with jackstands.
CAUTION: *Be sure that the car is securely supported. Remember, you will be working underneath it.*

2. Unfasten the bolts which attach the driveshaft universal joint yoke flange to the mounting flange on the differential drive pinion.
NOTE: *Be sure to matchmark the yoke flange to the mounting flange on the drive pinion.*

3. On models equipped with three universal joints, perform the following:
    a. Withdraw the driveshaft subassembly from the U-joint sleeve yoke.
    b. Unfasten the center support bearing from its bracket.

4. Remove the driveshaft end from the transmission.

5. Install an old U-joint yoke in the transmission or, if none is available, use a plastic bag secured with a rubber band over the hole to keep the transmission oil from running out.

6. Withdraw the driveshaft from beneath the vehicle.

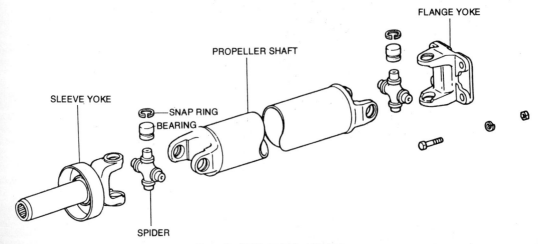

One-piece driveshaft—Starlet

7. Installation is performed in the following order: Apply multipurpose grease on the section of the U-joint sleeve which is to be inserted into the transmission.

8. Insert the driveshaft sleeve into the transmission.

CAUTION: *Be careful not to damage any of the seals.*

9. For models equipped with three U-joints and center bearings, perform the following:

a. Adjust the center bearing clearance with no load placed on the driveline components; the top of the rubber center cushion should be 0.04″ behind the center of the elongated bolt hole.

b. Install the center bearing assembly.

NOTE: *Use the same number of washers on the center bearing bracket as were removed.*

10. Secure the U-joint flange to the differential flange with the mounting bolts.

CAUTION: *Be sure that the bolts are of the same type as those removed and that they are tightened securely.*

11. Remove the jackstands and lower the vehicle.

U-JOINT OVERHAUL

NOTE: *As the U-joints on the Tercel 4x4 and most late model Corollas are non-serviceable,*

Shell Type

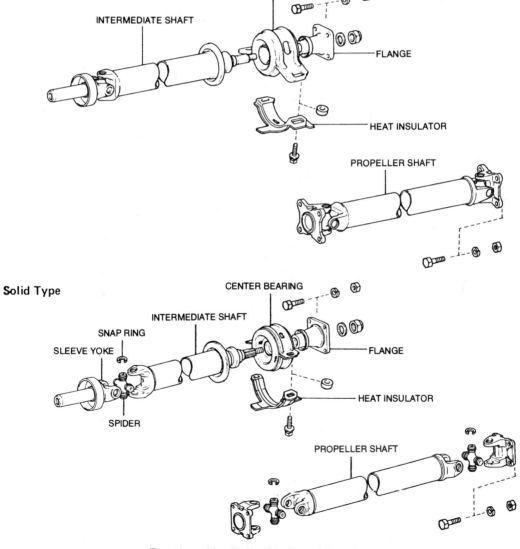

Two-piece driveshaft—Corolla and Tercel 4x4

the entire driveshaft must be replaced in the event of U-joint problems.

1. Matchmark the yoke and the driveshaft.
2. Remove the lockrings from the bearings.
3. Position the yoke on vise jaws. Using a bearing remover and a hammer, gently tap the remover until the bearing is driven out of the yoke about ½".
4. Place the tool in the vise and drive the yoke away from the tool until the bearing is removed.
5. Repeat Steps 3 and 4 for the other bearings.
6. Check for worn or damaged parts. Inspect the bearing journal surfaces for wear.
7. U-joint assembly is performed in the following order: Install the bearing cups, seals, and O-rings in the spider.
8. Grease the spider and the bearings.
9. Position the spider in the yoke.

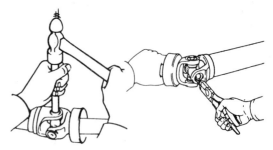

Removing the U-joint

12 MM SOCKET

Press the U-joint into the yoke using a vise

10. Start the bearings in the yoke and then press them into place, using a vise.
11. Repeat Step 4 for the other bearing.
12. If the axial play of the spider is greater than 0.002", select lockrings which will provide the correct play. Be sure that the lockrings are the same size on both sides or driveshaft noise will result.
13. Check the U-joint assembly for smooth operation.

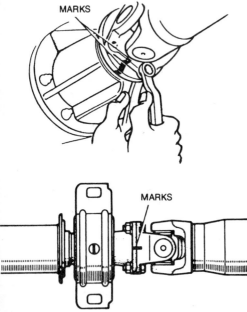

MARKS

MARKS

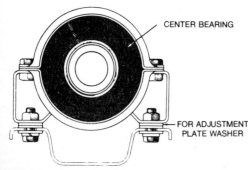

Always matchmark the driveshaft flanges before separating them

CENTER BEARING

FOR ADJUSTMENT PLATE WASHER

Center bearing adjustment

REAR AXLE

Axle Ratio

The drive axle of a car is said to have a certain axle ratio. This number (usually a whole number and a decimal fraction) is actually a comparison of the number of gear teeth on the ring gear and the pinion gear. For example, a 4.11 rear means that theoretically, there are 4.11 teeth on the ring gear and one tooth on the pinion gear or, put another way, the driveshaft must turn 4.11 times to turn the wheels once. Actually, on a 4.11 rear, there might be 37 teeth on the ring gear and 9 teeth on the pinion gear. By dividing the number of teeth on the pinion gear into the number of teeth on the ring gear, the numerical axle ratio (4.11) is obtained. This also provides a good method of ascertaining exactly which axle ratio one is dealing with. Another method of determining gear ratio is to jack up and support the car so that both rear wheels are off the ground. Make a chalk mark on the rear wheel and the drive shaft. Put the transmission in neutral. Turn the rear wheel one complete turn and count the number of turns that the driveshaft makes. The number of turns that the driveshaft makes in one complete revolution of the rear wheel is an approximation of the rear axle ratio.

Axle Shaft

REMOVAL AND INSTALLATION

Except Front Wheel Drive

1. Raise the rear of the car and support it securely by using jackstands.
   CAUTION: *Be sure that the vehicle is securely supported. Remember, you will be working underneath it.*
2. Drain the oil from the axle housing.
3. Remove the wheel cover, unfasten the lug nuts, and remove the wheel
4. Punch matchmarks on the brake drum

and the axle shaft to maintain rotational balance.
5. Remove the brake drum and related components.
6. Remove the rear bearing retaining nut.
7. Remove the backing plate attachment nuts through the access holes in the rear axle shaft flange.

Axle Bearing Retaining Nut Specifications

Model	Torque Range (ft. lbs.)
Corolla ('70–'74)	15–22
Corolla 1600	26–38
Tercel	22
Corolla 1800	44–53
Starlet	44–53

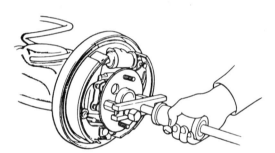

Using a slide hammer to remove the rear axle shaft

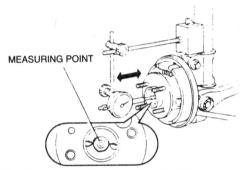

MEASURING POINT

Checking the bearing play—Corolla FWD

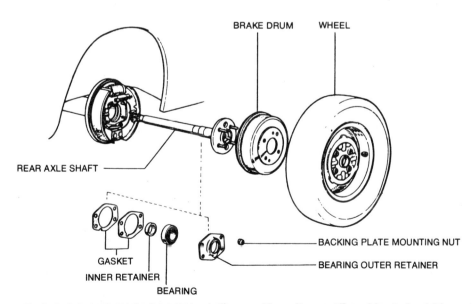

BRAKE DRUM   WHEEL

REAR AXLE SHAFT

GASKET

INNER RETAINER

BEARING

BACKING PLATE MOUNTING NUT

BEARING OUTER RETAINER

Exploded view of a typical rear axle shaft assembly—all except Tercel front wheel drive

8. Use a slide hammer with a suitable adaptor to withdraw the axle shaft from its housing.

CAUTION: *Use care not to damage the oil seal when removing the axle shaft.*

9. Repeat the procedure for the axle shaft on the opposite side. Be careful not to mix the components of the two sides.

10. Installation is performed in the reverse order of removal. Coat the lips of the rear housing oil seal with multipurpose grease prior to installation of the rear axle shaft. Torque the bearing retaining nut to the specifications given in the chart below.

Tercel

1. Raise the rear of the vehicle and support it with jackstands. Remove the wheel.

2. Remove the cap, cotter pin, nut lock and nut. Remove the axle hub together with the outer bearing, thrust washer and brake drum.

3. Disconnect the brake line from the rear wheel cylinder. Disconnect the parking brake cable.

4. Remove the four bolts attaching the axle shaft to the carrier and then remove the axle shaft and the brake backing plate.

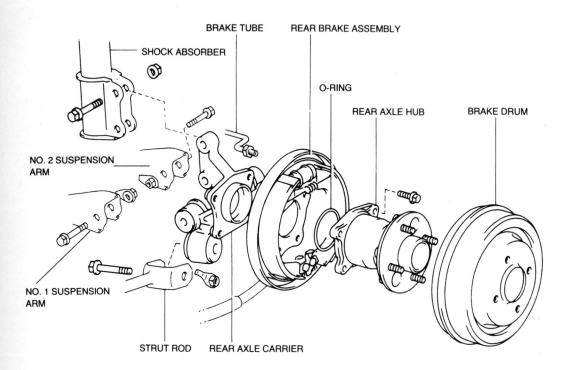

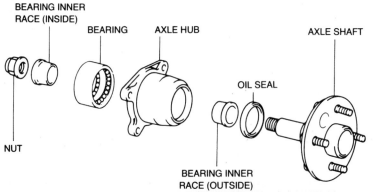

Exploded view of the rear axle shaft assembly—Corolla FWD

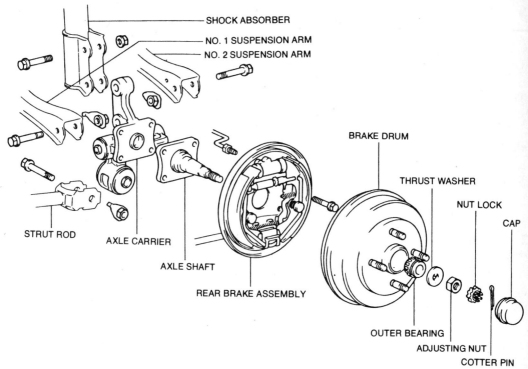

SHOCK ABSORBER
NO. 1 SUSPENSION ARM
NO. 2 SUSPENSION ARM
BRAKE DRUM
THRUST WASHER
NUT LOCK
CAP
STRUT ROD
AXLE CARRIER
AXLE SHAFT
REAR BRAKE ASSEMBLY
OUTER BEARING
ADJUSTING NUT
COTTER PIN

Exploded view of the rear axle shaft assembly—Tercel (except 4x4)

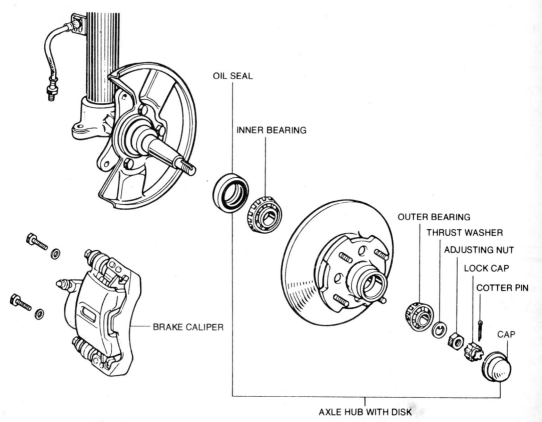

OIL SEAL
INNER BEARING
OUTER BEARING
THRUST WASHER
ADJUSTING NUT
LOCK CAP
COTTER PIN
BRAKE CALIPER
CAP
AXLE HUB WITH DISK

Exploded view of the front axle hub and bearing assembly—all except Tercel

5. Installation is in the reverse order of removal. Tighten the axle shaft-to-carrier nuts to 59 ft.lb. Bleed the brakes.

Corolla FWD

1. Raise and support the rear of the vehicle. Remove the brake drum.

2. Check that the bearing play in an axial direction is no more than 0.0020″.

3. Disconnect and plug the brake tube from the wheel cylinder.

4. Remove the four bolts holding the axle hub to the carrier. Remove the axle hub along with the brake assembly. Remove the O-ring.

5. Using a hammer and chisel, unstake the bearing retaining nut on the axle hub and remove the nut.

6. Using a two armed puller, remove the axle shaft form the axle hub.

7. To install, press the axle shaft into the hub and tighten the nut to 90 ft.lb. (123 Nm). Stake the nut.

8. Position a new O-ring into the axle carrier and then install the axle hub. Tighten the mounting bolts to 59 ft.lb. (80 Nm).

9. Installation of the remaining components is in the reverse order of removal.

FRONT AXLE

Front Axle Hub and Bearing
REMOVAL AND INSTALLATION
Rear Wheel Drive

1. Raise the front of the vehicle and support it with jackstands. Remove the wheel.

2. Remove the front disc brake caliper mounting bolts and position it safely out of the way.

3. Pry off the bearing cap and then remove the cotter pin, lock cap and the adjusting nut.

4. Remove the axle hub and disc together with the outer bearing and thrust washer.

NOTE: *Be careful not to drop the outer bearing during removal.*

5. Using a small prybar, pry out the oil seal from the back of the hub and then remove the inner bearing.

6. Installation is in the reverse order of removal. Please note the following:

a. Place some axle grease into the palm of your hand and then take the bearing and work the grease into it until it begins to ooze out the other side. Coat the inside of the axle hub and bearing cap with the same grease.

b. Install the bearing adjusting nut and tighten it to 22 ft.lb. Snug down the bearing by turning the hub several times. Loosen the

nut until it can be turned by hand and then, using spring scale, retighten it until the preload measures 0.8-1.9 lbs.

c. Use a new cotter pin when installing the lock cap.

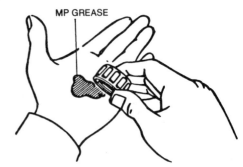

Packing the wheel bearing with grease

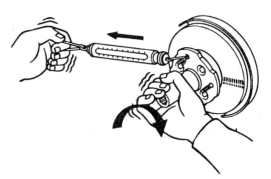

Use a spring scale to measure the wheel bearing preload—all except Tercel

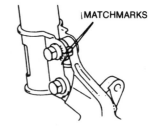

Matchmark the adjustment cam to the shock absorber bracket—front wheel drive

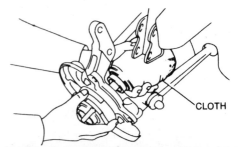

Sliding the axle hub into position—front wheel drive

Front Wheel Drive

1. Raise the front of the vehicle and support it with jackstands. Remove the wheel.

2. Remove the cotter pin from the bearing locknut cap and then remove the cap. Have an assistant step on the brake pedal and then loosen the locknut.

3. Remove the brake caliper mounting nuts and then position the caliper out of the way. Pull off the brake disc.

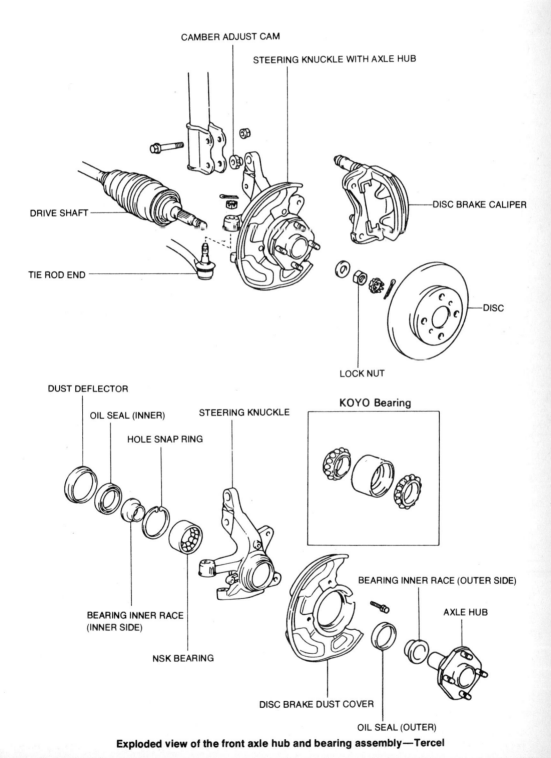

CAMBER ADJUST CAM

STEERING KNUCKLE WITH AXLE HUB

DRIVE SHAFT

DISC BRAKE CALIPER

TIE ROD END

DISC

LOCK NUT

DUST DEFLECTOR

OIL SEAL (INNER)

STEERING KNUCKLE

HOLE SNAP RING

KOYO Bearing

BEARING INNER RACE (OUTER SIDE)

AXLE HUB

BEARING INNER RACE (INNER SIDE)

NSK BEARING

DISC BRAKE DUST COVER

OIL SEAL (OUTER)

Exploded view of the front axle hub and bearing assembly—Tercel

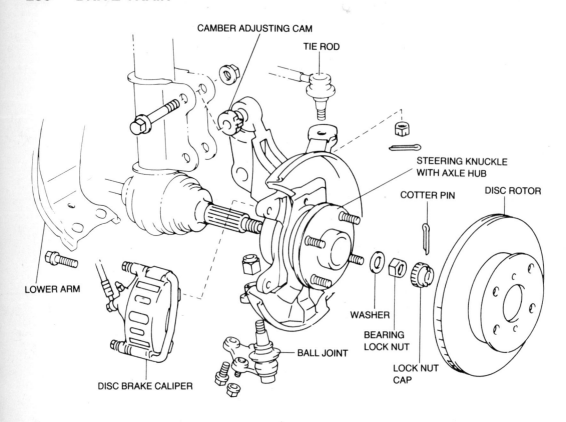

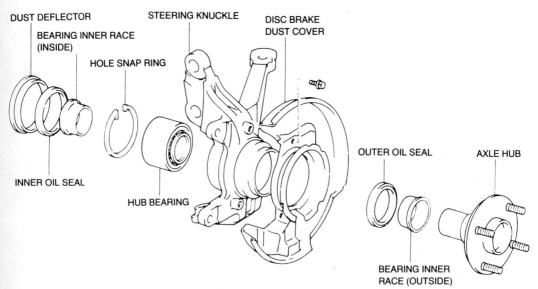

Exploded view of the front axle hub and bearing assembly—Corolla FWD

4. Remove the cotter pin and nut from the tie rod end and then, using a tie rod end removal tool, remove the tie rod.

5. Place matchmarks on the shock absorber

lower mounting bracket and the camber adjustment cam, remove the bolts and separate the steering knuckle from the shock.

6. Remove the two ball joint attaching nuts

and disconnect the lower arm from the knuckle.

7. Carefully grasp the axle hub and pull it out from the halfshaft.

NOTE: *Be sure to cover the halfshaft boot with a cloth to protect it from any damage.*

8. Clamp the steering knuckle in a vise. Remove the dust deflector. Remove the nut holding the steering knuckle to the ball joint. Press the ball joint from the steering knuckle.

9. Remove the deflector from the hub. Use a slide hammer to remove the inner oil seal. Remove the snap ring retainer with needle noise pliers.

10. Remove the disc brake dust shield. Use a two armed puller and remove the axle hub from the steering knuckle.

11. Remove the inner bearing races (inside and outside). Remove the oil seal from the knuckle.

12. Position the old bearing inner race (out-side) on the bearing. Use a hammer and drift to carefully knock out the bearing.

13. Press a new bearing into the steering knuckle.

14. Use a seal driver and install a new oil seal into the knuckle.

15. Install the brake dust cover. Apply grease to the oil seal lip and the bearing inner race. Press the hub into the knuckle.

16. Install a new snap ring. Press a new seal into position. Install the remaining components and the steering knuckle in the reverse order of removal. Please note the following:

a. Tighten the ball joint nut: 14 ft.lb. Replace the nut with a new one, and tighten to 82 ft.lb. Tighten the steering knuckle-to-shock absorber bolts to 105 ft.lb. (152 ft.lb. on diesel Corolla).

b. Tighten the bearing locknut to 137 ft.lb. and always use a new cotter pin.

Suspension and Steering

FRONT SUSPENSION

The front suspension system is of the MacPherson strut design. The struts used on either side are a combination spring and shock absorber with the outer casing of the shock actually supporting the spring at the bottom and thus forming a major structural component of the suspension. The wheel hub is attached to the bottom of the strut. A strut mounting bearing at the top and a ball joint at the bottom allow the entire strut to rotate in cornering maneuvers. The strut assembly, steering arm and the steering knuckle are all combined in one assembly; there is no upper control arm. A rubber bushed transverse link (control arm) connects the lower portion of the strut to the front crossmember via the ball joint; the link thus allows for vertical movement.

NOTE: *Exercise extreme caution when working with the front suspension. Coil springs and other suspension components are under extreme tension and result in severe injury if released unexpectedly.*

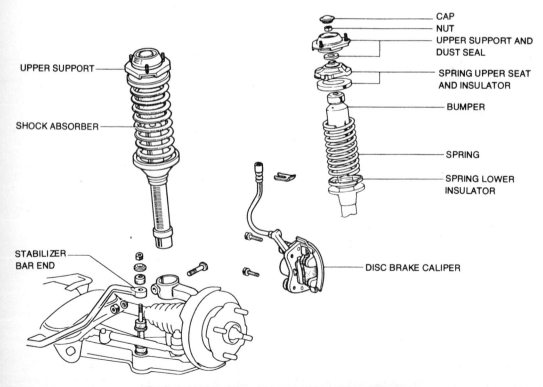

Exploded view of the strut assembly—1980–82 Tercel

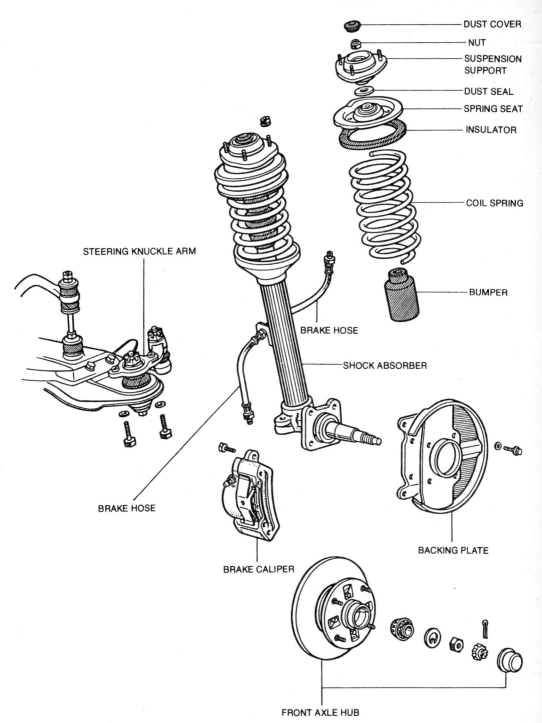

DUST COVER

NUT

SUSPENSION
SUPPORT

DUST SEAL

SPRING SEAT

INSULATOR

COIL SPRING

STEERING KNUCKLE ARM

BUMPER

BRAKE HOSE

SHOCK ABSORBER

BRAKE HOSE

BACKING PLATE

BRAKE CALIPER

FRONT AXLE HUB

Exploded view of the strut assembly—all rear wheel drive Corollas

Springs and Shock Absorbers
TESTING

The function of the shock absorber is to damper harsh spring movement and provide a means of dissipating the motion of the wheels so that the shocks encountered by the wheels are not totally transmitted to the body of the car and, therefore, to you and your passengers. As the wheel moves up and down, the shock ab-

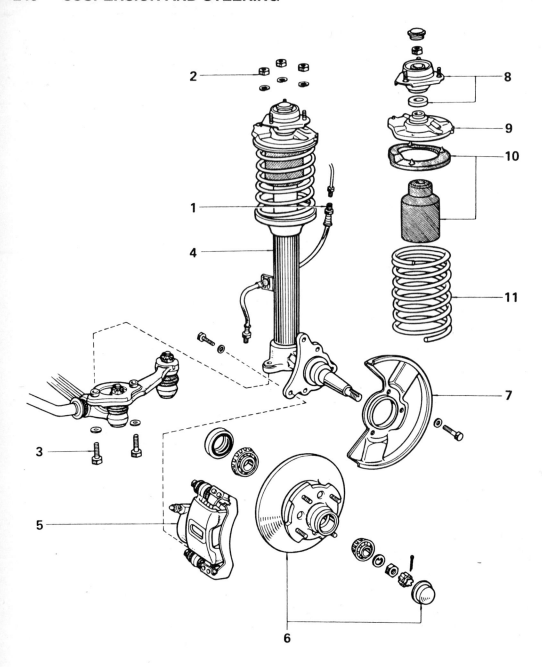

1. Brake Tube
2. Upper Support
3. Shell Lower Bolt Nut
4. Shock Absorber
5. Brake Caliper
6. Brake Disc & Hub
7. Backing Plate
8. Upper Support & Dust Seal
9. Spring Upper Seat
10. Spring Insulator & Spring Bumper
11. Spring

Components of the Starlet front suspension

sorber shortens and lengthens, thereby impos-
ing a restraint on excessive movement by its hydraulic action.

A good way to see if your shock absorbers are
working properly is to push on one corner of the
car until it is moving up and down for almost
the full suspension travel, then release it and
watch its recovery. If the car bounces slightly
about one more time and then comes to a rest,
you can be fairly certain that the shock is all

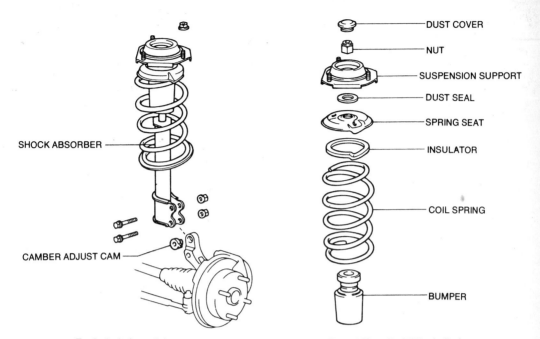

SHOCK ABSORBER

CAMBER ADJUST CAM

DUST COVER

NUT

SUSPENSION SUPPORT

DUST SEAL

SPRING SEAT

INSULATOR

COIL SPRING

BUMPER

Exploded view of the strut assembly—1983 and later Tercel (Corolla FWD similar)

right. If the car continues to bounce excessively, the shocks will probably require replacement.

MacPherson Struts

The struts are precious parts and retain the springs under tremendous pressure even when removed from the car. For this reason, several expensive tools and substantial specialized knowledge are required to safely and effectively work on these components. If spring and shock absorber work is required, it may not be a bad ideal to remove the strut involved yourself and then consider taking it to a repair facility which is fully equipped and familiar with the car.

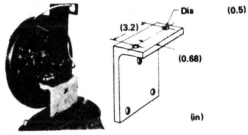

Fabricate the shock absorber stand and mount it in a vise as shown

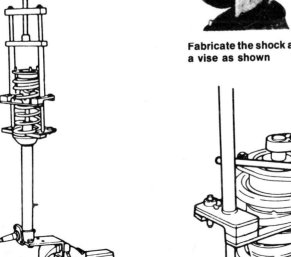

Spring compressor installed on the coil spring for removal

Hold the upper mount with a rod to unscrew the piston rod nut

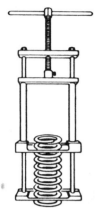

Spring compressor installed on the coil spring for installation—leave the upper coils free

REMOVAL AND INSTALLATION

1. Remove the hubcap and loosen the lug nuts.

2. Raise the front of the car and support it on the chassis jacking plates provided with jack stands.

CAUTION: *Do not support the weight of the car on the suspension arm; the arm will deform under its weight.*

3. Unfasten the lug nuts and remove the wheel.

4. Detach the front brake line from its clamp.

5. Remove the caliper and wire it out of the way.

6. Unfasten the three nuts which secure the upper shock absorber mounting plate to the top of the wheel arch.

7. Remove the two bolts which attach the shock absorber lower end to the steering knuckle low arm.

NOTE: *Press down on the suspension lower arm, in order to remove the strut assembly. This must be done to clear the collars on the steering knuckle arm bolt holes when removing the shock/spring assembly. The steering knuckle bolt holes have collars that extend about 0.20". Be careful to clear them when separating the steering knuckle from the strut assembly.*

Installation is performed in the reverse order of removal. Be sure to note the following, however:

1. Align the hole in the upper suspension support with the shock absorber piston rod end, so that they fit properly.

2. Always use a new nut and nylon washer on the shock absorber piston rod end when securing it to the upper suspension support. Torque the nut to 29-40 ft.lb.

CAUTION: *Do not use an impact wrench to tighten the nut.*

3. Coat the suspension support bearing with multipurpose grease prior to installation. Pack the space in the upper support with multipurpose grease, also, after installation.

4. Tighten the suspension support-to-wheel arch bolts to the following specification:
- Corolla (RWD): 11-16 ft.lb.
- Corolla (FWD): 23 ft.lb.
- Tercel: 12-16 ft.lb.

5. Tighten the shock absorber-to-steering knuckle arm bolts to the following specifications:
- Corolla (RWD): 50-65 ft.lb.
- Corolla (FWD): Gas 105 ft. lb.
  Diesel 152 ft.lb.
- Tercel: 105 ft.lb.
- All others: 65 ft.lb.

6. Adjust the front wheel bearing preload.

7. Bleed the brake system.

Coil Springs

REMOVAL AND INSTALLATION

CAUTION: *The coil springs are retained under considerable pressure. They can exert enough force to cause serious injury. Exercise extreme caution when disassembling the strut for coil spring removal.*

This procedure requires the use of a spring compressor. It cannot be performed without one. If you do not have access to this special tool, do not attempt to disassemble the strut.

1. Remove the strut assembly.

2. Fabricate a strut assembly mounting stand as illustrated. Bolt the assembly to the stand and then mount the stand in a vise.

CAUTION: *Do not attempt to clamp the strut assembly in a vise without the mounting stand as this will result in damage to the strut tube.*

3. Attach a spring compressor and compress the spring until the upper spring retainer is free of any spring tension.

4. Use a spring seat holder to hold the support and then remove the nut on the strut bearing plate.

5. Remove the bearing plate, the support, the upper spring retainer and then slowly and cautiously unscrew the spring compressor until all spring tension is relieved. Remove the spring and the dust cover.

NOTE: *Do not allow the piston rod to retract into the shock absorber. If it falls, screw a nut onto the rod and pull the rod out by the nut. Do not use pliers or the like to grip the rod as they will damage its surface, resulting in leaks, uneven operation or seal damage. Be extremely careful not to stress or contact the rod.*

6. Installation is in the reverse order of removal. Please note the following:

• Pack the bearing in the suspension support with mutlipurpose grease

• Use a new retaining nut and tighten it to 29-39 ft.lb.

Shock Absorbers

REMOVAL AND INSTALLATION

1970-82

CAUTION: *Disassemble the shock absorber in a clean place. Do not allow dust or dirt to get on the disassembled parts. The piston rod is high precision finished, even a slight scratch can cause fluid leakage so be careful when handling the piston rod.*

1. Remove the strut assembly and then the coil spring.

2. Remove the wheel hub and the brake disc.

3. Attach the strut tube to the mounting plate and clamp it in a vise.

4. Use a ring nut wrench and remove the ring nut at the top of the strut tube.

5. Use a needle and pick the gasket out of the strut tube.

6. Remove the guide, the rebound stopper and the piston rod.

7. Pull the cylinder out of the strut tube and then use a long blunt instrument to drive the base valve out of the bottom of the cylinder.

8. Empty all oil out of the tube.

Drive the base valve out of the shock cylinder

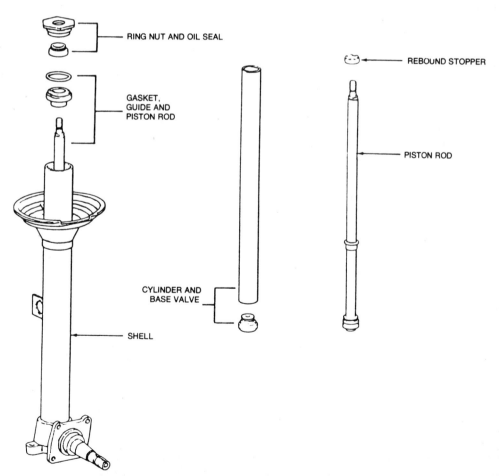

RING NUT AND OIL SEAL

GASKET, GUIDE AND PISTON ROD

REBOUND STOPPER

PISTON ROD

CYLINDER AND BASE VALVE

SHELL

Front shock absorber assembly

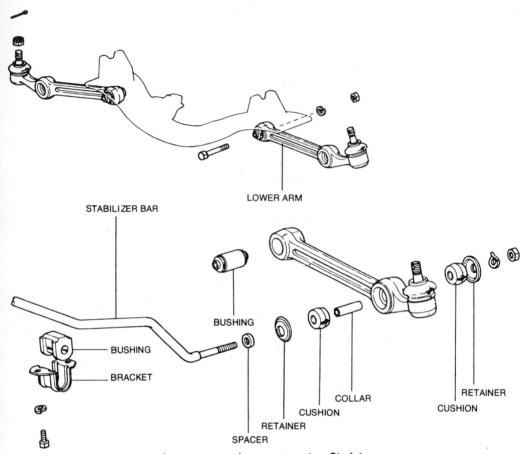

LOWER ARM

STABILIZER BAR

BUSHING

BUSHING

BRACKET

SPACER

RETAINER

CUSHION

COLLAR

RETAINER

CUSHION

Lower suspension components—Starlet

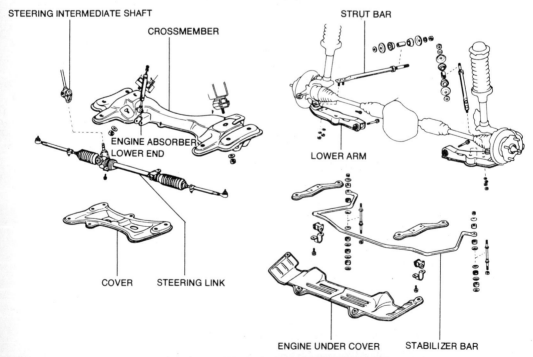

STEERING INTERMEDIATE SHAFT

CROSSMEMBER

STRUT BAR

ENGINE ABSORBER
LOWER END

LOWER ARM

COVER   STEERING LINK

ENGINE UNDER COVER   STABILIZER BAR

Lower suspension components—1980–82 Tercel

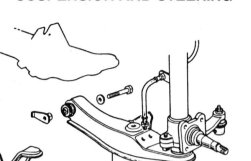

ENGINE UNDER COVER

LOWER ARM AND KNUCKLE ARM

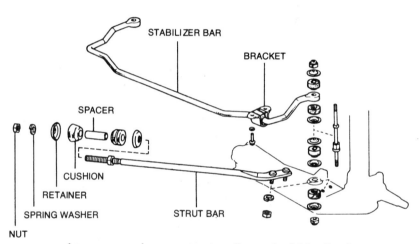

STABILIZER BAR

BRACKET

SPACER

CUSHION

RETAINER

SPRING WASHER

STRUT BAR

NUT

Lower suspension components—all rear wheel drive Corollas

NOTE: *Rebuilding kits are available through your local Toyota dealer.*
‹104‹

To install:

1. Press the base valve into the bottom of the cylinder.

2. Slide the cylinder into the strut tube.

3. Slide the piston rod and the rebound stopper into the cylinder.

4. Fill the cylinder with NEW shock absorber fluid (315cc Corolla and Carina; 230cc Tercel; 240cc Starlet).

5. Press the rod guide and its gasket into the top of the strut tube.

6. Tape the end of the piston rod to avoid damaging the oil seal inside the ring nut.

7. Coat the oil seal with multipurpose grease and then install the ring nut on the piston rod.

8. Using a ring nut wrench, tighten the ring nut until the top of the piston rod is 3.15-3.54". above the top of the strut tube. Torque the nut

to 73-108 ft.lb. on the Corolla, Carina and Starlet. Tighten to 66-97 ft.lb. on the Tercel.

9. Installation of the remaining components is in the reverse order of removal.

Ball Joints

INSPECTION

1970-79

1. Raise the car so that all the weight has been removed from the front wheels.

2. Apply upward and downward pressure to the outer end of the lower control arm. Be careful to avoid any compression of the coil spring.

3. There should be no noticeable play between the bottom of the strut assembly and the ball joint. If play exists, the ball joint will require replacement.

NOTE: *The ball joint on all Toyotas except the 1983 Tercel is permanently connected to the lower control arm. If either of them go bad, they must be replaced as a unit.*

Tercel

1980 AND LATER

1. Jack up the vehicle and place wooden blocks under the front wheels. The block height should be 7.09-7.87″.
2. Use jack stands for additional safety.
3. Make sure the front wheels are in a straight forward position.
4. Chock the wheels.
5. Lower the jack until there is approximately half a load on the front springs.
6. Move the lower control arm up and down to check that there is no ball joint play.

Lower Control Arm and Ball Joint
REMOVAL AND INSTALLATION

Corolla RWD, Carina and Starlet

The ball joint and control arm cannot be separated from each other. If one fails, then both must be replaced as an assembly, in the following manner:

1. Perform Steps 1-7 of the Corolla, Carina, Starlet, Front Coil Spring Removal procedure. Skip Step 6.
2. Remove the stabilizer bar securing bolts. On Starlet, disconnect the tie rod.
3. Unfasten the torque strut mounting bolts. On the Starlet, jack up the opposite wheel until the frame clears the jackstand.
4. Remove the control arm mounting bolt and detach the arm from the front suspension member. The Starlet uses a caster adjusting spacer, be careful not to lose it.
5. Remove the steering knuckle arm from the control arm with a ball joint puller.
6. Inspect the suspension components which were removed for wear or damage. Replace any parts, as required.

Installation is performed in the reverse order of removal. Note the following, however:
1. When installing the control arm on the suspension member, tighten the bolts partially at first.
2. Complete the assembly procedure and lower the car to the ground.
3. Bounce the front of the car several times. Allow the suspension to settle, then tighten the lower control arm bolts to 51-65 ft.lb. Tighten knuckle arm bolts to 42-56 ft.lb., the tie rod end-to-knuckle bolt to 37-50 ft.lb. and the stabilizer bar nut to 66-90 ft.lb.
CAUTION: *Use only the bolt which was designed to fit the lower control arm. If a replacement is necessary, see an authorized dealer for the proper part.*

4. Remember to lubricate the ball joint. Check front end alignment.

1980-82 Tercel

1. Jack up the vehicle and support it with jack stands.
CAUTION: *Do not jack up the car on the lower control arms.*
2. Remove the front wheels.
3. Remove the tie rod ends.
4. Remove the stabilizer bar end.
5. Remove the strut bar end.
6. Place a jack under the lower control arm for support.
7. Remove the bolt from the bottom of the steering knuckle.
8. Remove the bolt from the lower control arm.
9. Remove the control arm.
NOTE: *The lower ball joint can not be separated from the lower control arm. It must be replaced as a complete unit.*
10. The following torques are required: bottom steering knuckle nut 40-52 ft.lb., stabilizer bar 11-15 ft.lb., tie rod end 37-50 ft.lb., strut bar 29-39 ft.lb., lower control arm 51-65 ft.lb.

Corolla FWD and 1983-87 Tercel

1. Raise the front of the vehicle and support it with jackstands. Remove the wheel.
2. Remove the two bolts attaching the ball joint to the steering knuckle.

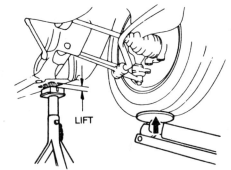

Raise the opposite wheel until the body lifts off the jackstand

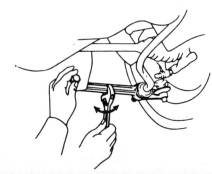

Wiggle the control arm while removing the mounting bolt

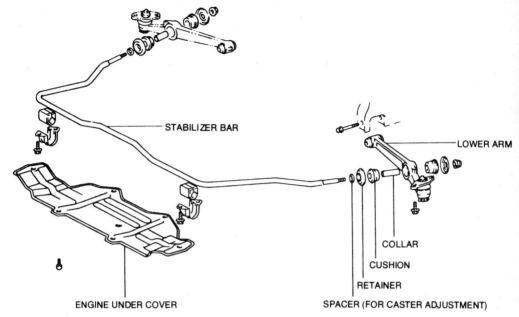

Lower suspension components—1983 and later Tercel

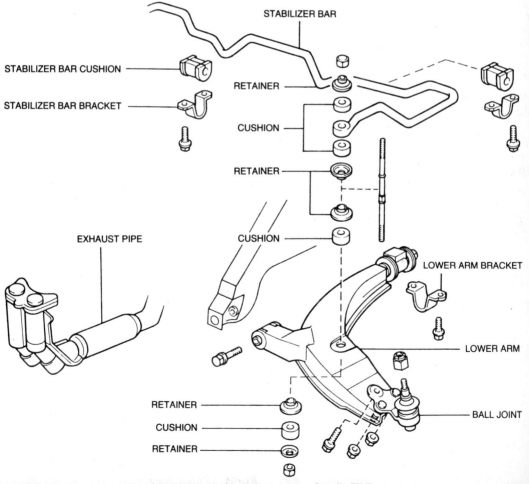

Lower suspension components—Corolla FWD

3. Remove the stabilizer bar nut, retainer and cushion.

4. Jack up the opposite wheel until the body of the car just lifts off the jackstand.

5. Loosen the lower control arm mounting bolt, wiggle the arm back and forth and then remove the bolt. Disconnect the lower control arm from the stabilizer bar.

NOTE: *When removing the lower control arm (on the Tercel), be careful not to lose the caster adjustment spacer.*

6. On the Tercel, carefully mount the lower control arm in a vise and then, using a ball joint removal tool, disconnect the ball joint from the arm.

7. Installation is in the reverse order of removal. Please note the following:

a. Tighten the ball joint-to-control arm nut to 51-65 ft.lb. and use a new cotter pin (Tercel only).

b. Tighten the steering knuckle-to-control arm bolts to 59 ft.lb. on the Tercel; 47 ft.lb. on the Corolla FWD.

c. Tighten the stabilizer bar bolt on the Corolla FWD to 13 ft.lb.

d. Before tightening the stabilizer bar nuts on the Tercel, or the control arm bracket bolts on the Corolla FWD, mount the wheels and lower the car. Bounce the car several times to settle the suspension and then tighten the stabilizer bolts on the Tercel to 66-90 ft.lb. On the Corolla FWD, tighten the front arm bracket bolt to 83 ft.lb. and the rear to 64 ft.lb.

e. Check the front end alignment.

Front End Alignment

Alignment should only be performed after it has been verified that all parts of the steering and suspension systems are in good operating condition. The car must be empty. The tires must be cold and inflated to the correct pressure and the test surface must be level and horizontal.

CASTER

Caster is the tilt of the front steering axis either forward or backward away from the front of the vehicle.

If the caster is found to be out of tolerance with the specifications, it may be adjusted by turning the nuts on the rear end of the strut bar (where it attaches to the body) on the Corolla RWD, Carina and the 1980-82 Tercel. The caster is decreased by lengthening the strut bar and increased by shortening it. One turn of the adjusting nut is equal to 8' of tilt on the Corolla RWD and Carina and 7' on the 1980-82 Tercel. 1' is $\frac{1}{60}$ of a degree.

Caster on the Starlet and the 1983 and later Tercel is adjusted by changing the number of spacers on the stabilizer bar. One spacer will change the caster 24' on the Starlet and 13' on the 1983 and later Tercel. One minute (1') is equal to $\frac{1}{60}$ of a degree.

NOTE: *If the caster still cannot be adjusted within the limits, inspect or replace any damaged or worn suspension parts.*

Caster is not adjustable on the Corolla FWD.

CAMBER

Camber is the slope of the front wheels from the vertical when viewed from the front of the vehicle. When the wheels tilt outward at the top, the camber is positive (+). When the wheels tilt inward at the top, the camber is neg-

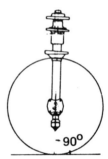

Caster is the forward or backward tilt of the steering axis

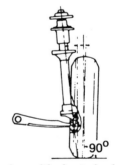

Camber is the slope of the front wheels when viewed from the front of the car

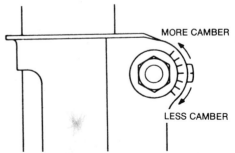

Camber adjusting bolt on the Corolla FWD and the 1983 and later Tercel

Wheel Alignment Specifications—1970–84

Model		Caster Range (deg)	Caster Pref Setting (deg)	Camber Range (deg)	Camber Pref Setting (deg)	Toe-In (in.)	Steering Axis Inclination	Wheel Pivot Ratio (deg) Inner Wheel	Wheel Pivot Ratio (deg) Outer Wheel
Corolla	1200	1½P–2⅓	—	½P–1½P	½P	0.04–0.20 ④	7½P–8½P	38½–41½ ⑤	30–36 ⑥
	1600 (1970–75)	1½P–2P ①	1¾P	½P–1½P	½P	0.04–0.20	7½P–8½P	38½–41½ ②	27½–33½
	(1976–79)	1¼P–1½P	2P	½P–1½P	1P	0.08–0.16 ③	7¼P–8¼P	37–39 ⑤	29¼–33¼ ⑥
	1800 exc. sta. wgn.	1°16'P–2°16'P	1°46'P	33'P–1°33'P	1°3'P	0–.08 ⑦	7°55'P–8°55'P	38–40	29–33
	1800 sta. wgn.	1°¹/₁₆'P–2°¹/₁₆'P	1°34'P	35'P–1°35'P	1°5'P	0–.08 ⑦	7°50'P–8°50'P	38–40	29–33
	1983	1°15'P–2°15'P ⑧	1°45'P ⑧	35'P–1°35'P	1°5'P	0–.08	8°20'P–8°30'P ⑨	37°5'–39°5'	33°30'
	1984 RWD	2°15'P–3°15'P ⑭	2°45'P ⑮	15'N–45'P	15'P	0–.08P	8°20'P–9°20'P	36°30'–40°30'	33°30' ⑯
	1984 FWD	25'P–1°25'P	55'P	1°N–0	30'N	.04N–.04P	12°5'P–13°5'P	—	—
Carina		½P–1½P	1P	0–1½P	1P	0.20–0.28	7½P	37–39	30–34
Tercel	1980–82	1°40'P–2°40'P	2°10'P	0–1°P	30'P	0.04–0.12	10°50'P–11°50'P	34–36	33
	1983–84	40'P–1°40'P ⑩	1°10'P ⑪	10'N–50'P	20'P	0.06N–0.04P	12°P–13°P	35°20'–37°20' ⑫	31°40'–33°40' ⑫
	4X4	1°55'–2°55'P	2°25'P	20'P–1°20'P	50'P	0.06N–0.04P	11°20'–12°20'	35°30'–37°30' ⑬	32°15'–34°15' ⑬
Starlet	1981–82 Sedan	1°40'P–2°20'P	2P	20'P–1°P	40'P	—	9¾P	36°50'	34
	Wagon	1°25'P–2°5'P	1°45'P	15'P–55'P	35'P	—	9°50'P	36°50'	33°55'
	1983–84	1°10'P–2°40'P	1°55'P	5'N–1°25'P	40'P	0.08N–0.24P	9°P–10°30'P	36°20'–38°20'	33°50'

P Positive
N Negative
① 1975 Wagon: ¾P–1½P
② 1975 inner: 37–39 deg
③ 1976–77 (radial): 0–0.08 in.
④ 1978–79 w/bias ply: 0.079"
   w/radial ply: 0.039"
⑤ 1978–79: 37–39
⑥ 1978–79: 29–33
⑦ w/bias tires: 0.12 ± 0.04
⑧ 50'P–2°20'P; 1°35'P: Sta. Wag.
⑨ 8°15'P–8°25'P: Sta. Wag.
⑩ W/Power Steering: 2°10'P–3°10'P
⑪ W/Power Steering: 2°40'P
⑫ W/Power Steering: Inner—34°50'–36°50'
   outer—31°55'–33°55'
⑬ W/Power Steering: inner—35°20'–37°20'
   outer—32°20'–34°20'
⑭ W/Power Steering: 3°10'P–4°10'P
⑮ W/Power Steering: 3°40'P
⑯ W/Power Steering: 33°

ative (–). The amount of positive and negative camber is measured in degrees from the vertical and the measurement is called camber angle. Camber is preset at the factory, therefore it is not adjustable on any models but the Corolla FWD and the 1983 and later Tercel. If the camber angle is out of tolerance, inspect or replace worn or damaged suspension parts.

Camber on the Corolla FWD and 1983 and later Tercel models is adjustable by means of a camber adjustment bolt on the lower strut mounting bracket. Loosen the shock absorber set nut and then turn the adjusting bolt until the camber is within specifications. Camber will change about 20' for each gradation on the cam. One minute (1') is equal to 1/60 of a degree.

TOE

Toe is the amount, measured in a fraction of an inch, that the front wheels are closer together at one end than the other. Toe-in means that the front wheels are closer together at the front of the tire than at the rear; toe-out means that the rear of the tires are closer together than the front.

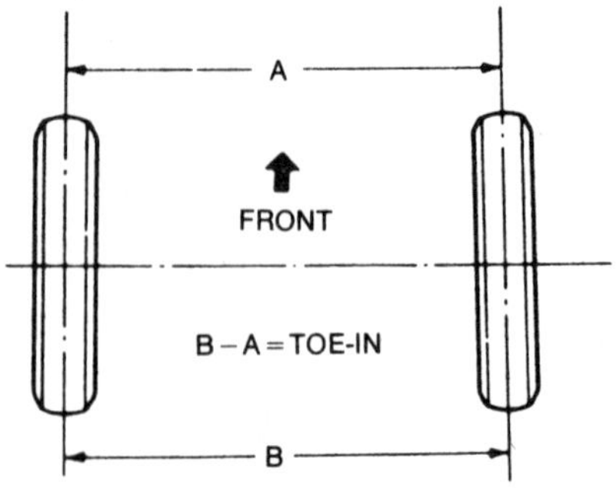

When the front of the tires are closer together than the rear, you have toe-in

Although it is recommended that this adjustment be made by your dealer or a qualified shop, you can make it yourself if you make very careful measurements. The wheels must be dead straight ahead. The car must have a full tank of gas, all fluids must be at their proper levels, all other suspensions and steering adjustments must be correct and the tires must be properly inflated to their cold specification.

1. Toe can be determined by measuring the

Wheel Alignment—1985–87

		Caster		Camber			Steering Axis
Year	Model	Range (deg.)	Preferred Setting (deg.)	Range (deg.)	Preferred Setting (deg.)	Toe-in (in.)	Inclination (deg.)
1985–86	Tercel (Sedan)	①	②	1/6N–5/6P	1/3P	0.06 out–0.04 in	12 1/2
	(Wagon)	③	④	1/4N–3/4P	1/4P	0.04 out–0.04 in	13
	(4wd)	1 15/16P–2 15/16P	2 7/16P	1/16P–1 1/16P	9/16P	0.08 out–0	11 13/16
	Corolla (RWD)	⑤	⑥	1/2N–1P	1/4P	0.04 out–0.12 in	9
	(FWD)	3/16P–1 11/16P	15/16P	1N–1/2P	1/4N	0.04 out–0.12 in	12 1/2
1987	Tercel (Sedan)	⑦	⑧	3/4N–3/4P	0	0.08 out–0.08 in	12 1/2
	(Wagon)	④	⑤	3/4N–3/4P	0P	0.12 out–0.04 in	12 1/2
	(4wd)	1 11/16P–3 3/16P	2 1/4P	3/16N–1 5/16P	9/16P	0.12 out–0.04 in	12
	Corolla (RWD)	⑤	⑥	1/2N–1P	1/4P	0.04 out–0.12 in	9
	(FWD)	1/8P–1 5/8P	7/8P	1N–1/2P	1/4N	0.04 out–0.12 in	12 1/2

① Man. Str.: 2/3P–1 2/3P
Pwr. Str.: 2 1/6P–3 1/6P
② Man. Str.: 1 1/6P
Pwr. Str.: 2 2/3P
③ Man. Str.: 1/6N–1 1/3P
Pwr. Str.: 1 1/4P–3P
④ Man. Str.: 2/3P
Pwr. Str.: 2 1/4P
⑤ Man. Str.: 2P–3 1/2P
Pwr. Str.: 3P–3 1/2P
⑥ Man. Str.: 2 3/4P
Pwr. Str.: 3 3/4P
⑦ Man. Str.: 1/4P–1 3/4P
Pwr. Str.: 1 3/4P–3 1/4P
⑧ Man. Str.: 1P
Pwr. Str.: 2 1/2P

distance between the centers of the tire treads, at the front of the tire and the rear. If the tread pattern of your car's tires makes this impossible, you can measure between the edges of the wheel rims, but be sure to move the car and measure in a few places to avoid errors caused by bent rims or wheel runout.

2. If the measurement is not within specifications, loosen the four retaining clamp locknuts on the adjustable tie rods.

3. Turn the left and right tie rods EQUAL amounts until the measurements are within specifications.

4. Tighten the lock bolts and then recheck the measurements. Check to see that the steering wheel is still in the proper position. If not, remove it and reposition it.

REAR SUSPENSION

Shock Absorbers

TESTING

Except Corolla FWD and 1983 and Later Tercel

Shock absorbers require replacement if the car fails to recover quickly after hitting a large bump or if it sways excessively following a directional change.

A good way to test the shock absorbers is to intermittently apply downward pressure to the side of the car until it is moving up and down for almost its full suspension travel. Release it and observe its recovery. If the car bounces once or twice after having been released and then comes to a rest, the shocks are all right. If

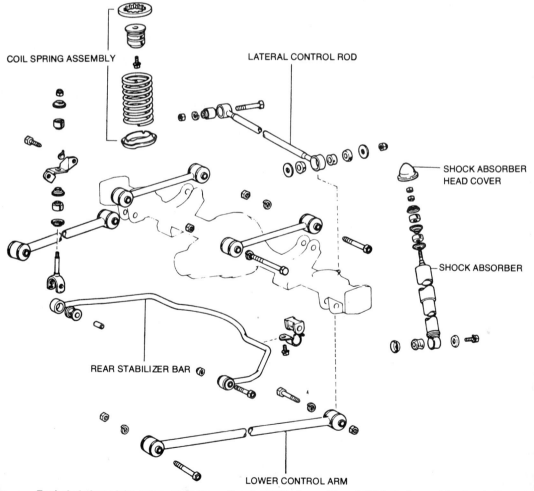

COIL SPRING ASSEMBLY

LATERAL CONTROL ROD

SHOCK ABSORBER HEAD COVER

SHOCK ABSORBER

REAR STABILIZER BAR

LOWER CONTROL ARM

Exploded view of the rear suspension—Corolla RWD shown; Tercel 4 X 4, Carina and Starlet similar

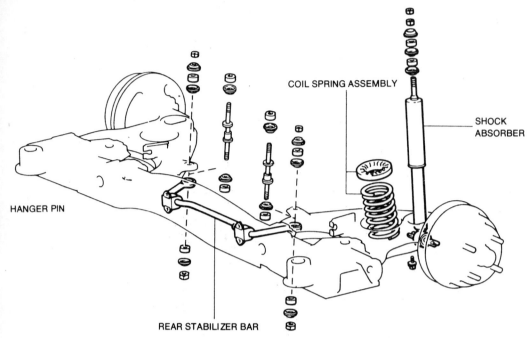

Exploded view of the rear suspension—1980–82 Tercel

COIL SPRING ASSEMBLY

SHOCK ABSORBER

HANGER PIN

REAR STABILIZER BAR

the car continues to bounce, the shocks will probably require replacement.

REMOVAL AND INSTALLATION

Except Corolla FWD and the 1983 and Later Tercel

1. Raise the rear of the car and support the rear axle with jackstands.

2. Unfasten the upper shock absorber retaining nuts. Use a screwdriver to keep the shaft from spinning.

NOTE: *On some models, upper retaining nut removal will require removing the rear seat. Always remove and install the shock absorbers one at a time. Do not allow the rear axle to hang in place as this may cause undue damage.*

3. Remove the lower shock retaining nut where it attaches to the rear axle housing.

4. Remove the shock absorber.

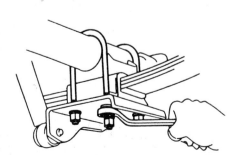

Removing the U-bolts from the spring seats

5. Inspect the shock for wear, leaks or other signs of damage.

6. Installation is in the reverse order of removal. Please note the following: Tighten the upper retaining nuts to 16-24 ft.lb. Tighten the lower retaining nuts to 22-32 ft.lb.

Springs

REMOVAL AND INSTALLATION

Leaf Springs

1. Loosen the rear wheel lug nuts.

2. Raise the rear of the vehicle. Support the frame and rear axle housing with stands.

CAUTION: *Be sure that the vehicle is securely supported.*

3. Remove the lug nuts and the wheel.

4. Remove the cotter pin, nut, and washer from the lower end of the shock absorber.

5. Detach the shock absorber from the spring seat pivot pin.

6. Remove the parking brake cable clamp.

NOTE: *Remove the parking brake equalizer, if necessary.*

7. Unfasten the U-bolt nuts and remove the spring seat assemblies.

8. Adjust the height of the rear axle housing so that the weight of the rear axle is removed from the rear springs.

9. Unfasten the spring shackle retaining nuts. Withdraw the spring shackle inner plate. Carefully pry out the spring shackle with a bar.

10. Remove the spring bracket pin from the

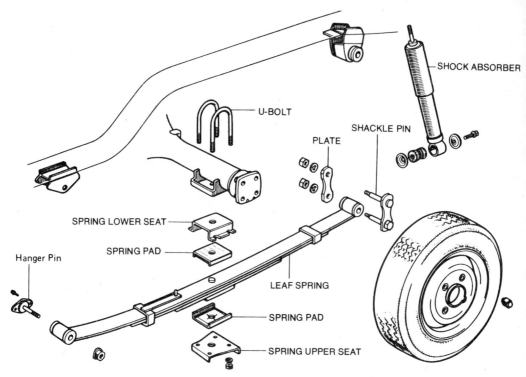

Exploded view of the rear suspension—Corolla station wagon

front end of the spring hanger and remove the rubber bushings.

11. Remove the spring.

CAUTION: *Use care not to damage the hydraulic brake line or the parking brake cable.*

Installation is performed in the following order:

1. Install the rubber bushings in the eye of the spring.

2. Align the eye of the spring with the spring hanger bracket and drive the pin through the bracket holes and rubber bushings.

NOTE: *Use soapy water as lubricant, if necessary, to aid in pin installation. Never use oil or grease.*

3. Finger tighten the spring hanger nuts and/or bolts.

4. Install the rubber bushings in the spring eye at the opposite end of the spring.

5. Raise the free end of the spring. Install the spring shackle through the bushings and the bracket.

6. Fit the shackle inner plate and finger tighten the retaining nuts.

7. Center the bolt head in the hole which is provided in the spring seat on the axle housing.

8. Fit the U-bolts over the axle housing. Install the lower spring seat.

9. Tighten the U-bolt nuts to 51-65 ft. lb.; the shackle bolts to 37-50 ft. lb.; the front

bracket pins to 29-39 ft. lb. and the rear bracket pins to 8-11 ft. lb.

NOTE: *Some models have two sets of nuts, while others have a nut and lockwasher.*

10. Install the parking brake cable clamp. Install the equalizer, if it was removed.

11. Install the shock absorber end at the spring seat. Tighten the nuts to the specified torque.

12. Install the wheel and lug nuts. Lower the car to the ground.

13. Bounce the car several times.

14. Tighten the spring bracket pins and shackles.

15. Repeat Step 13 and check all of the torque specifications again.

Coil Springs

1. Remove the hubcap and loosen the lug nuts.

2. Jack up the rear axle housing and support the frame with jackstands. Leave the jack in place under the rear axle housing.

CAUTION: *Support the car securely. Remember; you will be working underneath it.*

3. Remove the lug nuts and wheel.

4. Unfasten the lower shock absorber end.

5. If equipped with a stabilizer bar; remove the bracket bolts.

6. If equipped with a lateral control rod (Co-

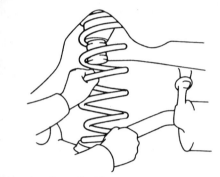

Removing the coil spring

rolla RWD and Tercel 4x4), disconnect the rod from the rear axle housing.

7. Slowly lower the jack under the rear axle housing until the axle is at the bottom of its travel.

8. Withdraw the coil spring, complete with its insulator.

9. Inspect the coil spring and insulator for wear and cracks, or weakness; replace either or both as necessary.

10. Installation is performed in the reverse order of removal. When reconnecting the lateral control rod, tighten the bolt finger tight.

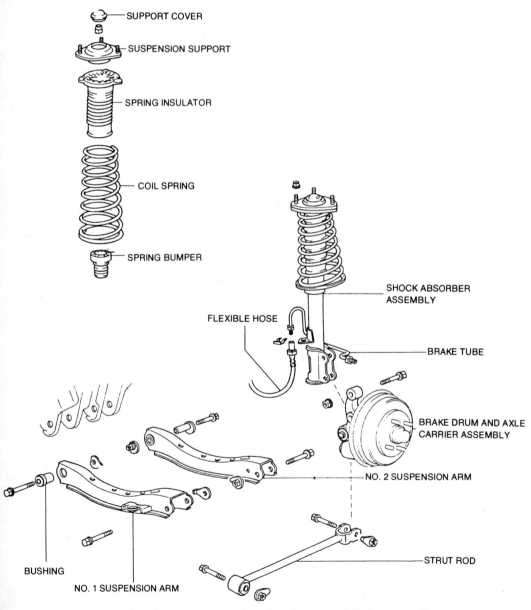

Exploded view of the rear suspension—Corolla FWD and 1983 and later Tercel

Make sure that the spring is installed correctly in the lower insulator (spring seat)

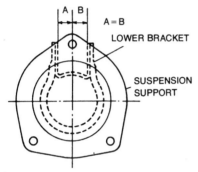

Aligning the suspension support with the strut lower bracket

When the car is lowered, bounce it a few times to stabilize the rear suspension. Raise the rear axle housing until the body is free and then tighten the nut to 47 ft.lb.

Lateral Control Rod
REMOVAL AND INSTALLATION
Corolla RWD and Tercel 4 x 4 Only

1. Raise the rear of the vehicle and support the axle housing with jackstands.
2. Disconnect the lateral rod from the rear axle housing.
3. Disconnect the lateral rod from the body and remove the rod.
4. Install the arm-to-body nut and finger tighten it.
5. Position the arm on the axle housing and install a washer, bushing, spacer, the arm, bushing, washer and then the nut. Finger tighten the nut.
6. Lower the vehicle and bounce it a few times to stabilize the suspension.
7. Raise the rear of the vehicle again then tighten the control rod-to-body nut to 83 ft.lb. and the control rod-to-axle housing nut to 47 ft.lb.

Upper and Lower Control Arms
REMOVAL AND INSTALLATION
Corolla RWD, Tercel 4 x 4 and Starlet Only

1. Raise the rear of the vehicle and support the body with jackstands. Support the rear axle housing with a jack.
2. Remove the bolt holding the upper control arm to the body.
3. Remove the bolt holding the upper control arm to the axle housing and then remove the upper control arm.
4. On the Starlet, disconnect the parking brake cable clamp from the lower control arm and position it out of the way.
5. Remove the bolt (and nut on Starlet) holding the lower control arm to the body.
6. Remove the bolt (and nut on Starlet) holding the lower control arm to the rear axle housing and then remove the lower control arm.
7. Position the upper control arm and install the arm-to-body and arm-to-axle housing bolts. Do not tighten the nuts.
8. Position the lower control arm and install the arm-to-body and arm-to-axle housing bolts. Do not tighten the nuts.
9. Reconnect the parking brake cable clamp to the axle housing on the Starlet.
10. Lower the vehicle and bounce it a few times to stabilize the suspension.
11. Raise and support the vehicle once again. Raise the rear axle housing until the body is just free from the jackstands.
12. Tighten the upper arm-to-body nut to 87 ft.lb. (87-122 ft.lb. on the Starlet). Do the same for the upper arm-to-axle housing nuts.
13. Tighten the lower arm-to-body nuts to 87 ft.lb. (55-75 ft.lb. on the Starlet). Do the same for the lower arm-to-axle housing nuts.

MacPherson Struts
REMOVAL AND INSTALLATION
1983 and Later Tercel and Corolla FWD

1. Working inside the car, remove the shock absorber cover and package tray bracket.
2. Raise the rear of the vehicle and support it with jackstands. Remove the wheel.
3. Disconnect the brake line from the wheel cylinder. Disconnect the brake line from the flexible hose at the mounting bracket on the strut tube. Disconnect the flexible hose from the strut.
4. Loosen the nut holding the suspension support to the shock absorber.
CAUTION: *Do not remove the nut.*
5. Remove the bolts and nuts mounting the strut on the axle carrier and then disconnect the strut.

6. Remove the three upper strut mounting nuts and carefully remove the strut assembly.

7. Installation is in the reverse order of removal. Please note the following:

a. Tighten the upper strut retaining nuts to 17 ft.lb.

b. Tighten the lower strut-to-axle carrier bolts to 105 ft.lb.

c. Tighten the nut holding the suspension support to the shock absorber to 36 ft.lb.

d. Bleed the brakes.

OVERHAUL

NOTE: *Coil spring and shock absorber removal and installation procedures are identical to those already detailed in the previous MacPherson Strut section (Front Suspension). Please refer to these procedures for any work involving the rear struts. If replacement of the shock absorber is required, a small hole (0.079-0.118") must be drilled in the bottom of the strut tube to relieve the gas pressure in the shock.*

STEERING

Steering Wheel

REMOVAL AND INSTALLATION

Three-Spoke

CAUTION: *Do not attempt to remove or install the steering wheel by hammering on it. Damage to the energy absorbing steering column could result.*

1. Unfasten the horn and turn signal multiconnector(s) at the base of the steering column shroud.

2. Loosen the trim pad retaining screws from the back side of the steering wheel.

3. Lift the trim pad and horn button assembly(ies) from the wheel.

4. Remove the steering wheel hub retaining nut.

5. Scratch matchmarks on the hub and shaft to aid in correct installation.

6. Use a steering wheel puller to remove the steering wheel.

7. Installation is performed in the reverse order of removal. Tighten the wheel retaining nut to 15-22 ft.lb., except for the Starlet and 1975-77 Corolla which should be tightened to 22-29 ft.lb.

Two-Spoke

The two-spoke steering wheel is removed in the same manner as the three-spoke, except that the trim pad should be pried off with a small prybar. Remove the pad by lifting it toward the top of the wheel.

Four-Spoke

CAUTION: *Do not attempt to remove or install the steering wheel by hammer on it. Damage to the energy absorbing steering column could result.*

Remove the pad on the two-spoke steering wheel the direction of arrow

Removing the four-spoke wheel with a puller

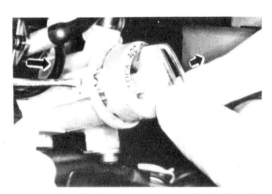

Depress the stop in order to remove the lock cylinder

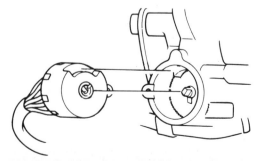

Align the switch before installation

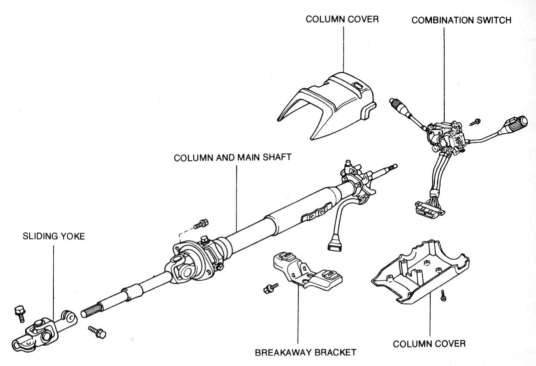

COLUMN COVER   COMBINATION SWITCH

COLUMN AND MAIN SHAFT

SLIDING YOKE

BREAKAWAY BRACKET   COLUMN COVER

Typical steering column assembly

1. Unfasten the horn and turn signal multiconnectors at the base of the steering column shroud (underneath the instrument panel).

2. Gently pry the center emblem off the front of the steering wheel.

3. Insert a wrench through the hold and remove the steering wheel retaining nut.

4. Scratch matchmarks on the hub and shaft to aid installation.

5. Use a steering wheel puller to remove the steering wheel.

6. Installation is the reverse of removal. Tighten the steering wheel retaining nut to 22-29 ft.lb.

Combination Switch

NOTE: *On some earlier models, the combination switch may only be the turn signal switch. Removal and installation procedures are the same for both.*

REMOVAL AND INSTALLATION

1. Disconnect the negative battery cable.

2. Unscrew the two retaining bolts and remove the steering column garnish.

3. Remove the upper and lower steering column covers.

4. Remove the steering wheel.

5. Trace the switch wiring harness to the multiconnector. Push in the lock levers and pull apart the connector.

6. Unscrew the four mounting screws and remove the switch.

7. Installation is in the reverse order of removal.

Ignition Lock/Switch

REMOVAL AND INSTALLATION

1. Disconnect the negative battery cable.

2. Unscrew the retaining screws and remove the upper and lower steering column covers.

3. Unscrew the two retaining screws and remove the steering column garnish.

4. Turn the ignition key to the ACC position.

5. Push the lock cylinder stop in with a small, round object (cotter pin, punch, etc.) and pull out the ignition key and the lock cylinder.

NOTE: *You may find that removing the steering wheel and the combination switch will facilitate easier removal.*

6. Loosen the mounting screw and withdraw the ignition switch from the lock housing.

To install:

1. Install the switch with the switch recess and the bracket tab positioned as shown in the illustration. Install the retaining screw.

2. Make sure that both the lock cylinder and the column lock are in the ACC position. Slide the cylinder into the lock housing until the stop tab engages the hole in the lock.

3. Installation of the remaining components is in the reverse order of removal.

Tie Rod Ends

REMOVAL AND INSTALLATION

Carina and 1970-82 Corolla

1. Working at the steering knuckle arm, pull out the cotter pin and then remove the castellated nut.

2. Using a tie rod end puller, disconnect the tie rod from the steering knuckle arm.

3. Repeat the first two steps on the other end of the tie rod (where it attaches to the relay rod).

To install:

1. Turn the tie rods in their adjusting tubes until they are of equal lengths.

2. Turn the tie rod ends so that they cross at 90°. Tighten the adjusting tube clamps so that they lock the ends in position.

3. Connect the tie rods and tighten the nuts to 37-50 ft.lb.

4. Check the toe. Adjust if necessary.

Tercel, Starlet, 1983 and Later Corolla

1. Raise the front of the vehicle and support it with jackstands. Remove the wheel.

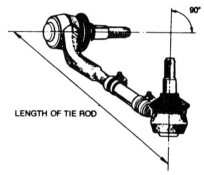

LENGTH OF TIE ROD

Make sure to position the tie-rod properly before installation

2. Remove the cotter pin and nut holding the tie rod to the steering knuckle.

3. Using a tie rod removal tool, press the tie rod out of the knuckle.

4. Matchmark the inner end of the tie rod to the end of the steering rack.

5. Loosen the pinch bolt and pull the tie rod off of the steering rack.

6. Repeat Steps 2-5 on the other side of the car.

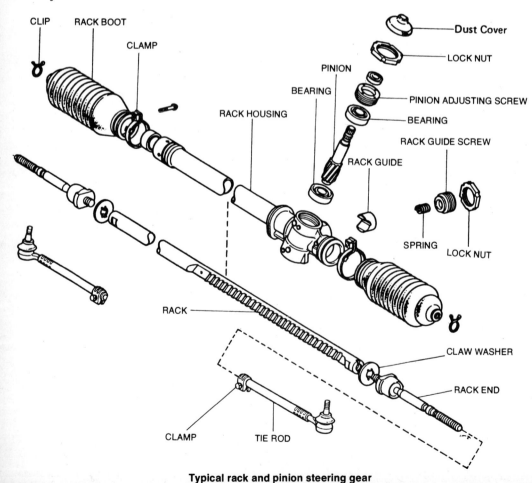

Typical rack and pinion steering gear

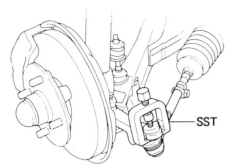

Removing the tie-rod end from the steering rack

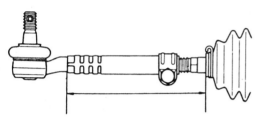

Tie-rod end measurement—1983 Tercel

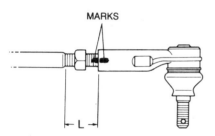

On the Corolla FWD, the distance (L) should measure 1.26 in.

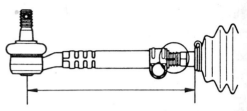

Tie-rod end measurement—Starlet and 1980–82 Tercel (note the matchmarks made during removal)

7. Install the tie rod ends onto the rack ends so that the tie rods are about 7.28" long on the 1983 Corolla 9.06" long on the 1984 Corolla RWD; 11.5" long on the Tercel and 9.72" long on the Starlet. Tighten the pinch bolts to 11-14 ft.lb. On the Corolla FWD, measure between the beginning of threading on the rod and the lip on the tie rod end. It should be approximately 1.26". Tighten the locknuts to 35 ft.lb.

8. Installation is in the reverse order of removal.

Power Steering Pump
REMOVAL AND INSTALLATION

1. Remove the fan shroud.
2. Unfasten the nut from the center of the pump pulley.
    NOTE: *Use the drive belt as a brake to keep the pulley from rotating.*
3. Withdraw the drive belt.
4. Remove the pulley and the Woodruff key from the pump shaft.
5. Detach the intake and outlet hoses from the pump reservoir.

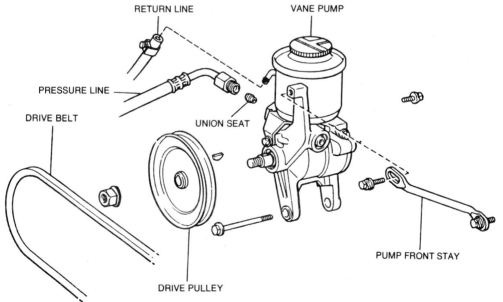

Power steering pump and related components

NOTE: *Tie the hose ends up high, so that the fluid cannot flow out of them. Drain of plug the pump to prevent fluid leakage.*

6. Remove the bolt from the rear mounting brace.

7. Remove the front bracket bolts and withdraw the pump.

Installation is performed in the reverse order of removal. Note the following, however:

1. Tighten the pump pulley mounting bolt to 25-39 ft.lb.

2. Adjust the pump drive belt tension. The belt should deflect 0.31-0.39" when 22 lbs. pressure is applied midway between the air pump and the power steering pump.

3. Fill the reservoir with Dexron®II automatic transmission fluid. Bleed the air from the system.

BLEEDING

1. Raise the front of the car and support it securely with jackstands.

2. Fill the pump reservoir with DEXRON®II automatic transmission fluid.

3. Rotate the steering wheel from lock-to-lock several times. Add fluid as necessary.

4. With the steering wheel turned fully to one lock, crank the starter while watching the fluid level in the reservoir.

NOTE: *Disconnect the high tension lead from the coil; do not start the engine. Operate the starter with a remote starter switch or have an assistant do it from inside of the car. Do not run the starter for prolonged periods.*

5. Repeat Step 4 with the steering wheel turned to the opposite lock.

6. Start the engine. With the engine idling, turn the steering wheel from lock-to-lock two or three times.

7. Lower the front of the car and repeat Step 6.

8. Center the wheel at the midpoint of its travel. Stop the engine.

9. The fluid level should not have risen more than 0.2". If it does, repeat Step 7 again.

10. Check for fluid leakage.

Troubleshooting Basic Wheel Problems

Problem	Cause	Solution
The car's front end vibrates at high speed	• The wheels are out of balance • Wheels are out of alignment	• Have wheels balanced • Have wheel alignment checked/adjusted
Car pulls to either side	• Wheels are out of alignment • Unequal tire pressure • Different size tires or wheels	• Have wheel alignment checked/adjusted • Check/adjust tire pressure • Change tires or wheels to same size
The car's wheel(s) wobbles	• Loose wheel lug nuts • Wheels out of balance • Damaged wheel • Wheels are out of alignment • Worn or damaged ball joint • Excessive play in the steering linkage (usually due to worn parts) • Defective shock absorber	• Tighten wheel lug nuts • Have tires balanced • Raise car and spin the wheel. If the wheel is bent, it should be replaced • Have wheel alignment checked/adjusted • Check ball joints • Check steering linkage • Check shock absorbers
Tires wear unevenly or prematurely	• Incorrect wheel size • Wheels are out of balance • Wheels are out of alignment	• Check if wheel and tire size are compatible • Have wheels balanced • Have wheel alignment checked/adjusted

Troubleshooting Basic Tire Problems

Problem	Cause	Solution
The car's front end vibrates at high speeds and the steering wheel shakes	• Wheels out of balance • Front end needs aligning	• Have wheels balanced • Have front end alignment checked

Troubleshooting Basic Tire Problems (cont.)

Problem	Cause	Solution
The car pulls to one side while cruising	• Unequal tire pressure (car will usually pull to the low side)	• Check/adjust tire pressure
	• Mismatched tires	• Be sure tires are of the same type and size
	• Front end needs aligning	• Have front end alignment checked
Abnormal, excessive or uneven tire wear See "How to Read Tire Wear"	• Infrequent tire rotation	• Rotate tires more frequently to equalize wear
	• Improper tire pressure	• Check/adjust pressure
	• Sudden stops/starts or high speed on curves	• Correct driving habits
Tire squeals	• Improper tire pressure	• Check/adjust tire pressure
	• Front end needs aligning	• Have front end alignment checked

Troubleshooting the Steering Column

Problem	Cause	Solution
Will not lock	• Lockbolt spring broken or defective	• Replace lock bolt spring
High effort (required to turn ignition key and lock cylinder)	• Lock cylinder defective	• Replace lock cylinder
	• Ignition switch defective	• Replace ignition switch
	• Rack preload spring broken or deformed	• Replace preload spring
	• Burr on lock sector, lock rack, housing, support or remote rod coupling	• Remove burr
	• Bent sector shaft	• Replace shaft
	• Defective lock rack	• Replace lock rack
	• Remote rod bent, deformed	• Replace rod
	• Ignition switch mounting bracket bent	• Straighten or replace
	• Distorted coupling slot in lock rack (tilt column)	• Replace lock rack
Will stick in "start"	• Remote rod deformed	• Straighten or replace
	• Ignition switch mounting bracket bent	• Straighten or replace
Key cannot be removed in "off-lock"	• Ignition switch is not adjusted correctly	• Adjust switch
	• Defective lock cylinder	• Replace lock cylinder
Lock cylinder can be removed without depressing retainer	• Lock cylinder with defective retainer	• Replace lock cylinder
	• Burr over retainer slot in housing cover or on cylinder retainer	• Remove burr
High effort on lock cylinder between "off" and "off-lock"	• Distorted lock rack	• Replace lock rack
	• Burr on tang of shift gate (automatic column)	• Remove burr
	• Gearshift linkage not adjusted	• Adjust linkage
Noise in column	• One click when in "off-lock" position and the steering wheel is moved (all except automatic column)	• Normal—lock bolt is seating
	• Coupling bolts not tightened	• Tighten pinch bolts

Troubleshooting the Steering Column (cont.)

Problem	Cause	Solution
Noise in column (cont.)	• Lack of grease on bearings or bearing surfaces	• Lubricate with chassis grease
	• Upper shaft bearing worn or broken	• Replace bearing assembly
	• Lower shaft bearing worn or broken	• Replace bearing. Check shaft and replace if scored.
	• Column not correctly aligned	• Align column
	• Coupling pulled apart	• Replace coupling
	• Broken coupling lower joint	• Repair or replace joint and align column
	• Steering shaft snap ring not seated	• Replace ring. Check for proper seating in groove.
	• Shroud loose on shift bowl. Housing loose on jacket—will be noticed with ignition in "off-lock" and when torque is applied to steering wheel.	• Position shroud over lugs on shift bowl. Tighten mounting screws.
High steering shaft effort	• Column misaligned	• Align column
	• Defective upper or lower bearing	• Replace as required
	• Tight steering shaft universal joint	• Repair or replace
	• Flash on I.D. of shift tube at plastic joint (tilt column only)	• Replace shift tube
	• Upper or lower bearing seized	• Replace bearings
Lash in mounted column assembly	• Column mounting bracket bolts loose	• Tighten bolts
	• Broken weld nuts on column jacket	• Replace column jacket
	• Column capsule bracket sheared	• Replace bracket assembly
	• Column bracket to column jacket mounting bolts loose	• Tighten to specified torque
	• Loose lock shoes in housing (tilt column only)	• Replace shoes
	• Loose pivot pins (tilt column only)	• Replace pivot pins and support
	• Loose lock shoe pin (tilt column only)	• Replace pin and housing
	• Loose support screws (tilt column only)	• Tighten screws
Housing loose (tilt column only)	• Excessive clearance between holes in support or housing and pivot pin diameters	• Replace pivot pins and support
	• Housing support-screws loose	• Tighten screws
Steering wheel loose—every other tilt position (tilt column only)	• Loose fit between lock shoe and lock shoe pivot pin	• Replace lock shoes and pivot pin
Steering column not locking in any tilt position (tilt column only)	• Lock shoe seized on pivot pin	• Replace lock shoes and pin
	• Lock shoe grooves have burrs or are filled with foreign material	• Clean or replace lock shoes
	• Lock shoe springs weak or broken	• Replace springs
Noise when tilting column (tilt column only)	• Upper tilt bumpers worn	• Replace tilt bumper
	• Tilt spring rubbing in housing	• Lubricate with chassis grease
One click when in "off-lock" position and the steering wheel is moved	• Seating of lock bolt	• None. Click is normal characteristic sound produced by lock bolt as it seats.
High shift effort (automatic and tilt column only)	• Column not correctly aligned	• Align column
	• Lower bearing not aligned correctly	• Assemble correctly
	• Lack of grease on seal or lower bearing areas	• Lubricate with chassis grease
Improper transmission shifting— automatic and tilt column only	• Sheared shift tube joint	• Replace shift tube
	• Improper transmission gearshift linkage adjustment	• Adjust linkage
	• Loose lower shift lever	• Replace shift tube

Troubleshooting the Power Steering Pump

Problem	Cause	Solution
Chirp noise in steering pump	• Loose belt	• Adjust belt tension to specification
Belt squeal (particularly noticeable at full wheel travel and stand still parking)	• Loose belt	• Adjust belt tension to specification
Growl noise in steering pump	• Excessive back pressure in hoses or steering gear caused by restriction	• Locate restriction and correct. Replace part if necessary.
Growl noise in steering pump (particularly noticeable at stand still parking)	• Scored pressure plates, thrust plate or rotor • Extreme wear of cam ring	• Replace parts and flush system • Replace parts
Groan noise in steering pump	• Low oil level • Air in the oil. Poor pressure hose connection.	• Fill reservoir to proper level • Tighten connector to specified torque. Bleed system by operating steering from right to left—full turn.
Rattle noise in steering pump	• Vanes not installed properly • Vanes sticking in rotor slots	• Install properly • Free up by removing burrs, varnish, or dirt
Swish noise in steering pump	• Defective flow control valve	• Replace part
Whine noise in steering pump	• Pump shaft bearing scored	• Replace housing and shaft. Flush system.
Hard steering or lack of assist	• Loose pump belt • Low oil level in reservoir **NOTE:** Low oil level will also result in excessive pump noise • Steering gear to column misalignment • Lower coupling flange rubbing against steering gear adjuster plug • Tires not properly inflated	• Adjust belt tension to specification • Fill to proper level. If excessively low, check all lines and joints for evidence of external leakage. Tighten loose connectors. • Align steering column • Loosen pinch bolt and assemble properly • Inflate to recommended pressure
Foaming milky power steering fluid, low fluid level and possible low pressure	• Air in the fluid, and loss of fluid due to internal pump leakage causing overflow	• Check for leaks and correct. Bleed system. Extremely cold temperatures will cause system aeration should the oil level be low. If oil level is correct and pump still foams, remove pump from vehicle and separate reservoir from body. Check welsh plug and body for cracks. If plug is loose or body is cracked, replace body.
Low pump pressure	• Flow control valve stuck or inoperative • Pressure plate not flat against cam ring	• Remove burrs or dirt or replace. Flush system. • Correct
Momentary increase in effort when turning wheel fast to right or left	• Low oil level in pump • Pump belt slipping • High internal leakage	• Add power steering fluid as required • Tighten or replace belt • Check pump pressure. (See pressure test)
Steering wheel surges or jerks when turning with engine running especially during parking	• Low oil level • Loose pump belt • Steering linkage hitting engine oil pan at full turn • Insufficient pump pressure	• Fill as required • Adjust tension to specification • Correct clearance • Check pump pressure. (See pressure test). Replace flow control valve if defective.

Troubleshooting the Power Steering Pump (cont.)

Problem	Cause	Solution
Steering wheel surges or jerks when turning with engine running especially during parking (cont.)	• Sticking flow control valve	• Inspect for varnish or damage, replace if necessary
Excessive wheel kickback or loose steering	• Air in system	• Add oil to pump reservoir and bleed by operating steering. Check hose connectors for proper torque and adjust as required.
Low pump pressure	• Extreme wear of cam ring • Scored pressure plate, thrust plate, or rotor • Vanes not installed properly • Vanes sticking in rotor slots • Cracked or broken thrust or pressure plate	• Replace parts. Flush system. • Replace parts. Flush system. • Install properly • Freeup by removing burrs, varnish, or dirt • Replace part

NOISE DIAGNOSIS

The Noise Is	Most Probably Produced By
• Identical under Drive or Coast	• Road surface, tires or front wheel bearings
• Different depending on road surface	• Road surface or tires
• Lower as the car speed is lowered	• Tires
• Similar with car standing or moving	• Engine or transmission
• A vibration	• Unbalanced tires, rear wheel bearing, unbalanced driveshaft or worn U-joint
• A knock or click about every 2 tire revolutions	• Rear wheel bearing
• Most pronounced on turns	• Damaged differential gears
• A steady low-pitched whirring or scraping, starting at low speeds	• Damaged or worn pinion bearing
• A chattering vibration on turns	• Wrong differential lubricant or worn clutch plates (limited slip rear axle)
• Noticed only in Drive, Coast or Float conditions	• Worn ring gear and/or pinion gear

Troubleshooting Basic Steering and Suspension Problems

Problem	Cause	Solution
Hard steering (steering wheel is hard to turn)	• Low or uneven tire pressure • Loose power steering pump drive belt • Low or incorrect power steering fluid • Incorrect front end alignment • Defective power steering pump • Bent or poorly lubricated front end parts	• Inflate tires to correct pressure • Adjust belt • Add fluid as necessary • Have front end alignment checked/adjusted • Check pump • Lubricate and/or replace defective parts
Loose steering (too much play in the steering wheel)	• Loose wheel bearings • Loose or worn steering linkage • Faulty shocks • Worn ball joints	• Adjust wheel bearings • Replace worn parts • Replace shocks • Replace ball joints
Car veers or wanders (car pulls to one side with hands off the steering wheel)	• Incorrect tire pressure • Improper front end alignment • Loose wheel bearings • Loose or bent front end components • Faulty shocks	• Inflate tires to correct pressure • Have front end alignment checked/adjusted • Adjust wheel bearings • Replace worn components • Replace shocks

Troubleshooting Basic Steering and Suspension Problems (cont.)

Problem	Cause	Solution
Wheel oscillation or vibration trans-mitted through steering wheel	• Improper tire pressures • Tires out of balance • Loose wheel bearings • Improper front end alignment • Worn or bent front end compo-nents	• Inflate tires to correct pressure • Have tires balanced • Adjust wheel bearings • Have front end alignment checked/ adjusted • Replace worn parts
Uneven tire wear	• Incorrect tire pressure • Front end out of alignment • Tires out of balance	• Inflate tires to correct pressure • Have front end alignment checked/ adjusted • Have tires balanced

Brakes

BRAKE SYSTEM

Understanding the Brakes

HYDRAULIC SYSTEM

Basic Operating Principles

Hydraulic systems are used to actuate the brakes of all modern automobiles. The system transports the power required to force the friction surfaces of the braking system together from the pedal to the individual brake units at each wheel. A hydraulic system is used for two reasons. First, fluid under pressure can be carried to all parts of an automobile by small hoses, some of which are flexible, without taking up a significant amount of room or posing routing problems. Second, a great mechanical advantage can be given to the brake pedal end of the system, and the foot pressure required to actuate the brakes can be reduced by making the surface area of the master cylinder pistons smaller than that of any of the pistons in the wheel cylinders or calipers.

The master cylinder consists of a fluid reservoir and either a single or double cylinder and piston assembly. Double type master cylinders are designed to separate the front and rear braking systems hydraulically in case of a leak.

Steel lines carry the brake fluid to a point on the vehicle's frame near each of the vehicle's wheels. The fluid is then carried to the slave cylinders by flexible tubes in order to allow for suspension and steering movements.

In drum brake systems, the slave cylinders are called wheel cylinders. Each wheel cylinder contains two pistons, one at either end, which push outward in opposite directions. In disc brake systems, the slave cylinders are part of the calipers. One or four cylinders are used to force the brake pads against the disc, but all cylinders contain one piston only. All slave cylinder pistons employ some type of seal, usually made of rubber, to minimize the leakage of fluid around the piston. A rubber dust boot seals the outer end of the cylinder against dust and dirt. The boot fits around the outer end of the piston on disc brake calipers, and around the brake actuating rod on wheel cylinders.

The hydraulic system operates as follows: When at rest, the entire system, from the piston(s) in the master cylinder to those in the wheel cylinders or calipers, is full of brake fluid. Upon application of the brake pedal, fluid trapped in front of the master cylinder piston(s) is forced through the lines to the slave cylinders. Here, it forces the pistons outward, in the case of drum brakes, and inward toward the disc, in the case of disc brakes. The motion of the pistons is opposed by return springs mounted outside the cylinders in drum brakes, and by internal springs or spring seals, in disc brakes.

Upon release of the brake pedal, a spring located inside of the master cylinder immediately returns the master cylinder piston(s) to the normal position. The pistons contain check valves and the master cylinder has compensating ports drilled in it. These are uncovered as the pistons reach their normal position. The piston check valves allow fluid to flow toward the wheel cylinders or calipers as the pistons withdraw. Then, as the return springs force the brake pads or shoes into the released position, the excess fluid reservoir through the compensating ports. It is during the time the pedal is in the released position that any fluid that has leaked out of the system will be replaced through the compensating ports.

Dual circuit master cylinders employ two pistons, located one behind the other, in the same cylinder. The primary piston is actuated directly by mechanical linkage from the brake pedal. The secondary piston is actuated by fluid trapped between the two pistons. If a leak develops in front of the secondary piston, it moves forward until it bottoms against the front of the master cylinder, and the fluid trapped between the pistons will operate the rear brakes. If the rear brakes develop a leak, the primary piston will move forward until direct contact with the secondary piston takes place, and it will force the secondary piston to actuate the front brakes. In either case, the brake pedal moves farther when the brakes are applied, and less braking power is available.

All dual-circuit systems use a distributor switch to warn the driver when only half of the brake system is operational. This switch is located in a valve body which is mounted on the firewall or the frame below the master cylinder. A hydraulic piston receives pressure from both circuits, each circuit's pressure being applied to one end of the piston. When the pressures are in balance, the piston remains stationary. When one circuit has a leak, however, the greater pressure in that circuit during application of the brakes will push the piston to one side, closing the distributor switch and activating the brake warning light.

In disc systems, this valve body also contains a metering valve and, in some cases, a proportioning valve. The metering valve keeps pressure from traveling to the disc brakes on the front wheels until the brake shoes on the rear wheels have contacted the drums, ensuring that the front brakes will never be used alone. The proportioning valve throttles the pressure to the rear brakes so as to avoid rear wheel lock-up during very hard braking.

These valves may be tested by removing the lines to the front and rear brake systems and installing special brake pressure testing gauges. Front and rear system pressures are then compared as the pedal is gradually depressed. Specifications vary with the manufacturer and design of the brake system.

Brake system warning lights may be tested by depressing the brake pedal and holding it while opening one of the wheel cylinder bleeder screws. If this does not cause the light to go on, substitute a new lamp, make continuity checks, and finally, replace the switch as necessary.

The hydraulic system may be checked for leaks by applying pressure to the pedal gradually and steadily. If the pedal sinks very slowly to the floor, the system has a leak. This is not to be confused with a springy or spongy feel due to the compression of air within the lines. If the system leaks, there will be a gradual change in the position of the pedal with a constant pressure.

Check for leaks along all lines and at wheel cylinders. If no external leaks are apparent, the problem is inside the master cylinder.

DISC BRAKES
Basis Operating Principles

Instead of the traditional expanding brakes that press outward against a circular drum, disc brake systems utilize cast iron disc with brake pads positioned on either side of it. Braking effect is achieved in a manner similar to the way you would squeeze a spinning phonograph record between your fingers. The disc (rotor) is a one-piece casting with cooling fins between the two braking surfaces. This enables air to circulate between the two braking surfaces making them less sensitive to heat buildup and more resistant to fade. Dirt and water do not affect braking action since contaminants are thrown off by the centrifugal action of the rotor or scraped off by the pads. Also, the equal clamping action of the two brake pads tends to ensure uniform, straight line stops. All disc brakes are inherently self-adjusting.

There are three general types of disc brake:
1: A fixed caliper, four piston type.
2: A floating caliper, single piston type.
3: A sliding caliper, single piston type.
The fixed caliper design uses two pistons mounted on either side of the rotor (in each side of the caliper). The caliper is mounted rigidly and does not move.

The sliding and floating designs are quite similar. In fact, these two types are often lumped together. In both designs, the pad on the inside of the rotor is moved into contact with the rotor by hydraulic force. The caliper, which is not held in a fixed position, moves slightly, bringing the outside pad into contact with the rotor. There are various methods of attaching floating calipers. Some pivot at the bottom or top, and some slide on mounting bolts, In any event, the end result is the same.

DRUM BRAKES
Basic Operating Principles

Drum brakes employ two brake shoes mounted on a stationary backing plate. These shoes are positioned inside a circular cast iron drum which rotates with the wheel assembly. The shoes are held in place by springs; this allows them to slide toward the drums (when they are applied) while keeping the linings and drums in alignment. The shoes are actuated by a wheel cylinder which is mounted at the top of the backing plate. When the brakes are applied, hydraulic pressure forces the wheel cylinder's two actuating links outward. Since these links bear directly against the top of the brake shoes, the tops of the shoes are then forced outward against the inner side of the drum. This action forces the bottoms of the two shoes to contact the brake drum by rotating the entire assembly slightly (known as servo action). When pressure within the wheel cylinder is relaxed, return springs pull the shoes back away from the drum.

Most modern drum brakes are designed to self-adjust themselves during application when the vehicle is moving in reverse. This motion causes both shoes to rotate very slightly with the drum, rocking an adjusting lever, thereby causing rotation of the adjusting screw by means of a star wheel.

POWER BRAKE BOOSTERS

Power brakes operate just as standard brake systems except in the actuation of the master cylinder pistons. A vacuum diaphragm is located on the front of the master cylinder and assists the driver in applying the brakes, reducing both the effort and travel he must put into moving the brake pedal.

The vacuum diaphragm housing is connected to the intake manifold by a vacuum hose. A check valve is placed at the point where the hose enters the diaphragm housing, so that during periods of low manifold vacuum brake assist vacuum will not be lost.

Depressing the brake pedal closes off the vacuum source and allows atmospheric pressure to enter on one side of the diaphragm. This causes the master cylinder pistons to move and apply the brakes. When the brake pedal is released, vacuum is applied to both sides of the diaphragm, and return springs return the diaphragm and master cylinder pistons to the released position. If the vacuum fails, the brake pedal rod will butt against the end of the master cylinder actuating rod, and direct mechanical application will occur as the pedal is depressed.

The hydraulic and mechanical problems that apply to conventional brake systems also apply to power brakes, and should be checked for if the tests below do not reveal the problem.

Test for a system vacuum leak as described below:

1. Operate the engine at idle with the transmission in Neutral without touching the brake pedal for at least one minute.

2. Turn off the engine, and wait one minute.

3. Test for the presence of assist vacuum by depressing the brake pedal and releasing it several times. Light application will produce less and less pedal travel, if vacuum was present. If there is no vacuum, air is leaking into the system somewhere.

Test for system operation as follows:

1. Pump the brake pedal (with engine off) until the supply vacuum is entirely gone.

2. Put a light, steady pressure on the pedal.

3. Start the engine, and operate it at idle with the transmission in Neutral. If the system is operating, the brake pedal should fall toward the floor is constant pressure is maintained on the pedal.

Power brake systems may be tested by hydraulic leaks just as ordinary systems are tested, except that the engine should be idling with the transmission in Neutral throughout the test.

Adjustments
DISC BRAKES

All disc brakes are inherently self-adjusting. No periodic adjustment is either necessary or possible.

DRUM BRAKES

The rear drum brakes used on all models in this manual except the Corolla 1200 are equipped with automatic adjusters actuated by the parking brake mechanism. No periodic adjustment of the drum brakes is necessary if this mechanism is working properly. If the brake shoe-to-drum clearance is incorrect, and applying and releasing the parking brake a few times does not adjust it properly, the parts will have to be disassembled for repair.

Corolla 1200

Corolla 1200 models are equipped with rear drum brakes which require manual adjustment. Perform the adjustment in the following order:

1. Chock the front wheels and fully release the parking brake.

2. Raise the rear of the car and support it with jackstands.

CAUTION: *Be sure that the car is securely supported. Remember; you will be working underneath it.*

3. Remove the adjusting hole plug from the backing plate.

4. Expand the brake shoes by turning the adjusting wheel with a starwheel adjusting tool or appropriate thin-bladed tool.

5. Pump the brake pedal several times, while expanding the shoes, so that the shoe contact the drum evenly.

NOTE: *If the wheel still turns when your foot is removed from the brake pedal, continue expanding the shoes until the wheel locks.*

6. Back off on the adjuster just enough so that the wheel rotates without dragging.

7. After this point is reached, continue backing off for five additional notches.

8. If the wheel still does not turn freely, back off one or two more notches. If after this, it still drags, check for worn or defective parts.

9. Pump the brake pedal again, and check wheel rotation.

10. Reverse Steps 1-3.

Master Cylinder

REMOVAL AND INSTALLATION

CAUTION: *Be careful not to spill brake fluid on the painted surfaces of the vehicle; it will damage the paint.*

1. Unfasten the hydraulic lines from the master cylinder.

2. Detach the hydraulic fluid pressure differential switch wiring connectors. On models with ESP, disconnect the fluid level sensor wiring connectors, as well.

3. Loosen the master cylinder reservoir mounting bolt.

4. Then, do one of the following:

a. On models with manual brakes remove the master cylinder securing bolts and the clevis pin from the brake pedal. Remove the master cylinder.

b. On models with power brakes, unfasten the nuts and remove the master cylinder assembly from the power brake unit (vacuum booster).

Installation is performed in the reverse order of removal. Note the following, however:

1. Before tightening the master cylinder

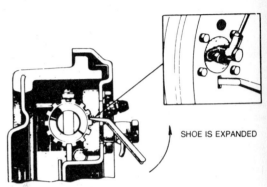

SHOE IS EXPANDED

Adjusting the brake shoe clearance

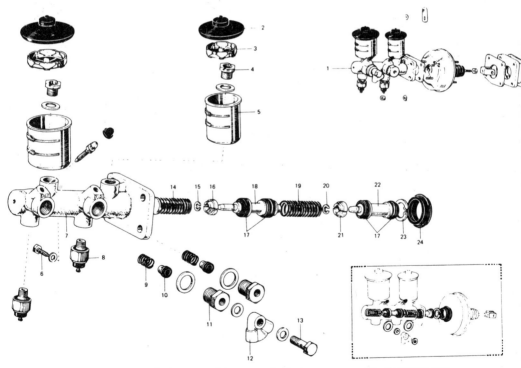

1. Master cylinder assembly	9. Spring	17. Cylinder cup
2. Reservoir cap	10. Check valve	18. No. 2 piston
3. Strainer	11. Plug	19. Spring
4. Reservoir set bolt	12. Union	20. Snap-ring
5. Reservoir	13. Union bolt	21. Retainer
6. Bolt	14. Spring	22. No. 1 piston
7. Master cylinder body	15. Snap-ring	23. Snap-ring
8. Pressure differential switch	16. Retainer	24. Rubber boot

Exploded view of an early tandem master cylinder

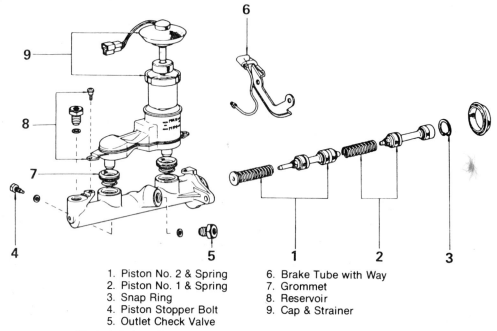

1. Piston No. 2 & Spring
2. Piston No. 1 & Spring
3. Snap Ring
4. Piston Stopper Bolt
5. Outlet Check Valve
6. Brake Tube with Way
7. Grommet
8. Reservoir
9. Cap & Strainer

Exploded view of a late model master cylinder—most models similar

mounting nuts or bolts, screw the hydraulic line into the cylinder body a few turns.

2. After installation is completed, bleed the master cylinder and the brake system as outlined following. Check the power booster piston rod-to-piston clearance, which should be 0.0039-0.020" at idle.

OVERHAUL

1. Remove the reservoir caps and floats. Unscrew the bolts which secure the reservoirs to the main body.

2. Remove the pressure differential warning switch assembly. Then, working from the rear of the cylinder, remove the boot, snapring, stop washer, piston No. 1, spacer, cylinder cup, spring retainer, and spring, in that order.

3. Remove the end plug and gasket from the front of the cylinder, then remove the front piston stop bolt from underneath. Pull out the spring, retainer, piston No. 2, spacer, and the cylinder cup.

4. Remove the two outlet fittings, washers, check valves and springs.

5. Remove the piston cups from their seats only if they are to be replaced.

6. After washing all parts in clean brake fluid, dry them with compressed air (if available). Inspect the cylinder bore for wear, scuff marks, or nicks. Cylinders may be hones slightly, but the limit if 0.006". In view of the importance of the master cylinder, it is recommended that it

be replaced, rather than overhauled, if worn or damaged.

7. Assembly is performed in the reverse order of disassembly. Absolute cleanliness is imperative. Coat all parts with clean brake fluid prior to assembly.

8. Bleed the hydraulic system after the master cylinder is installed, as detailed following.

Proportioning Valve

A proportioning valve is used on all models to reduce the hydraulic pressure to the rear brakes because of weight transfer during high speed stops. This helps to keep the rear brakes from locking up by improving front-to-rear brake balance.

The proportioning valve is located in the engine compartment, near the master cylinder.

REMOVAL AND INSTALLATION

1. Disconnect the brake lines from the valve unions.

2. Unfasten the valve mounting bolt, if used.

3. Remove the proportioning valve assembly. NOTE: *If the proportioning valve is defective, it must be replaced as an assembly; it cannot be rebuilt.*

4. Installation is the reverse of removal. Bleed the brake system after it completed.

Vacuum Booster

NOTE: *Vacuum boosters can be found only on models equipped with power brakes.*

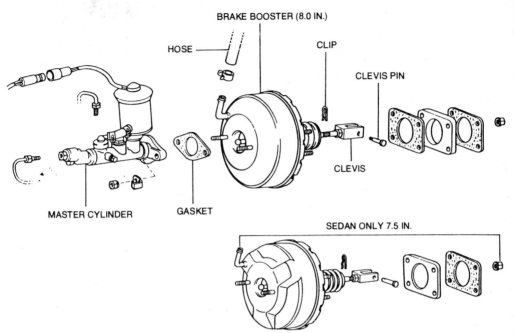

Exploded view of the master cylinder and vacuum booster assembly—late model Corolla shown

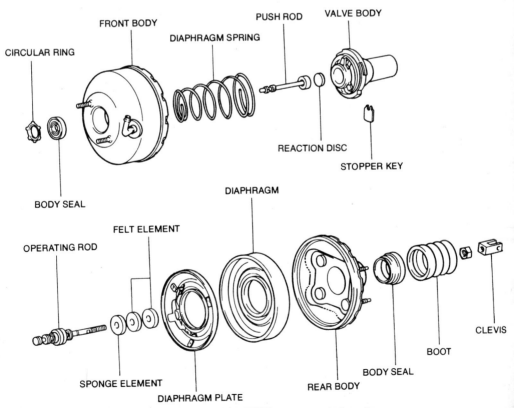

Exploded view of the AISIN-type vacuum booster

REMOVAL AND INSTALLATION

1. Remove the master cylinder as previously detailed.

2. Locate the clevis rod where it attaches to the brake pedal. Pull out the clip and then remove the clevis pin.

3. Disconnect the vacuum hose from the booster.

4. Loosen the four nuts and then pull out the vacuum booster, the bracket and the gasket.

5. Installation is in the reverse order of removal.

OVERHAUL

Aisin Type

1. Unscrew the nut at the front of the booster and remove the pushrod.

2. Loosen the retaining nut and then unscrew the clevis.

3. Pull off the rubber boot.

4. Pry out the air filter retainer from around the back of the booster and then remove the three filter elements.

5. Put an alignment mark across the front body, the band and the rear body.

6. Using Special Tool #09738-00010 or a few pieces of wood and some C-clamps, compress the rear body into the front body and remove the booster band. Separate the front and rear bodies from each other.

7. Carefully, remove the spring retainers, the reaction plate, the reaction levers and the rubber ring.

8. Use snapring pliers to remove the snapring in the diaphragm plate and then pull out the operating rod toward the rear.

9. Using a special retainer wrench, remove the retainer and then separate the diaphragm and the plate.

10. Assembly is in the reverse order of disassembly.

JKK Type

1. Loosen the retaining nut and unscrew the clevis. Remove the rubber boot.

2. Use a screwdriver to remove the air filter retainer and then pull out the two filter elements.

3. Put an alignment mark on the front and rear shells.

4. Use the Special Tool #09738-00010 or a few pieces of wood and some C-clamps to compress the rear shell into the front shell.

NOTE: *If the Special Tool is used, tighten its bolts to 35-52 ft.lb.*

5. Turn the front shell clockwise to separate the two shells and then remove the pushrod and the spring.

6. Remove the diaphragm from the diaphragm plate.

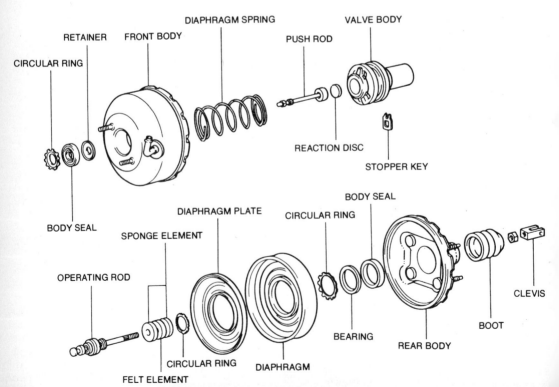

Exploded view of the JKK-type vacuum booster

7. Push the valve operating rod in and remove the stopper key.

8. Pull out the valve operating rod.

9. Assembly is in the reverse order of disassembly.

Bleeding

CAUTION: *Do not reuse brake fluid which has been bled from the brake system.*

1. Insert a clear vinyl tube into the bleeder plug on the master cylinder or the wheel cylinders.

NOTE: *If the master cylinder has been overhauled or if air is present in it, start the bleeding procedure with the master cylinder. Otherwise (and after bleeding the master cylinder), start with the wheel cylinder which is farthest from the master cylinder.*

2. Insert the other end of the tube into a jar which is half filled with brake fluid.

3. Slowly depress the brake pedal (have an assistant do it) and turn the bleeder plug ⅓-½ of a turn at the same time.

NOTE: *If the brake pedal is depressed too fast, small air bubbles will form in the brake fluid which will be very difficult to remove.*

4. Bleed the cylinder before hydraulic pressure decreases in the cylinder.

5. Repeat this procedure until the air bubbles are removed and then go on to the next wheel cylinder.

CAUTION: *Replenish the brake fluid in the master cylinder reservoir, so that it does not run out during bleeding.*

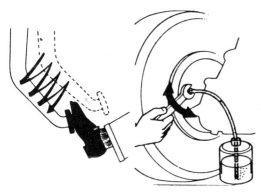

Bleeding the brakes

FRONT DISC BRAKES

Disc Brake Pads

INSPECTION

For proper inspection, the disc brake caliper and the brake pads themselves must be removed.

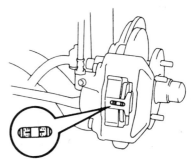

INSPECTION HOLE

For a quick check of the brake pads, use the inspection hole in the caliper—most late models similar

REMOVAL AND INSTALLATION

1970-79 Corolla and Carina

1. Raise and support the front of the vehicle on jackstands. Remove the front wheel.

2. Siphon a sufficient quantity of brake fluid from the master cylinder reservoir to prevent the brake fluid from overflowing the master cylinder when removing or installing pads. This is necessary as the piston must be forced into the cylinder bore to provide sufficient clearance to remove the pads.

3. Remove the four clips that hold the caliper guides in position.

4. Lightly tap out the guides (keys). Remember the correct positioning.

5. Lift the caliper off of the mounting bracket. It may be necessary to rock it back and forth a bit in order to seat the piston so it will clear the brake pads. Position the caliper out of the way and support it with wire so it doesn't hang by the brake lines.

6. Remove the brake pads from the mounting bracket. Do not remove the support springs.

7. A support plate is under each pad; they are not interchangeable and must be replaced correctly. Remove the support plates.

8. Inspect the brake disc (rotor) as detailed in the appropriate section.

9. Inspect the caliper and piston assembly for breaks, cracks or other damage. Overhaul or replace the caliper as necessary.

10. Replace the support plates in their original positions.

11. Place the new pads in the support bracket over the support springs.

12. Push the piston all the way back into its bore (a C-clamp may be necessary for this operation).

NOTE: *The piston must be turned back into its seated position on certain models. Check piston type before seating.*

13. Position the caliper over the pads and onto the mounting bracket.

14. Install the caliper guides (retaining keys) and then install the guide retaining pins.

15. Refill the master cylinder with fresh brake fluid.

16. Install the tire and wheel assembly and then pump the brake pedal several times to bring the pads into adjustment. Road test the vehicle.

NOTE: *If a firm pedal cannot be obtained, bleed the system as detailed in Bleeding the Brakes.*

Tercel and Corolla FWD

1. Raise and support the front of the vehicle on jackstands. Remove the wheel.

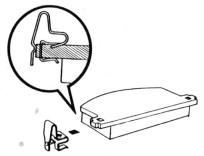

On Tercel and Corolla FWD models, the pad wear indicators must be installed so the arrow points in the direction of rotor rotation

2. Siphon a sufficient quantity of brake fluid from the master cylinder reservoir to prevent the brake fluid from overflowing the master cylinder when removing or installing the brake pads. This is necessary as the piston must be forced into the cylinder bore to provide sufficient clearance to remove the pads.

3. Remove the two caliper mounting bolts and then remove the caliper from the torque plate. It may be necessary to rock the caliper back and forth a bit in order to seat the piston so it will clear the brake pads. Position the caliper out of the way and support it with wire so it doesn't hang by the brake line.

4. Remove the two anti-squeal springs and then lift out the brake pads and the anti-squeal shims.

5. Remove the four pad support plates.

6. Check the brake disc (rotor) as detailed in the appropriate section.

7. Examine the dust boot for cracks or damage and then push the piston back into the cylinder bore. Use a C-clamp or other suitable tool to bottom the piston. If the piston is frozen, or if the caliper is leaking hydraulic fluid, the caliper must be overhauled or replaced.

8. Install four new pad support plate into the torque plate.

9. Install new pad wear indicator clips onto

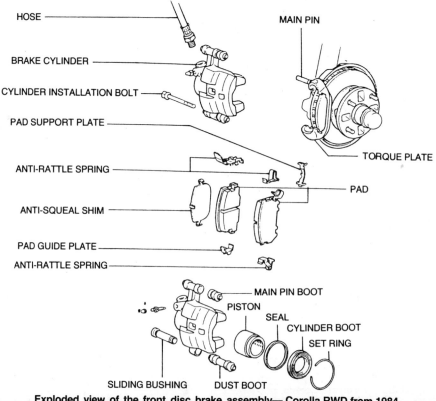

Exploded view of the front disc brake assembly— Corolla RWD from 1984

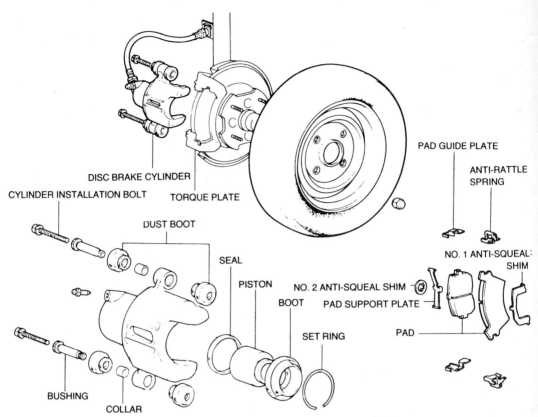

DISC BRAKE CYLINDER

CYLINDER INSTALLATION BOLT

TORQUE PLATE

DUST BOOT

SEAL

PISTON

NO. 2 ANTI-SQUEAL SHIM

BOOT

PAD SUPPORT PLATE

SET RING

BUSHING

COLLAR

PAD GUIDE PLATE

ANTI-RATTLE SPRING

NO. 1 ANTI-SQUEAL SHIM

PAD

Exploded view of the front disc brake assembly—Starlet

each pad. Install new anti-squeal shims onto the backing of each pad and then position the pads into the torque plate.

NOTE: *Make sure that the arrow on the pad wear indicator clip is pointing in the direction of rotor rotation when the pad is installed into the torque plate.*

10. Install the two anti-squeal springs.

11. Position the caliper on the torque plate, insert the mounting bolts and tighten them to 18 ft.lb.

12. Refill the master cylinder with fresh brake fluid.

13. Install the tire and wheel assembly and

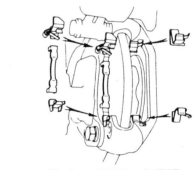

Hardware positioning—1984 Corolla RWD

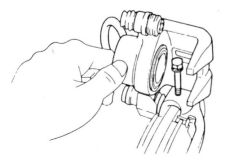

Use a bolt to secure the caliper—Corolla RWD from 1984

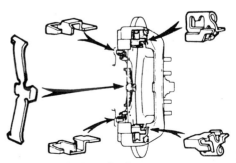

Hardware positioning—Starlet

NO. 2 ANTI-SQUEAL
SHIM

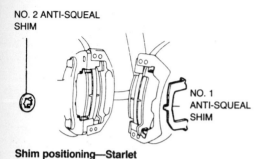

NO. 1
ANTI-SQUEAL
SHIM

Shim positioning—Starlet

then pump the brake pedal several times to bring the pads into adjustment. Road test the vehicle.

NOTE: *If a firm pedal cannot be obtained, bleed the system as detailed in Bleeding the Brakes.*

Starlet and Corolla RWD

1. Raise and support the front of the vehicle on jackstands. Remove the wheel.

2. Siphon a sufficient quantity of brake fluid from the master cylinder reservoir to prevent the brake fluid from overflowing the master cylinder when removing or installing the brake pads. This is necessary as the piston must be forced into the cylinder bore to provide sufficient clearance to remove the pads.

3. On the Starlet, remove the two caliper mounting bolts and then remove the caliper from the torque plate. It may be necessary to rock the caliper back and forth a bit in order to seat the piston so it will clear the brake pads. Position the caliper out of the way and support it with wire so it doesn't hang by the brake line. On the Corolla, remove the lower guide bolt. Swing the caliper upward and install a bolt into the torque plate to secure the caliper.

4. Lift out the brake pads and anti-squeal shims.

5. Remove the anti-rattle springs, pad guide plate and support plate.

6. Check the brake disc (rotor) as detailed in the appropriate section.

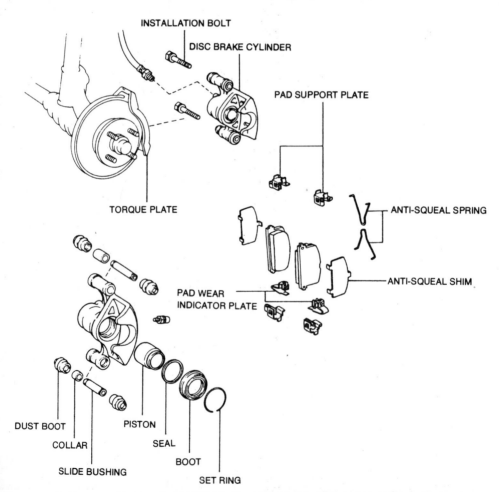

INSTALLATION BOLT

DISC BRAKE CYLINDER

PAD SUPPORT PLATE

TORQUE PLATE

ANTI-SQUEAL SPRING

ANTI-SQUEAL SHIM

PAD WEAR
INDICATOR PLATE

DUST BOOT

COLLAR

PISTON

SEAL

SLIDE BUSHING

BOOT

SET RING

Exploded view of the front disc brake assembly— Tercel and Corolla FWD from 1984

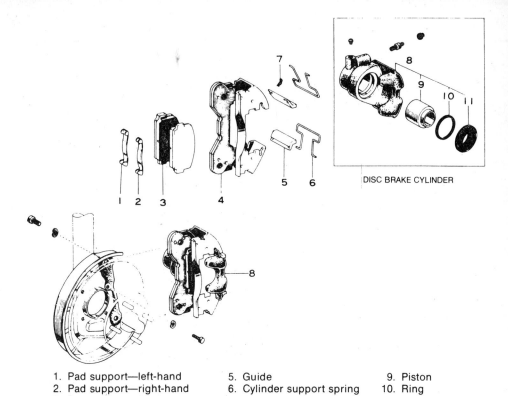

DISC BRAKE CYLINDER

1. Pad support—left-hand
2. Pad support—right-hand
3. Disc brake pad
4. Disc brake caliper mounting
5. Guide
6. Cylinder support spring
7. Clip
8. Caliper assembly
9. Piston
10. Ring
11. Cylinder boot

Exploded view of the front disc brake assembly—1970–79 Corolla and Carina

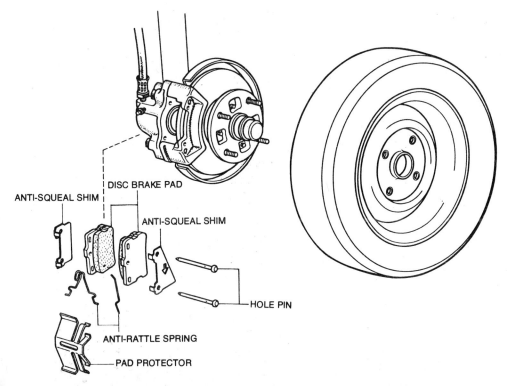

DISC BRAKE PAD

ANTI-SQUEAL SHIM

ANTI-SQUEAL SHIM

HOLE PIN

ANTI-RATTLE SPRING

PAD PROTECTOR

Exploded view of the front disc brake assembly—1980–83 Corolla

7. Examine the dust boot for cracks or damage and then push the piston back into the cylinder bore. Use a C-clamp or other suitable tool to bottom the piston. If the piston is frozen, or if the caliper is leaking hydraulic fluid, the caliper must be overhauled or replaced.

8. Install new pad support plates, guide plates and anti-rattle springs into the torque plate.

NOTE: *Be careful of the proper installation direction.*

9. On the Corolla, install new pad wear indicator clips onto each pad. Install a new anti-squeal shim onto the backing of the piston side pad and then position the pads into the torque plate.

10. On the Starlet, position the pads into the torque plate. Install the No. 1 anti-squeal shim onto the backing of the outer pad. Install the No. 2 shim to the backing of the piston-side pad.

11. On the Corolla, remove the bolt from the torque plate, swing the caliper into position, insert the guide bolt and tighten it to 14 ft.lb.

On the Starlet, position the caliper over the torque plate, insert the guide bolts and tighten them to 11-15 ft.lb.

12. Refill the master cylinder with fresh brake fluid.

13. Install the tire and wheel assembly and then pump the brake pedal several times to bring the pads into adjustment. Road test the vehicle.

NOTE: *If a firm pedal cannot be obtained, bleed the system as detailed in Bleeding the Brakes.*

Disc Brake Caliper

REMOVAL AND INSTALLATION

If you plan to overhaul the caliper, then you only need to remove the brake cylinder as detailed previously in the Brake Pad Removal and Installation section (1980-83 Corolla calipers are removed in the same way as the others). If the whole assembly must be removed (such as to remove the brake disc), unscrew the two mounting bolts on the back of the caliper mounting frame and pull the whole assembly off of the disc.

OVERHAUL

1. Remove the caliper cylinder from the car. On 1980-83 Corollas, you must first remove the

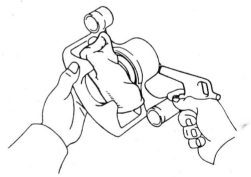

Use compressed air to remove the piston

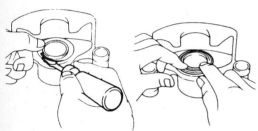

Removing the dust boot

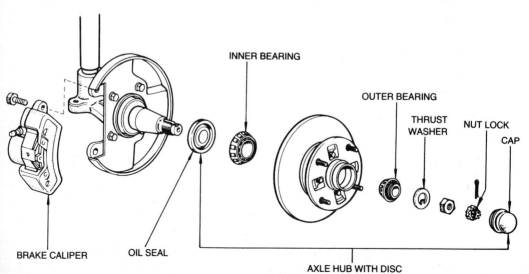

Brake disc and hub assembly—1980 and later Corolla RWD

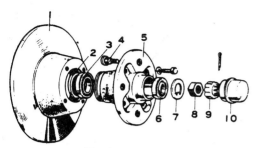

1. Disc
2. Oil seal
3. Tapered roller bearing
4. Hub bolt
5. Hub
6. Tapered roller bearing
7. Washer
8. Nut
9. Adjusting lock cap
10. Grease cap

Brake disc and hub assembly—Carina and 1970–79 Corolla

two bridge bolts in order to split the caliper halves.

2. Carefully remove the dust boot from around the cylinder bore.

3. Apply compressed air to the brake line union to force the piston out of its bore. Be careful, the piston may come out forcefully.

4. Remove the seal from the piston. Check the piston and cylinder bore for wear and/or corrosion. Replace components as necessary.

Assembly is performed in the following order:

1. Coat all components with clean brake fluid.

2. Install the seal and piston in the cylinder bore, after coating them with the rubber lubricant supplied in the rebuilding kit. Seat the piston in the bore with your fingers.

3. Fit the boot into the groove in the cylinder bore.

4. Install the caliper cylinder assembly.

Brake Disc

REMOVAL AND INSTALLATION

1. Remove the brake pads and the caliper, as detailed in the appropriate preceding section.

2. Loosen the bolts which secure the caliper mounting brackets. Withdraw the bracket, complete with the caliper support plates and springs attached.

3. Check the disc runout, as detailed following, at this point. Make a note of the results for use during installation.

4. Remove the grease cap from the hub. Remove the cotter pin and the castellated nut.

5. Remove the wheel hub with the brake disc attached. On the Tercel and Corolla FWD, sim-

ply unbolt the disc from the wheel hub. Perform the disc inspection procedure, as outlined in the following section.

Installation is performed in the following order:

1. Coat the hub oil seal lip with multipurpose grease and install the disc/hub assembly.

2. Adjust the wheel bearing preload, as detailed following.

3. Measure the disc runout. Check it against the specifications in the Disc and Pad Specifications chart and against the figures noted during removal.

NOTE: *If the wheel bearing nut is improperly tightened, disc runout will be affected.*

4. Install the caliper support, complete with springs. Tighten the securing nuts to 20-40 ft.lb.; 47 ft.lb., 1980 and later.

CAUTION: *Be careful not to distort the support springs during installation.*

5. Install the support plates and the brake pads in the same positions from which they were removed.

NOTE: *Install the pad support plate with the arrow pointing in the same direction as when it was removed.*

6. Install the remainder of the components as outlined in the appropriate preceding section.

7. Bleed the brake system.

8. Road test the car. Check the wheel bearing preload.

INSPECTION

Examine the disc. If it is worn, warped or scored, it must be replaced. Check the thickness of the disc against the specifications given in the Brake Specifications chart. If it is below specifications, replace it. Use a micrometer to measure the thickness.

The disc runout should be measured before the disc is removed and again, after the disc is installed. Use a dial indicator mounted on a stand to determine runout. If runout exceeds 0.006″ (all models), replace the disc.

NOTE: *Be sure that the wheel bearing nut is properly tightened. If it is not, an inaccurate*

Checking disc run-out

runout reading may be obtained. If different runout readings are obtained with the same disc, between removal and installation; this is probably the cause.

Wheel Bearings

REMOVAL AND INSTALLATION

Rear Wheel Drive

1. Remove the caliper and the disc/hub assembly, as previously detailed.

2. If either the disc or the entire hub assembly is to be replaced, unbolt the hub from the disc.

NOTE: *If only the bearings are to be replaced, to not separate the disc and hub.*

3. Using a brass rod as a drift, tap the inner bearing cone out. Remove the oil seal and the inner bearing.

NOTE: *Throw the old oil seal away.*

4. Drift out the inner bearing cup.

5. Drift out the outer bearing cup. Inspect the bearings and the hub for signs of wear or damage. Replace components, as necessary.

Installation is performed in the following order:

1. Install the inner bearing cup and then the outer bearing cup, by drifting them into place.

CAUTION: *Use care not to cock the bearing cups in the hub.*

2. Pack the bearings, hub inner well and grease cap with multipurpose grease.

3. Install the inner bearing into the hub.

4. Carefully install a new oil seal with a soft drift.

Preload Specifications

Model/Year	Initial Torque Setting (ft. lbs.)	Preload (oz.)
Starlet 1981–82	22	1–1.5
1983–84	22	0.8–1.9
Tercel 1980–87	22	13–30
Corolla 1975	19–23	6–13
1976–77	19–23	10–24
1978–87	19–23	11–25
Carina	19–24	10–22

5. Install the hub on the spindle. Be sure to install all of the washers and nuts which were removed.

6. Adjust the bearing preload, as detailed following.

7. Install the caliper assembly, as previously detailed.

PRELOAD ADJUSTMENT

1. With the front hub/disc assembly installed, tighten the castellated nut to the torque figure specified in the Preload Specifications chart.

2. Rotate the disc back and forth, two or three times, to allow the bearing to seat properly.

3. Loosen the castellated nut until it is only finger tight.

4. Tighten the nut firmly, using a box wrench.

5. Measure the bearing preload with a spring

Brake Specifications

(All measurements given are in. unless noted)

Model	Lug Nut Torque (ft. lbs.)	Master Cylinder Bore	Brake Disc Minimum Thickness	Brake Disc Maximum Run-Out	Brake Drum Diameter	Brake Drum Max. Machine O/S	Brake Drum Max. Wear Limit	Minimum Lining Thickness Front	Minimum Lining Thickness Rear
Corolla									
1200	65–86	0.626	0.350	0.0060	8.00	8.050	8.14	0.25	0.04
1600	65–86	0.813	0.350	0.0060	9.08	9.070	9.16	0.25	0.04
1800 ('80–'82),	66–86	—	0.453 ⑤	0.0059	9.00 ⑥	9.079 ⑦	—	0.04	0.04
1600 ('84–'87)	65–86	—	0.827	0.0060	—	9.079 ⑦	—	0.04	0.04
Carina	65–86	0.813	0.350	0.006	9.08	9.15	9.23	0.25	0.04
Tercel	65–86	—	0.354 ①	0.0059	7.087 ②	7.126 ③	—	0.04	0.04
Starlet	65–86	0.813	0.350 ④	0.0059	7.870	7.950	—	0.039	0.039

NOTE: Minimum lining thickness is as recommended by the manufacturer. Due to variations in state inspection regulations, the minimum allowable thickness may be different than recommended by the manufacturer.

① 1983 and later: 0.394
② Wagon and 4 x 4: 7.874
③ Wagon and 4 x 4: 7.913
④ 1983 and later: 0.354
⑤ RWD: 0.669   FWD: 0.492
⑥ FWD: 7.874
⑦ FWD: 7.913

scale attached to a wheel mounting stud. Check it against the specifications given in the Preload Specifications chart.

6. Install the cotter pin.

NOTE: *If the hold does not align with the nut (or cap) holes, tighten the nut slightly until it does.*

7. Finish installing the brake components and tI e wheel.

REAR DRUM BRAKES

Brake Drums

REMOVAL AND INSTALLATION

1. Remove the hub cap (if used) and loosen the lug nuts. Release the parking brake.

2. Block the front wheels, raise the rear of the car, and support it with jackstands.

Measuring wheel bearing preload with a spring scale

CAUTION: *Support the car securely.*

3. Remove the lug nuts and the wheel.

4. Unfasten the wheel bearing nut or the brake drum retaining screws.

5. Remove the brake drum. Tap the drum lightly with a mallet in order to free it. If the drum cannot be removed easily, insert a screwdriver into the hole in the backing plate and hold the automatic adjusting lever away from the adjusting bolt. Using another screwdriver relieve the brake shoe tension by turning the adjusting bolt clockwise. If the drum still will not come off, use a puller; but first make sure that the parking brake is released.

CAUTION: *Don't depress the brake pedal once the drum has been removed.*

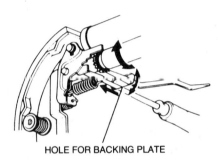

HOLE FOR BACKING PLATE

Backing off the brake shoes to remove the brake drum—most models similar

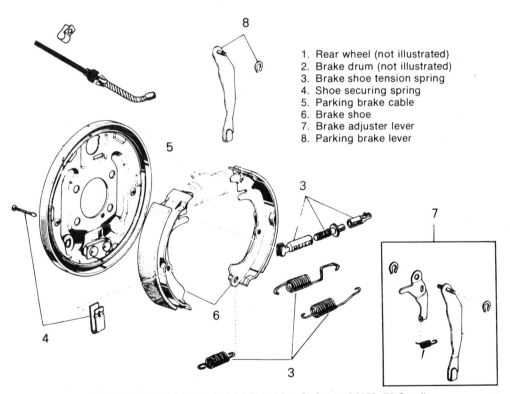

1. Rear wheel (not illustrated)
2. Brake drum (not illustrated)
3. Brake shoe tension spring
4. Shoe securing spring
5. Parking brake cable
6. Brake shoe
7. Brake adjuster lever
8. Parking brake lever

Exploded view of the rear brake assembly—Carina and 1970–79 Corolla

6. Inspect the brake drum as detailed following.

7. Brake drum installation is performed in the reverse order of removal.

INSPECTION

1. Clean the drum.

2. Inspect the drum for scoring, cracks, grooves and out-of-roundness. Replace or turn the drum, as required.

3. Light scoring may be removed by dressing the drum with fine emery cloth.

4. Heavy scoring will require the use of a brake drum lathe to turn the drum.

Brake Shoes

REMOVAL AND INSTALLATION

Tercel 4x4, 1984 and Later Tercel FWD Wagon, Corolla, Carina and Starlet

1. Perform the Brake Drum Removal procedure as previously detailed.

2. Unhook the shoe tension springs from the shoes with the aid of a brake spring removing tool.

3. Remove the brake shoe securing springs.

4. Disconnect the parking brake cable at the parking brake shoe lever.

5. Withdraw the shoes, complete with the parking brake shoe lever.

6. Unfasten the C-clip and remove the ad-juster assembly from the shoes. Inspect the shoes for wear and scoring. Have the linings replaced if their thickness is less than 0.04". Check the tension springs to see if they are weak, distorted or rusted.

7. Inspect the teeth on the automatic adjuster wheel for chipping or other damage.

Installation is performed in the following order:

NOTE: *Grease the point of the shoe which slides against the backing plate. Do not get grease on the linings.*

1. Attach the parking brake shoe lever and the automatic adjuster lever to the rear side of the shoe.

2. Fasten the parking brake cable to the lever on the brake shoe.

3. Install the automatic adjuster and fit the tension spring on the adjuster lever.

NOTE: *When assembling the rear shoe and the automatic adjuster, check the clearance between the shoe and the lever using a feeler gauge. Clearance should be 0-0.0138"; if not within specifications, adjustment can be made by replacing the shim on the adjusting lever shaft. Shims are available in 0.04" increments from 0.008-0.024" (there is also one measuring 0.035"). To replace the shim, remove the C-clip, install a shim of the proper thickness and then install a new C-clip.*

4. Install the securing spring on the rear

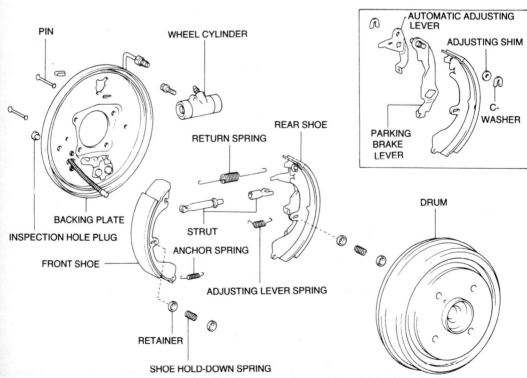

Exploded view of the rear brake assembly—Tercel wagon (FWD only) and Corolla FWD

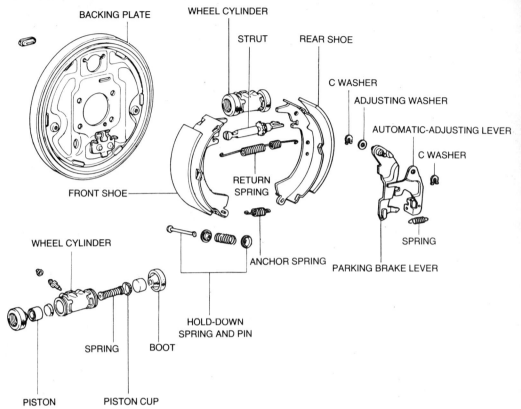

BACKING PLATE   WHEEL CYLINDER   STRUT   REAR SHOE   C WASHER   ADJUSTING WASHER   AUTOMATIC-ADJUSTING LEVER   C WASHER   RETURN SPRING   FRONT SHOE   SPRING   PARKING BRAKE LEVER   WHEEL CYLINDER   ANCHOR SPRING   HOLD-DOWN SPRING AND PIN   SPRING   BOOT   PISTON   PISTON CUP

Exploded view of the rear brake assembly—1980 and later Corolla RWD

shoe and then install the securing the spring on the front shoe.

NOTE: *The tension spring should be installed on the anchor, before performing Step 4.*

5. Hold one end of the tension spring over the rear shoe with the tool used during removal; hook the other end over the front shoe.

CAUTION: *Be sure that the wheel cylinder boots are not being pinched in the ends of the shoes.*

6. Test the automatic adjuster by operating the parking brake shoe lever.

7. Install the drum and adjust the brakes as previously detailed.

Tercel (Exc. 4x4, 1984 and later FWD Wagon)

1. Jack up your vehicle and support it with jackstands.

2. Remove the rear wheel.

3. Remove the bearing cap, cotter pin, locknut and adjusting nut.

4. Remove the brake drum.

NOTE: *When you remove the brake drum, the outer bearing, inner bearing and grease seal will come out at this time.*

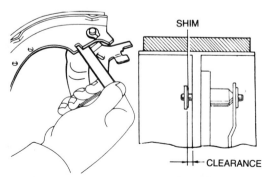

SHIM

CLEARANCE

Measuring the brake shoe to automatic adjuster lever clearance—typical Corolla RWD from 1984

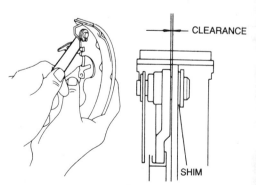

CLEARANCE

SHIM

Measuring the brake shoe to automatic adjuster lever clearance—typical except Corolla RWD from 1984

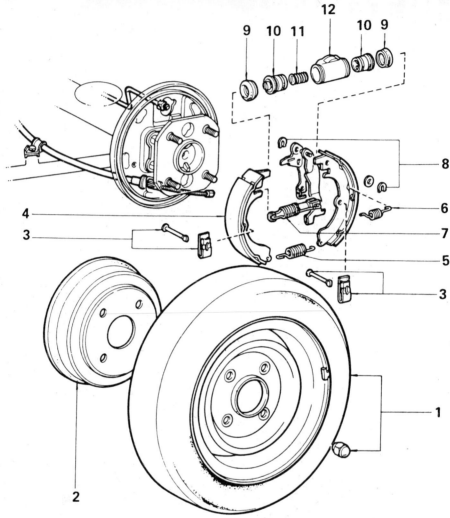

1. Wheel
2. Brake Drum
3. Shoe Hold Down Spring & Pin
4. Brake Shoe
5. Spring
6. Spring
7. Parking Brake Shoe Strut Set
8. Brake Shoe with Lever
9. Boot
10. Piston
11. Spring
12. Wheel Cylinder

Exploded view of the rear brake assembly—Starlet

5. Remove the brake shoe return spring and the hold down springs.

6. Remove the lower return spring.

7. Remove the front brake shoe.

8. Remove the parking brake strut.

9. Remove the rear shoe.

10. Disconnect the parking brake cable from the rear shoe.

11. Remove the parking brake lever from the rear shoe.

NOTE: *When reinstalling the parking brake lever be sure to use a new C-washer.*

12. Installation is the reverse of removal.

NOTE: *When assembling the rear shoe and the automatic adjuster, check the clearance* *between the shoe and the lever using a feeler gauge. Clearance should be 0-0.0138"; if not within specifications, adjustment can be made by replacing the shim on the adjusting lever shaft. Shims are available in 0.04" increments from 0.008-0.024" (there is also one measuring 0.035"). To replace the shim, remove the C-clip, install a shim of the proper thickness and then install a new C-clip.*

Wheel Cylinders

REMOVAL AND INSTALLATION

1. Plug the master cylinder inlet to prevent hydraulic fluid from leaking.

CHILTON'S
AUTO BODY REPAIR TIPS

Tools and Materials • Step-by-Step Illustrated Procedures
How To Repair Dents, Scratches and Rust Holes
Spray Painting and Refinishing Tips

With a little practice, basic body repair procedures can be mastered by any do-it-yourself mechanic. The step-by-step repairs shown here can be applied to almost any type of auto body repair.

TOOLS & MATERIALS

You may already have basic tools, such as hammers and electric drills. Other tools unique to body repair — body hammers, grinding attachments, sanding blocks, dent puller, half-round plastic file and plastic spreaders — are relatively inexpensive and can be obtained wherever auto parts or auto body repair parts are sold. Portable air compressors and paint spray guns can be purchased or rented.

Auto Body Repair Kits

The best and most often used products are available to the do-it-yourselfer in kit form, from major manufacturers of auto body repair products. The same manufacturers also merchandise the individual products for use by pros.

Kits are available to make a wide variety of repairs, including holes, dents and scratches and fiberglass, and offer the advantage of buying the materials you'll need for the job. There is little waste or chance of materials going bad from not being used. Many kits may also contain basic body-working tools such as body files, sanding blocks and spreaders. Check the contents of the kit before buying your tools.

BODY REPAIR TIPS

Safety

Many of the products associated with auto body repair and refinishing contain toxic chemicals. Read all labels before opening containers and store them in a safe place and manner.

• Wear eye protection (safety goggles) when using power tools or when performing any operation that involves the removal of any type of material.

• Wear lung protection (disposable mask or respirator) when grinding, sanding or painting.

Sanding

1 Sand off paint before using a dent puller. When using a non-adhesive sanding disc, cover the back of the disc with an overlapping layer or two of masking tape and trim the edges. The disc will last considerably longer.

2 Use the circular motion of the sanding disc to grind *into* the edge of the repair. Grinding or sanding away from the jagged edge will only tear the sandpaper.

3 Use the palm of your hand flat on the panel to detect high and low spots. Do not use your fingertips. Slide your hand slowly back and forth.

WORKING WITH BODY FILLER

Mixing The Filler

Cleanliness and proper mixing and application are extremely important. Use a clean piece of plastic or glass or a disposable artist's palette to mix body filler.

1 Allow plenty of time and follow directions. No useful purpose will be served by adding more hardener to make it cure (set-up) faster. Less hardener means more curing time, but the mixture dries harder; more hardener means less curing time but a softer mixture.

2 Both the hardener and the filler should be thoroughly kneaded or stirred before mixing. Hardener should be a solid paste and dispense like thin toothpaste. Body filler should be smooth, and free of lumps or thick spots.

Getting the proper amount of hardener in the filler is the trickiest part of preparing the filler. Use the same amount of hardener in cold or warm weather. For contour filler (thick coats), a bead of hardener twice the diameter of the filler is about right. There's about a 15% margin on either side, but, if in doubt use less hardener.

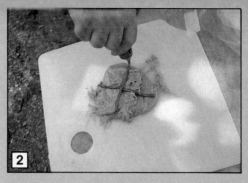

3 Mix the body filler and hardener by wiping across the mixing surface, picking the mixture up and wiping it again. Colder weather requires longer mixing times. Do not mix in a circular motion; this will trap air bubbles which will become holes in the cured filler.

Applying The Filler

1 For best results, filler should not be applied over ¼″ thick.

Apply the filler in several coats. Build it up to above the level of the repair surface so that it can be sanded or grated down.

The first coat of filler must be pressed on with a firm wiping motion.

Apply the filler in one direction only. Working the filler back and forth will either pull it off the metal or trap air bubbles.

REPAIRING DENTS

Before you start, take a few minutes to study the damaged area. Try to visualize the shape of the panel before it was damaged. If the damage is on the left fender, look at the right fender and use it as a guide. If there is access to the panel from behind, you can reshape it with a body hammer. If not, you'll have to use a dent puller. Go slowly and work the metal a little at a time. Get the panel as straight as possible before applying filler.

1 This dent is typical of one that can be pulled out or hammered out from behind. Remove the headlight cover, headlight assembly and turn signal housing.

2 Drill a series of holes ½ the size of the end of the dent puller along the stress line. Make some trial pulls and assess the results. If necessary, drill more holes and try again. Do not hurry.

3 If possible, use a body hammer and block to shape the metal back to its original contours. Get the metal back as close to its original shape as possible. Don't depend on body filler to fill dents.

4 Using an 80-grit grinding disc on an electric drill, grind the paint from the surrounding area down to bare metal. Use a new grinding pad to prevent heat buildup that will warp metal.

5 The area should look like this when you're finished grinding. Knock the drill holes in and tape over small openings to keep plastic filler out.

6 Mix the body filler (see Body Repair Tips). Spread the body filler evenly over the entire area (see Body Repair Tips). Be sure to cover the area completely.

7 Let the body filler dry until the surface can just be scratched with your fingernail. Knock the high spots from the body filler with a body file ("Cheesegrater"). Check frequently with the palm of your hand for high and low spots.

8 Check to be sure that trim pieces that will be installed later will fit exactly. Sand the area with 40-grit paper.

9 If you wind up with low spots, you may have to apply another layer of filler.

10 Knock the high spots off with 40-grit paper. When you are satisfied with the contours of the repair, apply a thin coat of filler to cover pin holes and scratches.

11 Block sand the area with 40-grit paper to a smooth finish. Pay particular attention to body lines and ridges that must be well-defined.

12 Sand the area with 400 paper and then finish with a scuff pad. The finished repair is ready for priming and painting (see Painting Tips).

Materials and photos courtesy of Ritt Jones Auto Body, Prospect Park, PA.

REPAIRING RUST HOLES

There are many ways to repair rust holes. The fiberglass cloth kit shown here is one of the most cost efficient for the owner because it provides a strong repair that resists cracking and moisture and is relatively easy to use. It can be used on large and small holes (with or without backing) and can be applied over contoured areas. Remember, however, that short of replacing an entire panel, no repair is a guarantee that the rust will not return.

1 Remove any trim that will be in the way. Clean away all loose debris. Cut away all the rusted metal. But be sure to leave enough metal to retain the contour or body shape.

2 Grind away all traces of rust with a 24-grit grinding disc. Be sure to grind back 3-4 inches from the edge of the hole down to bare metal and be sure all traces of paint, primer and rust are removed.

3 Block sand the area with 80 or 100 grit sandpaper to get a clear, shiny surface and feathered paint edge. Tap the edges of the hole inward with a ball peen hammer.

4 If you are going to use release film, cut a piece about 2-3″ larger than the area you have sanded. Place the film over the repair and mark the sanded area on the film. Avoid any unnecessary wrinkling of the film.

5 Cut 2 pieces of fiberglass matte to match the shape of the repair. One piece should be about 1″ smaller than the sanded area and the second piece should be 1″ smaller than the first. Mix enough filler and hardener to saturate the fiberglass material (see Body Repair Tips).

6 Lay the release sheet on a flat surface and spread an even layer of filler, large enough to cover the repair. Lay the smaller piece of fiberglass cloth in the center of the sheet and spread another layer of filler over the fiberglass cloth. Repeat the operation for the larger piece of cloth.

7 Place the repair material over the repair area, with the release film facing outward. Use a spreader and work from the center outward to smooth the material, following the body contours. Be sure to remove all air bubbles.

8 Wait until the repair has dried tack-free and peel off the release sheet. The ideal working temperature is 60°-90° F. Cooler or warmer temperatures or high humidity may require additional curing time. Wait longer, if in doubt.

9 Sand and feather-edge the entire area. The initial sanding can be done with a sanding disc on an electric drill if care is used. Finish the sanding with a block sander. Low spots can be filled with body filler; this may require several applications.

10 When the filler can just be scratched with a fingernail, knock the high spots down with a body file and smooth the entire area with 80-grit. Feather the filled areas into the surrounding areas.

11 When the area is sanded smooth, mix some topcoat and hardener and apply it directly with a spreader. This will give a smooth finish and prevent the glass matte from showing through the paint.

12 Block sand the topcoat smooth with finishing sandpaper (200 grit), and 400 grit. The repair is ready for masking, priming and painting (see Painting Tips).

Materials and photos courtesy Marson Corporation, Chelsea, Massachusetts

PAINTING TIPS

Preparation

1 SANDING — Use a 400 or 600 grit wet or dry sandpaper. Wet-sand the area with a 1/4 sheet of sandpaper soaked in clean water. Keep the paper wet while sanding. Sand the area until the repaired area tapers into the original finish.

2 CLEANING — Wash the area to be painted thoroughly with water and a clean rag. Rinse it thoroughly and wipe the surface dry until you're sure it's completely free of dirt, dust, fingerprints, wax, detergent or other foreign matter.

3 MASKING — Protect any areas you don't want to overspray by covering them with masking tape and newspaper. Be careful not get fingerprints on the area to be painted.

4 PRIMING — All exposed metal should be primed before painting. Primer protects the metal and provides an excellent surface for paint adhesion. When the primer is dry, wet-sand the area again with 600 grit wet-sandpaper. Clean the area again after sanding.

Painting Techniques

P aint applied from either a spray gun or a spray can (for small areas) will provide good results. Experiment on an old piece of metal to get the right combination before you begin painting.

SPRAYING VISCOSITY (SPRAY GUN ONLY) — Paint should be thinned to spraying viscosity according to the directions on the can. Use only the recommended thinner or reducer and the same amount of reduction regardless of temperature.

AIR PRESSURE (SPRAY GUN ONLY) — This is extremely important. Be sure you are using the proper recommended pressure.

TEMPERATURE — The surface to be painted should be approximately the same temperature as the surrounding air. Applying warm paint to a cold surface, or vice versa, will completely upset the paint characteristics.

THICKNESS — Spray with smooth strokes. In general, the thicker the coat of paint, the longer the drying time. Apply several thin coats about 30 seconds apart. The paint should remain wet long enough to flow out and no longer; heavier coats will only produce sags or wrinkles. Spray a light (fog) coat, followed by heavier color coats.

DISTANCE — The ideal spraying distance is 8"-12" from the gun or can to the surface. Shorter distances will produce ripples, while greater distances will result in orange peel, dry film and poor color match and loss of material due to overspray.

OVERLAPPING — The gun or can should be kept at right angles to the surface at all times. Work to a wet edge at an even speed, using a 50% overlap and direct the center of the spray at the lower or nearest edge of the previous stroke.

RUBBING OUT (BLENDING) FRESH PAINT — Let the paint dry thoroughly. Runs or imperfections can be sanded out, primed and repainted.

Don't be in too big a hurry to remove the masking. This only produces paint ridges. When the finish has dried for at least a week, apply a small amount of fine grade rubbing compound with a clean, wet cloth. Use lots of water and blend the new paint with the surrounding area.

WRONG

Thin coat. Stroke too fast, not enough overlap, gun too far away.

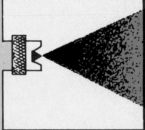

CORRECT

Medium coat. Proper distance, good stroke, proper overlap.

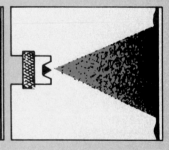

WRONG

Heavy coat. Stroke too slow, too much overlap, gun too close.

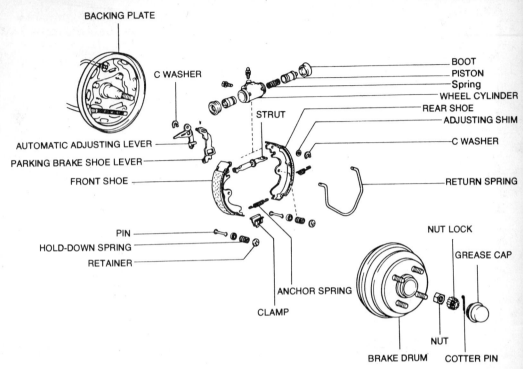

BACKING PLATE

C WASHER

BOOT
PISTON
Spring
WHEEL CYLINDER
REAR SHOE
ADJUSTING SHIM

STRUT

C WASHER

AUTOMATIC ADJUSTING LEVER
PARKING BRAKE SHOE LEVER
FRONT SHOE

RETURN SPRING

PIN
HOLD-DOWN SPRING
RETAINER

NUT LOCK

GREASE CAP

ANCHOR SPRING
CLAMP

NUT

BRAKE DRUM   COTTER PIN

Exploded view of the rear brake assembly—Tercel (exc. 4 x 4 and 1984 FWD wagon)

2. Remove the brake drums and shoes as detailed in the appropriate preceding section.

3. Working from behind the backing plate, disconnect the hydraulic line from the wheel cylinder.

4. Unfasten the screws retaining the wheel cylinder and withdraw the cylinder.

Installation is performed in the reverse order of removal. However, once the hydraulic line has been disconnected from the wheel cylinder, the union must be replaced. To replace the seat, proceed in the following manner:

1. Use a screw extractor with a diameter of 0.1″ and having reverse threads, to remove the union seat from the wheel cylinder.

2. Drive in the new union seat with a $\frac{5}{16}$″

bar, used as a drift. Remember to bleed the brake system after completing wheel cylinder, brake shoe and drum installation.

OVERHAUL

It is not necessary to remove the wheel cylinder from the backing plate if it is only to be inspected or rebuilt.

1. Remove the brake drum and shoes. Remove the wheel cylinder only if it is going to be replaced.

2. Remove the rubber boots from either end of the wheel cylinder.

3. Withdraw the piston and cup assemblies.

4. Take the compression spring out of the wheel cylinder body.

5. Remove the bleeder plug (and ball), if nec-

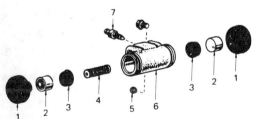

1. Wheel cylinder boot
2. Wheel cylinder piston
3. Cylinder cup
4. Compression spring
5. Union seat
6. Wheel cylinder body
7. Bleeder plug

Wheel-cylinder assembly

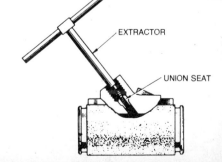

EXTRACTOR

UNION SEAT

Replacing the wheel cylinder union seat

essary. Check all components for wear or damage. Inspect the bore for signs of wear, scoring and/or scuffing. If in doubt, replace or hone the wheel cylinder (with a special hone). The limit for honing a cylinder is 0.005″ oversize. Wash all the residue from the cylinder bore with clean brake fluid and blow dry.

Assembly is performed in the following order:

1. Soak all components in clean brake fluid, or coat them with the rubber grease supplied in the wheel cylinder rebuilding kit.

2. Install the spring, cups (recesses toward the center), and pistons in the cylinder body, in that order.

3. Insert the boots over the ends of the cylinder.

4. Install the bleeder plug (and ball), if removed.

5. Assemble the brake shoes and install the drum.

REAR DISC BRAKES

Brake Pads

REMOVAL AND INSTALLATION

1. Raise and safely support the rear of the vehicle.

2. Remove the wheel and temporarily fasten the rotor in position with the lug nuts.

3. Check the pad thickness by looking through the center hole provided at the top of the caliper. Minimum thickness should be 0.039″.

4. Open the bleeder screw on the caliper and bleed off a small amount of brake fluid.

5. Disconnect the clip that attaches the parking brake cable. Pull the cable from the brake cable bracket at the caliper.

6. Remove the lower (towards ground) caliper mounting bolt. Pivot the caliper upward on the upper mounting bolt. Loosen the upper bolt slightly if required.

7. Take note of the position of the brake pads and mounting hardware while removing them. Remove the two brake pads, the two anti-squeal shims, two anti-rattle springs, pad support plate and two pad guide plates. Disassemble and assemble one side at a time so that the other side can be use for component part placement reference.

8. Check the rotor thickness and runout. Service as required. Assemble the brake pads in the support bracket in the reverse order of removal.

NOTE: *The caliper piston must be turned clockwise to retract it back into the caliper bore. Special Toyota tool SST 09719-14020 (09719-00020) or the equivalent is required).*

CAUTION: *Do not force by trying to push the caliper into the caliper bore or damage to the parking brake adjuster will occur.*

9. Turn the caliper piston clockwise, back into the caliper bore.

10. Lower the caliper and fit the brake pad protrusion (rear of inner pad) into the stopper groove in the caliper piston. (Align as required).

11. Finish lowering the caliper, taking care not to wedge the boot between the metal of the support bracket and caliper. Install the lower mounting bolt, tighten the mounting bolts to 14 ft.lb. Connect the parking brake cable. Adjust the parking brake by pulling and releasing the apply lever. Install the rear wheel. Fill the master cylinder and bleed the brake system.

Caliper

REMOVAL

1. Place a suitable container (to catch the brake fluid) under the brake hose to caliper mounting. Disconnect the brake line at the caliper.

2. Remove the brake pads and mounting hardware.

3. Remove the upper mounting bolt and remove the caliper.

OVERHAUL AND INSTALLATION

1. Remove the upper mounting bolt bushing and boot.

2. Remove the piston boot snapring and piston boot.

3. Use the special service tool or equivalent (mentioned in Pad Removal) to turn the caliper COUNTERCLOCKWISE out of the caliper bore.

4. Remove the piston seal from the caliper bore.

NOTE: *Special Service Tool SST 09756-00010, or the equivalent, is required to turn the internal parking brake adjusting nut so that snapring removal is possible.*

5. Postion the SST onto the parking brake adjuster nut (bottom of caliper bore) and tighten the nut slightly.

CAUTION: *Use the SST or suitable equivalent to ensure that the internally mounted spring will not fly out, causing injury or damage to the caliper bore. DO NOT tighten the adjuster TOO much!*

6. Remove the internal retainer snapring with suitable pliers. Remove the SST.

7. Remove the adjuster spring retainer, spring, spring plate and stopper together with the adjusting bolt.

8. Remove the strut. Remove the torsion spring from the parking brake crank lever.

9. Turn the crank to a position where it will

not catch on the stopper pin and remove it from the caliper.

10. Remove the crank boot.

11. Inspect all parts, service as required.

12. Install the parking crank boot into the caliper. Install the parking brake crank and torsion spring.

13. Check the clearance of the cable support bracket to caliper. Clearance should be 0.0197-0.0275″. Adjust the clearance with the cable support mounting bolt.

14. Install the strut into the caliper bore. Adjust the needle beraings so that they will not catch on the hole.

15. Install a new O ring on the adjuster bolt. Assemble the stopper, washer, spring and spring case to the adjuster bolt. Use the SST and fully tighten down by hand. Position the marked surface of the stopper upward. Align the notches on the spring case with the notches on the stopper.

16. Install the adjuster assembly into the caliper. Install the snapring with the opening in the snapring facing the bleeder hole. Remove the SST. Pull upward on the adjuster assembly and insure that it is secured.

17. Move the parking brake lever crank by hand to insure that the adjuster bolt moves smoothly.

18. Install the piston seal in the caliper bore groove.

19. Assemble the piston into the caliper bore by using the SST and slowly screwing in the piston CLOCKWISE. Screw in the piston until it will not desend any further. Align the center of the piston stopper groove with the positioning protrusion on the lower edge of the caliper.

20. Install the piston boot. Install the upper mounting bushing and boot.

21. Install the brake pads and caliper in the reverse order of removal. Tighten the mounting bolts to 14 ft.lb. Connect the parking brake cable. Connect the brake hose.

22. Fill the master cylinder reservoir. Adjust the parking brake and bleed the brake system. Check for fluid leakage.

Parking Brake
ADJUSTMENTS

NOTE: *On Corolla 1200 models, the rear brake shoes must be adjusted before performing this procedure. See the section on brake*

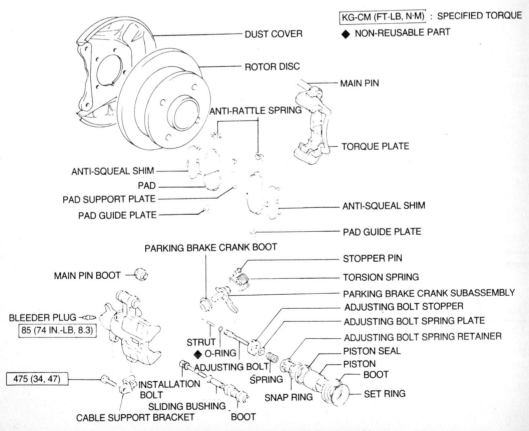

KG-CM (FT-LB, N·M) : SPECIFIED TORQUE
◆ NON-REUSABLE PART

DUST COVER
ROTOR DISC
MAIN PIN
ANTI-RATTLE SPRING
TORQUE PLATE
ANTI-SQUEAL SHIM
PAD
PAD SUPPORT PLATE
PAD GUIDE PLATE
ANTI-SQUEAL SHIM
PAD GUIDE PLATE
PARKING BRAKE CRANK BOOT
MAIN PIN BOOT
STOPPER PIN
TORSION SPRING
PARKING BRAKE CRANK SUBASSEMBLY
ADJUSTING BOLT STOPPER
BLEEDER PLUG
85 (74 IN.-LB, 8.3)
ADJUSTING BOLT SPRING PLATE
ADJUSTING BOLT SPRING RETAINER
STRUT
◆ O-RING
PISTON SEAL
PISTON
BOOT
ADJUSTING BOLT
475 (34, 47)
INSTALLATION BOLT
SPRING
SNAP RING
SET RING
SLIDING BUSHING
CABLE SUPPORT BRACKET
BOOT

Exploded view of the rear disc brake assembly

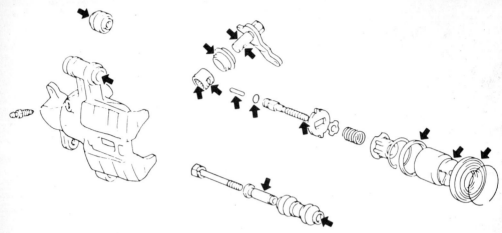

Exploded view of the rear disc brake-parking brake adjuster assembly

Parking Brake Adjustment

Model		Range of Adjustment (Notches)
Carina		3–7
Corolla	1200 ('70–'77)	7–8
	('78–'79)	4–12
	1600 ('70–'77)	2–4
	('78–'79)	4–12
	1800 ('80–'84)	4–7 ①
Tercel	('80–'82)	2–5
	Sedan ('83–'84)	5–8
	Wagon ('83–'84)	6–8
Starlet		3–6

NOTE: Two clicks equal one notch.
① 1984 RWD: 5–8

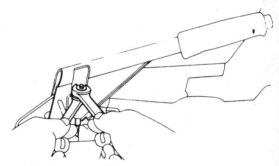

Adjusting the parking brake

adjustments at the beginning of this chapter for details.

1. Slowly pull the parking brake lever upward, without depressing the button on the end of it and while counting the number of notches required until the parking brake is applied.

NOTE: *Two clicks are equal to one notch.*

2. Check the number of notches against the specifications given in the Parking Brake Adjustment chart.

3. If the brake requires adjustment, loosen the cable adjusting nut cap which is located at the rear of the parking brake lever. Hold the cap with an open-end wrench.

4. Take up the slack in the parking brake cable by rotating the adjusting nut with another open-end wrench.

a. If the number of notches is less than specified, turn the nut counterclockwise.

b. If the number of notches is more than specified, turn the nut clockwise.

5. Tighten the adjusting cap, using care not to disturb the setting of the adjusting nut.

6. Check the rotation of the rear wheels to be sure that the brakes are not dragging.

Troubleshooting the Brake System

Problem	Cause	Solution
Low brake pedal (excessive pedal travel required for braking action.)	• Excessive clearance between rear linings and drums caused by inoperative automatic adjusters	• Make 10 to 15 alternate forward and reverse brake stops to adjust brakes. If brake pedal does not come up, repair or replace adjuster parts as necessary.
	• Worn rear brakelining	• Inspect and replace lining if worn beyond minimum thickness specification

Troubleshooting the Brake System (cont.)

Problem	Cause	Solution
Low brake pedal (excessive pedal travel required for braking action.) (cont.)	• Bent, distorted brakeshoes, front or rear • Air in hydraulic system	• Replace brakeshoes in axle sets • Remove air from system. Refer to Brake Bleeding.
Low brake pedal (pedal may go to floor with steady pressure applied.)	• Fluid leak in hydraulic system • Air in hydraulic system • Incorrect or non-recommended brake fluid (fluid evaporates at below normal temp). • Master cylinder piston seals worn, or master cylinder bore is scored, worn or corroded	• Fill master cylinder to fill line; have helper apply brakes and check calipers, wheel cylinders, differential valve tubes, hoses and fittings for leaks. Repair or replace as necessary. • Remove air from system. Refer to Brake Bleeding. • Flush hydraulic system with clean brake fluid. Refill with correct-type fluid. • Repair or replace master cylinder
Low brake pedal (pedal goes to floor on first application—o.k. on subsequent applications.)	• Disc brake pads sticking on abutment surfaces of anchor plate. Caused by a build-up of dirt, rust, or corrosion on abutment surfaces	• Clean abutment surfaces
Fading brake pedal (pedal height decreases with steady pressure applied.)	• Fluid leak in hydraulic system • Master cylinder piston seals worn, or master cylinder bore is scored, worn or corroded	• Fill master cylinder reservoirs to fill mark, have helper apply brakes, check calipers, wheel cylinders, differential valve, tubes, hoses, and fittings for fluid leaks. Repair or replace parts as necessary. • Repair or replace master cylinder
Decreasing brake pedal travel (pedal travel required for braking action decreases and may be accompanied by a hard pedal.)	• Caliper or wheel cylinder pistons sticking or seized • Master cylinder compensator ports blocked (preventing fluid return to reservoirs) or pistons sticking or seized in master cylinder bore • Power brake unit binding internally	• Repair or replace the calipers, or wheel cylinders • Repair or replace the master cylinder • Test unit according to the following procedure: (a) Shift transmission into neutral and start engine (b) Increase engine speed to 1500 rpm, close throttle and fully depress brake pedal (c) Slow release brake pedal and stop engine (d) Have helper remove vacuum check valve and hose from power unit. Observe for backward movement of brake pedal. (e) If the pedal moves backward, the power unit has an internal bind—replace power unit
Spongy brake pedal (pedal has abnormally soft, springy, spongy feel when depressed.)	• Air in hydraulic system • Brakeshoes bent or distorted • Brakelining not yet seated with drums and rotors • Rear drum brakes not properly adjusted	• Remove air from system. Refer to Brake Bleeding. • Replace brakeshoes • Burnish brakes • Adjust brakes

Troubleshooting the Brake System (cont.)

Problem	Cause	Solution
Hard brake pedal (excessive pedal pressure required to stop vehicle. May be accompanied by brake fade.)	• Loose or leaking power brake unit vacuum hose • Incorrect or poor quality brake-lining • Bent, broken, distorted brakeshoes • Calipers binding or dragging on mounting pins. Rear brakeshoes dragging on support plate.	• Tighten connections or replace leaking hose • Replace with lining in axle sets • Replace brakeshoes • Replace mounting pins and bushings. Clean rust or burrs from rear brake support plate ledges and lubricate ledges with molydisulfide grease. **NOTE:** If ledges are deeply grooved or scored, do not attempt to sand or grind them smooth—replace support plate.
	• Caliper, wheel cylinder, or master cylinder pistons sticking or seized • Power brake unit vacuum check valve malfunction	• Repair or replace parts as necessary • Test valve according to the following procedure: (a) Start engine, increase engine speed to 1500 rpm, close throttle and immediately stop engine (b) Wait at least 90 seconds then depress brake pedal (c) If brakes are not vacuum assisted for 2 or more applications, check valve is faulty
	• Power brake unit has internal bind	• Test unit according to the following procedure: (a) With engine stopped, apply brakes several times to exhaust all vacuum in system (b) Shift transmission into neutral, depress brake pedal and start engine (c) If pedal height decreases with foot pressure and less pressure is required to hold pedal in applied position, power unit vacuum system is operating normally. Test power unit. If power unit exhibits a bind condition, replace the power unit.
	• Master cylinder compensator ports (at bottom of reservoirs) blocked by dirt, scale, rust, or have small burrs (blocked ports prevent fluid return to reservoirs). • Brake hoses, tubes, fittings clogged or restricted • Brake fluid contaminated with improper fluids (motor oil, transmission fluid, causing rubber components to swell and stick in bores • Low engine vacuum	• Repair or replace master cylinder **CAUTION:** Do not attempt to clean blocked ports with wire, pencils, or similar implements. Use compressed air only. • Use compressed air to check or unclog parts. Replace any damaged parts. • Replace all rubber components, combination valve and hoses. Flush entire brake system with DOT 3 brake fluid or equivalent. • Adjust or repair engine
Grabbing brakes (severe reaction to brake pedal pressure.)	• Brakelining(s) contaminated by grease or brake fluid • Parking brake cables incorrectly adjusted or seized • Incorrect brakelining or lining loose on brakeshoes	• Determine and correct cause of contamination and replace brakeshoes in axle sets • Adjust cables. Replace seized cables. • Replace brakeshoes in axle sets

Troubleshooting the Brake System (cont.)

Problem	Cause	Solution
Grabbing brakes (severe reaction to brake pedal pressure.) (cont.)	• Caliper anchor plate bolts loose • Rear brakeshoes binding on support plate ledges	• Tighten bolts • Clean and lubricate ledges. Replace support plate(s) if ledges are deeply grooved. Do not attempt to smooth ledges by grinding.
	• Incorrect or missing power brake reaction disc • Rear brake support plates loose	• Install correct disc • Tighten mounting bolts
Dragging brakes (slow or incomplete release of brakes)	• Brake pedal binding at pivot • Power brake unit has internal bind	• Loosen and lubricate • Inspect for internal bind. Replace unit if internal bind exists.
	• Parking brake cables incorrrectly adjusted or seized • Rear brakeshoe return springs weak or broken	• Adjust cables. Replace seized cables. • Replace return springs. Replace brakeshoe if necessary in axle sets.
	• Automatic adjusters malfunctioning • Caliper, wheel cylinder or master cylinder pistons sticking or seized • Master cylinder compensating ports blocked (fluid does not return to reservoirs).	• Repair or replace adjuster parts as required • Repair or replace parts as necessary • Use compressed air to clear ports. Do not use wire, pencils, or similar objects to open blocked ports.
Vehicle moves to one side when brakes are applied	• Incorrect front tire pressure • Worn or damaged wheel bearings • Brakelining on one side contaminated	• Inflate to recommended cold (reduced load) inflation pressure • Replace worn or damaged bearings • Determine and correct cause of contamination and replace brakelining in axle sets
	• Brakeshoes on one side bent, distorted, or lining loose on shoe • Support plate bent or loose on one side • Brakelining not yet seated with drums or rotors • Caliper anchor plate loose on one side • Caliper piston sticking or seized • Brakelinings water soaked • Loose suspension component attaching or mounting bolts • Brake combination valve failure	• Replace brakeshoes in axle sets • Tighten or replace support plate • Burnish brakelining • Tighten anchor plate bolts • Repair or replace caliper • Drive vehicle with brakes lightly applied to dry linings • Tighten suspension bolts. Replace worn suspension components. • Replace combination valve
Chatter or shudder when brakes are applied (pedal pulsation and roughness may also occur.)	• Brakeshoes distorted, bent, contaminated, or worn • Caliper anchor plate or support plate loose • Excessive thickness variation of rotor(s)	• Replace brakeshoes in axle sets • Tighten mounting bolts • Refinish or replace rotors in axle sets
Noisy brakes (squealing, clicking, scraping sound when brakes are applied.)	• Bent, broken, distorted brakeshoes • Excessive rust on outer edge of rotor braking surface • Brakelining worn out—shoes contacting drum of rotor • Broken or loose holddown or return springs • Rough or dry drum brake support plate ledges	• Replace brakeshoes in axle sets • Remove rust • Replace brakeshoes and lining in axle sets. Refinish or replace drums or rotors. • Replace parts as necessary • Lubricate support plate ledges

Troubleshooting the Brake System (cont.)

Problem	Cause	Solution
Noisy brakes (squealing, clicking, scraping sound when brakes are applied.) (cont.)	• Cracked, grooved, or scored rotor(s) or drum(s)	• Replace rotor(s) or drum(s). Replace brakeshoes and lining in axle sets if necessary.
	• Incorrect brakelining and/or shoes (front or rear).	• Install specified shoe and lining assemblies
Pulsating brake pedal	• Out of round drums or excessive lateral runout in disc brake rotor(s)	• Refinish or replace drums, re-index rotors or replace

Body and Trim

EXTERIOR

Doors

REMOVAL AND INSTALLATION

1. With the door opened: Support the outer/lower edge of the door with a jack, placing a block of wood between the jack and the door.

2. Raise the jack until the wood is against, and putting slight upward pressure on the lower door edge. This will help support the door when the hinge mounting bolts are loosened.

3. On models so equipped, remove the door open check pin. Remove the body side hinge mounting bolts, lower hinge first.

4. Remove the door.

5. Install in the reverse order of removal. Adjust the door as required.

ADJUSTMENT

NOTE: *Special service tool SST 09812-22010 (for early models), SST 09812-00010 (for late models) or the equivalent is required to fit on the hinge bolts to aid in door position adjustment.*

1. To adjust the door in the forward-backward or up-down position, loosen the body hinge bolts slightly and use the SST to aid in proper door alignment

2. To adjust the door in the left-right or up-down position, loosen the door side hinge bolts and use the SST to aid in proper door alignment.

3. Tighten the door/body side hinge bolts and check alignment. Readjust if necessary. Check the position of the door lock striker.

4. If the striker is not in the correct position, loosen the mounting bolts slightly, and tap the striker (with a plastic hammer) into the correct position. Tighten the mounting bolts.

1. Door Stopper Pin
2. Door Panel Set Bolt
3. Door Panel

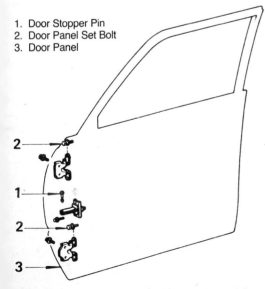

Tercel door mounting components—early model

1. Door Stopper Pin
2. Door Panel Set Bolt
3. Door Panel

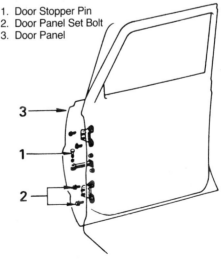

Starlet door mounting components

Door Locks

REMOVAL AND INSTALLATION

1. Have the window glass in the raised position. Remove the door trim panel and service hole cover.

2. Remove from the door lock assembly: The inside door opening control link, the door lock cylinder link, the door lock control link, the outside control link and the door lock mounting bolts/screws.

NOTE: *On models equipped with electric door locks, disconnect the negative battery cable prior to the start of servicing. Disconnect*

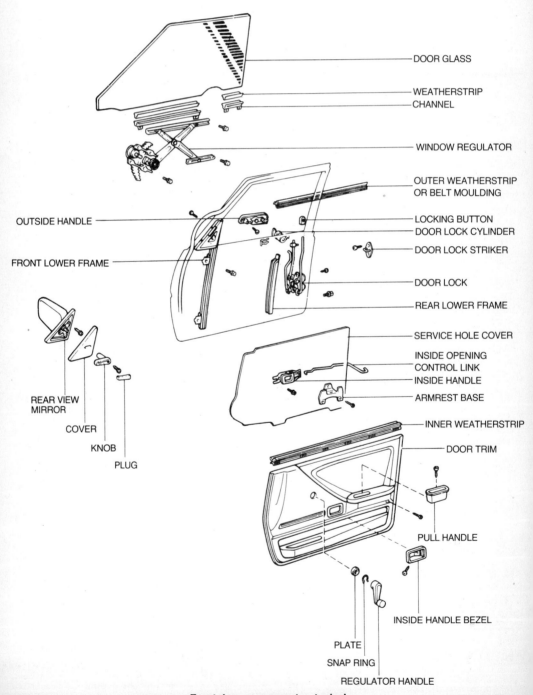

DOOR GLASS

WEATHERSTRIP
CHANNEL

WINDOW REGULATOR

OUTER WEATHERSTRIP
OR BELT MOULDING

OUTSIDE HANDLE

LOCKING BUTTON
DOOR LOCK CYLINDER
DOOR LOCK STRIKER

FRONT LOWER FRAME

DOOR LOCK

REAR LOWER FRAME

SERVICE HOLE COVER

INSIDE OPENING
CONTROL LINK
INSIDE HANDLE

REAR VIEW
MIRROR

ARMREST BASE

COVER

KNOB

PLUG

INNER WEATHERSTRIP

DOOR TRIM

PULL HANDLE

INSIDE HANDLE BEZEL

PLATE

SNAP RING

REGULATOR HANDLE

Front door components—typical

the links as described above. Remove the door lock knob, disconnect the door lock solenoid, remove the solenoid and the door lock.

3. Install the door lock in the reverse order. Check operation.

Hood

ADJUSTMENT

1. Loosen the hood hinge (hood side) mounting bolts slightly so that slight force is required

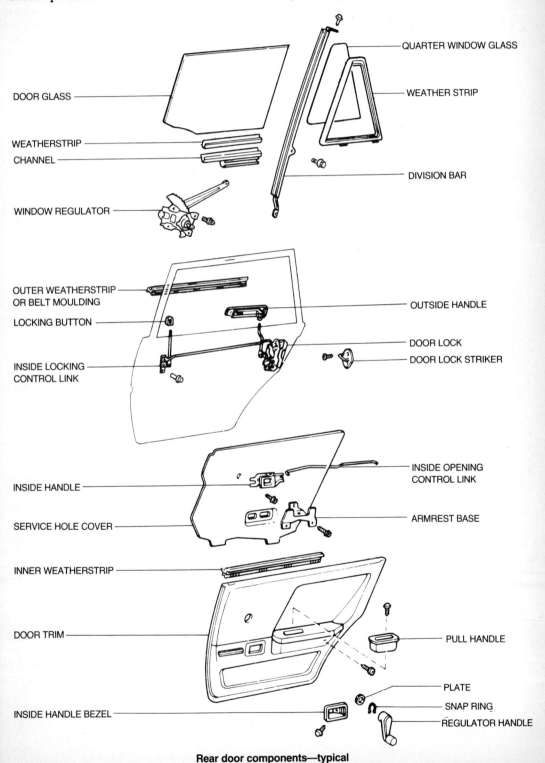

DOOR GLASS

WEATHERSTRIP

CHANNEL

WINDOW REGULATOR

OUTER WEATHERSTRIP OR BELT MOULDING

LOCKING BUTTON

INSIDE LOCKING CONTROL LINK

INSIDE HANDLE

SERVICE HOLE COVER

INNER WEATHERSTRIP

DOOR TRIM

INSIDE HANDLE BEZEL

QUARTER WINDOW GLASS

WEATHER STRIP

DIVISION BAR

OUTSIDE HANDLE

DOOR LOCK

DOOR LOCK STRIKER

INSIDE OPENING CONTROL LINK

ARMREST BASE

PULL HANDLE

PLATE

SNAP RING

REGULATOR HANDLE

Rear door components—typical

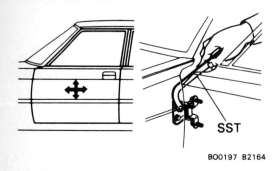

BOO197 B2164

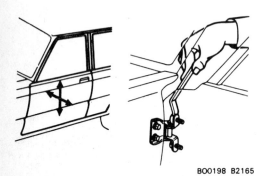

BOO198 B2165

Adjustment of door—typical late model

to move the hood. Pull the hood forward, or from side to side as required.

2. Make sure the space between the sides of the hood and the fenders are even, pull the hood forward or push rearward to align the front edge with the fender trim.

3. Tighten the hood hinge bolts, close the hood gently and check alignment. Readjust if necessary.

4. If the front edge of the hood is higher or lower than the fenders: Raise or lower the cushions that are mounted either at each side front on the inner fender/radiator support, or at the rear by the body side of the hood hinge(s).

Rear Hatch/Trunk Lid

ADJUSTMENT

1. Open the hatch/trunk lid. Loosen the door hinge mounting nuts slightly on the body side (hatch) lid side (trunk) of the vehicle.

2. The hatch/trunk lid may now be shifted as required.

3. Check the back hatch/trunk lid lock striker (cover panel removal may be required on some models) and adjust (if necessary) while observing the left and right lower back door and body clearance.

4. Tighten the hinge mounting nuts after adjustment is completed.

INTERIOR

Door Panels

REMOVAL AND INSTALLATION

1. Lower the door glass to the full down position.

2. Remove the window regulator handle. Use a clean cloth and position the edge between the rear of the window crank handle and door panel. Move the cloth backward and forward and around the handle base until the retaining snap ring is remove from its slot.

3. Remove the arm rest and inside door handle (unless the mounting bolts are covered by the door panel on later models) and bezel.

4. If the vehicle is equipped with an internal adjustable rear view mirror: Remove the set screw and adjusting knob, tape a screwdriver tip, pry loose the retainer and remove the inside cover. Remove the mounting screws/nuts and the mirror. If the mirror is motor driven, unplug the wire connecter.

5. Insert a taped screwdriver behind the door trim panel retainers and gently pry loose from the door. Disconnect the electric window control switch connector if equipped. Remove the panel. Remove the inner door handle after disconnecting the control link (late models).

6. Remove the inner weatherseal covering the door service access panel if further servicing is required.

7. Install the door panel in the reverse order of removal.

Door Glass/Window Regulator

REMOVAL AND INSTALLATION

1. Remove the door trim panel and weatherseal.

2. If the vehicle is equipped with power windows, disconnect the negative battery cable.

3. On early models: If the upper inner and outer weatherstrip is not contained on the door panel, remove them from the door.

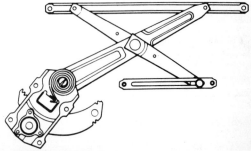

BOO194

Typical window regulator

4. Remove the lower glass channel through bolts that mount the lower edge of the glass to the regulator. Remove the glass by lifting upward and outward.

5. On late models: Raise the glass. Remove the glass edge run from the frame. Remove the frame mounting bolt and the frame. Lower the glass and remove the run. Lower the glass into the door and remove the glass channel mounting bolts. Remove the gall by pull it upward and outward through the top of the door.

6. If the vehicle is equipped with power windows, disconnect the wiring harness to the motor.

7. Remove the equalizer arm bracket mounting bolts.

8. Remove the regulator to door mounting bolts and remove the regulator through the service access hole in the inner door frame.

9. Inspect the regulator gears for wear, service as required. Install in the regulator and door glass in the reverse order of removal. Lubricate the regulator gears before installing the regulator.

How to Remove Stains from Fabric Interior

For rest results, spots and stains should be removed as soon as possible. Never use gasoline, lacquer thinner, acetone, nail polish remover or bleach. Use a 3′ x 3″ piece of cheesecloth. Squeeze most of the liquid from the fabric and wipe the stained fabric from the outside of the stain toward the center with a lifting motion. Turn the cheesecloth as soon as one side becomes soiled. When using water to remove a stain, be sure to wash the entire section after the spot has been removed to avoid water stains. Encrusted spots can be broken up with a dull knife and vacuumed before removing the stain.

Type of Stain	How to Remove It
Surface spots	Brush the spots out with a small hand brush or use a commercial preparation such as K2R to lift the stain.
Mildew	Clean around the mildew with warm suds. Rinse in cold water and soak the mildew area in a solution of 1 part table salt and 2 parts water. Wash with upholstery cleaner.
Water stains	Water stains in fabric materials can be removed with a solution made from 1 cup of table salt dissolved in 1 quart of water. Vigorously scrub the solution into the stain and rinse with clear water. Water stains in nylon or other synthetic fabrics should be removed with a commercial type spot remover.
Chewing gum, tar, crayons, shoe polish (greasy stains)	Do not use a cleaner that will soften gum or tar. Harden the deposit with an ice cube and scrape away as much as possible with a dull knife. Moisten the remainder with cleaning fluid and scrub clean.
Ice cream, candy	Most candy has a sugar base and can be removed with a cloth wrung out in warm water. Oily candy, after cleaning with warm water, should be cleaned with upholstery cleaner. Rinse with warm water and clean the remainder with cleaning fluid.
Wine, alcohol, egg, milk, soft drink (non-greasy stains)	Do not use soap. Scrub the stain with a cloth wrung out in warm water. Remove the remainder with cleaning fluid.
Grease, oil, lipstick, butter and related stains	Use a spot remover to avoid leaving a ring. Work from the outisde of the stain to the center and dry with a clean cloth when the spot is gone.
Headliners (cloth)	Mix a solution of warm water and foam upholstery cleaner to give thick suds. Use only foam—liquid may streak or spot. Clean the entire headliner in one operation using a circular motion with a natural sponge.
Headliner (vinyl)	Use a vinyl cleaner with a sponge and wipe clean with a dry cloth.
Seats and door panels	Mix 1 pint upholstery cleaner in 1 gallon of water. Do not soak the fabric around the buttons.
Leather or vinyl fabric	Use a multi-purpose cleaner full strength and a stiff brush. Let stand 2 minutes and scrub thoroughly. Wipe with a clean, soft rag.
Nylon or synthetic fabrics	For normal stains, use the same procedures you would for washing cloth upholstery. If the fabric is extremely dirty, use a multi-purpose cleaner full strength with a stiff scrub brush. Scrub thoroughly in all directions and wipe with a cotton towel or soft rag.

Mechanic's Data

General Conversion Table

Multiply By	To Convert	To	
LENGTH			
2.54	Inches	Centimeters	.3937
25.4	Inches	Millimeters	.03937
30.48	Feet	Centimeters	.0328
.304	Feet	Meters	3.28
.914	Yards	Meters	1.094
1.609	Miles	Kilometers	.621
VOLUME			
.473	Pints	Liters	2.11
.946	Quarts	Liters	1.06
3.785	Gallons	Liters	.264
.016	Cubic inches	Liters	61.02
16.39	Cubic inches	Cubic cms.	.061
28.3	Cubic feet	Liters	.0353
MASS (Weight)			
28.35	Ounces	Grams	.035
.4536	Pounds	Kilograms	2.20
—	To obtain	From	Multiply by

Multiply By	To Convert	To	
AREA			
.645	Square inches	Square cms.	.155
.836	Square yds.	Square meters	1.196
FORCE			
4.448	Pounds	Newtons	.225
.138	Ft./lbs.	Kilogram/meters	7.23
1.36	Ft./lbs.	Newton-meters	.737
.112	In./lbs.	Newton-meters	8.844
PRESSURE			
.068	Psi	Atmospheres	14.7
6.89	Psi	Kilopascals	.145
OTHER			
1.104	Horsepower (DIN)	Horsepower (SAE)	.9861
.746	Horsepower (SAE)	Kilowatts (KW)	1.34
1.60	Mph	Km/h	.625
.425	Mpg	Km/1	2.35
—	To obtain	From	Multiply by

Tap Drill Sizes

National Coarse or U.S.S.

Screw & Tap Size	Threads Per Inch	Use Drill Number
No. 5	40	.39
No. 6	32	.36
No. 8	32	.29
No. 10	24	.25
No. 12	24	.17
1/4	20	8
5/16	18	.F
3/8	16	5/16
7/16	14	.U
1/2	13	27/64
9/16	12	31/64
5/8	11	17/32
3/4	10	21/32
7/8	9	49/64

National Coarse or U.S.S.

Screw & Tap Size	Threads Per Inch	Use Drill Number
1	8	7/8
1 1/8	7	63/64
1 1/4	7	1 7/64
1 1/2	6	1 11/32

National Fine or S.A.E.

Screw & Tap Size	Threads Per Inch	Use Drill Number
No. 5	44	.37
No. 6	40	.33
No. 8	36	.29
No. 10	32	.21

National Fine or S.A.E.

Screw & Tap Size	Threads Per Inch	Use Drill Number
No. 12	28	.15
1/4	28	3
6/16	24	1
3/8	24	.Q
7/16	20	.W
1/2	20	29/64
9/16	18	33/64
5/8	18	37/64
3/4	16	11/16
7/8	14	13/16
1 1/8	12	1 3/64
1 1/4	12	1 11/64
1 1/2	12	1 27/64

Drill Sizes In Decimal Equivalents

Inch	Decimal	Wire	mm
1/64	.0156		.39
	.0157		.4
	.0160	78	
	.0165		.42
	.0173		.44
	.0177		.45
	.0180	77	
	.0181		.46
	.0189		.48
	.0197		.5
	.0200	76	
	.0210	75	
	.0217		.55
	.0225	74	
	.0236		.6
	.0240	73	
	.0250	72	
	.0256		.65
	.0260	71	
	.0276		.7
	.0280	70	
	.0292	69	
	.0295		.75
	.0310	68	
1/32	.0312		.79
	.0315		.8
	.0320	67	
	.0330	66	
	.0335		.85
	.0350	65	
	.0354		.9
	.0360	64	
	.0370	63	
	.0374		.95
	.0380	62	
	.0390	61	
	.0394		1.0
	.0400	60	
	.0410	59	
	.0413		1.05
	.0420	58	
	.0430	57	
	.0433		1.1
	.0453		1.15
3/64	.0465	56	
	.0469		1.19
	.0472		1.2
	.0492		1.25
	.0512		1.3
	.0520	55	
	.0531		1.35
	.0550	54	
	.0551		1.4
	.0571		1.45
	.0591		1.5
	.0595	53	
	.0610		1.55
1/16	.0625		1.59
	.0630		1.6
	.0635	52	
	.0650		1.65
	.0669		1.7
	.0670	51	
	.0689		1.75
	.0700	50	
	.0709		1.8
	.0728		1.85

Inch	Decimal	Wire	mm
	.0730	49	
	.0748		1.9
	.0760	48	
	.0768		1.95
5/64	.0781		1.98
	.0785	47	
	.0787		2.0
	.0807		2.05
	.0810	46	
	.0820	45	
	.0827		2.1
	.0846		2.15
	.0860	44	
	.0866		2.2
	.0886		2.25
	.0890	43	
	.0906		2.3
	.0925		2.35
	.0935	42	
3/32	.0938		2.38
	.0945		2.4
	.0960	41	
	.0965		2.45
	.0980	40	
	.0981		2.5
	.0995	39	
	.1015	38	
	.1024		2.6
	.1040	37	
	.1063		2.7
	.1065	36	
	.1083		2.75
7/64	.1094		2.77
	.1100	35	
	.1102		2.8
	.1110	34	
	.1130	33	
	.1142		2.9
	.1160	32	
	.1181		3.0
	.1200	31	
	.1220		3.1
1/8	.1250		3.17
	.1260		3.2
	.1280		3.25
	.1285	30	
	.1299		3.3
	.1339		3.4
	.1360	29	
	.1378		3.5
	.1405	28	
9/64	.1406		3.57
	.1417		3.6
	.1440	27	
	.1457		3.7
	.1470	26	
	.1476		3.75
	.1495	25	
	.1496		3.8
	.1520	24	
	.1535		3.9
	.1540	23	
5/32	.1562		3.96
	.1570	22	
	.1575		4.0
	.1590	21	
	.1610	20	

Inch	Decimal	Wire & Letter	mm
	.1614		4.1
	.1654		4.2
	.1660	19	
	.1673		4.25
	.1693		4.3
	.1695	18	
11/64	.1719		4.36
	.1730	17	
	.1732		4.4
	.1770	16	
	.1772		4.5
	.1800	15	
	.1811		4.6
	.1820	14	
	.1850	13	
	.1850		4.7
	.1870		4.75
3/16	.1875		4.76
	.1890		4.8
	.1890	12	
	.1910	11	
	.1929		4.9
	.1935	10	
	.1960	9	
	.1969		5.0
	.1990	8	
	.2008		5.1
	.2010	7	
13/64	.2031		5.16
	.2040	6	
	.2047		5.2
	.2055	5	
	.2067		5.25
	.2087		5.3
	.2090	4	
	.2126		5.4
	.2130	3	
	.2165		5.5
7/32	2188		5.55
	.2205		5.6
	.2210	2	
	.2244		5.7
	.2264		5.75
	.2280	1	
	.2283		5.8
	.2323		5.9
	.2340	A	
15/64	.2344		5.95
	.2362		6.0
	.2380	B	
	.2402		6.1
	.2420	C	
	.2441		6.2
	.2460	D	
	.2461		6.25
	.2480		6.3
1/4	.2500	E	6.35
	.2520		6.
	.2559		6.5
	.2570	F	
	.2598		6.6
	.2610	G	
	.2638		6.7
17/64	.2656		6.74
	.2657		6.75
	.2660	H	
	.2677		6.8

Inch	Decimal	Letter	mm
	.2717		6.9
	.2720	I	
	.2756		7.0
	.2770	J	
	.2795		7.1
	.2810	K	
9/32	.2812		7.14
	.2835		7.2
	.2854		7.25
	.2874		7.3
	.2900	L	
	.2913		7.4
	.2950	M	
	.2953		7.5
19/64	.2969		7.54
	.2992		7.6
	.3020	N	
	.3031		7.7
	.3051		7.75
	.3071		7.8
	.3110		7.9
5/16	.3125		7.93
	.3150		8.0
	.3160	O	
	.3189		8.1
	.3228		8.2
	.3230	P	
	.3248		8.25
	.3268		8.3
21/64	.3281		8.33
	.3307		8.4
	.3320	Q	
	.3346		8.5
	.3386		8.6
	.3390	R	
	.3425		8.7
11/32	.3438		8.73
	.3445		8.75
	.3465		8.8
	.3480	S	
	.3504		8.9
	.3543		9.0
	.3580	T	
	.3583		9.1
23/64	.3594		9.12
	.3622		9.2
	.3642		9.25
	.3661		9.3
	.3680	U	
	.3701		9.4
	.3740		9.5
3/8	.3750		9.52
	.3770	V	
	.3780		9.6
	.3819		9.7
	.3839		9.75
	.3858		9.8
	.3860	W	
	.3898		9.9
25/64	.3906		9.92
	.3937		10.0
	.3970	X	
	.4040	Y	
13/32	.4062		10.31
	.4130	Z	
	.4134		10.5
27/64	.4219		10.71

Inch	Decimal	mm
	.4331	11.0
7/16	.4375	11.11
	.4528	11.5
29/64	.4531	11.51
15/32	.4688	11.90
	.4724	12.0
31/64	.4844	12.30
	.4921	12.5
1/2	.5000	12.70
	.5118	13.0
33/64	.5156	13.09
17/32	.5312	13.49
	.5315	13.5
35/64	.5469	13.89
	.5512	14.0
9/16	.5625	14.28
	.5709	14.5
37/64	.5781	14.68
	.5906	15.0
19/32	.5938	15.08
39/64	.6094	15.47
	.6102	15.5
5/8	.6250	15.87
	.6299	16.0
41/64	.6406	16.27
	.6496	16.5
21/32	.6562	16.66
	.6693	17.0
43/64	.6719	17.06
11/16	.6875	17.46
	.6890	17.5
45/64	.7031	17.85
	.7087	18.0
23/32	.7188	18.25
	.7283	18.5
47/64	.7344	18.65
	.7480	19.0
3/4	.7500	19.05
49/64	.7656	19.44
	.7677	19.5
25/32	.7812	19.84
	.7874	20.0
51/64	.7969	20.24
	.8071	20.5
13/16	.8125	20.63
	.8268	21.0
53/64	.8281	21.03
27/32	.8438	21.43
	.8465	21.5
55/64	.8594	21.82
	.8661	22.0
7/8	.8750	22.22
	.8858	22.5
57/64	.8906	22.62
	.9055	23.0
29/32	.9062	23.01
59/64	.9219	23.41
	.9252	23.5
15/16	.9375	23.81
	.9449	24.0
61/64	.9531	24.2
	.9646	24.5
31/32	.9688	24.6
	.9843	25.0
63/64	.9844	25.0
1	1.0000	25.4

GLOSSARY OF TERMS

AIR/FUEL RATIO: The ratio of air to gasoline by weight in the fuel mixture drawn into the engine.

AIR INJECTION: One method of reducing harmful exhaust emissions by injecting air into each of the exhaust ports of an engine. The fresh air entering the hot exhaust manifold causes any remaining fuel to be burned before it can exit the tailpipe.

ALTERNATOR: A device used for converting mechanical energy into electrical energy.

AMMETER: An instrument, calibrated in amperes, used to measure the flow of an electrical current in a circuit. Ammeters are always connected in series with the circuit being tested.

AMPERE: The rate of flow of electrical current present when one volt of electrical pressure is applied against one ohm of electrical resistance.

ANALOG COMPUTER: Any microprocessor that uses similar (analogous) electrical signals to make its calculations.

ARMATURE: A laminated, soft iron core wrapped by a wire that converts electrical energy to mechanical energy as in a motor or relay. When rotated in a magnetic field, it changes mechanical energy into electrical energy as in a generator.

ATMOSPHERIC PRESSURE: The pressure on the Earth's surface caused by the weight of the air in the atmosphere. At sea level, this pressure is 14.7 psi at 32°F (101 kPa at 0°C).

ATOMIZATION: The breaking down of a liquid into a fine mist that can be suspended in air.

AXIAL PLAY: Movement parallel to a shaft or bearing bore.

BACKFIRE: The sudden combustion of gases in the intake or exhaust system that results in a loud explosion.

BACKLASH: The clearance or play between two parts, such as meshed gears.

BACKPRESSURE: Restrictions in the exhaust system that slow the exit of exhaust gases from the combustion chamber.

BAKELITE: A heat resistant, plastic insulator material commonly used in printed circuit boards and transistorized components.

BALL BEARING: A bearing made up of hardened inner and outer races between which hardened steel ball roll.

BALLAST RESISTOR: A resistor in the primary ignition circuit that lowers voltage after the engine is started to reduce wear on ignition components.

BEARING: A friction reducing, supportive device usually located between a stationary part and a moving part.

BIMETAL TEMPERATURE SENSOR: Any sensor or switch made of two dissimilar types of metal that bend when heated or cooled due to the different expansion rates of the alloys. These types of sensors usually function as an on/off switch.

BLOWBY: Combustion gases, composed of water vapor and unburned fuel, that leak past the piston rings into the crankcase during normal engine operation. These gases are removed by the PCV system to prevent the build-up of harmful acids in the crankcase.

BRAKE PAD: A brake shoe and lining assembly used with disc brakes.

BRAKE SHOE: The backing for the brake lining. The term is, however, usually applied to the assembly of the brake backing and lining.

BUSHING: A liner, usually removable, for a bearing; an anti-friction liner used in place of a bearing.

BYPASS: System used to bypass ballast resistor during engine cranking to increase voltage supplied to the coil.

CALIPER: A hydraulically activated device in a disc brake system, which is mounted straddling the brake rotor (disc). The caliper contains at least one piston and two brake pads. Hydraulic pressure on the piston(s) forces the pads against the rotor.

CAMSHAFT: A shaft in the engine on which are the lobes (cams) which operate the valves. The camshaft is driven by the crankshaft, via a belt, chain or gears, at one half the crankshaft speed.

CAPACITOR: A device which stores an electrical charge.

CARBON MONOXIDE (CO): a colorless, odorless gas given off as a normal byproduct of combustion. It is poisonous and extremely dangerous in confined areas, building up slowly to toxic levels without warning if adequate ventilation is not available.

CARBURETOR: A device, usually mounted on the intake manifold of an engine, which mixes the air and fuel in the proper proportion to allow even combustion.

CATALYTIC CONVERTER: A device installed in the exhaust system, like a muffler, that converts harmful byproducts of combustion into carbon dioxide and water vapor by means of a heat-producing chemical reaction.

CENTRIFUGAL ADVANCE: A mechanical method of advancing the spark timing by using flyweights in the distributor that react to centrifugal force generated by the distributor shaft rotation.

CHECK VALVE: Any one-way valve installed to permit the flow of air, fuel or vacuum in one direction only.

CHOKE: A device, usually a moveable valve, placed in the intake path of a carburetor to restrict the flow of air.

CIRCUIT: Any unbroken path through which an electrical current can flow. Also used to describe fuel flow in some instances.

CIRCUIT BREAKER: A switch which protects an electrical circuit from overload by opening the circuit when the current flow exceeds a predetermined level. Some circuit breakers must be reset manually, while other reset automatically

COIL (IGNITION): A transformer in the ignition circuit which steps of the voltage provided to the spark plugs.

COMBINATION MANIFOLD: An assembly which includes both the intake and exhaust manifolds in one casting.

COMBINATION VALVE: A device used in some fuel systems that routes fuel vapors to a charcoal storage canister instead of venting them into the atmosphere. The valve relieves fuel tank pressure and allows fresh air into the tank as fuel level drops to prevent a vapor lock situation.

COMPRESSION RATIO: The comparison of the total volume of the cylinder and combustion chamber with the piston at BDC and the piston at TDC.

CONDENSER: 1. An electrical device which acts to store an electrical charge, preventing voltage surges.
2. A radiator-like device in the air conditioning system in which refrigerant gas condenses into a liquid, giving off heat.

CONDUCTOR: Any material through which an electrical current can be transmitted easily.

CONTINUITY: Continuous or complete circuit. Can be checked with an ohmmeter.

COUNTERSHAFT: An intermediate shaft which is rotated by a mainshaft and transmits, in turn, that rotation to a working part.

CRANKCASE: The lower part of an engine in which the crankshaft and related parts operate.

CRANKSHAFT: The main driving shaft of an engine which receives reciprocating motion from the pistons and converts it to rotary motion.

CYLINDER: In an engine, the round hole in the engine block in which the piston(s) ride.

CYLINDER BLOCK: The main structural member of an engine in which is found the cylinders, crankshaft and other principal parts.

CYLINDER HEAD: The detachable portion of the engine, fastened, usually, to the top of the cylinder block, containing all or most of the combustion chambers. On overhead valve engines, it contains the valves and their operating parts. On overhead cam engines, it contains the camshaft as well.

DEAD CENTER: The extreme top or bottom of the piston stroke.

DETONATION: An unwanted explosion of the air fuel mixture in the combustion chamber caused by excess heat and compression, advanced timing, or an overly lean mixture. Also referred to as "ping".

DIAPHRAGM: A thin, flexible wall separating two cavities, such as in a vacuum advance unit.

DIESELING: A condition in which hot spots in the combustion chamber cause the engine to run on after the key is turned off.

DIFFERENTIAL: A geared assembly which allows the transmission of motion between drive axles, giving one axle the ability to turn faster than the other.

DIODE: An electrical device that will allow current to flow in one direction only.

DISC BRAKE: A hydraulic braking assembly consisting of a brake disc, or rotor, mounted on an axle, and a caliper assembly containing, usually two brake pads which are activated by hydraulic pressure. The pads are forced against the sides of the disc, creating friction which slows the vehicle.

DISTRIBUTOR: A mechanically driven device on an engine which is responsible for electrically firing the spark plug at a predetermined point of the piston stroke.

DOWEL PIN: A pin, inserted in mating holes in two different parts allowing those parts to maintain a fixed relationship.

DRUM BRAKE: A braking system which consists of two brake shoes and one or two wheel cylinders, mounted on a fixed backing plate, and a brake drum, mounted on an axle, which revolves around the assembly. Hydraulic action applied to the wheel cylinders forces the shoes outward against the drum, creating friction and slowing the vehicle.

DWELL: The rate, measured in degrees of shaft rotation, at which an electrical circuit cycles on and off.

ELECTRONIC CONTROL UNIT (ECU): Ignition module, module, amplifier or igniter. See Module for definition.

ELECTRONIC IGNITION: A system in which the timing and firing of the spark plugs is controlled by an electronic control unit, usually called a module. These systems have not points or condenser.

ENDPLAY: The measured amount of axial movement in a shaft.

ENGINE: A device that converts heat into mechanical energy.

EXHAUST MANIFOLD: A set of cast passages or pipes which conduct exhaust gases from the engine.

FEELER GAUGE: A blade, usually metal, of precisely predetermined thickness, used to measure the clearance between two parts. These blades usually are available in sets of assorted thicknesses.

F-Head: An engine configuration in which the intake valves are in the cylinder head, while the camshaft and exhaust valves are located in the cylinder block. The camshaft operates the intake valves via lifters and pushrods, while it operates the exhaust valves directly.

FIRING ORDER: The order in which combustion occurs in the cylinders of an engine. Also the order in which spark is distributed to the plugs by the distributor.

FLATHEAD: An engine configuration in which the camshaft and all the valves are located in the cylinder block.

FLOODING: The presence of too much fuel in the intake manifold and combustion chamber which prevents the air/fuel mixture from firing, thereby causing a no-start situation.

FLYWHEEL: A disc shaped part bolted to the rear end of the crankshaft. Around the outer perimeter is affixed the ring gear. The starter drive engages the ring gear, turning the flywheel, which rotates the crankshaft, imparting the initial starting motion to the engine.

FOOT POUND (ft.lb. or sometimes, ft. lbs.): The amount of energy or work needed to raise an item weighing one pound, a distance of one foot.

FUSE: A protective device in a circuit which prevents circuit overload by breaking the circuit when a specific amperage is present. The device is constructed around a strip or wire of a lower amperage rating than the circuit it is designed to protect. When an amperage higher than that stamped on the fuse is present in the circuit, the strip or wire melts, opening the circuit.

GEAR RATIO: The ratio between the number of teeth on meshing gears.

GENERATOR: A device which converts mechanical energy into electrical energy.

HEAT RANGE: The measure of a spark plug's ability to dissipate heat from its firing end. The higher the heat range, the hotter the plug fires.

HUB: The center part of a wheel or gear.

HYDROCARBON (HC): Any chemical compound made up of hydrogen and carbon. A major pollutant formed by the engine as a byproduct of combustion.

HYDROMETER: An instrument used to measure the specific gravity of a solution.

INCH POUND (in.lb. or sometimes, in. lbs.): One twelfth of a foot pound.

INDUCTION: A means of transferring electrical energy in the form of a magnetic field. Principle used in the ignition coil to increase voltage.

INJECTION PUMP: A device, usually mechanically operated, which meters and delivers fuel under pressure to the fuel injector.

INJECTOR: A device which receives metered fuel under relatively low pressure and is activated to inject the fuel into the engine under relatively high pressure at a predetermined time.

INPUT SHAFT: The shaft to which torque is applied, usually carrying the driving gear or gears.

INTAKE MANIFOLD: A casting of passages or pipes used to conduct air or a fuel/air mixture to the cylinders.

JOURNAL: The bearing surface within which a shaft operates.

KEY: A small block usually fitted in a notch between a shaft and a hub to prevent slippage of the two parts.

MANIFOLD: A casting of passages or set of pipes which connect the cylinders to an inlet or outlet source.

MANIFOLD VACUUM: Low pressure in an engine intake manifold formed just below the throttle plates. Manifold vacuum is highest at idle and drops under acceleration.

MASTER CYLINDER: The primary fluid pressurizing device in a hydraulic system. In automotive use, it is found in brake and hydraulic clutch systems and is pedal activated, either directly or, in a power brake system, through the power booster.

MODULE: Electronic control unit, amplifier or igniter of solid state or integrated design which controls the current flow in the ignition primary circuit based on input from the pickup coil. When the module opens the primary circuit, the high secondary voltage is induced in the coil.

NEEDLE BEARING: A bearing which consists of a number (usually a large number) of long, thin rollers.

OHM: (Ω) The unit used to measure the resistance of conductor to electrical flow. One ohm is the amount of resistance that limits current flow to one ampere in a circuit with one volt of pressure.

OHMMETER: An instrument used for measuring the resistance, in ohms, in an electrical circuit.

OUTPUT SHAFT: The shaft which transmits torque from a device, such as a transmission.

OVERDRIVE: A gear assembly which produces more shaft revolutions than that transmitted to it.

OVERHEAD CAMSHAFT (OHC): An engine configuration in which the camshaft is mounted on top of the cylinder head and operates the valve either directly or by means of rocker arms.

OVERHEAD VALVE (OHV): An engine configuration in which all of the valves are located in the cylinder head and the camshaft is located in the cylinder block. The camshaft operates the valves via lifters and pushrods.

OXIDES OF NITROGEN (NOx): Chemical compounds of nitrogen produced as a byproduct of combustion. They combine with hydrocarbons to produce smog.

OXYGEN SENSOR: Used with the feedback system to sense the presence of oxygen in the exhaust gas and signal the computer which can reference the voltage signal to an air/fuel ratio.

PINION: The smaller of two meshing gears.

PISTON RING: An open ended ring which fits into a groove on the outer diameter of the piston. Its chief function is to form a seal between the piston and cylinder wall. Most automotive pistons have three rings: two for compression sealing; one for oil sealing.

PRELOAD: A predetermined load placed on a bearing during assembly or by adjustment.

PRIMARY CIRCUIT: Is the low voltage side of the ignition system which consists of the ignition switch, ballast resistor or resistance wire, bypass, coil, electronic control unit and pick-up coil as well as the connecting wires and harnesses.

PRESS FIT: The mating of two parts under pressure, due to the inner diameter of one being smaller than the outer diameter of the other, or vice versa; an interference fit.

RACE: The surface on the inner or outer ring of a bearing on which the balls, needles or rollers move.

REGULATOR: A device which maintains the amperage and/or voltage levels of a circuit at predetermined values.

RELAY: A switch which automatically opens and/or closes a circuit.

RESISTANCE: The opposition to the flow of current through a circuit or electrical device, and is measured in ohms. Resistance is equal to the voltage divided by the amperage.

RESISTOR: A device, usually made of wire, which offers a preset amount of resistance in an electrical circuit.

RING GEAR: The name given to a ring-shaped gear attached to a differential case, or affixed to a flywheel or as part a planetary gear set.

ROLLER BEARING: A bearing made up of hardened inner and outer races between which hardened steel rollers move.

ROTOR: 1. The disc-shaped part of a disc brake assembly, upon which the brake pads bear; also called, brake disc.
2. The device mounted atop the distributor shaft, which passes current to the distributor cap tower contacts.

SECONDARY CIRCUIT: The high voltage side of the ignition system, usually above 20,000 volts. The secondary includes the ignition coil, coil wire, distributor cap and rotor, spark plug wires and spark plugs.

SENDING UNIT: A mechanical, electrical, hydraulic or electromagnetic device which transmits information to a gauge.

SENSOR: Any device designed to measure engine operating conditions or ambient pressures and temperatures. Usually electronic in nature and designed to send a voltage signal to an on-board computer, some sensors may operate as a simple on/off switch or they may provide a variable voltage signal (like a potentiometer) as conditions or measured parameters change.

SHIM: Spacers of precise, predetermined thickness used between parts to establish a proper working relationship.

SLAVE CYLINDER: In automotive use, a device in the hydraulic clutch system which is activated by hydraulic force, disengaging the clutch.

SOLENOID: A coil used to produce a magnetic field, the effect of which is produce work.

SPARK PLUG: A device screwed into the combustion chamber of a spark ignition engine. The basic construction is a conductive core inside of a ceramic insulator, mounted in an outer conductive base. An electrical charge from the spark plug wire travels along the conductive core and jumps a preset air gap to a grounding point or points at the end of the conductive base. The resultant spark ignites the fuel/air mixture in the combustion chamber.

SPLINES: Ridges machined or cast onto the outer diameter of a shaft or inner diameter of a bore to enable parts to mate without rotation.

TACHOMETER: A device used to measure the rotary speed of an engine, shaft, gear, etc., usually in rotations per minute.

THERMOSTAT: A valve, located in the cooling system of an engine, which is closed when cold and opens gradually in response to engine heating, controlling the temperature of the coolant and rate of coolant flow.

TOP DEAD CENTER (TDC): The point at which the piston reaches the top of its travel on the compression stroke.

TORQUE: The twisting force applied to an object.

TORQUE CONVERTER: A turbine used to transmit power from a driving member to a driven member via hydraulic action, providing changes in drive ratio and torque. In automotive use, it links the driveplate at the rear of the engine to the automatic transmission.

TRANSDUCER: A device used to change a force into an electrical signal.

TRANSISTOR: A semi-conductor component which can be actuated by a small voltage to perform an electrical switching function.

TUNE-UP: A regular maintenance function, usually associated with the replacement and adjustment of parts and components in the electrical and fuel systems of a vehicle for the purpose of attaining optimum performance.

TURBOCHARGER: An exhaust driven pump which compresses intake air and forces it into the combustion chambers at higher than atmospheric pressures. The increased air pressure allows more fuel to be burned and results in increased horsepower being produced.

VACUUM ADVANCE: A device which advances the ignition timing in response to increased engine vacuum.

VACUUM GAUGE: An instrument used to measure the presence of vacuum in a chamber.

VALVE: A device which control the pressure, direction of flow or rate of flow of a liquid or gas.

VALVE CLEARANCE: The measured gap between the end of the valve stem and the rocker arm, cam lobe or follower that activates the valve.

VISCOSITY: The rating of a liquid's internal resistance to flow.

VOLTMETER: An instrument used for measuring electrical force in units called volts. Voltmeters are always connected parallel with the circuit being tested.

WHEEL CYLINDER: Found in the automotive drum brake assembly, it is a device, actuated by hydraulic pressure, which, through internal pistons, pushes the brake shoes outward against the drums.

ABBREVIATIONS AND SYMBOLS

A: Ampere

AC: Alternating current

A/C: Air conditioning

A-h: Ampere hour

AT: Automatic transmission

ATDC: After top dead center

μA: Microampere

bbl: Barrel

BDC: Bottom dead center

bhp: Brake horsepower

BTDC: Before top dead center

BTU: British thermal unit

C: Celsius (Centigrade)

CCA: Cold cranking amps

cd: Candela

cm^2: Square centimeter

cm^3, cc: Cubic centimeter

CO: Carbon monoxide

CO_2: Carbon dioxide

cu.in., in^3: Cubic inch

CV: Constant velocity

Cyl.: Cylinder

DC: Direct current

ECM: Electronic control module

EFE: Early fuel evaporation

EFI: Electronic fuel injection

EGR: Exhaust gas recirculation

Exh.: Exhaust

F: Fahrenheit

F: Farad

pF: Picofarad

μF: Microfarad

FI: Fuel injection

ft.lb., ft. lb., ft. lbs.: foot pound(s)

gal: Gallon

g: Gram

HC: Hydrocarbon

HEI: High energy ignition

HO: High output

hp: Horsepower

Hyd.: Hydraulic

Hz: Hertz

ID: Inside diameter

in.lb.; in. lb.; in. lbs: inch pound(s)

Int.: Intake

K: Kelvin

kg: Kilogram

kHz: Kilohertz

km: Kilometer

km/h: Kilometers per hour

kΩ: Kilohm

kPa: Kilopascal

kV: Kilovolt

kW: Kilowatt

l: Liter

l/s: Liters per second

m: Meter

mA: Milliampere

mg: Milligram

mHz: Megahertz

mm: Millimeter

mm^2: Square millimeter

m^3: Cubic meter

$M\Omega$: Megohm

m/s: Meters per second

MT: Manual transmission

mV: Millivolt

μm: Micrometer

N: Newton

N-m: Newton meter

NOx: Nitrous oxide

OD: Outside diameter

OHC: Over head camshaft

OHV: Over head valve

Ω: Ohm

PCV: Positive crankcase ventilation

psi: Pounds per square inch

pts: Pints

qts: Quarts

rpm: Rotations per minute

rps: Rotations per second

R-12: A refrigerant gas (Freon)

SAE: Society of Automotive Engineers

SO_2: Sulfur dioxide

T: Ton

t: Megagram

TBI: Throttle Body Injection

TPS: Throttle Position Sensor

V: 1. Volt; 2. Venturi

μV: Microvolt

W: Watt

∞: Infinity

<: Less than

>: Greater than

Index

Chilton's Repair & Tune-Up Guides

The Complete line covers domestic cars, imports, trucks, vans, RV's and 4-wheel drive vehicles.

RTUG Title	Part No.	RTUG Title	Part No.
AMC 1975-82	7199	**Corvair 1960-69**	6691
Covers all U.S. and Canadian models		Covers all U.S. and Canadian models	
Aspen/Volare 1976-80	6637	**Corvette 1953-62**	6576
Covers all U.S. and Canadian models		Covers all U.S. and Canadian models	
Audi 1970-73	5902	**Corvette 1963-84**	6843
Covers all U.S. and Canadian models.		Covers all U.S. and Canadian models	
Audi 4000/5000 1978-81	7028	**Cutlass 1970-85**	6933
Covers all U.S. and Canadian models including turbocharged and diesel engines		Covers all U.S. and Canadian models	
Barracuda/Challenger 1965-72	5807	**Dart/Demon 1968-76**	6324
Covers all U.S. and Canadian models		Covers all U.S. and Canadian models	
Blazer/Jimmy 1969-82	6931	**Datsun 1961-72**	5790
Covers all U.S. and Canadian 2- and 4-wheel drive models, including diesel engines		Covers all U.S. and Canadian models of Nissan Patrol; 1500, 1600 and 2000 sports cars; Pick-Ups; 410, 411, 510, 1200 and 240Z	
BMW 1970-82	6844	**Datsun 1973-80 Spanish**	7083
Covers U.S. and Canadian models		**Datsun/Nissan F-10, 310, Stanza, Pulsar 1977-86**	7196
Buick/Olds/Pontiac 1975-85	7308	Covers all U.S. and Canadian models	
Covers U.S. and Canadian full size rear wheel drive models		**Datsun/Nissan Pick-Ups 1970-84**	6816
Cadillac 1967-84	7462	Covers all U.S and Canadian models	
Covers all U.S. and Canadian rear wheel drive models		**Datsun/Nissan Z & ZX 1970-86**	6932
Camaro 1967-81	6735	Covers all U.S. and Canadian models	
Covers all U.S. and Canadian models		**Datsun/Nissan 1200, 210, Sentra 1973-86**	7197
Camaro 1982-85	7317	Covers all U.S. and Canadian models	
Covers all U.S. and Canadian models		**Datsun/Nissan 200SX, 510, 610, 710, 810, Maxima 1973-84**	7170
Capri 1970-77	6695	Covers all U.S. and Canadian models	
Covers all U.S. and Canadian models		**Dodge 1968-77**	6554
Caravan/Voyager 1984-85	7482	Covers all U.S. and Canadian models	
Covers all U.S. and Canadian models		**Dodge Charger 1967-70**	6486
Century/Regal 1975-85	7307	Covers all U.S. and Canadian models	
Covers all U.S. and Canadian rear wheel drive models, including turbocharged engines		**Dodge/Plymouth Trucks 1967-84**	7459
Champ/Arrow/Sapporo 1978-83	7041	Covers all $^1/_2$, $^3/_4$, and 1 ton 2- and 4-wheel drive U.S. and Canadian models, including diesel engines	
Covers all U.S. and Canadian models		**Dodge/Plymouth Vans 1967-84**	6934
Chevette/1000 1976-86	6836	Covers all $^1/_2$, $^3/_4$, and 1 ton U.S. and Canadian models of vans, cutaways and motor home chassis	
Covers all U.S. and Canadian models		**D-50/Arrow Pick-Up 1979-81**	7032
Chevrolet 1968-85	7135	Covers all U.S. and Canadian models	
Covers all U.S. and Canadian models		**Fairlane/Torino 1962-75**	6320
Chevrolet 1968-79 Spanish	7082	Covers all U.S. and Canadian models	
Chevrolet/GMC Pick-Ups 1970-82 Spanish	7468	**Fairmont/Zephyr 1978-83**	6965
Chevrolet/GMC Pick-Ups and Suburban 1970-86	6936	Covers all U.S. and Canadian models	
Covers all U.S. and Canadian $^1/_2$, $^3/_4$ and 1 ton models, including 4-wheel drive and diesel engines		**Fiat 1969-81**	7042
Chevrolet LUV 1972-81	6815	Covers all U.S. and Canadian models	
Covers all U.S. and Canadian models		**Fiesta 1978-80**	6846
Chevrolet Mid-Size 1964-86	6840	Covers all U.S. and Canadian models	
Covers all U.S. and Canadian models of 1964-77 Chevelle, Malibu and Malibu SS; 1974-77 Laguna; 1978-85 Malibu; 1970-86 Monte Carlo; 1964-84 El Camino, including diesel engines		**Firebird 1967-81**	5996
		Covers all U.S. and Canadian models	
		Firebird 1982-85	7345
		Covers all U.S. and Canadian models	
Chevrolet Nova 1986	7658	**Ford 1968-79 Spanish**	7084
Covers all U.S. and Canadian models		**Ford Bronco 1966-83**	7140
Chevy/GMC Vans 1967-84	6930	Covers all U.S. and Canadian models	
Covers all U.S. and Canadian models of $^1/_2$, $^3/_4$, and 1 ton vans, cutaways, and motor home chassis, including diesel engines		**Ford Bronco II 1984**	7408
		Covers all U.S. and Canadian models	
Chevy S-10 Blazer/GMC S-15 Jimmy 1982-85	7383	**Ford Courier 1972-82**	6983
Covers all U.S. and Canadian models		Covers all U.S. and Canadian models	
Chevy S-10/GMC S-15 Pick-Ups 1982-85	7310	**Ford/Mercury Front Wheel Drive 1981-85**	7055
Covers all U.S. and Canadian models		Covers all U.S. and Canadian models Escort, EXP, Tempo, Lynx, LN-7 and Topaz	
Chevy II/Nova 1962-79	6841	**Ford/Mercury/Lincoln 1968-85**	6842
Covers all U.S. and Canadian models		Covers all U.S. and Canadian models of FORD Country Sedan, Country Squire, Crown Victoria, Custom, Custom 500, Galaxie 500, LTD through 1982, Ranch Wagon, and XL; MERCURY Colony Park, Commuter, Marquis through 1982, Gran Marquis, Monterey and Park Lane; LINCOLN Continental and Towne Car	
Chrysler K- and E-Car 1981-85	7163		
Covers all U.S. and Canadian front wheel drive models			
Colt/Challenger/Vista/Conquest 1971-85	7037		
Covers all U.S. and Canadian models			
Corolla/Carina/Tercel/Starlet 1970-85	7036	**Ford/Mercury/Lincoln Mid-Size 1971-85**	6696
Covers all U.S. and Canadian models		Covers all U.S. and Canadian models of FORD Elite, 1983-85 LTD, 1977-79 LTD II, Ranchero, Torino, Gran Torino, 1977-85 Thunderbird; MERCURY 1972-85 Cougar,	
Corona/Cressida/Crown/Mk.II/Camry/Van 1970-84	7044		
Covers all U.S. and Canadian models			

continued on next page

RTUG Title	Part No.	RTUG Title	Part No.
1983-85 Marquis, Montego, 1980-85 XR-7; LINCOLN 1982-85 Continental, 1984-85 Mark VII, 1978-80 Versailles		**Mercedes-Benz 1974-84** Covers all U.S. and Canadian models	6809
Ford Pick-Ups 1965-86 Covers all ¹/₂, ³/₄ and 1 ton, 2- and 4-wheel drive U.S. and Canadian pick-up, chassis cab and camper models, including diesel engines	6913	**Mitsubishi, Cordia, Tredia, Starion, Galant 1983-85** Covers all U.S. and Canadian models	7583
		MG 1961-81 Covers all U.S. and Canadian models	6780
Ford Pick-Ups 1965-82 Spanish	7469	**Mustang/Capri/Merkur 1979-85** Covers all U.S. and Canadian models	6963
Ford Ranger 1983-84 Covers all U.S. and Canadian models	7338	**Mustang/Cougar 1965-73** Covers all U.S. and Canadian models	6542
Ford Vans 1961-86 Covers all U.S. and Canadian ¹/₂, ³/₄ and 1 ton and cutaway chassis models, including diesel engines	6849	**Mustang II 1974-78** Covers all U.S. and Canadian models	6812
		Omni/Horizon/Rampage 1978-84 Covers all U.S. and Canadian models of DODGE omni, Miser, 024, Charger 2.2; PLYMOUTH Horizon, Miser, TC3, TC3 Tourismo; Rampage	6845
GM A-Body 1982-85 Covers all front wheel drive U.S. and Canadian models of BUICK Century, CHEVROLET Celebrity, OLDSMOBILE Cutlass Ciera and PONTIAC 6000	7309	**Opel 1971-75** Covers all U.S. and Canadian models	6575
		Peugeot 1970-74 Covers all U.S. and Canadian models	5982
GM C-Body 1985 Covers all front wheel drive U.S. and Canadian models of BUICK Electra Park Avenue and Electra T-Type, CADILLAC Fleetwood and deVille, OLDSMOBILE 98 Regency and Regency Brougham	7587	**Pinto/Bobcat 1971-80** Covers all U.S. and Canadian models	7027
		Plymouth 1968-76 Covers all U.S. and Canadian models	6552
		Pontiac Fiero 1984-85 Covers all U.S. and Canadian models	7571
GM J-Car 1982-85 Covers all U.S. and Canadian models of BUICK Skyhawk, CHEVROLET Cavalier, CADILLAC Cimarron, OLDSMOBILE Firenza and PONTIAC 2000 and Sunbird	7059	**Pontiac Mid-Size 1974-83** Covers all U.S. and Canadian models of Ventura, Grand Am, LeMans, Grand LeMans, GTO, Phoenix, and Grand Prix	7346
GM N-Body 1985-86 Covers all U.S. and Canadian models of front wheel drive BUICK Somerset and Skylark, OLDSMOBILE Calais, and PONTIAC Grand Am	7657	**Porsche 924/928 1976-81** Covers all U.S. and Canadian models	7048
		Renault 1975-85 Covers all U.S. and Canadian models	7165
GM X-Body 1980-85 Covers all U.S. and Canadian models of BUICK Skylark, CHEVROLET Citation, OLDSMOBILE Omega and PONTIAC Phoenix	7049	**Roadrunner/Satellite/Belvedere/GTX 1968-73** Covers all U.S. and Canadian models	5821
		RX-7 1979-81 Covers all U.S. and Canadian models	7031
GM Subcompact 1971-80 Covers all U.S. and Canadian models of BUICK Skyhawk (1975-80), CHEVROLET Vega and Monza, OLDSMOBILE Starfire, and PONTIAC Astre and 1975-80 Sunbird	6935	**SAAB 99 1969-75** Covers all U.S. and Canadian models	5988
		SAAB 900 1979-85 Covers all U.S. and Canadian models	7572
Granada/Monarch 1975-82 Covers all U.S. and Canadian models	6937	**Snowmobiles 1976-80** Covers Arctic Cat, John Deere, Kawasaki, Polaris, Ski-Doo and Yamaha	6978
Honda 1973-84 Covers all U.S. and Canadian models	6980	**Subaru 1970-84** Covers all U.S. and Canadian models	6982
International Scout 1967-73 Covers all U.S. and Canadian models	5912	**Tempest/GTO/LeMans 1968-73** Covers all U.S. and Canadian models	5905
Jeep 1945-87 Covers all U.S. and Canadian CJ-2A, CJ-3A, CJ-3B, CJ-5, CJ-6, CJ-7, Scrambler and Wrangler models	6817	**Toyota 1966-70** Covers all U.S. and Canadian models of Corona, MkII, Corolla, Crown, Land Cruiser, Stout and Hi-Lux	5795
		Toyota 1970-79 Spanish	7467
Jeep Wagoneer, Commando, Cherokee, Truck 1957-86 Covers all U.S. and Canadian models of Wagoneer, Cherokee, Grand Wagoneer, Jeepster, Jeepster Commando, J-100, J-200, J-300, J-10, J20, FC-150 and FC-170	6739	**Toyota Celica/Supra 1971-85** Covers all U.S. and Canadian models	7043
		Toyota Trucks 1970-85 Covers all U.S. and Canadian models of pick-ups, Land Cruiser and 4Runner	7035
Laser/Daytona 1984-85 Covers all U.S. and Canadian models	7563	**Valiant/Duster 1968-76** Covers all U.S. and Canadian models	6326
Maverick/Comet 1970-77 Covers all U.S. and Canadian models	6634	**Volvo 1956-69** Covers all U.S. and Canadian models	6529
Mazda 1971-84 Covers all U.S. and Canadian models of RX-2, RX-3, RX-4, 808, 1300, 1600, Cosmo, GLC and 626	6981	**Volvo 1970-83** Covers all U.S. and Canadian models	7040
		VW Front Wheel Drive 1974-85 Covers all U.S. and Canadian models	6962
Mazda Pick-Ups 1972-86 Covers all U.S. and Canadian models	7659	**VW 1949-71** Covers all U.S. and Canadian models	5796
Mercedes-Benz 1959-70 Covers all U.S. and Canadian models	6065	**VW 1970-79 Spanish**	7081
Mereceds-Benz 1968-73 Covers all U.S. and Canadian models	5907	**VW 1970-81** Covers all U.S. and Canadian Beetles, Karmann Ghia, Fastback, Squareback, Vans, 411 and 412	6837

Chilton's Repair Manuals are available at your local retailer or by mailing a check or money order for **$15.95** per book plus **$3.50** for 1st book and **$.50** for each additional book to cover postage and handling to:

Chilton Book Company
Dept. DM
Radnor, PA 19089

NOTE: When ordering be sure to include your name & address, book part No. & title.